Frederic Amory in Memoriam

Old Norse-Icelandic Studies

THE WILDCAT CANYON ADVANCED SEMINARS

Advisory Board
Richard Hardack, *Secretary*
Thomas A. Dubois
Stephen J. Epstein
Terry Gunnell
Merrill Kaplan
John Lindow
Ulf Palmenfelt
Mark Sandberg
Timothy R. Tangherlini

Publication Series
Occasional Monograph Series
Cultural Studies
Folklore
Mythology
Nordic Studies
Classic Studies Reprints

OCCASIONAL MONOGRAPH SERIES

Volume 2

Frederic Amory in Memoriam

Old Norse-Icelandic Studies

Edited by

John Lindow
&
George Clark

NORTH PINEHURST PRESS
BERKELEY • LOS ANGELES

Publisher's Cataloging-in-Publication data

Frederic Amory in memoriam : Old Norse-Icelandic studies / Edited by John
Lindow & George Clark.
    pages cm.
    Series : Wildcat Canyon Advanced Seminars Occasional Monographs
    ISBN 978-0-692-52016-1
    Includes bibliographical references.

1. Mythology, Norse. 2. Literature and folklore --Iceland. 3. Old Norse
literature. 4. Folklore, Norway. 5. Norwegian literature --History and criticism.
6. Literature, Medieval --History and criticism. 7. English literature --Old
English, ca. 450-1100 --History and criticism. I. Amory, Frederic. II. Lindow,
John. III. Clark, George, 1932-. IV. Series.

PT7154 .F74 2015
839.609 --dc23   2015950703

COVER PHOTOGRAPHY BY TIMOTHY R. TANGHERLINI
COVER DESIGN BY TIMOTHY R. TANGHERLINI

North Pinehurst Press
Berkeley and Los Angeles

Printed on acid-free paper

ISBN: 978-0-692-52016-1
LCCN: 2015950703

Veiztu, ef þú vin átt,
þann er þú vel trúir,
ok vill þú af hánum gótt geta,
geði skaltu við þann blanda
ok gjǫfum skipta,
fara at finna opt.

Frederic Amory

Contents

HANS FIX

Introduction

John Lindow and *George Clark*

Habent sua fata libelli. The essays in this volume were originally intended to be included in a special issue of a journal to honor our colleague Fred Amory; upon Fred's death in 2009, it was agreed that the special number of the journal would honor Fred's memory. The essays went through the referee process and some copy-editing, but the editorial team was unable to bring the volume to completion and stepped down after a number of years had passed. When the current editors inherited the project, the authors represented here agreed to go forward, but it was necessary to allow time for possible revisions, both before and after the new referee process, and the former copy-editing was no longer useful. In the end, the process has taken far longer than anyone imagined, but our gratitude for Fred's friendship and pleasure in honoring his memory remain steadfast.

Frederic Amory was born in 1925 and received the A.B. in English from Harvard in 1950, with an honors thesis on the poetry of Wallace Stevens. One year later he earned the A.M. in Comparative Literature, concentrating in French, Italian, and English. Thereafter he spent two years working for a bank in Brazil, a time that was to have a major impact on his overall research profile. From 1957 to 1962 he did graduate work in English at the University of California at Berkeley, and from 1962 until 1994 he taught in the San Francisco area, first at Mills College in Oakland, then at Hayward State University, finally at the University of San Francisco, from which he retired in 1994. In 1984 he was a Fulbright Lecturer in English at the University of Iceland.

Fred taught subjects ranging from English literature in various periods to Linguistics, but his scholarly range was far broader—astonishingly so. His first articles treated Thomas Mann's "Der Tod in Venedig," the Benedictine theologian Guibert of Nogent's *Vita*, and the Brazilian author Euclides da Cunha's novel *Os Sertões*, to which he would return (see below), and later contributions ranged from French literature to Greek literature to patristics. Fred's 1975 article on *Skaufalabálkur* was the first of numerous substantial contributions to the study of Old Norse-Icelandic literature. Several of these were breakthrough works, for example in the application of speech-act theory to saga literature or linguistic theory to kennings, on each of which topics he contributed more than one substantial publication:

> "Narrative Syntax in the Typical Saga Scene" (in *Journal of English and Germanic Philology* 79, 1980)
> "Speech Acts and Violence in the Sagas" (in *Arkiv för nordisk filologi* 106, 1991)
> "Towards a Grammatical Classification of Kennings as Compounds" (in *Arkiv för nordisk filologi* 97, 1982)
> "Kennings, Referentiality, and Metaphor" (in *Arkiv för nordisk filologi* 103, 1987)
> "On the Linguistic Understanding of Kennings" (in *Geremanic Studies in Honor of Anatoly Liberman,* ed. Kurt G. Goblirsch and Marvin Taylor, 1992)

Also on skaldic kennings, in one article Fred traced a possible aspect of the skaldic kenning system across three traditions: Old Norse-Icelandic, Latin, and Old Irish:

> "Tmesis in M.Lat., ON, and O.Ir. Poetry: An Unwritten *notatio norrœna*" (in *Arkiv för nordisk filologi* 94, 1979)

Fred was also among the first to take on the relationship of medieval Latin to Old Norse-Icelandic:

"Saga Style in Some Kings' Sagas and Early Medieval Latin
Literature" (in *Acta Philologica Scandinavica* 32, 1978)

"The Viking Hasting in Franco-Scandinavian Legend" (in *Saints,
Scholars and Heroes: Studies in Medieval Culture in Honor of Charles
W. Jones,* ed. Margot H. King and Wesley H. Stevens, 1979)
"The *dönsk tunga* in Early Medieval Normandy: A Note" (in
*American Indian and Indoeuropean Studies: Papers in Honor of Madison
S. Beeler,* ed. Kathryn Klar *et al.,* 1980)

With his breadth of knowledge, Fred was uniquely qualified to
contribute to our knowledge of such matters as beast epic and
Greek influences, and he was a pioneer in the investigation of the
"post-classical" sagas:

"'Skaufalabálkur,' its Author and its Sources" (in *Scandinavian
Studies* 47, 1975)
"Things Greek and the *Riddarasögur*" (in *Speculum* 59, 1984)
"Pseudoarchaism and Fiction in *Króka-Refs saga*" (in *Mediaeval
Scandinavia* 12, 1988)

As regards the classical sagas, we may cite his important study
of the representation of the Icelandic outlaw, putting *Gísla saga* and
Grettis saga in their European literary context:

"The Medieval Icelandic Outlaw: Life-Style, Saga, and Legend"
(in *From Sagsa to Society: Comparative Approaches to Early Iceland,* ed.
Gísli Pálsson, 1992)

On poetry in Eddic meters, Fred contributed an insightful study
of *Sólarljóð* and a forceful and important argument for the early
origin of *Rígspula.*

"Norse-Christian Syncretism and Interpretatio Christiania in
Sólarljóð (in *Gripla* 7, 1990)
"The Historical Worth of *Rígspula*" (in *Alvíssmál* 10, 2001)

Fred's abiding interest in myth, mythography, and theories of myth led to several fascinating contributions.

"Myth and Story" (in *Occident* new series 8, 1974)
"The Medieval Hamlet: A Note on the Use and Abuse of a Myth" (in *Deutsche Vierteljahrsschrift für Geistesgeschichte und Literaturwissenschaft* 51, 1977)
"The Trickster Figure" (in *Journal of the Folklore Institute of Indiana University*, preprint series 5, 1979), reprinted as "Three Profiles of the Trickster" (in *Arv 44,* 1988)

In this context we note also Fred's assistance to Mary P. Coote in the translation of M. I. Steblin-Kamensij's *Myth* (1985).

Fred had in mind a book on the Icelandic outlaw, and it would have been a good one. His last work was a biography of the Brazilian author who had long fascinated him: *Euclides da Cunha: uma odisseia nos trópicos* (2009). A few months after Fred's death it was awarded the Euclides da Cunha prize from the Brazilian Academy of Letters.

We dedicate this volume of essays to the memory of our friend Fred Amory.

A stanza attributed to Eyvindr Finnsson skáldaspillir; and again the origins of *dróttkvætt*

Richard Perkins

> Meðan árar knarra,
> hoyra ritur karra,
> hoyra ternur kria,
> gita, hvat tær siga.
> – HANS A. DJURHUUS

> Der Ursprung der Poesie ist
> in der Arbeit zu suchen.
> – KARL BÜCHER

SECTION I: THE PROSE CONTEXT OF THE VERSE

At the end of *Haralds saga gráfeldar* (ch. 16) in Snorri Sturluson's *Heimskringla*, we find this cock-and-bull story told of Eyvindr skáldaspillir[1]: Famine holds sway in Hálogaland and it snows there

---

[1] The basis for the present article is a paper given at the eleventh Saga Conference held in Sydney in 2000 (cf. Richard Perkins, "A verse attributed to Eyvindr skáldaspillir; and again the origin of *dróttkvætt*" in the preprints for the conference: *Old Norse myths, literature and society: Proceedings of the 11ᵗʰ International Saga Conference, 2-7 July 2000, University of Sydney. Supplement*, ed. Geraldine Barnes and Margaret Clunies Ross [Sydney: Centre for Medieval Studies, 2000], 1-18). Since the Sydney conference, it has been substantially revised and appears here under a new title. It is dedicated to the memory of Fred Amory in gratitude for his friendship over many years.

3

at midsummer. Eyvindr declaims a verse about this (*Snýr á Svǫlnis vǫru*, etc.; found also in *Fagrskinna*; = *Eyv Lv 12).[2] He also composes a *drápa* about "all the Icelanders" and every Icelandic farmer gives silver in coined form (a *skattpenningr*) to reward him. At the assembly the silver is refined, forged into a cloak-brooch (*feldardálkr*) and sent to the poet. Eyvindr has it cut up and buys livestock with the proceeds. The saga continues:

Þá kom ok þar um vár við útver nǫkkurr broddr af síld. Eyvindr skipaði róðrarferju húskǫrlum sínum ok landsbúum ok røri þannug til, sem síldin var rekin. Hann kvað:

Lǫtum langra nóta
lǫgsóta verfótum
at spáþernum sporna
sporðfjǫðruðrum norðan –
vita, ef akrmurur jǫkla,
ǫl-Gerðr, falar verði,
ítr, þær'r upp um róta
unnsvín, vinum mínum.

And when all his money is used up, Eyvindr even has to give his arrows in exchange for herring. About this he declaims a third stanza (*Fengum feldarstinga*, etc.; found only in *Heimskringla*; = *Eyv Lv 14) which concludes the saga.

---

[2] *Heimskringla. Nóregs konunga sǫgur af Snorri Sturluson*, ed. Finnur Jónsson, 4 vols., Samfund til udgivelse af gammel nordisk litteratur 23 (København: S. L. Møller, 1893-1901), I: 252-4 (hereafter abbreviated as *Hkr1*); Snorri Sturluson, *Heimskringla*, ed. Bjarni Aðalbjarnarson, 3 vols., Íslenzk fornrit 26-28 (Reykjavík: Hið íslenzka Fornritafélag, 1941-51), I: 221-4 (hereafter abbreviated as *Hkr2*). In references to individual skaldic stanzs in this article, Finnur Jónsson abbreviations in *LP,* (see below, note 13), pp. xiii-xvi, are often used, not however in italics but prefixed by an astertisk (e.g., *Eyv Lv 12). This, of course, by no means implies that the attributions of stanzas to particular skalds suggested by these abbreviations are accepted.

Little space need be wasted in dwelling on the improbabilities, indeed certain absurdities, of this story. As hinted by Jón Helgason,[3] the *drápa* that Eyvindr is said to have composed is unlikely ever to have existed. Even less credible is the reward said to have been paid for it (cf. *Hkr2* I: 222, note 2, where it is calculated that the cloak-brooch would have weighed more than 10 kilogrammes); cf. also Helgi Guðmundsson.[4] These and other factors make it unlikely that the third verse was in fact composed under the circumstances described in the prose. It seems probable that most of the passage is the pure invention of Snorri, for some reason put together as a frame to accommodate the second and third verses (which, however, are unlikely to be of Snorri's composition). And there are probably lessons to be learnt here from the way Snorri appears to be playing fast and loose in his presentation and use of skaldic verses here and apparently consciously so. If this passage is really (as it is received opinion that it is) the work of Snorri Sturluson, then it must serve to demonstrate how untrustworthy he might often have been in his attribution of skaldic poetry to named poets. And we must remember that something like two-thirds of extant skaldic poetry from before Snorri's time has been transmitted to us through his single pen. In my view, one of the greatest impediments to the advance of skaldic studies in the twentieth century was the misplaced confidence that appears to have been reposed in the attributions made in medieval sources (and not least by Snorri Sturluson) of *dróttkvætt*-verses to individual poets. At all events, we may feel ourselves free to consider the second verse of the passage (referred to henceforth for convenience as "Verse 2" (= *Eyv Lv 13) more or less, although perhaps not entirely, *in vacuo*. And there is certainly very little reason to assume that it was originally composed by Eyvindr Finsson as defined, for example, as the poet of *Hákonarmál*.

---

[3] Jón Helgason, "Norges og Islands digtning" in *Litteraturhistorie: Norge og Island*, ed. Sigurður Nordal, Nordisk kultur VIII: B (Uppsala: Almqvist & Wiksell, 1953) 3-179, at 135-6.

[4] Helgi Guðmundsson, *Um haf innan. Vestrænir menn og íslenzk menning á miðöldum* (Reykjavík: Háskólaútgáfan, 1997), 321-322.

Section II: Analysis of Verse 2

Verse 2 (*Eyv Lv 13) is found, then, in *Heimskringla*, and only in that work. It is preserved in Codex Frisianus (AM 45 folio; *c.* 1300-1325) and must have been preserved in Kringla (*c.* 1250-1270) and Jöfraskinna (*c.* 1300-1325), which two vellums exist only fragmentarily, but are represented by copies on which we have to rely in the present context: of Kringla, e.g. AM 35 folio (written by Ásgeir Jónsson, *c.* 1688-1704); of Jöfraskinna, e.g. AM 37 folio (written by Jens Nielsøn in 1567-1568).[5] The location of the verse in these manuscripts is: 45: 21ra; 35: p. 236; 37: 72v.[6] Images of the relevant parts of these three manuscripts, as well as of AM 761 b quarto which also contains the verse, are to be found at *SPSMA*.[7] In addition to *Hkr1* and *Hkr2*, verse is edited in *Den norsk-islandske skjaldedigtning*, A, 1: 74; B, 1: 64,[8] in Krause, *Die Dichtung*, 270-273 and doubtless elsewhere.[9] It is presented with the following prose word order in *Hkr2*: *Lǫtum lǫgsóta sporna norðan verfótum at sporðfjǫðruðrum spápernum langra nóta, – vita, ef akrmurur jǫkla, þær'r unnsvín um róta upp, verði falar vinum mínum, ítr ǫl-Gerðr.*

I offer the following line-by-line commentary of the verse and its diction, etc.:

---

5 Cf. Diana Whaley, *Heimskringla: An Introduction* (London: Viking Society for Northern Research, 1991), 41-7.
6 Cf. Arnulf Krause, *Die Dichtung des Eyvindr skáldaspillir. Edition-Kommentar-Untersuchungen* (Leverkusen: Mark Reinhardt, 1990), 270.
7 *Skaldic Poetry of the Scandinavian Middle Ages*, https://www.abdn.ac.uk/skaldic/db.php
8 Finnur Jónsson, ed., *Den norsk-islandske skjaldedigtning*, 4 vols., vols. A, 1-2, Tekst efter håndskrifterne, vols. B, 1-2, Rettet tekst (København: Gyldendalske boghandel, 1912-15; Reprint, København: Rosenkilde og Bagger, 1967-73) (hereafter abbreviated *Skj*).
9 Cf. e.g. *Codex Frisianus: En samling af norske konge-sagaer*, ed. C. R. Unger (Christiania [Oslo]: P. T. Malling, 1871), 95.

1-3. *lǫtum lǫgsóta sporna verfótum*: cf. *Óleifr lét Vísund sporna á unnir* in a verse attributed to Sighvatr (*Hkr2*, II: 268; *Sigv 12, 3; *Skj*, A, I: 257; B, I: 239); *lǫtum*: Konráð Gíslason stresses that the mood of this verb is imperative (not indicative)[10]; *lǫgsóti*, "steed of the sea," "ship"; *sporna*, "tread" (verb); *verfótr*, "sea-foot," "oar." (With a basic sense "strike with the foot" for *sporna*, the instrumental *verfótum* with a sense "oars" is particularly apposite and Krause's interpretation "Schiffskiel" much less acceptable;[11] cf. also Konráð Gíslason, 1866.)

1-4. *sporðfjaðraðar spápernur langra nóta*, "feathered with a tail"; *sporðfjǫðruð perna langra nóta*, "tern of the long nets, feathered with a tail," "fish," and since there is a similarity between the tern and the herring, especially with respect to the tail,[12] "herring." (Because herring are caught almost exclusively with nets, the determinant *langra nóta* is apposite.) *Spápernur* is glossed by Finnur Jónsson as "varslende tærner."[13] Flornes (1939)[14] thinks that terns are so called because of their habit of collecting over shoals of fish and thus giving fishermen intelligence (*spá*) of the fish's whereabouts. Birds (and not least sea-birds), their calls, movements and very presence were thought to give all manner of information, ranging from far-reaching omens arrived at by superstitious and yet elaborate ornithomancy (cf. the expression "omen-bird" used by e.g. Hose

---

[10] Konráð Gíslason, "Strøbemærkninger til oldnordiske Digte," *Aarbøger for nordisk Oldkyndighed og Historie* 1866, 188-97.

[11] Krause, *Die Dichtung*, 271.

[12] See Hans M. Flornes, "'Spåterne': Merknader til ei lausavise av Eyvind Finnsson," *Maal og minne* 1939, 15-16.

[13] Finnur Jónsson, *Lexicon poeticum antiquæ linguæ septentrionalis. Ordbog over det norsk-islandske skjaldesprog oprindelig forfattet af Sveinbjörn Egilsson*, 2nd ed. (København: S. L. Møller, 1931), 529 (hereafter abbreviated as *LP*).

[14] Cf. Odd Nordland in *Kulturhistorisk lexikon för nordisk medeltid*, 22 vols. (Malmö: Allhem, 1956-1978) (hereafter abbreviated as *KL*), s.v. *Spådom*.

and McDougall[15]) to pointers based on common-sense deductions about, for instance, the whereabouts of other animals or (at sea) the direction of the nearest land. On the other hand, the likening of the tern to the herring implied by this kenning might rather suggest some sort of special relationship (and thus collusion) between the two animals: the terns might also be thought of as warning the herring of the fishermen's approach. Animals, particularly birds, were often thought of as warning others of approaching danger (as, indeed, they sometimes do in reality). For example, in Icelandic folklore, the great black-backed gull (*svartbakur*) was thought to have entered into an agreement with the seal by which, in return for certain favours, it would warn the seal of the approach of any seal-hunters.[16]

5. *vita*: Finnur Jónsson (*Hkr1*, IV: 70) refers to this as an "anakolutisk infin." with a sense "jeg, el. vi, vil prøve"; *akrmurur jökla: akr jökla*, "field of (floating) ice," "sea" (cf. the kenning *land ísa* for "sea" in *Skáldskaparmál*[17]); *mura*, "cinquefoil," probably more specifically, "*Potentilla anserina*" (cf. Holmboe[18]; *KL*, s.v. *Madplanter, vilde* [cols 209-210]). The root of this plant was eaten in Scandinavia in former centuries by livestock, the poor and in times of hardship. Knud Leem, writing in the mid-eighteenth century, says of the Norwegian word *mure*: "Saa kaldes paa Sundmør een liden smal enkelt Roed, som er guulagtig af Farve, og sødagtig af Smag næsten som een Nød-kierne, hvilken Roed voxer der i *Agrene*" (my

---

15 Charles Hose and W. McDougall, "The relations between men and animals in Sarawak," *The Journal of The Anthropogical Institute of Great Britain and Ireland* 31 (1901): 173-213.
16 Cf. Lúðvík Kristjánsson, *Íslenzkir sjávarhættir*, 5 vols. (Reykjavík: Bókaútgáfa Menningarsjóðs, 1980-86), I: 438, 449 (hereafter abbreviated as *ÍS*).
17 Snorri Sturluson, *Edda. Skáldskaparmál*, ed. Anthony Faulkes, 2 vols. (Exeter: Viking Society for Northern Research, 1998), 36 (hereafter abbreviated as *SnE*, 1998).
18 Jens Holmboe, "Mura (*Potentilla anserina* L.) og dens bruk som matnyttig plante i ældre og nyere tid," *Svensk botanisk tidskrift* 22 (1928-29): 160-8.

emphasis); and Hannaas implies that the same plant was known in Innvik (Sogn og Fjordane) as *grisemure* because its roots were used as fodder for pigs (cf. *–svín* in line 8).[19] The roots of the cinquefoil would be just below the surface of the ground just as herring would be just below the surface of the sea (cf. Krause, 1990, 271).

5-8. *vita ef akrmurur jǫkla verði falar vinum mínum*: Finnur Jónsson's (*Skj*, B, I: 65) translation, "lad os se, om ikke sildene…fås tilkøbs hos mine venner," is perhaps not unreasonable within the context of the prose of *Heimskringla* surrounding the verse. But if we consider the verse more or less *in vacuo* (as I have suggested we should), Kock's understanding of the words *verði falar vinum mínum* (i.e. "are available to, can be caught by my men")[20] seem clearly correct, as is his translation of all eight words, "för att se, om mitt folk kan fånga lite sill."

6. *ǫl-Gerðr*: kenning for "woman." Skaldic verses are sometimes addressed to women, even though the poet seems to be in circumstances (e.g. as here, out at sea) where no woman is present (on this, see further Section IX). And in some half dozen instances, a woman is, as here, apostrophized with a kenning containing the element *Gerðr* as a base-word.[21] The determinant *ǫl-* refers to the woman's role as a server of beer at table (cf. Meissner, 417). – Codex Frisianus has the variant reading *eld-Gerðr*. If this is a genuine

---

[19] See *Professor Knud Leems Norske maalsamlingar fraa 1740-aari (Handskr. nr. 597, 4to i Kallske samling)*, ed. Torleiv Hannaas, Skrifter utgjevne for Kjeldeskriftfondet 48 (Kristiania [Oslo]: Jacob Dybwad, 1923), 130-131.

[20] Ernst A. Kock, *Notationes norrænæ. Anteckningar till Edda och skaldediktning*, 28 vols., Lunds Universitets årsskrift n.f., avd. 1, 19 nr. 2 to 39 nr. 3 (Lund: Gleerup, 1923-44), §3050 (hereafter abbreviated as *NN*).

[21] Cf. Rudolf Meissner, *Die Kenningar der Skalden: ein Beitrag zur skaldischen Poetik*, Rheinische Beiträge und Hülfsbücher zur germanischen Philologie und Volkskunde I (Bonn: Kurt Schroeder, 1921), 406; *LP*, 179-180; Roberta Frank, "Why skalds address women," *Poetry in the Scandinavian Middle Ages. Atti del 12° Congresso internazionale di studi sull'alto Medioevo*, ed. Teresa Paroli (Spoleto: Centro Studi, 1990) 67-83, at 79-83.

kenning for "woman" – and it is paralleled by *eld-Gefn* in *Mgóð 2 (*Skj*, A, I: 330; B, I: 304) – then *eld-* ("fire-") may be conceived as part of an incomplete kenning for "gold" (cf. Meissner, 413; kennings for "woman" are frequently incomplete; cf. Meissner, 419-420). On the other hand, Krause's (1990, 272) suggestion that *eld-Gerðr* refers to the "Göttin des Herdfeuers" is not to be dismissed; it might then refer to the woman's role as one who tends the house's fire (cf. the sense of *ǫl-Gerðr*).

8. *unnsvín*, literally "wave-pigs." This word has been interpreted in various ways. For example, Finnur Jónsson (*LP*, 583) takes it as "skib" and (*LP*, 472) is able to point to an instance in modern Icelandic of the expression *að róta upp* used of vessels scooping fish up out of the sea.[22] Monsen improbably understands *unnsvín* as "fishing net."[23] I now think it most likely that a whale or some whale-like creature, and then very possibly a dolphin, is referred to.[24] Dolphins feed mainly on fish (not least herring) which they find by their echolocation (and possibly also disorientate by the same means, making them easier to catch). At least some species have well-defined snouts and in this respect perhaps somewhat resemble pigs. And there may be a comparison between the sounds made by a dolphin and a pig. The word *unnsvín* meaning "whale" or "dolphin" (rather than "boat") would probably be paralleled by *brimsvín* in verse 27 of *Hymiskviða* (cf. *KFD*, 13-14); and also by Danish *marsvin*, "porpoise" (literally: "pig of the sea"). In this context, we may note the antiquated expression in English *herring-*

---

[22] See Bjarni Sæmundsson, "Fiskirannsóknir 1909 og 1910," *Andvari* 37 (1911): 51-103, at 97.

[23] Erling Monsen, with A. H. Smith, Snorre Sturluson *Heimskringla: or, The Lives of the Norse Kings* (Cambridge: W. Heffer & Sons, 1932), 114.

[24] See Svale Solheim, *Kvalen i folketru og dikting*, Ord og sed 111 (Oslo: Nemndi til gransking av norsk nemningsbruk, 1942), 12-13 (hereafter abbreviated as *KFD*); cf. Richard Perkins, "Rowing chants and the origins of *dróttkvæðr háttr*," *Saga-Book* 21 (1982-5): 155-221, at 199-200 (hereafter abbreviated as *R*, with an immediately following page reference).

hog for the dolphin (cf. Josselyn[25]: " . . . we saw many Grandpisces or Herring-hogs, hunting the scholes of Herrings").[26] But it is not impossible that the poet ingeniously meant both the ideas, i.e. both "dolphin" (or "whale" or "porpoise") and "boat" to be present.

The following rendering of the verse into English may be offered:

> Let us row our vessel (let us have our sea-steed tread with oars) from the north to the herring, feathered with tails, to find out, O lady, whether fish, which dolphins/whales (*or* ships) root up, may be caught by my comrades.

SECTION III: THE ORIGIN OF *DRÓTTKVÆÐR HÁTTR* IN ROWING CHANTS

At the third Saga Conference in Oslo in 1976, I put forward the thesis that the metre *dróttkvæðr háttr* had its origin in time-keeping verses or chants used to regulate rowing in the Scandinavian ships of the period in which it arose.[27] I developed this idea further in an article which appeared in *Saga-Book* in 1982-

---

[25] John Josselyn, *An Account of two Voyages to New-England* (London: Giles Widdows, 1674), 10.

[26] Dolphins found in Icelandic waters (cf. pp. 26-27 below) include the Common dolphin (*Delphinus delphis*), the White-beaked dolphin (*Lagenorhynchus albirostris*), the Atlantic white-sided dolphin (*Lagenorhynchus acutus*), and the Bottlenose dolphin (*Tursiops truncatus*). The commonest of these is perhaps the White-beaked dolphin which "eagerly follows ships and boats" (cf. Sigurður Ægisson, Jón Ásgeir í Aðaldal, Jón Baldur Hlíðberg, *Icelandic Whales, Past and Present*, trans. Daniel Teague [Reykjavík: Forlagið, 1997], 16-23, 61-66).

[27] Cf. Richard Perkins, "Rowing chants, the first Kings' Sagas?," *The Third International Saga Conference, Oslo, July 26th-31st, 1976* (Oslo: n. p., 1976).

1985 (=R). And I wrote a note relevant to this theme which also appeared in *Saga-Book (Notes and reviews)* in 1987 (=NQ).[28] In framing my theory (R155-157), I make three assumptions: (*a*) that rowing was a particularly common activity when *dróttkvæðr háttr* came into existence; (*b*) that poetry in *dróttkvæðr háttr* is, of course, a form of metrical composition; (*c*) that labour processes, including rowing, can give rise to new modes of rhythmical composition. In support of my theory, I then turn first (R158-163) to a verse preserved in *Bjarnar saga Hítdælakappa*[29] i.e. *Hristi handar fasta*, etc. (= *Bjhit 2,2 here abbreviated *Bj*) of which I now give this rendering:

> The man has given the lady sexual pleasure; Eykyndill's bottom beats hard on the down cushion; meanwhile (*meðan*) let us cause (*vinnum*) the stout oar to sigh at the gunwhale. There is a reason for that: I must keep the ship moving forward.

I produce nine reasons to support the idea that *Bj* was, as the editor(s) of *ÍF* III, argue, "ort við árina, meðan á róðri stóð" or (put another way) a rowing chant. I cannot go into these in detail here, but they include the following: (A) The fact that the verse says that rowing is in progress while it is being declaimed. (B) that *Bj* contains the first person plural of a verb denoting the work in hand (in this case rowing); this is a common feature of work chants. (C) That *Bj* is what, for want of a better term, I call a *"meðan-verse"*: such verses juxtapose descriptions of two activities (one or both of them often some act of labour of the sex act) and connect them with a word meaning "while" (Icelandic: *meðan*). (I give other examples from Old Norse poetry and American whalers' songs and shanties; and also one from Saxo Grammaticus's *Gesta Danorum*; cf.

---

[28] Richard Perkins, "Steigar-Þórir's Couplet and Steinn Herdísarson II: Notes and Queries," *Saga-Book (Notes and reviews)* 22 (1987): 109-15 (hereafter abbreviated as *NQ*).
[29] *Bjarnar saga Hítdælakappa* in *Borgfirðinga sǫgur*, ed. Sigurður Nordal and Guðni Jónsson, ÍF 3 (Reykjavík: Hið íslenzka Fornritafélag, 1972), 109-211, at 123-124.

Section IX). Such *meðan*-verses are clearly related to work chants.[30] After dealing with *Bj*, I consider various other verses in *dróttkvætt* which I think could have been used as rowing chants, not least one preserved uniquely in Flateyjarbók and attributed to a certain Þórarinn (*Skj*, A, I: 153; B, I: 145; *Þór; R196: *Sitr við ár, enn etjum*, etc.). The conclusion of this part of my argument is, then, that the Vikings could well have rowed to the accompaniment of verses composed in *dróttkvætt*.

But this conclusion does not, of course, necessarily suffice to demonstrate that *dróttkvætt* had its origins in rowing chants. In R165-171, however, I go on to suggest how certain features of (poetry in) *dróttkvætt* might be explained if *dróttkvætt*-poetry had its origins in rowing chants:

(I) The final trochee of the *dróttkvætt*-line (and indeed the metres most distinctive feature) could have had its origin as a regularly recurring constant of the type which appears at the end of lines of work chants. Such constants, frequently uttered at the moment of greatest exertion often consist of inarticulate grunts and mark the end of a line which was otherwise variable. The following example is from the Thonga people of southern Africa recorded by the Swiss missionary, Henri Junod:

Ba hi shanisa! Ehe!
Ba ku hi hlupha! Ehe!
Ba nwa makhofi! Ehe!

---

[30] As is suggested by the title of Katarina Villner's contribution of 1980 ("*När lantman trygg på landet står, en sjöman emot böljan flår.*" *Antagonismen mellan sjöman och bönder belyst av folkliga sjömansvisor* [unpublished Uppsats för fortsättningskurs i etnologi, Institutet för Folklivsforskning, Stockholms Universitet, 1980]), similar patterns or themes are to be found in Swedish shanties and other seamen's songs from recent centuries (with Swedish *när* corresponding to Icelandic *meðan* and English *while*).

Ba nga hi nyiki! Ehe![31]

(II) Another feature of *dróttkvætt* is that the number of syllables in each line is fixed within narrow limits and in the vast majority of cases is six. The standardization of the length of each line would regularize the incidence of the constant and make for the strict coordination which would have been so necessary in rowing.

(III) The third feature to be mentioned here is not a prosodic one. It is rather the extensive use of kennings and *heiti* in the diction of poetry composed in *dróttkvætt*. And here my theory ties in with one already propounded by various scholars. This is that skaldic diction had its origin in the language of taboo used by those wishing to avoid normal everyday language for superstitious reasons. Such languages (which for convenience may be called "*noa*-languages") are particularly common amongst hunters and fishermen (who use *noa*-expressions not least for their quarry) but also amongst warriors and seamen in general. And *noa*-expressions are particularly used of feared and revered phenomena. On the basis of Jakob Jakobsen's description of 1897 of the *noa*-language used at sea by Shetland fishermen in the nineteenth century,[32] Axel Olrik (also 1897) sought to account for various special expressions listed in the poem

---

[31] Henri A. Junod, *The Life of a South African tribe*, 2nd ed., 2 vols. (London: Macmillan, 1927), here quoted from Junod II: 189, 284. (While Junod gives the fourth word of the second line as *hlupa* on p. 189, he gives it as *hlupha* on p. 284.) The man whom Junod heard murmuring the verse had just been chastised by his European masters; he appears to have been a member the Nkuna clan of the Thonga tribe (cf. Junod, 1927, I: 19). Junod gives this translation: "They treat us badly! Ehe! They are hard on us! Ehe! They drink their coffee! Ehe! And they give us none! Ehe!" George Thomson (*Studies in Ancient Greek Society. The Prehistoric Ægean*, 4th ed. [London: Lawrence and Wishart, 1978], 447-8) refers to this verse in his discussion of the origins of poetry.

[32] Jakob Jakobsen, *Det norrøne sprog på Shetland* (København: Wilhelm Prior, 1897).

Alvíssmál and also represented by skaldic *heiti*.[33] Erik Noreen saw the origin of kennings for "snake" of the type *lyngfiskr* in *noa*-expressions for the same animal (e.g. Norwegian *lyngål*).[34] In an important work of 1940, Svale Solheim was able to demonstrate the extensive use of *noa*-language amongst Norwegian fishermen of recent centuries.[35] And in *KFD* of 1942, he argued that various expressions for "whale" in Old Norse poetry (e.g. *brimsvín* in *Hymiskviða*, verse 27; *unnsvín* in Verse 2) had their origins in *noa*-language. Finally Alberta Johanna Portengen in her contribution of 1915 put forward an elaborate argument for the origin in *noa*-language not merely of skaldic kennings and *heiti* but of the diction of Germanic poetry as a whole.[36] This she does on the basis of a wide-ranging discussion of *noa*-language the world over and not least of N. Adriani's study of a sea-*noa*-language used by a people living in the Sangir Archipelago (Kepulauan Sangihe) off the north-eastern tip of Sulawesi (Celebes) in present-day Indonesia.[37] In addition to their everyday language (called Sangirese), the people in question had a special *noa*-language (called Sasahara) which they used first and foremost at sea but also in their poetry but also in

---

[33] Axel Olrik, "Det norröne sprog på Shetland og den nordiske kultur," *Nordisk tidskrift för vetenskap, konst och industri utgifven af Letterstedtska Föreningen* 20 (1897): 339-44. We may note the use of *noa*-expressions (including *nomina agentis*; cf. R, note 24 on pages 207-208; Meissner, *Die Kenningar*, 6ff., 110ff.) aboard an Orkney deep-sea trawler in the twenty-first century (cf. Redmond O'Hanlon, *Trawler. A journey through the North Atlantic* [London: Penguin, 2004], 99-100).

[34] Erik Noreen, *Studier i fornvästnordisk diktning*, 3 vols., Uppsala universitets årsskrift 1921: Filosofi, språkvetenskap och historiska vetenskaper 4; 1922: Filosofi, språkvetenskap och historiska vetenskaper 4; 1923: Filosofi, språkvetenskap och historiska vetenskaper 3 (Uppsala: Akademiska bokhandeln, 1921-1923), I: 3-17.

[35] Svale Solheim, *Nemningsfordomar ved fiske* (Oslo: Jacob Dybwad, 1940), hereafter abbreviated as *NF*.

[36] Alberta Johanna Portengen, *De Oudgermaansche dichtertaal in haar ethnologisch verband* (Leiden: H. L. van Nifterik, 1915) (hereafter abbreviated as *ODEV*).

[37] N. Adriani, *Sangireesche spraakkunst* (Leiden: A. H. Adriani, 1893).

their poetry (and not least poetry which accompanied paddling or rowing; cf. R, note 26). Now while it is impossible to accept Portengen's arguments in their entirety, her contribution to this theory was to draw attention to Sasahara as a concrete example of what seems to be the derivation of poetic diction from a *noa*-language. Not least from the researches of Jakob Jakobsen and Svale Solheim, we may infer with confidence that a *noa*-language used at sea existed in the milieu in which *dróttkvætt*-poetry arose. And if we assume that *dróttkvæðr háttr* had its origin in rowing chants used at sea, then this would go far in explaining the abundant use of kennings in skaldic poetry.

In R171-174, I turn to a different kind of evidence in support of my thesis, the fact that skaldic kennings appear to evince a certain preoccupation not only with things maritime in general but phenomena familiar to the rower in particular. This sometimes despite the fact that the metaphor involved is sometimes somewhat inapposite. Thus in kennings for "sword" the base-word in various cases is a word for "oar," despite the relatively un-sword-like nature of an oar (see R172). There are three or four kennings for "tongue" where the base-word is a word for "oar" (see R172-173). The word *dorg* which *LP* (83) glosses as "fiskesnöre (på en lang stang, som slæbes med båden, idet denne ros frem)" is used as a determinant in three kennings for "sea," in none of which particularly appositely (cf. *SnE*, 1998, 36). And a 'woman' is characterized as the *popta* ("rowing-bench") of riches (or the like) in at least four kennings (cf. *LP*, 642-643). In R174-179 I draw my conclusions: First I mention two alternative theories on the origin of *dróttkvætt*. I am afraid that I am dismissive of these, particularly of Hallvard Lie's arguments that "dróttkvættstilen" had its inspiration in the visual arts of the period in which it arose. Second, I anticipate and answer various possible objections which may be made to my theory. I shall return to these in Section VIII. Finally, I draw attention to certain advantages my theory has: (a) It ties in well with the existing (and to some extent favoured) theory that kennings and *heiti* had their origin in *noa*-expressions and *noa*-language. (b) It fully accepts, as seems necessary, that *dróttkvætt* developed from *fornyrðislag*. (c) The body of evidence in favour of it appears to be more varied and greater than that in favour of rival theories. (d) It would explain why poetry in *dróttkvætt* appears to have a special preoccupation with the sea, not only in its subject matter, but also in its diction.

In Excursus 1 of *R* (180-184), I show how the topical and laudatory themes of some *dróttkvætt* poems, as well as the hints for reward which they sometimes contain, may be shared by rowing chants and give examples of this from various places around the world. And in Excursus 2 (R184-189) I suggest how two features of the *dróttkvætt*-stanza (that is, the system of internal rhymes (*aðalhendingar* and *skothendingar*; the eight lines of the stanza) may have had some functional purpose if such stanzas were used (as I posit they were) to regulate the work of rowers.

SECTION IV: VERSE 2 AS A ROWING CHANT

At various places in my contribution of 1982-1985, I argue or assume that Verse 2 is a rowing chant (see especially *R*171). In this section, I develop this argument and under two headings as follows:

(a) Likeness of Verse 2 to an Icelandic miðavísa

By the Icelandic word *miðavísa*, we understand a mnemonic verse used to help find the position of a fishing ground (*mið*) in relationship to hills, mountains and other features on land visible from the sea. Such verses are known not only from Iceland, but also from the Faroe Islands and Norway. The oldest example is preserved in *Bárðar saga Snæfellsáss*;[38] its metre is akin to *dróttkvætt* and it has a place in editions of the skaldic corpus (cf. e.g. *Skj*, A, II:

---

[38] Cf. *Bárðar saga Snæfellsáss*, in *Harðar saga: Bárðar saga, Þorskfirðinga saga, Flóamanna saga*, ed. Þórhallur Vilmundarson and Bjarni Vilhjálmsson, ÍF 13 (Reykjavík: Hið íslenzka Fornritafélag, 1991), 99-172, at 124-5; *Bárð 3.

450; B, II: 482). Perhaps the fullest collection of Icelandic *miðavísur* is that of Lúðvík Kristjánsson in *ÍS*, III: 194-200. One of the *miðavísur* recorded by Lúðvík (*ÍS*, III: 198) is this from eastern Iceland:

> Róum út og norður
> Fáskrúðs flyðru sporður,
> Köttur á Kambfjall
> Höttur á Hanfjall,
> Sauðaból og Súlunes
> saman Njáll og Bera
> þar skaltu vera.[39]

It is unnecessary to discuss the place-names of this verse (nor have I been able to discover the more precise import of the words *Fáskrúðs flyðru sporður*, although one wonders if a comparison with the Norwegian *noa*-place-name *Sildsporden* used at sea [cf. *NF*, 162] might not be of interest in this context.) But at least some similarities with Verse 2 here under discussion may be discerned: both verses begin with a word or periphrasis meaning "let us row"; both indicate the direction of rowing (*norður, norðan*); and both have rhyme on the elements *norð-* and *sporð-*. *Miðavísur* must have been rehearsed (or at least muttered) while rowing was actually in progress and it is reasonable to assume that it was possible to row to them. Here then we find a likeness between Verse 2 and a verse which may have been used as some sort of rowing chant.

---

[39] Formulae similar to *þar skaltu vera* are found elsewhere in *miðavísur*: in the skaldic *miðavísa* in *Bárðar saga Snæfellsáss*: *þar skaltu þá liggja* (cf. *ÍF* 13: 125); in Faroese: *har skalt tú fiskin fanga* (cf. V. U. Hammershaimb, *Færøsk anthologi*, 2 vols., Samfund til udgivelse af gammel nordisk litteratur, 15 [København: S. L. Møller, 1891] I: 338 [hereafter abbreviated as *FA*]); in Norwegian: *Der fisker'u best* (cf. Hovda, 1961, 228).

(b) Likeness of Verse 2 to a Faroese children's verse

In his book *Rytmens trollmakt*,[40] Gustaf Cederschiöld discerned an affinity between certain Scandinavian cradle songs on the one hand and rowing chants on the other. He writes:

Bland andra grupper [of cradle songs] förtjänar den att särskildt uppmärksammas, som börjar med:

Ro, ro till fiskeskär,
många fiskar få vi där,

eller någon variation af samma tanke. Också i Norge äro dessa visor rikt representerade. I fortsättningen uppräknas vanligen de fiskar, man skall fånga. Dessa visor tyckas snarare ha uppkommit vid verklig rodd eller då man lekt "rodd" med små barn genom att taktmässigt föra deras armar fram och tillbaka. Om detta är den egentliga användningen, har öfverflyttningen til vaggningen kunnat bero på likhet i takt, på analogien mellan vagga och båt, vaggning och rodd, samt kanske också på ordet *Ro,* som ju i annan betydelse börjar många vaggvisor.

And later in his book, Cederschiöld (*RT*, 97) refers to the proposition that "ursprungliga svenska (och norska) roddarsånger kunna dölja sig under vissa nutida vaggvisor, som handla om rodd."

In a contribution of 1987 (= *NQ*), I point to certain similarities between a skaldic couplet attributed to Steigar-Þórir (*Vǫrum félagar fjórir / forðum – einn við stýri; Skj,* A, I: 434; B, I: 403; *Steigþ*) on the one hand and certain Icelandic children's verses used in a seal-hunting game on the other. I then use Cederschiöld's arguments

---

[40] Gustaf Cederschiöld, *Rytmens trollmakt: några bidrag till människans historia*, Populärt vetenskapliga föreläsningar vid Göteborgs Högskola, ny följd I (Stockholm: Albert Bonnier, 1905), 80 (hereafter abbreviated as *RT*).

just mentioned in support of the suggestion that Steigar-Þórir's couplet might, in fact, be part of a rowing chant. I now offer a similar sort of argument in connection with a Faroese children's verse and Verse 2. The children's verse in question, edited by V. U. Hammershaimb is as follows:

Rogva út á balta, veiða fiskin salta,
rogva út á tanga, veiða fiskin langa,
rogva út á háa, veiða fiskin gráa;
rogvið suður, og rogvið norður at vita,
hvàt íð harrin vil geva ogum báðum.[41]

Hammershaimb's Danish translation is this:

Ro ud på havet at fange den salte fisk, ro ud på tange at fange fisken den lange, ro ud på medet at fange fisken den grå, ro mod syd og ro mod nord at forsøge, hvad gud vil give os begge.

And my English translation would be:

Row out onto the sea, catch the salt fish, / row out to the headland, catch the long fish, / row out to the fishing ground, catch the grey fish; / row to the south, and row to the north to find out / what the Lord will give to us both.

Now I have yet to establish under what precise circumstances this verse might have been used, whether in children's games, or in dandling children or simply as a cradle song. But however this may be, certain structural and other likenesses to Verse 2 are undeniable: Both begin with an invocation to row and to the prospective

---

[41] V. U. Hammershaimb, "Barneviser og ramser," *Antiquarisk Tidsskrift udgivet af Det kongelige nordiske Oldskrift-Selskab 1849-1851* (1852): 310-315, at 312.

catching of fish; both refer to the direction of the rowing (Verse 2: *norðan*; the Faroese verse: *suður, norður*); more interestingly, both employ the infinitive (*at*) *vita* in very much the same context within the structure of the verse; and both end by mentioning the potential beneficiary of the catch in the dative (Verse 2: *vinum mínum*; Faroese verse: *ogum báðum*).

Here, then, are two pieces of evidence on the basis of which it may be argued that Verse 2 was used as a rowing chant. It will be noted that the comparative material I adduce is relatively varied in nature (an Icelandic *miðavísa*; a Faroese children's verse); and, with respect to (b), my arguments are paralleled by a comparison of an *Icelandic* children's verse with a piece of poetry rather different from Verse 2. Such factors, I would suggest, somewhat reinforce my arguments on this matter. The Faroese children's verse belongs, of course, to the type mentioned by Cederschiöld (*Ro, ro till fiskeskär*, etc.) which is probably found throughout Scandinavia.[42] And the Icelandic *miðavísa* finds parallels in at least the Faroe Islands and Norway.

SECTION V: THE DICTION OF VERSE 2 AND *NOA*-LANGUAGE

My contention, then, is that Verse 2 was used as a rowing chant and then, it would appear, by fishermen on their way out to the fishing-banks in the hope of making a catch. Now in Section III above, I have pointed out that my suggestion that *dróttkvætt* had its origin in rowing chants accords well with an already existing theory on the origin of skaldic *heiti* and kennings in *noa*-language. And what is of interest here is that it is difficult to imagine many situations in which *noa*-language is more likely to have been used than that I envisage for the rehearsal of Verse 2. In substantiation of this statement, I present the following considerations in itemized form:

---

[42] Cf e.g. Per Hovda, *Norske fiskeméd: landsoversyn og to gamle médbøker*, Skrifter frå Norsk stadnamnarkiv 2 (Oslo: Universitetsforlaget 1961), 126-7.

(1) Verse 2 would have been declaimed at sea: it is precisely at sea that *noa*-languages are particularly used. Jakobsen (1897, 84) referred to the *noa*-language of the Shetland fishermen as "et systematisk gennemført søsprog" and Adriani to Sasahara (cf. pp. 14-15 above) as "een volledige zee-tal." The many *noa*-expressions collected by Solheim in *NF* were, of course, primarily used at sea. *And there can be little doubt that in the environment in which* dróttkvætt *had its origins and that in which skaldic poetry was cultivated, the Norse, at least to some extent, used* noa-*language while at sea.*

(2) Verse 2 was declaimed while people were at work: *noa*-language was often used while people were involved in some labour or enterprise and then not necessarily at sea. To give random examples, we note that those engaged in brewing ale, harvesting crops, mining minerals often used *noa*-language. Carelessness in such situations could lead to failure of the enterprise, bad luck with the weather and accidents. In this connection, it is worth citing *in extenso* a passage from Solheim's *NF* (176) concerning Norwegian fishermen:

Når fiskarane i gamle dagar var ute på sjøen og fiska, så hadde dei ei kjensle av at sjølve arbeidet var noko høgtideleg, noko som låg heilt utanom det vanlege. Utan tvil kjende dei det som dei var i ei verd for seg sjølv, i ein annan heim. Men livet i denne andre heimen var fullt av spaning og otte. Støtt måtte fiskaren vera på vakt, for kringom han på alle kantar låg det og lurde sterke og farlege makter, som berre venta på eit høve til å gjera skade. Og skade, det var det same som mislukka fiske, uver, skipbrot og mannespille.

And Solheim continues:

Fiskarane var samstundes bønder, dei hadde gard og buskap og avgrøde som dei hadde ansvar og omsut for. Kvar dei stod og gjekk i sitt arbeid som fiskarar, kunne dei ikkje kjenna seg heilt trygge for det dei åtte og hadde kjært. Det kunne så lett bera til ymse uhende heime på garden med grøda, buskapen og huslyden. Krøtera kunne gå seg bort og koma ut for rovdyr og anna vondt.

(3) Verse 2 was used amongst fishermen, probably hoping to catch herring. *Noa*-language was particularly used amongst certain groups of people, for example, warriors, hunters, seamen in general and fishermen in particular. Olrik and Solheim described the sea-*noa*-language of respectively Shetlandic and Norwegian fishermen. And Solheim (*NF*, 38) refers to the use of *noa*-language precisely amongst herring-fishermen (in Scotland).

(4) Verse 2 mentions various phenomena for which we might expect *noa*-expressions to be particularly used. These may be considered in itemized form as follows:

(a) *lǫgsóti*, "boat," "ship" (possibly also *unnsvín*; see above pp. 9-10). There was a great reluctance amongst Scandinavian fishermen and seamen to mention their vessels by their ordinary names; Solheim (*NF*, 14-39) gives numerous examples. And an example from outside Scandinavia: the war-canoes of the Maoris were surrounded by many taboos. Cf. *R*, note 21.

(b) *verfótr*, "oar." The same taboos on mentioning sailing-vessels by their usual names also often extended to a ship's or boat's equipment and then not least to its oars. Solheim (*NF*, 21-22) adduces examples of various *noa*-expressions for 'oar' from Norway, Orkney and Shetland and in this context writes as follows:

> Det er turvande å streka sterkt under at alt som hadde med riggen å gjera, og alt som høyrde med til årar og roing, hadde overlag mykje å seia for god lukke på sjøen. Det var saker som dei laut vera varsame med, ting som til kvar tid laut vera i god stand dersom fiskarane skulle kunna kjenna seg nokolunde trygge på sjøen. Ei mast, eit

segl, eit fall, årar o.s.b. som ikkje vart ettersedde og skifte
ut når det trongst, ville lett kunna gjera navigasjonen
livsfarleg. Reint praktiske omsyn har gjort at fiskarane i
serleg grad laut vera på vakt, også når det galdt
nemningane. Og så lyt vi ikkje gløyma at her var eit rikt
operasjonsfelt for uvener [cf. the *vinir* of Verse 2, line 8]
og medtevlarar som hadde vondt i hugen. Dersom slike i
løynd fekk høve til å tukla med desse ting, så kunne det
verkeleg verta fare på ferde.

In Sasahara there was a special word for "paddle (of a canoe)"
(cf. Adriani, 1893, 61; R170).

(c) *akr jǫkla*, "sea" (in kenning for "fish" or "herring"). *Noa*-
expressions are not only very frequently used *at* sea (cf. (1) above),
but also *of* the sea (and then not least by fishermen of fishing-
banks). Solheim (*NF*, 116ff.) produces material from various places
in the Scandinavian world and the British Isles. At least three of the
Shetlandic *noa*-words to which Axel Olrik draws attention in
connection with the diction of *Alvíssmál* meant "sea" (viz. *djub, mar,
log*; cf. R168-169). And a *noa*-expression for the sea used in the
Hebrides, i.e. "Mary's Storehouse," is interestingly described in one
source as a "Roman Catholic kenning" (cf. *NF*, 117).

(d) *unnsvín*, probably "whale," "dolphin" (rather than "boat,"
"ship"). *Noa*-expressions were particularly used of large or
dangerous animals, whether of the land or sea. The normal
Germanic word for "bear" (cf. e.g. Swedish *björn*, German *Bär*) was
originally a *noa*-expression (meaning "the brown one"). And whales
and similar large sea-animals were referred to by *noa*-expressions,
not only because of the awe they were held in by seafarers but also
when they were being hunted. In his short monograph on whales in
Norwegian folklore (*KFD*), Svale Solheim mentions various *noa*-
expressions for whales used, for example, by modern and
motorized Norwegian whale-hunters (*KFD*, 8) or by Shetlandic
fishermen (viz. *fjedin*, "the fat one"). He also points out that the

Danish *marsvin*, "porpoise," which is a parallel to *unnsvín* "er sikkert
eit opphavleg løyndenamn." Like the person declaiming Verse 2
and his companions, the *unnsvín* might be in search of herring (and
perhaps even swimming close to their vessel; cf. Note 26). They
might, then, have regarded it as a competitor and a threat to their
enterprise and thus have used a *noa*-expression for it. In the fishing
communities of northern of Scotland, any mention of the word
porpoise might mean failure to catch fish or some disaster.[43] Certainly
the whale-hunting Indians of Vancouver Island used *noa*-epressions
for their quarry (cf. R, note 29). And in Sasahara there were special
words for "shark" and "sawfish" (see Adriani, 1893, 56).

(e) *pernur langra nóta; akrmurur jǫkla*, "fish," and more probably
"herring." Amongst hunters, fishermen, and indeed gatherers of
inanimate objects the world over, perhaps the greatest taboo was on
mentioning the object of the search itself by its usual name and *noa*-
expressions were frequently used, for example, by hunters of their
quarry and by fishermen of the fish they were out to catch. The
intention was here very much to conceal their aims from hostile
spirits, competitors and, of course, the object of the pursuit or
search.[44]

---

[43] Morag Cameron, "Highland fisher-folk and their superstitions," *Folklore* 14 (1903): 300-06, at 304.
[44] As general a source as the Swedish *Nationalencyklopedin* has this to say in
connection with *noa*-language: "Noaord förekom tidigare rätt ofta i
samband med jakt och fiske och har där sin grund i föreställningen att
djuren förstod mänskligt språk. Genom att använda noaord kunde jägaren
eller fiskaren dölja sina avsikter för bytesdjuret" ("Noaord" in
Nationalencyklopedin, ed. Christer Engström, 20 vols. [Höganäs: Bokförlaget
Bra Böcker, 1989-96], 14: 193). And Adriani (1893, 7) writes of Sasahara
(cf. pp. 14-15 above): "Deze taal wordt op zee gesproken, opdat de
geesten de plannen der varenden niet zullen afluisteren en die uit
kwaadwilligheid verijdelen" ("This language is spoken at sea, so that the
genii may not eavesdrop on the plans of the seamen and, out of spite,
frustrate them").

Numerous examples are given in *ODEV* (see particularly pp. 78-128). For example, those out looking for camphor in Borneo would refer to the object of their search not by its normal name but as "the thing that smells." Hunters in Norway would speak of their quarry simply as *dyret* (cf. R, note 23). And particularly fishermen used *noa*-expressions for the fish they were out to catch, not only in fresh water but more particularly at sea. Solheim (*NF*, 39-57) gives ample evidence from Norway of *noa*-expressions for fish in general and for different sorts of fish in particular. It is true that *noa*-expressions for "herring" seem to be strangely absent from the modern Norwegian material, But Solheim (*NF*, 53-54) is able to offer explanations for this and, to some extent on the basis of Estonian material, comes to the very reasonable conclusion that "dei norske fiskarane ein gong verkeleg har hatt motvilje mot å nemna silda." – In this connection a source referred to by Portengen (*ODEV*, 126) is of special interest: This refers to the Kenyahs, a tribe that lived around the headwaters of the River Baram in Sarawak and which was studied by Hose and McDougall at the end of the nineteenth century. According to these authorities (1901, 205), this people attributed to animals mental processes and powers of reasoning very similar to their own and believed that animals were capable of understanding them: That they entertained these beliefs in a very practical manner is shown by their conduct in preparing for a fishing excursion:

> If, for example, they are preparing to poison the fish of a section of the river with the "tuba" root, they always speak of the matter as little as possible and use the most indirect and fanciful modes of expression; thus they will say, "There are many leaves fallen here," meaning, "There are plenty of fish in this part of the river." And these elaborate precautions are taken lest the birds should overhear their remarks and inform the fish of their intentions when of course the fish would not stay to be

caught but would swim away to some other part of the river.

Here in Sarawak, the birds appear to have been thought of as posing a threat similar to that which the *spápernur* of Verse 2 might have done, i.e. that of warning the fish of impending danger from the fishermen (cf. pp. 15 above). And we also note that the "indirect and fanciful mode of expression" used by the Kenyahs relies on a botanical metaphor just as the kenning *akrmurur jǫkla* for "fish" or "herring" in Verse 2 does (cf. also *ODEV*, 125).

On the basis of the material presented in this Section, then, I would argue that the diction of Verse 2 could well have had the active function of *noa*-language within the context in which Verse 2 would appear to have been rehearsed. Indeed, we appear to have echoes of actually attested *noa*-expressions in the diction of the verse: the element *lǫg-* in *lǫgsóti* is paralleled by Shetlandic *log* and Norwegian *løgje*, both used as *noa*-terms (cf. *NF*, 113-115; *KFD*, 2-3); and, as noted, *unnsvín* is paralleled by Danish *marsvín*, "porpoise," which as Solheim (*KFD*, 10) argues, is doubtless originally a *noa*-expression. And it will be seen how the arguments I produce here (and the comparisons I make) often chime in with those of various of the scholars who discern the origins of skaldic diction in *noa*-language (viz. Olrik, Portengen, Noreen, Solheim). In many ways, then, Verse 2 appears to help bridge the gulf which many have seen between skaldic practices and *noa*-language (however favourably inclined they may be to the idea of the *origin* of kennings and *heiti* in *noa*-expressions). And here we should remember that much skaldic poetry was clearly composed or rehearsed at sea where the use of at least some *noa*-expressions was the rule, with penalties of varying severity for infringements (cf. (1) above). We should also bear in mind that in the relatively unstratified society of free men in which skaldic poetry must have arisen, the difference between fisherman and courtier would not have been great. Particularly fishermen and whalers would probably have made very competent Vikings. And if, incidentally, the idea of a work chant couched in *noa*-language might

seem unduly complicated, it should be noted that there is in fact
some evidence for such phenomena, and for example, orders given
to rowers often contained *noa*-expressions (cf. *NF*, 21, 39; *R*, notes
26, 29).

SECTION VI: THE PROVENANCE OF VERSE 2

Various critics who, unlike me, appear to take seriously Snorri's
attribution of Verse 2 to Eyvindr skáldaspillir assume that it had its
origin in Norway in the second half of the tenth century (and then
perhaps more precisely in the 970s on the island of Alsten in
Norway's present-day Nordlands fylke.[45] But as I have suggested
above, there is certainly no compelling reason to think that it was
composed by any named or known poet. And, as far as I can see,
there is nothing in the verse (e.g. on matters of flora or fauna) to
demonstrate that is was composed in Norway rather than Iceland
(in which country it was first committed to vellum). Further, as a
possible indication of a later rather than earlier date, I would point
to the presence of the particle *um* (thus in AM 35 folio and 37 folio)
in the verse's seventh line: this, as far as I can see (and I must admit
to being on uncertain ground here) is very possibly unetymological
and yet appears essential to the metre of the verse. In view of these
factors, my suggestion is that while Verse 2 probably had older
models, it (in the form and with the wording it has been preserved
to us) could well have first been composed as late as the twelfth or
perhaps even thirteenth century and then as a rowing chant used
amongst Icelandic fishermen. More particularly, one might be
tentatively inclined to associate it with fishermen operating out of
such fishing-places (*ver*) in south-western Iceland as Grindavík,
Selvogur, Eyrarbakki or Þykkvibær who rowed southwards (cf. line
4: *norðan*) in search of herring (cf. *ÍS*, II, 29-42). It was from such an
environment that Snorri might have got to know the verse, perhaps

---

[45] Cf. Finnur Jónsson, *Den oldnorske og oldislandske litteraturs historie*, 2nd ed.,
3 vols. (København: G. E. C. Gad, 1920-1924), I: 449; Holmboe, 1928-
1929, 165; Flornes, 1939; Frank, 1990, 67.

as early as his boyhood years at Oddi. Another possibility is that it might be current amongst fishermen of Hvalfjörður where herring could well have been fished in the medieval period (cf. *KL*, s.v. *Sildefiske. Island*). But these ideas are, to say the least, conjectural.

SECTION VII: PRECONDITIONS FOR THE POSSIBLE GENESIS OF *DRÓTTKVÆTT* IN ROWING CHANTS

In this section, I take the opportunity of mentioning on a perhaps rather random basis a few factors which seem to be relevant to the culture and society in which poetry in *dróttkvætt* might have had its origins and the composition of poetry in that metre may have been first practised.

The sail came relatively late to Scandinavia, but lack of it did not inhibit intense maritime activity in the southern part of the region stretching back to the Bronze Age. The numerous Scandinavian petroglyphs of the Bronze Age depicting ships with their stylised "crew lines" (Swedish: *bemanningsstreck*) representing large teams of paddlers could well have had ritual significance. Tacitus in chapter 44 of *Germania* refers to the fleets of the Sviones, again powered by paddle. And even at the time of the advent of sail, the rowed ships of the Gotlandic picture-stones, proportionately few though they may be in number, are also of interest in this context.

A well-based and widely accepted etymology for *Russia* takes the word back to the Scandinavian word for "rowing" or "rower" or "to row" and relates it, of course, to the word *Rus*, those hardy Scandinavian rowers of the Russian rivers in the Viking Age (some of whom would have covered, for example, the distance of more than 900 kilometers upstream from the mouth of the River Dnieper to Kiev and further; it was travelling this route that Haraldr Sigurðarson may quite possibly have composed or rehearsed his *gamanvisur*; cf. *Hkr2* III: 89). And an etymology for *víkingr*, "Viking," (proposed by Daggfeldt,[46] and favoured by e.g. Gösta Holm[47]) sees this word as denoting "one who rows shifts (*vikur*) at the oar" (on long-distance journeys). Taking these arguments a little further, one might contend that it was very much the need for, and use of, rowing which was so important for the Scandinavian expansion in the Viking Age (cf. R155-157). And in my view it was this environment which gave rise to *dróttkvætt*. Here we may note Christer Westerdahl's characterization of Scandinavian society of the early Viking Age as "a rowing society."[48] (In this context it is interesting to compare the historical and economic factors which A. L. Lloyd singles out as giving rise to the shanties,[49] although with respect to the shanties the time-scale was probably rather shorter.)

And then we may think of the Scandinavian institution of levy with its essential dependence on rowing as a means of locomotion. We may, for example, consider this statement by Christer Westerdahl:

> The Scandinavian realms appear rather early on to have based their pattern of state organization on levy (*ledung, leidang*) war fleets, which later developed into the first fully-fledged system of taxation (*skatteledung*). Here the contours of the war galley permeate the whole fabric of

---

[46] Bertil Daggfeldt, "Vikingen – roddaren," *Fornvännen* 78 (1983): 92-94.

[47] Gösta Holm, "Tre bidrag till norrön etymologi," *Eyvindarbók. Festskrift til Eyvind Fjeld Halvorsen, 4. mai 1992*, ed. Finn Hødnebø et al. (Oslo: Institutt for nordistikk og litteraturvitenskap, Universitetet i Oslo, 1992), 118-22, at 120-1.

[48] Christer Westerdahl, "Society and sail. On symbols as Specific Social Values and Ships as Catalysts of Social Units," in *The Ship as Symbol in Prehistoric and Medieval Scandinavia. Papers from an International Research Seminar at the Danish National Museum, Copenhagen, 5th-7th May 1994*, ed. Ole Crumlin-Pedersen and Birgitte Munch Thye, Publications from the National Museum: Studies in Archaeology and History I (Copenhagen: Nationalmuseet, 1995), 41-50, at 43-5.

[49] A. L. Lloyd, *Folk Song in England* (St Albans: Paladin, 1975), 273-80.

society down to its smallest components, every rowlock and oar representing a farm or collection of farms, every rower's bench a village.[50]

And Westerdahl interestingly contines, although not perhaps altogether clearly:

> These microcosms, supplying the ordinary soldiers/rowers for the fleet, also had to be equalized to a fair and even burden. Thereby, the *ledung* levy system obviously gave an impetus to the first agrarian partition reforms of the North, in Sweden called *bolskifte* and *solskifte*, traces of which occur in the hazy beginnings of the Middle Ages.

If, as Westerdahl appears to suggest here, the levy-system could give rise to wide-ranging administrative and social developments in Scandinavia, this would parallel the idea of rowing giving rise to metrical developments. Certainly the levy looms large in skaldic poetry going back from the thirteenth century quite possible as far as the tenth.[51] It is also interesting that when Snorri Sturluson sets out in his *Háttatal* to instruct young poets in the techniques of skaldic metre, he seems to have something of a preoccupation with rowing and also the levy (cf. Snorri Sturluson *Edda. Háttatal*[52] xi, 14, 16, 31, 56; R200). (And two of Snorri's kennings in *Háttatal*, i.e. *ár*

---

[50] Christer Westerdahl, "Treenails and history. A Maritime Archaeological Hypothesis," in *In honorem Evert Baudou*, ed. Margareta Backe *et al.*, Archaeology and Environment 4 (Umeå: Department of Archaeology, University of Umeå, 1985) 395-414, at 395.

[51] Cf. Rikke Malmros, "Leding og skjaldekvad: Det elvte århundredes nordiske krigsflåder, deres teknologi og organisation og deres placering i samfundet, belyst gennem den samtidige fyrstedigtning," *Aarbøger for nordisk Oldkyndighed og Historie 1985* (1986): 89-139.

[52] Snorri Sturluson, *Edda. Háttatal*, ed. Anthony Faulkes, 2nd ed. (Exeter: Viking Society for Northern Research, 1999) (hereafter abbreviated as *SnE* 1999).

sára [*Ht 61: for "sword"] and *ræði tǫlu* [*Ht 81: for 'tongue] seem to show a preoccupation with the oar; cf. p. 15 above).

Dreingjabørnini í Føroyum verða borin í heim við ár í hendi goes the Faroese proverb: "The baby-boys in the Faroes are born into this world with oars in their hands." Rowing was an absolutely essential part of daily life in the Faroes up to the last century and probably the same may be said of the society in western Norway where *dróttkvætt* probably had its origins. In that same society, cradle songs and children's games may well have been related to rowing and prepared boys for a life at the oar from the start (cf. Section IV above). And for many of them who were unlucky enough to end their days in shipwreck and drowning an oar would often have been their companion in death.[53]

---

[53] Hammershaimb (*FA*, I: xxxiii) paints this word-picture of life in a Faroese community in the nineteenth century: "For at kunne drive havfiskeri i vinter- og vårtiden må der bruges store både mandede med 8-10 mand; for at gå til fjælds at samle fårene til slagtning eller til uldens afrykning kræves lige så mange folk og ofte mange flere; til handelssted, efter læge, til skyds med præst, embedsmænd og rejsende ligeledes; til indbjærgning af høet . . . ligeledes. Og dette fællesskab har sin store betydning for samlivet; der udveksles tanker og følelser under samarbejdet, snart i alvor og snart i spøg, og arbejdet selv lettes derved, som ordsproget siger: *"tungur er tigandi róður"* [cf. R155]; alt dette har en oplivende, dannende indflydelse på det selskabelige samliv, og den gensidige hjælpsomhed, som alle trænge til og til gengæld altid ere redebonne til at udvise, knytter et indbyrdes bånd af hengivenhed og deltagelse mellem bygdemænd, der kan være velsignet og dyrebart, når bygden besjæles af en god ånd." (Hammershaimb goes on to mention the poetry, including "vittige og bidende dögnviser" (cf. R180-181), which arose in this milieu.) It was in a similar environment of co-operation for successful fishing and farming and one in which rowing was so essential, that I see poetry in *dróttkvætt* having its origins and then probably in south-western Norway. – There was, at all events, a highly developed "rowing culture" in the Faroe Islands. As an indication of this we may note Joensen's statement (Jóan Pauli Joensen, *Färöisk folkkultur* [Lund:

SECTION VIII: CONCLUSIONS

In Sections IV and V, then, it has been argued that the verse attributed to Eyvindr skáldaspillir (i.e. Verse 2) could well have been used as a rowing chant by herring-fishers and also that the skaldic diction in which it is couched could well have had the active function of *noa*-language used by the fishermen for superstitious purposes. And in Section VII, I show that rowing must have had great, not to say exceptional, importance in the culture of the society in which *dróttkvætt* had its origins. Given these results, then, I reassert my thesis that: *rowing, through rowing chants, gave rise to* dróttkvæðr háttr. In Verse 2 it seems that we have preserved one of several verses in *dróttkvætt* which bear clear signs of having been used as rowing chants. The clearest example is perhaps the verse attributed to Bjǫrn Arngeirsson Hítdœlakappi (i.e. *Bj* mentioned in Section III above and discussed in R158-163). Another is the verse attributed to Þórarinn also already mentioned (*Sitr við ǫ́r, enn etjum*, etc.; *Þór*; *Skj*, A, I: 153; B, I: 145; R196). And for other possible examples, see R, note 45. As Jón Helgason (1953, 146) remarks: "i det hele taget er havsprøjtet, styrtesøerne, de knagende åretoller yndede emner . . . " in skaldic *lausavísur*. In chapter 12 of *Hávarðar saga Ísfirðings*,[54] one of a group of rowers asks the helmsman, Hávarðr, to chant a verse and he responds with a *dróttkvætt*-stanza (= *Háv* 7). Moreover, and as noted, my hypothesis explains various features of *dróttkvætt*, the final cadence and the standardized number of syllables in each line. Again as noted, it ties in well with an already existing theory (i.e. proposed by others than myself) on the origin of skaldic diction in *noa*-language. And as I have stressed,

---

Liber Läromedel, 1980], 84): "Besättningsmedlemmarna [of fishing boats] satt påbestämda platser under rodden, men under fisket fick de byta plats. Varje bygd hade sina fasta regler för hur varje enskild man skulle flytta sig." (We may also note that in Shetland, *noa*-expressions were used in orders given to rowers, e.g. for changing places on board; cf. *NF*, 39.)

[54] *Hávarðar saga Ísfirðings*, in *Vestfirðinga sǫgur*, ed. Björn K. Þórólfsson and Guðni Jónsson, ÍF 6 (Reykjavík: Hið íslenzka Fornritafélag, 1943), 289-359, at 331-2.

it: (i) fully accepts, as seems necessary, that *dróttkvætt* developed from *fornyrðislag*; and (ii) also explains the general preoccupation of skaldic poetry and its diction not only with the sea, but also with things familiar to the rower. I might at this point stress that no concerted written arguments have (as far as I know) really been marshalled against my theory since I first put it forward in Oslo in 1976.[55] In R175-179 (cf. also R, note 28), however, I anticipate and answer possible objections to my hypothesis. I could not, for example, accept an objection to my theory that there was too great a social gap between the milieu in which skaldic poetry had its origin and that familiar to the oarsman (cf. R175-176 and note 41;

---

[55] I should note, however, that Stephen N. Tranter (*Clavis metrica: Háttatal, Háttalykill and the Irish metrical tracts*, Beiträge zur nordischen Philologie 25 (Basel: Helbing & Lichtenhahn, 1997), 173, footnote 48) writes of himself as follows: "As a former oarsman and coxwain, I have my problems imagining any form of cadence being used at the 'moment of maximum exertion' [cf. R166-167]." Tranter continues: "One attempts nowadays to spread the exertion over the whole period the oar-blade is in the water, so that the analogy of the axe or hammer-stroke is misleading. In the course of the stroke two moments are particularly crucial; the point at which the blade is 'locked' into the water, and the moment at which it is struck out. If Viking techniques were in any way comparable, a work-chant serving the purpose would have to have a double stressed cadence." But as I point out in R165, it seems probable that Viking techniques were indeed different from those used by those involved in rowing races on rivers. Alan Binns ("Introduction" in Holger Arbman, *The Vikings*, trans. and ed. Alan Binns, Ancient Peoples and Places 21 [London: Thames and Hudson, 1961] 11-25, at 14) writes: "Recent experience with teams of trained rowers in facsimile vessels has shown that the stroke required is the short quick one needed for rowing at sea as distinct from racing on rivers." He also writes of the oars of ships similar to the Gokstad ship: "The oars are by no means the heavy sweeps with a long and ponderous stroke that some have imagined." And Tranter's arguments here appear to imply that, irrespective of the question of the *origin* of *dróttkvætt*, it was not even possible to row to the rhythm of verse in that metre. This, as I have been at pains to point out (both in the present contribution and in R), is a proposition which runs very much counter to a substantial body of evidence to the contrary.

Malmros, 1986, 104: "Skjaldene kender da heller ikke nogen arbejdsdeling mellem roere og krigere; både ledingshærens og den kongelige hirds mænd kan sidde ved årerne og prises for deres roning"). And I would dismiss any objection that, if my theory is correct, one would expect to find more verses in *dróttkvætt* which show unequivocal signs of being rowing chants. In fact, the evidence that *dróttkvætt*-stanzas were used as rowing chants is relatively large and varied. And at any rate, more humdrum examples of work chants rarely find their way into medieval texts.[56] The most serious objection that might be raised against my theory, and certainly the one that has most given me pause, is that work songs tend to be rather simple from a formal point of view, whereas poetry in *dróttkvætt* displays considerable formal complexity, not least with respect to its word order. But there are considerations which, taken together, more or less invalidate this objection. First, it is certainly possible to exaggerate the complexity of skaldic word order.[57] Second, I should stress that my theory does not presuppose that *dróttkvætt* as we have it did not develop out of something simpler. Indeed, it seems obvious that it did. Complex phenomena develop from simpler ones. And there are pieces of poetry in *dróttkvætt*, or metres related to it, which seem to be (connected with) maritime work songs and yet whose word order is simpler than that of most poetry in the metre: *Hfr Lv 4: *Færum festar órar*, etc; *ÓTr 1: *Einn í ølpu grænni*, etc.; Þráinn Sigfússon's couplet in ch. 88 of *Brennu-Njáls saga: Lǫtum geisa Gamminn*, etc. [58]; *Bárð 4: *Út reri einn á báti*, etc. (cf. R177-178, 200-202). It should also be noted that work

---

[56] It is, of course, precisely because the function of many work chants is "to distract the mind from the tedium of the job" (so Lloyd, *Folk Song in England*, 271) and many of them concern themselves with any matter but the work in hand. This is doubtless a factor which helps to explain why the number of undisguised work chants passed down to us from the Middle Ages and antiquity appears so relatively small.

[57] Cf. R177; Jón Helgason, *Norrøn litteraturhistorie* (København: Levin & Munksgaard, 1934), 63.

[58] *Brennu-Njáls saga*, ed. Einar Ól. Sveinsson, (Reykjavík: Hið íslenzka Fornritafélag, 1954), 220.

chants can take quite complex forms, not least when they are related to particular work drills. But the strongest reason for dismissing this objection is, of course, as follows (cf. R178-179): We have preserved at least three verses in *dróttkvætt* which there is every reason to believe were used as rowing chants. The word-order of these verses is no less complicated than that of other *dróttkvætt*-poetry. (For example, Verse 2 has enjambment in its seventh and eighth line.[59]) Therefore we can say that by these very facts, *ipso facto*, Old Norse rowing chants could be formally rather complex and have had relatively free word order. The objection is, then, invalidated. It is precisely against the background of the factors described in Section VII that elaborate rowing chants could have come into existence. In view, then, of the evidence adduced in *R*, *NQ* and the present paper, I think it would take a bold man to state categorically that the rowers of the thalassocracies of south-western Norway in which skaldic poetry probably had its origins cannot have rowed to time-keeping verses in metres akin to those of *dróttkvætt*-verses as we know them.

SECTION IX: VERSE 2 ADDRESSED TO A WOMAN

In this section, by way of something of a postscript, I turn to another aspect of the verse attributed to Eyvindr, the fact that it is addressed to a woman (*ítr ǫl-Gerðr*; Codex Frisianus has *ítr eld-Gerðr*). There is, of course, nothing in the context of the verse to make one think that there may be a woman present on the ship being rowed out to fish for herring.

One of the papers given on the first day of the seventh Saga Conference in Spoleto in 1988 was a contribution (published in 1990) by Roberta Frank entitled "Why skalds address women." Frank's central conclusion appears to be (69):

---

[59] Cf. Kari Ellen Gade, *The Structure of Old Norse* dróttkvætt *Poetry*, Islandica 49 (Ithaca and London: Cornell University Press, 1995), 197.

. . . when a skald addresses a woman, his "O lady" apostrophe is not so much a greeting as a kind of shorthand, a mnemonic of masculinity. When he says "O lady" he really means "Notice me. Admire me, advise me, advertise me. Look lady, how good I am at being a man."

Now of course the exact reason for a particular person doing a particular thing in the far past will often be difficult to divine. But we have good cause to think that Frank's suggestion here is along the right lines. Even so, we might well find further solution to this problem within the framework of my suggestion that skaldic verses were used as rowing chants in particular and as work chants in general. Certainly the arduous, and very often unpleasant, business of rowing and other maritime tasks (bailing, for example) might well have prompted feminine admiration on land as masculine activities. Now in his classic study of the work chant, Karl Bücher writes of collective work songs that "sie suchen die Genossen . . . durch Hinweis auf die gute Meinung der Zuschauer anzuspornen."[60] I would suggest that this is precisely the aim of two stanzas attributed to Þjóðólfr Arnórsson which I think are rowing chants or related to rowing chants (cf. R163, 196-198) and which Frank refers to (together with a third also attributed to Þjóðólfr) in her paper (Frank, 72-74). These appear to refer to Haraldr Sigurðarson's levy (*leiðangr*) departing on his expedition to Denmark in about 1060 (cf. *Hkr2*, III, 141ff.). The verses may be roughly translated as follows (although there are other interpretations):

(1; *ÞjóðA 4, 19) On Saturday, the lord of the troop throws off the long awnings, there where the stately women see (*prúðar ekkjur líta*) the sides of the dragon ship from the town. The young king steered the brand-new longship west out of the Nið and the comrades' oars plash in the water.

---

[60] Karl Bücher, *Arbeit und Rhythmus*, 6th edition (Leipzig: Emmanuel Reinicke, 1924), 247.

(2; *ÞjóðA 4, 20) The chief's men can pull straight oars from the sea. The woman stands and admires the movement of the oars as a wonderful thing (*Ekkja stendr ok undrask áraburð sem furðu.*) There will be rowing in peace, O lady, before the solid tarred oars are broken in two. The woman gives that her approval (*Þǫll leggr leyfi á þat*).

Frank imaginatively suggests that the warriors rowing off to battle as they pull at their oars (the *hǫkesjur* of *Steinn 2; cf. *Hkr2*, III: 147; *NQ*, 114f.) "feel the gaze of women at the back of their heads, and an oceanic weight of expectations pressing them forward." And well out of sight of women and far from land they would have the same obligations and the same need for approval. Allusion in their rowing chants to the women at home could only improve their labours. Bücher (1924, 242f.; cf. *R*, note 52) mentions a rowing chant used on Chinese junks which refers to the rower's son (rather than his wife) and which "erweckt in den Schiffleuten Heimatgefühle" and as a result they "unwillkürlich rudern...kräftiger und rascher." And the words of the sea-shanties frequently turn the mariners' thoughts to women at home.[61]

---

[61] This is hardly the place to give much attention to the obvious preoccupation in the sea-shanties with women. These maritime work songs often, of course, directly address women, and then absent women: *Haul on the bow-line, O Kitty, You are my darling* (Cecil J. Sharp, *English Folk-Chanteys* [London: Simpkin Marshall, 1914], 42-43); *There is fire in the galley, There is fire down below, Fetch a bucket of water, girls, There's fire down below* (Sharp, *English Folk-Chanteys*, 27); *In Plymouth town there lived a maid, Bless you, young women,...* (Sharp, *English Folk-Chanteys*, 28-29). Sometimes a woman is addressed and the task in hand is compared with the sex act (cf. R158-161): *Oho, Julyah! Pretty Miss Julyah! Take'em off, Julyah! Lay back, Julyah!* (cf. Lloyd, *Folk Song in England*, 280-281). And there are often hints, jokes or other references to the infidelities, real or imagined, of wives and girl-friends. – For the preoccupation with women on board, for example, an Orcadian fishing-vessel in the twenty-first century, see Redmond

But an almost explicit answer to the question "why do skalds address women?" is perhaps to be found in the verse in the sixth book of Saxo's *Gesta Danorum* already mentioned above (p. 12).[62] This consists of 19 lines in Saxo's Latin where it is ascribed to the second King Fridlevus of Denmark, who has been refused the hand of Frogertha, daughter of Amundus, king of Norway, but who has released Amundus's young son from captivity by a giant whom he deprives of two limbs and much treasure. Fridlevus declaims the poetry as he gets the former captive to help him row back to his ships with his spoils. As, for example Axel Olrik has suggested,[63] the poem in Saxo is probably based on one or more Icelandic *lausavísur*. Quite who the original author of the Icelandic poetry was and under what circumstances it was first composed is, of course, impossible to say. Certainly Saxo's surrounding prose narrative, confused as it is, is quite probably secondary to, or an adaptation of, the verse and we have good reason to feel ourselves free to consider it, like Verse 2, largely *in vacuo* (although we note that Saxo says that it was declaimed while rowing was in progress). At all events the Latin verse itself reveals affinity with an Icelandic *meðan*-verse which might very well have been used as a rowing chant (R158-163). It juxtaposes the activities of different persons with the conjunction *dum*; and it contains at least four expressions for "to row" in the first person plural present tense. It is quoted *in extenso* in R161-162, but I here give just its last six lines:

O'Hanlon's *Trawler* (2004, especially 255-277). In a review of O'Hanlon's book, Torgny Nordin (2004) writes of the milieu described by O'Hanlon: "Det nordatlantiska djuphavsfisket är en kompakt manlig företeelse men trots det, eller kanske just därför, är kvinnorna genom sin frånvaro ständigt närvarande . . . " (Torgny Nordin, "O'Hanlon på djupt vatten" [review of O'Hanlon, 2004] in *Svenska Dagbladet. Kultur* (4th August, 2004): 4.) For references to women ashore in Scandinavian shanties and songs of recent centuries, cf., for example, Villner, *"När lantman trygg,"* 8.

[62] *Saxonis Gesta Danorum*, ed. J. Olrik and H. Ræder, and Franz Blatt, 2 vols. (Havniæ: Levin & Munksgaard, 1931-57), I: 148-9.

[63] Axel Olrik, *Kilderne til Sakses oldhistorie: en literaturhistorisk undersøgelse*, 2 vols. (København: G. E. C. Gad, 1892-1894), I: 73-8.

Ergo leves totoque manus conamine nisi
rimemur mare, castra prius classemque petentes,
quam roseum liquidis Titan caput exserat undis,
ut, cum rem rumor vulgaverit atque Frogertha
noverit egregio partam conamine prædam,
blandior in nostrum moveat præcordia votum.

Fisher's translation:

Let us speed then and churn the sea with all / the
strength of our hands, seeking our ships and the camp /
before the sun has pushed his rosy head / from the clear
waves, so that when the story is known / and Frogerth
hears of the plunder won through our gallant / attempt,
she may turn her heart more sweetly to our prayers.[64]

We note that the name *Frogertha* (Icelandic *Freygerðr*?) contains the
element *–gerð(r)* which appears so relatively frequently in the
kennings for women (including Verse 2's *ǫl-Gerðr*) to whom skaldic
verses are addressed (cf. p. 9 above). Now Saxo sets the verse in a
heroic context and then with adaptation: the gains are the spoils
won from the giant whom the declaimer of the verse has just
overcome; Frogertha is a Norwegian princess, and the *votum* a
proposal for a royal marriage. But in the humbler context I suggest
as the more likely original framework for verses of this type, things
would have been different. The spoils that the declaimer of the
verse and his comrades hope to return home with are more the
plunder of the sea, the catch which will provide sustenance for their
womenfolk and their families. Bonny laddies and lassies will dance
to their homecoming daddies. And just as the Frogertha of Saxo's
verse will be more kindly disposed to the prayers of the rowers, so
the woman of Verse 2, as an *ǫl-Gerðr* will perhaps have beer waiting

---

[64] Saxo Grammaticus, *The History of the Danes,* trans. Peter Fisher, ed. Hilda
Ellis Davidson, 2 vols. (Cambridge: D. S. Brewer, 1979-80), I: 168.

for her man (or possibly, as an *eld-Gerðr*, a warm fire[65]). And, if suitably impressed by her man's *remigii conamen* (cf. Saxo, 6, line 32), she will quite possibly accord a more amorous welcome. The women of the rowers of Verse 2 are, of course, absent from the herring-boat. But their men-folk can still dream of them, hope for their approval, anticipate their adulation. And this, in turn, will make them, like the rowers of the Chinese junks just mentioned, row more efficiently, or to use Bücher's words, "kräftiger und rascher."

LATER NOTE

Since writing this paper its original form, I have given closer attention to another passage in Gustaf Cederschiöld's book *Rytmens trollmakt* which I refer to on pp. 18-20 above. On p. 96 of *Rytmens trollmakt*, after stressing the fact that rowing chants are found amongst "nästan alla jordens folk" and that they are amongst the most necessary of work chants, Cederschiöld writes:

Också svenskarna, som annars tyckas vara bland de trögaste och ovilligaste till gemensam sång, höras stundom sjunga, då de föra årorna. Enkom för rodd författade svenska sånger hafva likväl icke blifvit mig tillgängliga, om jag icke såsom "sång" skall rubricera en af doktor AUGUST BONDESON välvilligt meddelad "roddaretrall":

Niu, niu, niu, *nej!*
Niu, niu, niu, *nå!*

---

[65] Cf. this *cri de cœur* from a Swedish seaman actually at sea recorded in "Nanna Bendixons visbok" (cf. Villner, *"När lantman trygg,"* 23): "Då tänker jag på vännen min. Ack, om hon vore här! / Hon skulle mig uppvärma och torka mina klär."

Annars hör man hvarjehanda dikter, som alls icke ha
något afseende på rodden eller sjölifvet, sjungas af
svenska roddare; hvad som helst, blott takten kan
afpassas för rodden och visan förnöjer de roende, kan
förekomma.

The last sentence here chimes in with a point similar to that I make
(on pp. 33 above; cf. note 56), that rowing chants do not necessarily
refer to the task of rowing and that the more humdrum work
chants tend not to be preserved. But in the "roddaretrall" cited by
Cederschiöld we seem to have a singularly monotonous rowing
chant preserved, it appears, from Sweden of the nineteenth century.
Now my admittedly rather superficial inquiries have not led me to
any further knowledge about Bondeson's "roddaretrall" or its
context and provenance. It is not impossible, although perhaps not
very likely, that a perusal of Bondeson's unpublished manuscript
collections now housed in Uppsala might throw further light on the
item. But even the text as Cederschiöld presents it has some
relavance to my discussion of skaldic poetry. As far as I can see,
Cederschiöld's italicization of "nej" and "nå" in the "roddaretrall"
can serve no other purpose than to indicate special stress by the
rowers on the elements in question. This being so, they surely mark
the moment of exertion in the stroke. (If this is right, then it, of
course, militates against certain arguments put forward by Stephen
N. Tranter; cf. note 55.) And it is precisely in such elements that I
see the origin of the final trochee of the *dróttkvætt*-line (cf. p. 13
above and R166-167). (It is true that the pattern here is rather
different from that of the work chant I cite on page 13: whereas
that has similar elements marking the moment of exertion and
variation in the rest of the line, Bondeson's "roddaretrall" has the
converse: the main part of the line is constant, while the "exertion-
element" is variable.) Here, then, we have a rowing chant the
pattern of which in certain respects resembles that which I argue
could have been the basis for couplets (and subsequently whole
stanzas) of poetry in *dróttkvætt* (cf. R177-179 and my remarks on the
couplet from chapter 88 of *Brennu-Njáls saga*: *Lptum geisa Gamminn*, /

gerrat Þráinn vægja.) And that rowing chant comes from Scandinavian territory.

The Pleasure of the Gold Cup:
A Skaldic Affirmation?

Russell Poole

Descriptions of feasting and revelry in Old English poetry are built up, as has long been observed, from individual distinctive motifs such as *benc* ("bench"), *hearpe* ("harp"), *meodu* ("mead"), *horn* ("drinking-horn") and *bune* ("cup"), all these in a system of metonymy subordinate to the key terms *heall* ("hall") and *dryhten* ("lord").[1] Among associated abstract nouns denoting activities or emotions, prominent are *gliw* ("music, entertainment, pleasure"), *dream* ("joy, bliss, revelry, mirth"), *wundor* ("wonder, prodigy"), *wynn* "joy, delight" and *gamen*/*gomen* ("amusement, merriment, mirth, joy").[2] The use of clusters of lexical items like these has ideological

[1] In writing on this topic I salute the memory of Frederic Amory, whose enterprising and original scholarship on the skaldic corpus is evidenced in such publications as "Tmesis in MLat., ON, and OIr. Poetry: An unwritten *notatio norrœna*," *Arkiv for nordisk Filologi* 94 (1979): 42-49; "Kennings, Referentiality and Metaphors," *Arkiv for nordisk filologi* 103 (1988): 87-101; and "Second Thoughts on *Skáldskaparmál*," *Scandinavian Studies* 62 (1990): 331-39 (Review of Margaret Clunies Ross, *Skáldskaparmál: Snorri Sturluson's ars poetica and Medieval Theories*). I am grateful to the Social Sciences and Humanities Research Council Canada and Western University (formerly The University of Western Ontario) for funding towards the research presented in this paper. I am also grateful to the anonymous peer-reviewers for their commentary; all remaining errors are attributable to me alone.
[2] See Kathryn Hume, "The concept of the hall in Old English poetry," *Anglo-Saxon England* 3 (1974): 63-74 for a concise and representative presentation of the material; also R. I. Page, *Life in Anglo-Saxon England* (London: Batsford, 1970), 155-59. Here and elsewhere definitions of Old

Russell Poole 45

significance, as indicating the power and affluence of kings, earls, and other magnates – the "gold-givers of spectacular munificence" invoked by Kathryn Hume[3] — and the security and confidence that their followers feel under their leadership. While the articulation of this ideologeme may well have ancient origins, as envisaged by Michael J. Enright,[4] it may also have gained additional reinforcement and new modes of expression as a result of early medieval diffusion. The evidence from both material and textual culture is that new ideas as to the most prestigious architecture and artifacts to be associated with a great leader made their way through the various European and insular societies and onward to their Scandinavian counterparts. In this essay I propose, as a possible instance of this diffusion, an explanation of a difficult skaldic stanza on the hypothesis that it conveys praise of a Norwegian leader's "golden cup." I shall begin by analysing the stanza and conclude by investigating the aesthetic and ideological significance of such prestigious drinking vessels in relevant contemporary cultures.

Eyjólfr dáðaskald ("Poet of deeds") composed his *Bandadrápa* ("Ode of Bands") in honour of the great Norwegian leader Eiríkr jarl (Earl Eirik). Commemorated in the extant fragments are just some of the earl's great deeds. The recital seems to have terminated in the early eleventh century, probably a year or so before the inception of the closing phase of his career,[5] which sees him sailing

English words are taken, wherever possible, from the *Dictionary of Old English: A to G online*, ed. Angus Cameron, Ashley Crandell Amos, Antonette diPaolo Healey, et al., http://www.doe.utoronto.ca/.

[3] Hume, "The concept of the hall," 71. For comparable analysis of expressions of leadership and patronage in the later Middle Ages see Victoria L. Weiss, "The Play World and the Real World: Chivalry in *Sir Gawain and the Green Knight*," *Philological Quarterly* 72 (1993): 403-18.

[4] "Lady with a Mead-Cup: Ritual, Group Cohesion and Hierarchy in the Germanic Warband," *Frühmittelalterliche Studien* 22 (1988): 170-203.

[5] Eyjólfr dáðaskáld, *Bandadrápa*, ed. Russell Poole, in *Skaldic Poetry of the Scandinavian Middle Ages* I: *Poetry from the Kings' Sagas 1: From Mythical Times to c. 1035* (hereafter SKALD), ed. Diana Whaley (Turnhout: Brepols, 2012), 454-68, at 454; cf. Finnur Jónsson, *Den oldnorske og oldislandske Litteraturs Historie*. 3 vols, 2nd ed. (Copenhagen: Gad, 1920-24), I 555.

to England in 1014 to support the campaigns of Knútr inn ríki (Canute the Great), assuming the position of a jarl in Northumbria and eventually disappearing from history not long after 1023.[6] This "English" period is covered by other skalds but seemingly not by Eyjólfr. The stanza to be discussed here relates to Eiríkr's assumption, as a young man, of control over Raumaríki (Romerike) and Vingulmǫrk (Vingulmark). This he achieved through the good offices of the then king of Denmark, Haraldr Gormsson, who, to judge from the stanza, appears to have been supported in the election by other magnates in Denmark and Norway. In effect Eiríkr's status was changed from "sea-king" (*sækonungr*) to territorial ruler, tributary to the Danish king,[7] as recounted in the stanza:

Folkstýrir vas fára
†finnsk ǫlknarrar linna†
suðr at sævar naðri
†setbergs† gamall vetra,
áðr at Yggjar brúði
élhvetjanda setja
Hildar hjalmi faldinn
hoddmildingar vildu.

The troop-leader [ruler] was, [when] a few years old, in the south on the adder of the sea [ship], . . . before the treasure-bestowers [generous men] wished to place the inciter of the storm of Hildr <valkyrie> [(lit. "storm-inciter of Hildr") battle > warrior], attired in his helmet,

[6] Frank Stenton, *Anglo-Saxon England*, 3rd ed. (Oxford: Clarendon Press, 1971), 390, 398 and 418-19; Alistair Campbell, ed., *Encomium Emmae reginae*, Camden 3rd ser. 72 (London: Offices of the Royal Historical Society, 1949), 70; Bjarni Aðalbjarnarson, ed., *Snorri Sturluson. Heimskringla*, 3 vols (Reykjavík: Hið íslenzka fornritafélag, 1941-51), ÍF 27:32, n. 1.
[7] See Claus Krag, "The early unification of Norway," in *The Cambridge History of Scandinavia*, vol. 1, *Prehistory to 1520*, ed. Knut Helle (Cambridge: Cambridge University Press, 2003), 184-201, at 193 for evidence that these two provinces were under Danish overlordship at this period.

over the bride of Yggr <= Óðinn> [= Jǫrð (jǫrð, "land")].[8]

Scholarship has found the first *helmingr* of this stanza remarkably recalcitrant, as can be seen from the diversity of attempted solutions I will now canvass. Two variant readings exist, *olknattar* in 325VIII 1 for majority *ǫlknarrar* and *sinna* in Jöfraskinna for majority *linna*, but both can be rejected on stemmatic grounds and therefore do not constitute any particular help or hindrance in seeking a solution.

A review of the scholarly history of interpretation can start with Finnur Jónsson, who combined two of the three genitive-case nouns shown above in the obelized part of the *helmingr*, *linna* ("of snakes") and *setbergs* ("of the saddle-hill"),[9] to form a kenning for "gold." This interpretation clearly works well, in and of itself, since the proposed kenning is of a well-attested type.[10] As we shall see, however, it was by-passed by subsequent investigators. With this kenning Finnur tentatively linked *finnz*, construed as a proper noun *Finns*, genitive of *Finnr*, and interpreted as a *heiti* (poetic by-name) for "elf"; no evidence for such a *heiti* exists, however. A "Finnr" or "elf" of gold would then putatively be a kenning for "generous lord" and *ǫlknarrar* ("ale ship," genitive case from nominative singular *ǫlknǫrr*) would refer to this lord's hall, "that type of ship in which ale is served." In fact, though, a determinant (or defining element) "liquor" does not appear to be used in kennings for "house, hall" in the extant corpus,[11] perhaps because it might have led to a confusing overlap with kennings for "drinking vessel." Additionally, Finnur separated the preposition *at* from *sævar naðri* so as to govern this phrase, citing the idiom *at Bjarnar* ("at Bjarni's

---

[8] Text and translation are from Eyjólfr dáðaskáld, *Bandadrápa*, ed. Poole, 460-61.
[9] A *setberg* is a flat-topped hill, resembling a seat or saddle in shape. The translation is conventional, though unfortunate insofar as it might lead to confusion with the "saddle" formation in a mountain range.
[10] Cf. Rudolf Meissner, *Die Kenningar der Skalden. Ein Beitrag zur skaldischen Poetik* (Bonn: K. Schroeder, 1921), 237-41.
[11] Meissner, *Die Kenningar*, 430.

[place]").[12] That however is not a true parallel; furthermore, separation of a preposition from the immediately following noun phrase is counter to what we know of skaldic idiom. Finnur's interpretation of the complete *helmingr* is then, in English translation, "The leader, just a few years old, spent time with his dragon ship in the south (Denmark) in the generous ruler's hall." Here we might demur that Eiríkr could hardly be described as a mere babe in arms, when he has already dispatched a rival at age ten or eleven;[13] also his double placing on the ship and in the hall seems awkward. Altogether, with so many counts against it, Finnur's suggested solution is scarcely viable.

E.A. Kock followed Finnur in taking *finnz* as genitive of a proper name and in interpreting *ǫlknǫrr* as "hall" but otherwise rejected his predecessor's explanation. He proposed a kenning *setbergs Finnr*, "giant," i.e. "Finnr (Finnish man) of the mountain"; this is sustainable as a recognized kenning type, where an ethnic descriptor (such as "Briton," "Scot" or "Saxon") is "corrected" by a synonym or near-synonym for "rock" or mountain."[14] From this beginning, Kock goes on to explain the giant's *ǫlknǫrr* ("ale-ship [hall]") as "mountain," the mountain's *folk* as Norwegians, and their *stýrir* as Eiríkr. This hypothesized kenning is unsatisfactory on more than one ground, however. For one thing, as we have seen, parallels are lacking for an interpretation of *ǫlknarrar* ("ale ship") as "hall." Moreover, by skaldic convention the *folk* in the "mountain's folk" type of kenning should be "giants," not "Norwegians."[15] And when the structure of the whole proposed kenning is considered, it is hard to reconcile with the fundamental principles of kenning formation: interpretation of *ǫlknǫrr Finns setbergs* as "mountain" involves the assumption that one kenning (for "hall") can be "corrected" by another (for "giant") to yield a third (for

---

12 Finnur Jónsson, ed., *Den norsk-islandske skjaldedigtning*, Vols. A.1-2, Tekst efter håndskrifterne. Vols. B.1-2, Rettet tekst (Copenhagen: Gyldendal, 1912-15) (henceforward *Skj*), BI, 191.
13 Eyjólfr dáðaskáld, *Bandadrápa*, ed. Poole, 456.
14 Meissner, *Die Kenningar*, 256-58.
15 Meissner, *Die Kenningar*, 256-59.

"mountain"), whereas in reality the process of correction characteristic of kennings occurs at the level of the individual lexical item, not of kennings as a whole.[16] (A kenning *hǫll Finns setbergs "hall of the Finnish man of the saddle-hill" > "giant" > "mountain" would by contrast be acceptable in terms of this principle,[17] if tending towards circularity.)[18] Kock further proposed emendation of *linna* to *sinna* ("travel") (as we have seen, Jöfraskinna in fact offers this reading). He drew these interpretations together to explain the *helmingr* as follows, in English translation: "The ruler of the mountain-land's people (Norwegians) got to travel, when he was only a few years old, southwards on the dragon of the sea."[19] This is scarcely tenable in view of Kock's selection of a weakly supported variant reading and the assumption of multiple deviations from attested skaldic idiom, added to which are the contextual reasons I have adduced against Finnur Jónsson's interpretation.

Bjarni Aðalbjarnarson significantly diverged from these previous interpreters by reading *finnz* as the verb *finnsk*,[20] rather than the noun *finns*, and this construal accords with the tendency of the relevant manuscripts to use <z> not for genitive <s> but instead

---

[16] Meissner, *Die Kenningar*, 41-42. For the structure of kennings more generally see Meissner, *Die Kenningar*, 2-3; similarly Bjarne Fidjestøl, "Kenningsystemet: Forsøk på ein lingvistisk analyse," *Maal og Minne* (1974): 5-50, reprinted as "The kenning system: An Attempt at a Linguistic Analysis," in *Selected Papers*, ed. Odd Einar Haugen and Else Mundal (Odense: Odense University Press, 1997), 16–67, at 17-19; Edith Marold, *Kenningkunst: Ein Beitrag zu einer Poetik der Skaldendichtung*. Quellen und Forschungen zur Sprach- und Kulturgeschichte der germanischen Völker, new ser. 80 (Berlin: de Gruyter 1983), 25-26.

[17] Meissner, *Die Kenningar*, 89.

[18] See Meissner, *Die Kenningar*, 73-74 for some roughly analogous examples.

[19] E.A. Kock, *Notationes norrœnæ. Anteckninger till Edda och skaldediktning* (Lund: Gleerup, 1923-41), §552; cf. Kock, *Den norsk-isländska skaldediktingen*, 2 vols. (Lund: Gleerup, 1946-1950), I:101.

[20] Bjarni Aðalbjarnarson, *Heimskringla*, ÍF 26:250-51.

for the reflexive inflection of verbs.[21] Bjarni then separated the
compound *ǫlknarrar* into its two elements, so obtaining a
complement (*ǫl*) for the verb (*finnsk*). The result is an apparently
parenthetic clause *finnsk ǫl knarrar linna setbergs*. Bjarni goes on to
explain *setbergs linna*, read as "snakes of the saddle-hill," as
"dwarves," whose *knǫrr* ("ship") is "poetry" and its *ǫl* the "drink of
poetry." The weak points here are threefold. First, there is a
redundancy in the double specification, "poetry" and "drink of
poetry," that cannot be paralleled in the extant corpus.[22] Secondly,
the word combination *setbergs linna* (whether in that order or
reversed) is likely to have been received by any skaldic audience as
an instantiation of the standard and utterly familiar "dragon's
residence" type of kenning for "gold" – a point noted earlier. Also
unsatisfactory, thirdly, is the assumption of a base-word "snakes" in
a kenning for "dwarves": besides lacking analogues in the extant
corpus, as a matter of principle the implicit comparison of dwarves
and snakes that it presupposes would be hard to reconcile with the
mentions of dwarves to be found in our sources. The sense of the
complete parenthetic clause, on Bjarni's construal, would be (in
English translation) "poetry is found," i.e. "I am composing
poetry." Such content would undoubtedly be generically
appropriate in skaldic poetry, which frequently features
extradiegetic comments on the poet's composition or delivery of
the poem. The main clause, on Bjarni's construal, would be (in
English translation): "The leader was a few years old in the south
on his ship." Once again, multiple weak points militate against this
solution of the *helmingr*. Nevertheless, Bjarni's analysis of it as
containing a main clause and a parenthesis, with recognition of
finnsk as the finite verb – placed, what is more, in its appropriate
slot as the first word of the parenthesis – , represents a distinct gain.

Seemingly unaware of Bjarni's contribution, Kock's pupil Åke
Ohlmarks proposed a radically divergent solution. In it the words
setbergs sævar naðr are combined and interpreted as a kenning for

---

[21] I am grateful to Diana Whaley for this information (pers. comm. 9
March 2011).
[22] Meissner, *Die Kenningar*, 428.

"sledge." Such a combination violates the same principle of kenning formation as Kock had done, since the two genitive-case nouns *setbergs sævar* should form a kenning in their own right ("saddle-hill of the sea" > "wave," perhaps) "correcting" the base-word *naðr*, rather than, as supposed by Ohlmarks, *sævar* "correcting" *naðr* and then *setbergs* "correcting" *sævar naðr* in an imagined logical sequence: 1. "adder of the sea" > "ship," 2. "ship of the saddle-hill" > "sledge." Add to this that there is otherwise no evidence to indicate that the concept "sledge" lay within the semantic domain covered by kennings.[23] Meanwhile *ǫlknarrar finnr* is interpreted as a kenning for "host, house-holder"[24] and this likewise has no analogue in skaldic usage. Ohlmarks used these interpretations to reach the following construal of the *helmingr* (in English translation): "He went, a few years old, to the "Finnlapp's" mead-ship (hall) in the south [on] the dragon of the mountain storm's breaking sea (sledge?), the good helmsman of the battle troops."[25] Such a fantastical rendering requires no further comment. On one point, however, Ohlmarks makes an advance over his predecessors, in recognizing that the earl cannot sensibly be described as only a few years old when he takes his ship south. Unfortunately Ohlmarks's attempt to resolve the problem by moving the stanza back two places to the beginning of the poem (as extant), before Eiríkr's early teenage exploit, and attempting to expunge the reference to Denmark raises more difficulties than it solves.

While these four engagements with the enigma presented by the stanza are enterprising and explore a wide range of possibilities, none of them, as we have seen, yields a convincing result. That being the case, and in the absence of any obvious alternative interpretation of the text as it stands, the next step is to ask whether any of the manuscript readings might be wrong. The choice of

---

[23] For the notion of a kenning "domain" and its significance for the kenning system as a whole see Fidjestøl, "The kenning system," at 19.
[24] Åke Ohlmarks, *Tors skalder och Vite-Krists: trosskiftestidens isländska furstelovskalder, 980-1013. Tolkade samt försedda med literaturhistorisk inledning och strofupplösande detaljkommentarer* (Stockholm: Geber, 1958), 502-03.
[25] Ohlmarks, *Tors skalder*, 281.

potentially suspect readings is quite restricted – always, of course, on the assumption that the *helmingr* has not undergone a wholesale scribal remodelling. That is because most of the constituent words are guaranteed by alliteration, metrics or internal rhyme, and sometimes a combination thereof. The narrowness of selection is compounded by lexical constraints – in other words, the paucity of vocabulary items in the language that could fit these slots – and constraints on word order, notably adherence to the permissible slots for verbs. Ignoring "grammar words," the sole items not held firmly in place by one or more of these factors are *ǫlknarrar* and *gamall*: the guarantee for them is limited to metrical configuration, plus the weaker constraint that a word in their slot cannot carry alliteration (a rule with which they indeed comply).

With this analysis in mind, let us consider the *helmingr* anew. Bjarni's proposed division into main clause and parenthesis is shown below with bolding of the latter:

> Folkstýrir vas fára
> **finnsk ǫlknarrar linna**
> suðr at sævar naðri
> **setbergs** gamall vetra…

Within the parenthesis the three genitive-case nouns can readily be interpreted in accord with normal kenning usage. They yield two kennings: 1. *linna setbergs* ("saddle-hill of snakes") > "gold" (reviving Finnur Jónsson's analysis) and 2. *ǫlknarrar* ("ale-ship") > "vessel (for liquor)."[26] These taken in combination correspond to the compound *gullker* (or alternatively *gullskáli* and *gullstaup*) "gold drinking vessel." The syntactic outlier is the verb *finnsk* ("is found"), which resists construction with these nouns (since they are genitive rather than nominative case) but is in itself doubly guaranteed by alliteration and internal rhyme. No other word exists, aside from the rejected *finns*, that could have occupied this slot, and therefore a

---

[26] Cf. Meissner, *Die Kenningar*, 434-35.

function must be found for *finnsk* by searching the main clause for a possible complement.

The words provisionally allocated to the main clause, *Folkstýrir vas fára . . . suðr at sævar naðri . . . vetra gamall*, literally "The troop-leader [ruler] was in the south [while] a few winters old on the adder of the sea [ship]," hold together well in and of themselves. But when we look onwards to the second *helmingr* of the stanza, it becomes apparent that the "few winters" require to be understood not as a specification of Eiríkr's age (the absurdity of this has already been noted) but of the length of time that he was a sea-king before being given control of landed kingdoms. Use of the genitive in indications of time duration, as required by the present context, although far less prevalent than the accusative, occurs sporadically.[27] So our analysis of the words outside the parenthesis needs to be revised to the following: *Folkstýrir vas fára . . . suðr at sævar naðri . . . vetra*, literally "The troop-leader [ruler] was (only) a few years in the south on the adder of the sea [ship]."

What then happens to the word *gamall* ("old")? A parsimonious hypothesis would be that it was erroneously written in the ancestor of all our manuscripts for original **gaman*. The two words are obviously very similar in appearance and sound, added to which they are metrically equivalent. The reading *gamall* could have crept in to supplant *gaman* during transmission, under attraction from its lexical collocate *vetra*. Misunderstanding of the phrase *fára vetra* as an allusion to Eiríkr's youthfulness at the time of his exploits in the south would be understandable when his tender years happen to have been emphasized in the first two extant stanzas of the poem. If the noun **gaman* is then taken with the parenthesis rather the main clause, it immediately supplies the needed nominative complement of the verb *finnsk*, yielding the nucleus of the clause: "pleasure is found." Precisely the same collocation occurs in the modern Icelandic idiom *finna/finnst gaman* ("enjoy"), with object

---

[27] Marius Nygaard, *Norrøn syntax* (Kristiania: H. Aschehoug, 1905), §140, 152.

governed by *til* (noun) or *að* (verbal infinitive).[28] Comparable also is the standard idiom *þykkja gaman* ("enjoy"),[29] seen in *Guðrúnarkviða onnur*:

Húnskar meyjar, þær er hlaða spioldum
ok gera gull fagrt, svá at þér gaman þikki.[30]

Hunnish maidens who lace tablets and make fine gold, so that it seems a pleasure to you.

Here the logical though unexpressed subject of the impersonal verb *þikki* is presumably the product of the work – i.e. gorgeous pieces of weaving and gold ornaments, or perhaps gold thread woven into the textile.

Turning now to the remainder of the parenthesis, the phrase *linna setbergs olknarrar* ("of the gold drinking-vessel") would represent a genitive of description or specification, indicating the source of pleasure. The use of this type of genitive in combination with *gaman* occurs rarely: just two attestations are cited in the ONP database: *gaman veraldar* ("pleasure of the world") and *þersa heims gaman* ("pleasure of this world").[31] The pattern of occurrence is significant, in that, with their "learned-style" Christian content, they smack of an adoption from Old English idiom. The same English linkage, albeit from an earlier era, could be made in the case of the construction I am postulating in Eyjólfr. A close syntactic parallel in

---

[28] Jón Hilmar Jónsson, *Orðastaður: Orðabók um íslenska málnotkun* (Reykjavík: Mál og menning, 1994), s. *gaman*.

[29] Richard Cleasby and Gudbrand Vigfússon, *An Icelandic-English dictionary*. 2nd edn, with a supplement by William A. Craigie (Oxford: Clarendon Press 1962), s. *gaman*. Cf. Johan Fritzner, *Ordbog over det gamle norske sprog*. 2nd edn, 1883-96, 3 vols, reprint including vol. 4, *Tillegg og rettelser*, ed. Didrik Arup Seip and Trygve Knudsen (Oslo 1954), s. *gaman*.

[30] Gustav Neckel, ed., *Edda: Die Lieder des Codex Regius nebst verwandten Denkmälern I: Text*. Rev. Hans Kuhn, 5th edition (Heidelberg: C. Winter, 1962), 228, v. 26. My normalization.

[31] *Ordbog over det norrøne prosasprog*, http://www.onp.hum.ku.dk

Old English poetry, with double use of the genitive, would be the following passage from *Beowulf: næs hearpan wyn, / gomen gleobeames*[32] ("there was no joy of the harp, pleasure of the tuneful wood"). Skaldic anglicisms of tenth- and eleventh-century date are a reasonably familiar phenomenon,[33] and I shall mention some clear instances of them presently.

The result of the foregoing discussion of the *helmingr* is as follows, with the parenthesis now marked in the conventional manner:

Folkstýrir vas fára
(finnsk ǫlknarrar linna)
suðr at sævar naðri
(setbergs gama*n*) vetra . . .

The troop-leader [ruler] was (only) a few years in the south on the adder of the sea [ship] – pleasure of the ale-ship [drinking-vessel] of the saddle-hill of snakes [gold] is found . . .

As noted, this putative mention of the "pleasure of the drinking-vessel" is placed parenthetically in a stanza otherwise concerned with the exploits of the jarl. Several factors – the use of the two kennings, the choice of an impersonal verb, and the abrupt switch in narrative level from diegetic to extradiegetic – could make such an allusion appear too cryptic to be fully credible, but in fact

---

32 Elliott Van Kirk Dobbie, ed., *Beowulf and Judith*, Anglo-Saxon Poetic Records 4 (New York: Columbia University Press 1953), 70, ll. 2262-63.
33 The classic study is Dietrich Hofmann, *Nordisch-englische Lehnbeziehungen der Wikingerzeit*, Bibliotheca Arnamagnæana 14 (Copenhagen: E. Munksgaard, 1955). Cf. also Matthew Townend, *Language and History in Viking Age England: Linguistic Relations Between Speakers of Old Norse and Old English* (Turnhout: Brepols, 2002); Russell Poole, "Crossing the Language Divide: Anglo-Scandinavian Language and Literature," in *Cambridge History of Early Medieval English Literature, 500-1150*, ed. Clare A. Lees (Cambridge: Cambridge University Press, 2012), 579-606.

these are all standard features of skaldic poetry. In the present poem, moreover, the presence of shifts of narrative level and focus is systematically foregrounded by the use of the split refrain (*klofastef*). Less expected is the topic of the proposed extradiegesis. Typically what features in this slot is a different pleasure of the hall, the delivery of poetry (as suggested for this stanza by Bjarni Aðalbjarnarson).[34] Nevertheless, a poet could with perfect appropriateness choose instead the related topic of the ceremonial drinking at the leader's feast, where the poem is likely to have been declaimed. The two topics, ceremonial drinking and the delivery of poetry, are in fact associatively linked through the prevalent use of "poetry" kennings based on cups and liquor,[35] with their basis in the myth of the poetic mead.[36] Another potential avenue of association is via the topos of parody drinking ceremonies where ravens, eagles and wolves slurp the blood of the slain on the battlefield, a theme which has countless iterations in praise poetry and is often placed parenthetically, in subordinate clauses or within kennings.[37]

A description of ceremonial drinking in the hall, at a gathering convened by Haraldr harðráði ("Hard-rule") Sigurðarson at Haugr (Haug), one of his royal farmsteads, is found in a later *klofastef* poem, the *Stúfsdrápa* of Stúfr inn blindi Þórðarson kattar ("Stúfr the blind, son of Þórðr Cat"):

---

[34] The classic treatment of skalds' statements about their poetry is Gert Kreutzer, *Die Dichtungslehre der Skalden. Poetologische Terminologie und Autorenkommentare als Grundlage einer Gattungspoetik* (Kronberg: Scriptor Verlag, 1974).

[35] Meissner, *Die Kenningar*, 429-30.

[36] On the topic of the poetic mead see Roberta Frank, "Snorri and the Mead of Poetry," in *Speculum Norrænum: Norse Studies in Memory of Gabriel Turville-Petre*, ed. Ursula Dronke et al. (Odense: Odense University Press, 1981), 155-70; also Judy Quinn, "Liquid Knowledge: Traditional Conceptualisations of Learning in Eddic Poetry," in *Along the Oral-Written Continuum: Types of Texts, Relations and their Implications*, ed. S. Rankovic, L. Melve and E. Mundal, Utrecht Studies in Medieval Literacy 20 (Turnhout: Brepols, 2010), 175-217.

[37] For one out of countless examples, see Eyvindr skáldaspillir Finnsson, *Háleygjatal* v. 9, ed. Russell Poole, in SKALD I:I:195-213, at 207.

Vissak hildar hvessi
– hann vas nýztr at kanna –
af góðum byr Gríðar
gagnsælan mér fagna,
þás blóðstara brœðir
baugum grimmr at Haugi
gjarn með gylltu horni
gekk sjalfr á mik drekka.

I knew the victory-blessed inciter of war [warrior] to
welcome me with a good wind of Gríðr <giantess>
[mind] – he was the most bountiful to know –, when the
feeder of the blood-starling [raven > warrior], ferocious
to rings, himself went willingly to toast me with the gilded
horn at Haug.[38]

There is no doubting the potential pleasure to be gained from
having a toast drunk in one's honour or from the liquid contents of
the drinking vessel, which might be ale or a prestigious southern
wine or possibly the "aged mead" invoked in eddaic poetry. All the
same, these might not have been the only pleasures to be elicited by
a golden cup. Feasts like the one Stúfr commemorates were the
natural occasion for the aristocratic host to display and use prestige
items and for them to be received with admiration on the part of
the guests and the attendant court poet. Sources of appeal and
gratification would be the precious materials and exquisite aesthetic
values exhibited by the drinking-vessel. Stúfr, we observe, takes the
time to register that the horn raised by the king is gilded. It would
be during such toasts and also the stereotypic passing of the
drinking vessel amongst guests in the hall that its splendour would
most immediately elicit wonder and admiration. As Geoffrey of
Monmouth says laconically, through the mouth of Merlin, *Candebit*
argentum in circuitu et diuersa torcularia uexabit, "Silver will shine as it

---

[38] Stúfr inn blindi, *Stúfsdrápa,* in SKALD II: *Poetry from the Kings' Sagas 2:*
From c. 1035 to c. 1300, ed. Kari Ellen Gade (Turnhout: Brepols, 2009),
350-58, at 351, v. 1. The translation is Gade's.

passes round and trouble various wine-presses."[39]

The circulation of the cup is a familiar motif in both Old English and Old Norse poetry, and from the latter corpus Gunnarr's royal command in *Atlakviða* may serve as an example:

"Rístu nú, Fjǫrnir,
láttu á flet vaða
greppa gullskálir
með gumna hǫndum."[40]

"Rise now, Fjǫrnir, have the golden cups of warriors (poets?) pass along the hall with the hands of men."

Such a display would have been symbolically important, as betokening the resources, munificence and prestige of the leader. As recounted in the previous stanza of *Atlakviða*,

Kvaddi þá Gunnarr,
sem konungr skyldi,
mærr í miǫðranni,
af móði stórum.[41]

Gunnarr then greeted them as a king should, renowned in his meadhall, with great spirit.

Comparable is the behaviour of Jǫrmunrekkr (Ermanaric) in the Old Norse *Hamðismál*:

[39] Michael D. Reeve, ed., and Neil Wright, trans., *Geoffrey of Monmouth. The History of the Kings of Britain. An edition and translation of De gestis Britonum [Historia regum Britanniae]* (Woodbridge: Boydell Press, 2007), 159. The translation above modifies Reeve and Wright's (158).
[40] Ursula Dronke, ed., *The Poetic Edda, with translation, introduction, and commentary*, vol. 1, *Heroic Poems* (Oxford: Clarendon Press, 1969), 5, v. 10. My normalization.
[41] Dronke, *Poetic Edda*, 5, v. 9. My normalization.

Hló þá Iǫrmunrekkr,
hendi drap á kampa,
beiddiz at brǫngo,
bǫðvaðisk at víni,
skók hann skǫr iarpa,
sá á skiǫld hvítan,
lét hann sér í hendi
hvarfa ker gullit.[42]

Then Iǫrmunrekkr laughed, slapped his beard with his
hand, summoned up his belligerence, waxed fierce over
the wine, shook his brown hair, looked at his white shield,
flourished the golden cup in his hand.

An appreciative commentary on other types of prestige item to
be seen in a ruler's hall is found in a stanza from Sigvatr's
Austfararvísur, conventionally dated to ca. 1019:

Búa hilmis sal hjǫlmum
hirðmenn, þeirs svan grenna
(hér sék) bens, ok brynjum
(beggja kost á veggjum).
Því á ungr konungr engi
— ygglaust es þat — dyggra
húsbúnaði at hrósa;
hǫll es dýr með ǫllu.

Courtiers, who feed the swan of the wound [raven or
eagle], decorate the hall of the ruler with helmets and
mail-shirts; here I see the choicest of both on the walls.
And so no young king has worthier hangings to boast of;
that is without a doubt; the hall is costly in every respect.[43]

---

[42] Dronke, *Poetic Edda*, 165, v. 20. My normalization.
[43] Sigvatr Þórðarson, *Austrfararvísur*, in SKALD I:I:578-613, at 606-07, v.
16. The translation is Fulk's.

The poet surveys the helmets and mailshirts on show to the retainers in the leader's hall and finds the ensemble of these accoutrements and the building that houses them *dýr* ("costly"), in other words "splendid, precious."[44] A prose passage with comparable motifs is the description of Heimir's opulent hall in *Vǫlsunga saga: Var þat at skemtan haft at sjá brynjur ok hjalma ok stóra hringa ok undarliga mikil gullstaup ok alls konar hervápn* ("People found it enjoyable to view the mailcoats and helmets, big rings, astoundingly large golden cups and weapons of every kind").[45]

The Sigvatr stanza has a second relevance to my argument, in terms of the decided English inflection to be detected in it. The compound *hirðmenn* is one of the earliest attestations of the adoption into Old Norse of Old English *hiredmenn* ("household retainers"), and it can be ascribed to a re-organization of the court on Anglo-Saxon principles under King Óláfr.[46] Sigvatr is also the first named skald to use the word *hǫll* ("hall") in reference to a jarl's or a king's hall, and here too his immediate prompt is doubtless English influence at the court of Óláfr (cf. OE *heall*). To be sure, the usage has a precedent in the probably mid tenth-century anonymous memorial poem *Eiríksmál*,[47] but this likewise may be a case of English influence, since the Eiríkr commemorated in *Eiríksmál* – King Eiríkr blóðøx ("Blood-axe") – was based in Northumbria for the latter part of his career.[48]

---

[44] Bjarni Aðalbjarnarson, *Snorri Sturluson. Heimskringla*, ÍF 27:140-41; cf. *Skj* AI, 238, BI, 224.
[45] R.G. Finch, *The Saga of the Volsungs: Vǫlsunga Saga* (London 1965), 42.
[46] Hofmann, *Nordisch-englische Lehnbeziehungen*, 57-58. Cf. John Lindow, *Comitatus, individual and honor: Studies in north Germanic institutional vocabulary* (Berkeley, University of California Press, 1976), 52-60.
[47] *Eiríksmál*, ed. R. D. Fulk, in SKALD I:I:1003-13, at 1012, v. 8; cf. Hofmann, *Nordisch-englische Lehnbeziehungen*, 50; Matthew Townend, "Whatever Happened to York Viking Poetry?" *Saga-Book* 27 (2003): 48–90, at 52-54.
[48] *Eiríksmál*, ed. Fulk, 1003-04 and references there given.

Moving now from interpretation of Eyjólfr's text to a broader material-culture perspective, we can observe at the outset that a gold drinking vessel has to have been a rather singular piece of property to be in possession of. We could term it a case of "conspicuous possession." In ordinary life, at least in Anglo-Saxon England, there were evidently not too many of them around. Naturally, as Raymond Page remarks, "the poor made do with wood or pottery,"[49] but even in the case of the rich it is only rarely that we can substantiate their possession of golden or for that matter gilded cups. To that extent Philip Grierson seems too enthusiastic in claiming that in England during the two centuries before the Norman Conquest "every person or household of any pretensions to rank and wealth possessed many ornaments – drinking cups, armlets, baldrics, scabbards, and so on – either entirely of gold or heavily gilded."[50] Even the well-known cup left by Wynflæd to her son in her will had a core of wood, though it featured applied gold in quantities that made detaching and melting it down a worthwhile business.[51] Even in the poetic texts not all that glisters is gold. In *Vǫlundarkviða*, for example, silver was apparently good enough for Vǫlundr and presumably Níðuðr when the virtuoso smith crafted splendid plated drinking vessels for the cruel king. Of the rather plentiful literary references to plating with generic unspecified precious metals, a plating of silver or even copper rather than gold can usually not be ruled out. An instance occurs in a description of a feast in *Beowulf*: *gamen eft astah, / beorhtode bencsweg; byrelas sealdon / win of wunderfatum*,[52] "Merriment arose again, revelry at the bench brightened; the cup-bearers poured wine from wondrous vessels." The unusual compound noun *wunderfæt*

---

[49] Page, *Life in Anglo-Saxon England*, 152.

[50] Philip Grierson, "Carolingian Europe and the Arabs: the Myth of the Mancus," *Revue belge de philologie et d'histoire* 32 (1954): 1059-74, at 1060.

[51] Roberta Frank, "Three 'Cups' and a Funeral in *Beowulf*," in *Latin Learning and English Lore: Studies in Anglo-Saxon Literature for Michael Lapidge*, ed. Katherine O'Brien O'Keeffe and Andy Orchard (Toronto: University of Toronto Press, 2005), I:407-20, at 408. Cf. Page, *Life in Anglo-Saxon England*, 152.

[52] Dobbie, *Beowulf and Judith*, 37, ll. 1160-62.

presupposes the awed and admiring gaze of participants at the royal
feast, but they might be admiring silver. Similarly, in the classic
epitome of the hall in the Old English poem *The Wanderer*, the
"bright cup" could be silver rather than gold:

> Hwær cwom mearg? Hwær cwom mago? Hwær cwom
>   maþþumgyfa?
> Hwær cwom symbla gesetu? Hwær sindon seledreamas?
> Eala beorht bune! Eala byrnwiga!
> Eala þeodnes þrym![53]

> Where has the horse gone? Where has the man gone?
> Where has the treasure-giver gone? Where has the setting
> of feasts gone? Where are the joys of the hall? Alas bright
> cup! Alas the warrior in his mailshirt! Alas the glory of the
> lord!

On the other hand, when the estranged retainer in *Beowulf* seeks
to regain his lord's favour by purloining a *fæted wæge* ("plated
vessel") from the dragon's hoard,[54] the vessel should probably be
envisaged as gold, given the notorious predilection of dragons for
this metal (which provides the underlying logic for kennings such as
Eyjólfr's *linna setbergs* ["saddle-hill of snakes"]).[55]

More definite references to gold cups can also be found. From
Norse literature we have already considered instances in *Atlakviða*,
Hamðismál and *Vǫlsunga saga*. From Welsh literature we can add a
reference in the *Gododdin*, a poem of uncertain early medieval date

---

[53] George Philip Krapp and Elliott Van Kirk Dobbie, ed., *The Exeter Book*,
Anglo-Saxon Poetic Records 3 (New York: Columbia University Press,
1936), 136, ll. 92-95.
[54] Dobbie, *Beowulf and Judith*, 70, ll. 2282.
[55] For an interesting "antiquarian" example cf. *Jómsvíkingadrápa* 37, where
the meaning is possibly that Gull-Búi ("Gold-Búi") transforms himself
into a dragon in order to guard his treasure (Bjarni byskup Kolbeinsson,
Jómsvíkingadrápa, ed. Emily Lethbridge, in SKALD I:I:954-97, at 990-91.

that concerns itself with sixth-century events.[56] There, in praising the famed warriors who went to Catraeth, the poet asserts that *gwin a med o eur vu eu gwirawt* ("wine and mead out of gold was their drink").[57] Ifor Williams explains the cryptic "out of gold" as "o lestri aur" ("out of a golden vessel"), commenting further that this would be a demonstration of the power and affluence of Caer Eidyn, the chieftain's base.[58] By contrast, tellingly, another chieftain is said to have had only silver vessels in which to serve mead, even though he deserved gold: *Aryant am y ued eur dylyi* ("Silver for his mead: he deserved gold").[59]

The examples of possible gold cups cited so far are largely legendary. There is also historical documentation, however, for an élite class of possessors of these precious and prestigious objects – namely prelates and other high functionaries of the Church, often as beneficiaries of a royal donor. From the eighth century onwards, encouraged by conciliar decrees, the canon law of the Western Church provided that chalices and likewise patens, if not of gold or silver, must at least be composed of metal.[60] In his Second Old English Pastoral Letter Ælfric enjoins to that effect: *Beo his calic geworht of ecum antimbre, gylden oþþe sylfren, glæsen oþþe tinen* ("Let his chalice be made of enduring material, of gold or silver, glass or tin").[61] The so-called Canons of Edgar, actually a code compiled by Archbishop Wulfstan in the first decade of the eleventh century,

---

[56] G.R. Isaac, "Readings in the history and transmission of the *Gododdin*," *Cambrian Medieval Celtic Studies* 37 (1999): 55-78, at 77. Cf. Oliver Padel, "A New Study of the *Gododdin*," *Cambrian Medieval Celtic Studies* 35 (1998): 45-55, at 55.

[57] Ifor Williams, ed., *Canu Aneirin: gyda rhagymadrodd a nodiadau* (Aberystwyth: Gwasg Prifysgol Cymru 1938), 10, line 236.

[58] Williams, *Canu Aneirin*, 136.

[59] Williams, *Canu Aneirin*, 32, line 798.

[60] Cf. Alexandra Meier, *Die Entwicklung der Form und des Materials des sakralen Kelches vom frühen Mittelalter bis heute* (Munich: GRIN, 1996), 4-5.

[61] Bernhard Fehr, ed., *Die Hirtenbriefe Aelfrics in altenglischer und lateinischer Fassung*, Bibliothek der angelsächsischen Prosa 9 (Hamburg: H. Grand, 1914, reprinted with supplement by Peter Clemoes, Darmstadt: Wissenschaftliche Buchgesellschaft, 1966), 161-62.

draw on Ælfric in providing that *ælc calic gegoten beo þe man husl on halgige, and on treowenum ne halgige man ænig* ("all chalices in which the sacrifice is consecrated be poured [i.e. made of molten metal], and no [sacrifice] should be consecrated in wooden [vessels]"); an addition to this in the margin of manuscript Junius 121 reads *gylden oðða seolfren tinen* ("of gold or silver [or] tin").[62] The rationale was that the paten and chalice had to be worthy vessels for respectively the Body and the Blood of the Lord and not made of lowly materials, such as wood or clay, that might bring the Eucharist into contempt. Silver-gilt was a common compromise, often with the gilding inside, since it was there that the Body and Blood made immediate contact with their humanly-produced vessel.[63]

Among literary references to such vessels, Aldhelm includes mention of a gold chalice in his titulus on a church of St Mary built by Bugga, daughter of Centwine, the late seventh-century king of Wessex:[64] *Aureus atque calix gemmis fulgescit opertus / Ut caelum rutilat stellis ardentibus aptum*[65] ("And a golden chalice, encrusted with gems, shines, just as the sky glows, studded with blazing stars"). This praise, with its extravagant image of the night sky to capture the splendour of the sacred vessel, was evidently so memorable that Æthelwulf (Ædiluulf) subsequently alluded to it in three different

---

[62] Roger Fowler, *Wulfstan's Canons of Edgar*, Early English Text Society 266 (London: Oxford University Press 1972), 11, 35, and cf. xxvi-xxxiv.

[63] Cf. Meier, *Die Entwicklung der Form*, 4-5.

[64] Michael Lapidge and James L. Rosier, *Aldhelm. The Poetic Works* (Cambridge: D. S. Brewer, 1985), 40; cf. Andy Orchard, *The Poetic Art of Aldhelm* (Cambridge: Cambridge University Press, 1994), 243. Their translation of the second line to read "so that it seems to reflect the heavens with their bright stars" (49) puts the logic of the imagery on a different basis, but to my knowledge the Latin verb *rutilo* ('redden, glow red') cannot be rendered as "reflect."

[65] "In Ecclesia Mariae a Bugge Extructa," within the editorial compilation *Carmina ecclesiastica* III, 72-73, in *Aldhelmi Opera*, ed. Rudolf Ehwald, Monumenta Germaniae Historica, Auctores antiquissimi 15 (Berlin: Weidmann, 1919), 18. I owe this and the following example to Frank, "Three 'Cups' and a Funeral," 407-08.

passages of his *De abbatibus* ("On the Abbots").[66] Even though he
had purloined the golden words of his predecessor, perhaps we can
assume that the vessels he was referring to were real. Bede
mentions another golden chalice (*calicem aureum consecratum ad
ministerium altaris*) amidst the treasures he says were brought to Kent
by Paulinus, archbishop of York, after King Edwin's death at the
hands of Penda. He additionally remarks that in his day they were
still on show (*monstrantur*) "in the church of the Kentish people." In
the Old English version it is Edwin's widow Æthelburh who
personally brings the chalice, along with the other treasures.[67]
Whether this modification of Bede's account is due to a cultural
assumption on the part of the translator (or his copy-text) or to a
misunderstanding of the Latin remains uncertain.[68] A considerable
number of similar references to chalices, as to other sacred vessels,
could be cited,[69] and, as remarked above, these were typically the
subject of gifts or donations from royalty or the high aristocracy.
Such donors might have their Welsh representative in the chieftain
Rhufawn Hir ("the Tall"), who, we are told in the *Gododdin*, *rodei eur
e allawr*[70] ("was wont to give gold to the altar").[71] As counterpart

---

[66] For Æthelwulf's emulations of this passage, see Orchard, *The Poetic Art*,
264, 267-68; cf. also Andy Orchard, "Old English and Latin Poetic
Traditions," in *A Companion to Medieval Poetry*, ed. Corinne Saunders
(Oxford: Blackwell, 2010), 65-82, at 74.

[67] Bertram Colgrave and R. A. B. Mynors, ed., *Bede's Ecclesiastical History of
the English People* (Oxford: Clarendon Press, 1969), 204-05: cf. *gylden cælic
gehalgad to wigbedes þenunge* (Thomas Miller, ed., *The Old English Version of
Bede's Ecclesiastical History of the English People*, Early English Text Society
original series 95, 96, 110, 111 (London: Oxford University Press, 1890),
vol. I, 1, 150), "a golden chalice consecrated for service at the altar."

[68] I am grateful to Greg Waite for pointing out the latter possibility to me
(pers. comm. 20 September 2013).

[69] C.W. Dodwell, *Anglo-Saxon Art. A new perspective* (Manchester:
Manchester University Press, 1982), 203-09.

[70] Williams, *Canu Aneirin*, 15, l. 378.

[71] The translation is that of John T. Koch, "On the Prehistory of Brittonic
Syntax," in *Studies in Brythonic Word Order*, ed. James Fife and Erich Poppe,
Current Issues in Linguistic Theory 83 (Amsterdam: John Benjamins,
1991), 1-44, at 27.

gifts from the Carolingian empire, we can note the gold chalice studded with numerous pearls presented by Duke Salomon of Brittany (fl. 857-74), along with many other items, to his new monastic foundation at Plélan.[72] Eberhard of Friuli (825-866) likewise bequeaths gold chalices in his will, amongst other treasures, evidently intending them for religious use even though they go to members of his family.[73]

Outside the literature, some notable early medieval examples of chalices with gilding or applied gold have survived down to the present day, either in church treasuries or in the archaeological record. The Tassilo Chalice, for instance, dating from the late eighth century and of insular design, is cast in bronze, to the exterior of which gold and silver have been applied.[74] It was given by Tassilo III, duke of the Bavarians (748-88), and his wife, the Lombard princess Liutperga, to the monastery of Kremsmünster, probably at the time of its foundation by Tassilo in 777.[75] The ninth-century Trewhiddle Chalice, though primarily of silver, originally had an applied mount, and this and the interior of the cup were gilt.[76] The

---

[72] Pierre Riché, *The Carolingians. A family who forged Europe*, trans. Michael Idomir Allen (Philadelphia 1993), 340. For the context of these gifts, see Daniel C. DeSelm, "Unwilling Pilgrimage: Vikings, Relics, and the Politics of Exile During the Carolingian Era (c. 830-940)," (Diss. University of Michigan, 2009), 106-08.

[73] Riché, *The Carolingians*, 340-41. For the context of these gifts, see Christina La Rocca and Luigi Provero, "The Dead and their Gifts. The will of Eberhard, count of Friuli, and his wife Gisela, daughter of Louis the Pious (863-864)," in *Rituals of Power: From Late Antiquity to the Early Middle Ages*, ed. Frans Theuws and Janet L. Nelson (Leiden: Brill, 2000), 225-80.

[74] Herbert Schutz, *The Carolingians in Central Europe, Their History, Arts, and Architecture: A Cultural History of Central Europe, 750-900* (Leiden: Brill, 2004), 44. For an illustration see Dodwell, *Anglo-Saxon Art*, plate H (opposite 53).

[75] Marios Costambeys, Matthew Innes and Simon MacLean, *The Carolingian World* (Cambridge: Cambridge University Press, 2011), fig. 3, 71.

[76] D. M. Wilson, *Anglo-Saxon Art* (London: Thames & Hudson, 1984), 10.

probably ninth- or tenth-century Chalice of Ardagh, though once again consisting primarily of silver alloyed with copper, has panels of gold filigree among its exterior embellishments.[77]

Some of these gilded cups appear to have been appropriated by Vikings, as is scarcely surprising when one bears in mind the huge amount of plunder they took from monasteries and churches. A probable – and very notable – instance is the Jelling cup, found in the double barrow of Gorm the Old (ca. 900-936) and his Christian wife Thyra. Though primarily of silver, the cup is gilded inside, and the stem and foot and the figures on the outside are also partially gilded. At only 4.3 cm high and weighing 120.56 grams, it probably began life as a travelling chalice (*calix viaticus*).[78] The Vale of York cup, an outstanding recent discovery, is also primarily silver but exhibits the remains of gilding both inside and out. The hoard from which it comes, with a deposition date of ca. 928, has contents consistent with other attested Viking hoards in northern England from the first three decades of the tenth century. The cup is thought to emanate from a church or monastery in the northern Frankish Empire and to represent either tribute paid to the Vikings or loot taken by them. Its closest parallel in both form and design is with the silver-gilt cup that forms part of the Halton Moor Hoard, Lancashire; it is thought that this latter cup was taken from Normandy by Vikings. Both cups are related to a group of six late eighth- to mid-ninth-century Carolingian vessels.[79] The Vale of York cup seems to have survived into the 920s and the Halton

[77] Wilson, *Anglo-Saxon Art*, plate 151 and 120, 129; cf. National Museum of Ireland – Ard-Mhúsaem na hÉireann, "Silver chalice (The Ardagh Chalice), Reerasta, Ardagh, Co. Limerick," http://www.museum.ie/. Accessed 18 August 2013.
[78] Karen Stemann-Petersen and Anne Pedersen, "Jellingbægeret," Danish National Museum, http://jelling.natmus.dk/om-jelling/jellingbaegeret/. Accessed 13 August 2013.
[79] Barry Ager, "A Preliminary Note on the Artefacts from the Vale of York Viking Hoard," in *Studies in Early Medieval Coinage 2. New Perspectives*, ed. Tony Abramson (Woodbridge: Boydell and Brewer, 2011), 123-36, at 125-27, and references there given.

Moor cup for a century after that – down, in fact, into Eiríkr's final decade of public life – as vessels in use before they were hidden away in their respective hoards.

The history of the Vale of York and Halton Moor cups suggests that the Vikings saw them, along with the other treasures in their respective hoards, as items to be retained and no doubt prized in their own right, not simply as a source of silver bullion.[80] The eighth-century Codex Aureus (Stockholm, Swedish Royal Library, MS A. 35)[81] is a reminder from a different class of artifact that not all precious or sacred objects appropriated by Vikings got consigned to hacking or melting or burning. According to the testimony of the benefactors, the Codex was bought back in the late ninth century, along with other books, *for ðon ðe wit noldan ðæt ðas halgan beoc lencg in ðære hæðenesse wunaden* ("because we did not wish that these holy books would remain longer in heathendom").[82] For this statement to make sense, the books must have been in heathen hands for some time already. Evidently the sea-kings were capable of retaining a range of foreign cultural items intact and even appreciating them as prestigious aesthetic artifacts.

So I conclude this essay with two possibilities: first, Eyjólfr's poem may have mentioned a golden cup amongst the accoutrements of Eiríkr jarl; secondly, it would not have been strange for the jarl, like other sea-kings, to be the possessor of a golden cup.

---

[80] Gareth Williams and Barry Ager, *The Vale of York Hoard* (London: British Museum Press, 2010), 17.

[81] For the precious materials and exquisite artistry of this book, see Francis Wormald, *The Miniatures in St Augustine's Gospels* (Cambridge: Cambridge University Press, 1954), 8; cf. Carl Nordenfalk, "A note on the Stockholm Codex Aureus," *Nordisk Tidsskrift for Bok- och Biblioteksväsen* 38 (1951): 145-55; James Campbell, ed., *The Anglo-Saxons* (London: Penguin, 1982), 136-37.

[82] *Sweet's Anglo-Saxon Reader in Prose and Verse*, rev. Dorothy Whitelock (Oxford: Clarendon Press, 1967), 205.

Skáru á skíði:
Vǫluspá 20 and the Fixing of Fate

John Lindow

Among the pleasant memories of my professional life is writing a long review together with Fred Amory of one of the volumes of commentary, on mythological Eddic poetry, issued by the Frankfurt team.[1] The following essay comprises a kind of commentary to a line in *Vǫluspá* and indeed roams from time to time over lines and stanzas that Fred and I contemplated then.

Both redactions of *Vǫluspá* contain a sequence of stanzas about Askr and Embla, who are given life by the gods and fate by the norns. In each redaction these stanzas follow the *dvergjatal*, and in each something markedly different follows: in Codex Regius the stanzas about Gullveig, Heiðr, and the first war in the world, and in Hauksbók the stanzas that apparently deal with the Masterbuilder myth (stanzas 25-26 in the standard editions). Thus stanzas 17-20 form a whole, a marked-off sequence. I offer the standard text of these stanzas from the edition of Neckel and Kuhn, followed by the translation of Ursula Dronke.

> 17. Unz þrír[2] qvómo   ór því liði,
> ǫflgir oc ástgir,   æsir, at húsi;
> fundo á landi,   lítt megandi,

---

[1] Frederic Amory and John Lindow, "Review of: Klaus von See, et al., *Kommentar zu den Liedern der Edda. Band 3. Götterlieder.*" *Göttingsche Gelehrte Anzeigen* 258 (2006): 100-27.
[2] Both manuscripts: þriár.

Asc oc Emblo,   ørløglausa.

18. Ǫnd þau né átto,   óð þau né hǫfðo,
lá né læti   né lito góða;
ǫnd gaf Óðinn,   óð gaf Hœnir,
lá gaf Lóðurr oc lito góða.

19. Asc veit ec standa,   heitir Yggdrasill,
hár baðmr, ausinn   hvítaauri;
þaðan koma dǫggvar,   þærs í dala falla,
stendr æ yfir, grœnn,   Urðar brunni.

20. Þaðan koma meyiar,   margs vitandi,
þriár, ór þeim sæ,   er und þolli stendr;
Urð héto eina,   aðra Verðandi
– scáro á scíði –,   Sculd ina þriðio;
þær lǫg lǫgðo,   þær líf kuro
alda bornom, ørlǫg seggia.[3]

Until there came out of that company, mighty and loving
Æsir to a house. They found on land, little capable, Ash
and Embla, without destiny.

Breath they had not, spirit they had not, no film of flesh
nor cry of voice, nor comely hues. Breath Óðinn gave,
spirit Hœnir gave, film of flesh Lóðurr gave and comely
hues.

An ash I know there stands, Ygdrasill is its name, a tall
tree, showered with shining loam. From there come the
dews that drop in the valleys. It stands forever green over
Urðr's well.

---

[3] *Edda: Die Lieder des Codex Regius nebst verwandten Denkmälern*, ed. Gustav
Neckel and Hans Kuhn, 5th ed. (Heidelberg: Carl Winter –
Universitätsverlag, 1983), 4-5.

From there come maidens deep in knowledge, three,
from the lake that lies under the tree.Urðr they called one,
'Had to be', the second Verðandi, 'Coming to be', – skaru
á skíði – Skuld the third, 'Has to be'. They laid down laws,
they chose out lives for mankind's children, men's
destinies.[4]

I have altered Dronke's translation insofar as I have left "skáru
á skíði" in the original. Before turning to a detailed analysis of these
words, I note briefly that scholars have been able to agree only that
they are likely to concern the three norns Urðr, Verðandi, and
Skuld,[5] and that they therefore must bear some relationship to other
information about the norns, including the additional clauses in the
stanza having to do with establishing laws and choosing lives and
fates for human beings. In this light the variant readings in
Hauksbók must obviously be mentioned at the outset. They have
the women emerge from a hall (*ór þeim sal*) which is not under the
tree but on it (*á þeim þolli*) or perhaps near it. They also have the
norns "declare fate" in the last line (*ørlǫg segia*, as opposed to *ørlǫg
seggika* in Regius). These variants do not affect the reading of the
clause *skáru á skíði* I intend to propose.

The initial question concerns the subject of the clause.
Sveinbjörn Egilsson saw the verb *skáru* as a subjectless parallel to
hétu and thought that as people named the norns, they carved those
names (*skáru*) onto wood or a wooden tablet, presumably with
runes.[6] Although Finnur Jónsson accepted this reading,[7] few others

---

4 *The Poetic Edda*, vol. 2: *Mythological Poems, Edited with Translation,
Introduction and Commentary*, ed. Ursula Dronke, (Oxford: Clarendon Press,
1997), 11-12.
5 For a thorough discussion of these three figures, see Karen Bek-
Pedersen, *The Norns in Old Norse Mythology* (Edinburgh: Dunedin, 2011),
73-91.
6 Sveinbjörn Egilsson, *Lexicon Poeticum Angiquae Linguae Sepentrionalis*
(Hafniae, 1860), s.v. *skera* and *skíð*, quoted in Anne Holtsmark, "Skáro á
skíði: Til Tolkningen av Voluspá str. 20," *Maal og minne* 1951: 81-89, at 82.

have done so, and one of the few areas of unanimity regarding this disputed clause in the last seventy years or so has been assigning the subject of the clause to the three norns.

The second question regards the object of the clause. Most scholars have treated it as a dative singular from the neuter noun *skíð* ("piece of wood"). However, some have seen in it a plural: Sigurður Nordal seems to operate with this concept, and one finds it, for example, in the English translations of Hermann Pálsson, Carolyn Larrington and Andy Orchard.[8] Karen Bek-Pedersen agrees and cites a personal communication from Sverrir Tómasson to the effect that *skíði* may be either singular or plural.[9] These scholars clearly see the underlying noun as neuter *skíði* and the form as accusative plural. I see two possible objections to this reading.

The first is semantic. To the best of my knowledge, *skíði* is only attested in *Hamðismál* 15, where it means "sheath" (the same stanza also attests the kenning *skíðijárn* ("sheath-iron") for sword). A survey of the lexicographical tools does not turn up any other meanings for simplex *skíði*. Nor do these tools show the modern meaning "ski" for neuter *skíði* in Old Icelandic, and the compounds with genitive plural *skíða-* ("ski") as first component could be built on *skíð* as easily as on *skíði* with that meaning. It seems highly unlikely that the norns would carve on a wooden sheath for a sword, or on a ski, if we assume that the meaning existed in Old Norse-Icelandic.

---

7 Finnur Jónsson, *Lexicon Poeticum Angiquae Linguae Sepentrionalis: Ordbog over det gamle norsk-islandske skjaldesprog*, 2nd ed. (Copenhagen: G. E. C. Gad), 505-06, s.v. *skera.*

8 Hermann Pálsson, *Völuspá: The Sibyl's Prophecy* (Edinburgh: Lockharton, 1996), 71 ("pieces of wood"); Carolyne Larrington, *The Poetic Edda: Translated with an Introduction and Notes* (Oxford: Oxford University Press, 1996), 6 ("wooden slips"); Andy Orchard, *The Elder Edda: A Book of Viking Lore* (London etc.: Penguin), 20 ("wood-tablets").

9 Bek-Pedersen, *Norns*, 115 fn. 3.

My second objection, and one that I advance with less confidence, is syntactic. *Skera* normally takes an accusative object, but what the verb phrase *skera á* takes is far less clear, given the possibility of the preposition *á* to govern both dative and accusative. The one other attestation in poetry of the verb phrase of which I am aware is the chilling scene in *Atlamál* (strophe 79) in which Guðrún dispatches her two sons: "scar hon á háls báða" ("she cut both their throats"). Here we find the accusative, as in the many attestations of this expression in prose. Probably we have the accusative here because of the motion of the knife toward the throat.[10]

On the other hand, *skera á* also can be found with dative, if not in poetry. Using the DONP, I found the following examples.[11] The first regards King Óláfr Haraldsson's ship Karlshǫfði:

Þar var á framstafni scorit konungs haufuð.[12]

---

[10] Since Guðrún makes drinking cups from the skulls of the boys, we might imagine that "skera e-n á háls" has the sense of "decapitate," but the adverb *síðan* in the scene of the disgraceful death of Hákon jarl in the pigsty in one of the versions of Oddr's *Óláfs saga Tryggvasonar* seems to belie this notion: "Ok þá tók hann einn kníf ok skar jarlinn á hals, ok síðan sneið hann af honum hǫfuðit . . . . ("and then he took a certain knife and cut the jarl's throat, and thereafter he cut off his head . . . .") (*Færinga saga: Óláfs saga Tryggvasonar eptir Odd Munk Snorrasonar*, ed. Ólafur Halldórsson, Íslenzk fornit 25 (Reykjavík: Hið íslenzka fornritafélag, 2006), 202.)

[11] Where possible I have cited editions more modern than those excerpted by the DONP and therefore the text reads slightly differently from what is on the scanned cards—not, however, in a way that concerns the case governed by *á*.

[12] *Saga Óláfs konungs hins Helga: Den store saga om Olav den hellige: Efter pergramenthåndskrift i Kungliga biblioteket i Stockholm nr. 2 4to med varianter fra*

The head of the kings was inscribed on the prow.

The others concern images of the god Þórr. The first, found in *Fóstbræðra saga*, is on a chair used by the witch Gríma to conceal the presence of Þormóðr:

Enn á brúðum stólsins var skorinn Þórr, ok var þat mikit líkneski.[13]

And on the arms of the chair was incised Þórr, and that was a great likeness.

The other involves a carving of Þórr on the high-seat pillars of Þórólfr Mosdtrarskegg, which he throws overboard upon reaching the coast of Iceland in order to locate the place where he should take land.

Þórólfr kastaði þá fyrir borð ǫndvegissúlum sínum, þeim er staðit hǫfðu í hofinu. Þar var Þórr skorinn á annarri.[14]

Þórólfr then threw overboard his high-seat pillars, which had stood in his hall [in Norway]. Þórr was incised on one.

Finally, in *Reykdæla saga* there is a dative indicating where the

---

andre håndskrifter, ed. Oscar Albert Johnsen and Jón Helgason (Oslo: Dybwad, 1941), 89.
[13] *Fóstbræðra saga*, ed. Björn K. Þórólfsson and Guðni Jónsson, Íslenzk fornrit 6 (Reykjavík: Hið íslenzka fornritafélag, 1943), 245.
[14] *Eyrbyggja saga*, ed. Einar Ól. Sveinsson and Matthías Þórðarson, Íslenzk fornrit 4 (Reykjavík: Hið íslenzka fornritafélag, 1935), 7. The Sturlubók redaction of *Landnámabók* recounts this episode but simply says "Þórr var skorinn á" ("Þórr was incised in it"). *Íslendingabók: Landnámabók*, ed Jakob Benediktsson, Íslenzk fornrit 1 (Reykjavík: Hið íslenzka fornritafélag, 1968), 124.

incising was done, but *skera á* seems to be used absolutely, which could remove this attestation from the dossier of relevant passages.

Bað hann Þórgeirr reisa upp þar ás, ok skera á karlhǫfða á endanum.[15]

He asked Þorgeirr to erect a beam there, and to carve a man's head on the end.

To sum up, if *skíði* is accusative, the norns cut into or more likely most of the way through a wooden scabbard, or perhaps a ski-like wooden object. If *skíði* is dative, the norns incised something, perhaps an image, in a wood object. The latter seems far more likely to me, and the passage should in my view be interpreted accordingly.

Some scholars have thought that the norns incised runes,[16] but then one would expect not the verb *skera* but rather *rista* or perhaps *fá*,[17] and this objection seems powerful. Sigurður Nordal and others have thought of the description Tacitus gives us of writing on slips of wood for oracular purposes, as well as the casting of lots in later sagas, including especially some in *Heimskringla*,[18] but here again the language is a problem: if what I argued in the previous paragraph is correct, the carving of the norns was only on a single *skíð*, whereas Tacitus writes of a number of slips,[19] and the vocabulary is wrong in

---

[15] *Reykdœla saga*, ed. Björn Sigfússon, Íslenzk fornrit 10 (Reykjavík: Hið íslenzka fornritafélag, 1940), 228.

[16] E.g., Gustav Neckel, "Kleine Beiträge zur germanischen Altertumskunde," *Beiträge zur Geschichte der deutschen Sprache und Literatur* 33 (1908): 459-82, at 459-66.

[17] Sigurður Nordal, *Völuspá*, 2nd printing (Reykjavík: Helgafell, 1952), 71.

[18] Sigurður Nordal, *Völuspá*, 71; Dronke, *Poetic Edda*, 2:xxx; Carolyne Larrington, *Poetic Edda*, 128-29.

[19] Holtsmark, "Skáro á skíði," 82-83.

the Icelandic passages, which speak of *hlutir* that are *markaðir*[20]–
again more than one. This led Anne Holtsmark to the notion in
recent Norwegian folk practice of scoring on wood to mark the
passage of time: calendar sticks and the like.[21] This reading has the
enormous advantage of linguistic continuity, since the verb in
question was *skera* or its cognates, although Karen Bek-Pedersen
has recently objected on the grounds that ordinarily we would
expect *skora* rather than *skera* for counting.[22] Thus the norns, in
Holtsmark's reading, mark the duration of life for Askr and Embla
by scoring years and perhaps months, just as they chose life and
established laws and fates. Here Elizabeth Jackson's argument is of
interest. Jackson sees the clause "skáru á skíði" as an instrument for
linking two lists in stanza 20 and argues that "ørlǫg seggja" is the
object of the verb skera: "skáru á skíði ørlǫg seggja" (they incised
on a slip of wood men's destinies").[23] I do not believe, however,
that it is necessary to read the stanza this way grammatically in
order to reach the sense she proposes. Interlocking lists or not, the
norns' incising clearly has to do, in my view, with the fixing of fate.

I will begin at the basic semantic level, but unlike Holtsmark I
will start with the noun *skíð*. I will also visit the verb, *skera*, at the
end my discussion.

Skíð is formed from a dental extension of the Indo European
root **skei* ("cut, part, separate") and has numerous cognates in the
Germanic languages.[24] The basic idea is the splitting of a section of

---

[20] *Haralds saga Sigurðarsonar*, in *Heimskringla* vol. 3, ed. Bjarni
Aðalbjarnarson, Íslenzk fornrit 28 (Reykjavík: Hið íslenska fornritafélag,
1951), 73.

[21] Holtsmark, "Skáro á skíði," 81-89.

[22] Bek-Pedersen, *Norns*, 115.

[23] Elizabeth Jackson, "'Skáro á scíði ørlǫg seggia:' The Composition of
Vǫlospá 20 and the Implications of the Hauksbók Variant," *Alvíssmál* 9
(1999): 73-88.

[24] Julius Pokorny, *Indogermanisches etymoligisches Wörterbuch*, vol. 1 (Bern:
Francke, 1951), 921; Jan de Vries, *Altnordisches etymologisches Wörterbuch*
(Leiden: Brill, 1962), 491.

a log, and the result, depending on the technology used, is either a piece of firewood or a plank. Old Norse-Icelandic *skíð* attests both senses, as does, for example, archaic English *shide*.[25] A specialized use of a plank was as a ski or snowshoe, and that meaning was common in Old Norse-Icelandic.

The word *skíð* is attested beyond *Vǫluspá* 20 in two other Eddic passages. The meaning of the word is obscure enough in these three passages in Eddic poetry that La Farge and Tucker suggest three different meanings;[26] the one kenning in Eddic poetry, *sárskíð* ("wound-board," i.e., sword) is in this regard unhelpful because of the principle of member-for-member equivalence among base words of kennings.

The two other simplex passages are *Hávamál* 60 and *Rígsþula* 14. I begin with *Rígsþula* 14, where the meaning "board" or "plank" seems most likely; LaFarge and Tucker's gloss is "one of the boards forming a door frame."[27]

Gecc Rígr at þat   réttar brautir
kom hann at hǫllo,   hurð var á scíði;
inn nam at ganga,   eldr var á gólfi;
hión sáto þar,   heldo at sýslo.[28]

With that Rígr went straight roads, he came to a hall, the door was on a plank, he went in, the fire was on the floor; a couple sat there, kept on with their work.

What exactly it means for the door to be on a plank has long

---

[25] *Oxford English Dictionary*, vol. 9 (Oxford: Clarendon Press, 1933), 689.
[26] Beatrice La Farge and John Tucker, *Glossary to the Poetic Edda Based on Hans Kuhn's Kurzes Wörterbuch*, Skandinavistische Arbeiten, 15 (Heidelberg: Carl Winter – Universitätsverlag, 1992), 234.
[27] La Farge and Tucker, *Glossary*, 234.
[28] *Edda*, ed. Neckel and Kuhn, 262. My translation, as throughout if not otherwise noted.

been debated, primarily as to whether the door is open or shut and whether this door, in the home of Afi and Amma, where Karl will be born, represents a progression from the door of Ái and Edda, to whom Þræll will be born; their door was á gætti, which is another expression that has called forth numerous ingenious conjectures.[29] The Frankfurt team in their commentary unhelpfully translate the line "hurð var á skíði" as "Die Tür war am Scheit."[30]

Hávamál 60 follows two passages on the benefits of early rising ("Ár skal rísa") and precedes stanzas on behavior at a thing meeting. It runs as follows.

> þurra scíða   ok þakinna næfra,
>   þess kann maðr miǫt,
> oc þess viðar,   er vinnaz megi
>   mál oc misseri.[31]

Here as far as I can tell there is near unanimity that *skíð* must be firewood. That is a common enough meaning in prose and one certainly suggested by the German cognate *Scheit*; also, this is wood that should stay dry ("þurra scíða"). However, this creates something of a problem in reading the rest of the line. David Evans wrote:

> Unless we suppose the picture is one of a pile of pieces of bark waiting to be used and which, just like a wood-pile, have to be roofed against the weather, we must take *þakinna* here in a active sense ("bark *for roofing*") rather

---

[29] Klaus von See, Beatrice La Farge, Eva Picard, and Katja Schultz, *Kommentar zu ddn Liedern der Edda*, vol. 3: *Götterlieder (Vǫlundarkviða, Alvíssmál, Balddrs draumar, Rígsþula, Hyndlulióð, Grottasǫngr)* (Heidelberg: Universitätsverlag C. Winter), 524-25, 566-67.

[30] Von See et al., *Eddakommentar*, 565.

[31] *Edda*, ed. Neckel and Kuhn, 26.

than in the passive sense usual in the past participle, which the word appears to be.[32]

Evans goes on to rehearse the evidence for construing *þakinna* as active, but since the verb *þekja* is quite well known, the argument is recondite. If we take the participle as having its usual passive sense, I believe that we might venture the following translation.

Of dry boards / and of thatched barks, /of this a man can know the measure, / and of that wood, / which may suffice / for a quarter or half a year.

If we accept *scíð* here as boards rather than firewood, we reduce the number of references to firewood to one (*við* in long line 3) and thus remove an inelegant redundancy.

The boards in question could have to do with the threshold, as in *Rígsþula*, or with the walls of the house, in contrast with the thatched bark of the roof. A man may know their measure by observing whether rain or wind enters the house. Thus I would break up the first half-stanza into two parts: a man should know whether his dwelling will keep him dry, and he should know whether he has firewood to keep him warm.

In skaldic poetry, *skíð* served primarily as base word in kennings for ship ("*skíð* of the sea") and, less frequently, for swords (*skíð* of

---

[32] David A. H. Evans, *Hávamál*, Viking Society for Northern Research, Text Series 7 (London: Viking Society for Northern Research, 1986), 102. This text and the translation I shall propose rely on the common emendation of manuscript *miotðc* to *miot. oc.* The manuscript actually has *miotyðc*, the dot under the letter *v* indicating it should be omitted, and scholars have long assumed that the scribe simply forgot to place a dot under the *ð*. For example, Karl Hildebrand, ed., *Edda* (Paderborn: Ferdinand Schöningh, 1876), 94; Ludvig F. A. Wimmer and Finnur Jónsson, *Håndskriftet nr. 2365 4to gl. kgl. samling på det store kgl. bibliotehek i København (Codex Regius af den ældre Edda): I fototypisk og diplomatisk gengivelse* (Copenhagen: S. L. Møller, 1891), lix.

battle). Finnur Jónsson thought that the ship kennings drew on the meaning of *skíð* as "ski,"[33] which is certainly attested in the skaldic corpus; in the famous stanza in which he enumerated his skills, Rǫgnvaldr kali boasted: "Skríða kannk á skíðum" ("I am able to glide on skis").[34] However, any plank would do as base word of such kennings. The same is presumably true of the sword kennings. Kormákr used *hjalmar skíð* (*skíð* of the rudder), for the boat's tiller with which he struck Þorvaldr,[35] and amongst the *þulur* one finds *hjǫlumvǫlr* as a shipboard *heiti*.[36]

In prose, *skíð* seems to be used mostly for snowshoe or ski, although the dictionaries usually list "firewood" or "split piece of wood" first. Before modern technology, skis were just planks. Thus the etymological meaning of *skíð* was still current. Related to such attested verbs as Old English *ofscíðan* and German *scheiten*, a *skíð* is a piece of wood that has been worked by human hand, such as a plank in a building, or for that matter a shield. I think Finnur Jónsson's long and somewhat fussy gloss in his *Lexicon Poeticum* must be correct: "langstrakt, tyndt træstykke frembragt ved flækning"[37] ("a lengthy, thin piece of wood produced by splitting").

I wish to propose that all three attestations of the word *skíð* in Eddic poetry have the same meaning: "plank." And even if I am wrong about *Hávamál* 60 – a possibility I readily concede – in *Vǫluspá* 20 a plank makes more sense that a piece of firewood, and it makes a great deal more sense than a "slip of wood" or something small enough to cast lots on. What the norns carved on was a plank or board, as Gísli Sigurðsson saw when in his edition of

[33] Finnur Jónsson, *Lexicon Poeticum*, 508.
[34] Judith Jesch, "Rǫgnvaldr jarl Kali Kolsson," in *Skaldic Poetry of the Scandinavian Middle Ages*, vol. 2, *Poetry from the Kings' Sagas*, ed. Kari Ellen Gade (Turnhout: Brepols), 575-608, at 576.
[35] His lausavísa 57; see *Kormáks saga*, ed. Einar Ól. Sveinsson, Íslenzk fornrit, 8 (Reykjavík: Hið íslenzka fornritafélag, 1939), 294.
[36] Þul. IV z 7, in Finnur Jónsson, ed., *Den norsk-islandske skjaldedigtning* (Copenhagen: Gyldendal, 1912-15), vol. A1, 673; vol. B1, 668.
[37] Finnur Jónsson, *Lexicon Poeticum*, 508.

Eddic poems he correctly glossed *skíð* with modern *fjöl* in Vǫluspá 20.[38]

The *skíð* in *Rígsþula* is definitely in a house, and I argue that the same is likely to be so for the *skíð* in *Hávamál*. Furthermore, Dronke argues a direct parallel between the arrival of Rígr *at húsi* in *Rígsþula* and the arrival of the æsir *at húsi* in *Vǫluspá* 17.[39] If the *skíð* in *Vǫluspá* 20 is in a house, there may be a connexion with *Vǫluspá* 17, when the three æsir come *at húsi*, where they find Askr and Embla. Whose house or building is this? If it belongs to Askr and Embla, we may rightly wonder who built it.[40] On the other hand, there certainly appears to be a connection between Askr and Embla and the house, and there is no indication that Askr and Embla have moved or been moved between stanzas 17 and 20. There is thus a possibility that the *skíð* into which the norns incised was a part of the building to which the Æsir came when they found Askr and Embla lying on the shore.

In her discussion of the stanza, Holtsmark drew attention to the *dyraskíð* as a place where people scored marks for various purposes, and she actually mentioned the *Rígsþula* passage as relevant to the discussion of *Vǫluspá* 20.[41] It thus seems not out of the question to wonder whether the norns incised into planking near the door or somewhere else in a house or building relevant to Askr and Embla. If *Rígsþula* is a valid parallel at all, it is the house in which Askr and Embla will procreate and bring about the generations of mankind. To score marks of whatever kind in the house where Askr and Embla are to live is to make their fate visible to them.

Besides scoring something onto some piece of wood, the norns also set down laws and chose life for the sons of humans, fates for warriors. Laws were until the twelfth century oral in form and even

---

[38] *Eddukvæði*, ed. Gísli Sigurðsson ([Reykjavík:] Mál og menning, 1999), 10.
[39] Dronke, *Poetic Edda*, II:122.
[40] Sigurður Nordal, *Völuspá*, 71.
[41] Holtsmark, "Skáro," 85.

after that time some principles of orality – that is, mutability and contextual understanding of them – continued in practice. Setting down the laws must surely have been a speech act undertaken by the norns. As for choosing the fates of men, this must be parallel to the act of choosing the slain on the battlefield and here must surely refer to the fates of Askr and Embla. What I am trying to say here is that there is a verbal component to the norns' action, as in fact the Hauksbók redaction makes explicit.[42]

Þær lǫg lǫgðu   þær líf kuru
allda bǫrnum   ørlǫg at segia.

They set down laws, / they chose life, / for the children of men, / to declare fates.

This variant of the poem, at least, makes it appear likely that the norns both declared the fates of Askr and Embla and also recorded those fates in some way by scoring wood.[43] There is a vast difference between the two media: what one hears can easily be altered in the retelling, but what one sees cannot easily be altered in the re-seeing. The dichotomy is usually expressed using the spoken and written word,[44] but in fact what is important about writing is that it allows recursive access, and so does visual representation.

The calendrical marks Holtsmarks discusses are simply slashes

---

[42] *Norrœn fornkvæði: Islandsk samling af folkelige oldtidsdigte om Norden guder og heroer: Almindelig kaldet Sæmundar edda hins fróða*, ed. Sophus Bugge (Christiania: Aschehoug, 1867), 21. Cf. also Jackson, "Scáro."

[43] This redaction of the poem, but not of course that of Regius, could be read to support the repeated assertion of Paul Bauschatz in *The Well and the Tree: World and Time in Early Germanic Culture* (Amherst: University Press of New England, 1982), that the norns daily say the primal laws (e.g., 25). Insofar as this hypothesis points to a speech act of the norns, it conforms to my own reading of the passage.

[44] This insight, now hardly new, goes back to the seminal article of Jack Goody and Ian Watt, "The Consequences of Literacy," *Comparative Studies in Society and History* 5 (1963): 304-45.

cut into wood, presumably against the grain. However, if we are thinking of a house, and perhaps especially of the area around the door, and if we take into consideration the usage of *skera á* in the saga passages I cited above, we may imagine that they incised images that accompany the words that Hauksbók at least suggests they used for the fates of Askr and Embla and that both redactions of *Vǫluspá* imply through the connection with laws. Karen-Bek Pedersen came upon this idea and brought into her discussion of the passage the carving of images of Þórr in *Fóstbrœðra saga*, chapter 23 and the image of his beloved carved by Tjǫrvi inn háðsami according to *Landnámabók*.

Read this way, the phrase perhaps points back to *Vǫluspá* 17 where Askr and Embla are created, seemingly from two tree trunks, but it might also recall wooden statues found in bogs and the occasional references to carved images of gods.

I propose a completely different parallel, namely the images incised in the hall of Óláfr pái at Hjarðarholt according to *Laxdœla saga*, images which formed the subject of the skaldic poem composed by Úlfr Uggason and recited at the wedding of Óláfr's daughter Þuriðr to the viking Geirmundr gnýr.[45] These images are called *sǫgur* "narratives" and are carved within the interior of the hall: "Váru þar markaðar ágætligar sǫgur á þilviðinum og svá á ræfrinu"[46] ("There splendid stories were incised on the vertical wall planks and rafters"). Besides being *markaðar* (from *merkja*, "mark, draw"), the image-narratives are also said to be *skrifaðar* (from *skrifa*, here with the meaning "scratch" rather than "write"),[47] and the whole was *vel smiðat*, "well crafted." I propose this parallel, despite the verbal differences, for its juxtaposition of word and image, which I have tried to present above as a context for understanding what the norns did when they carved on a plank.

---

[45] *Laxdœla saga*, ed. Einar Ól. Sveinsson, Íslenzk fornrit 5 (Reykjavík: Hið íslenzka fornritafélag, 1934), 79.

[46] *Laxdœla saga*, 79.

[47] *Laxdœla saga*, 80.

The stanzas of Úlfr's Húsdrápa retained in Snorri's edda suggest that three scenes, at least, were incised in the wood at Hjarðarholt: Loki's enigmatic battle with Heimdallr for the Brísinga men, Þórr's battle with the Midgard serpent, and Baldr's funeral. Of these, Baldr's funeral could be an indication of his fate, and if Þórr kills the serpent in Úlfr's version of this well-known myth,[48] the worm's final fate would be there as well.

Indeed, there is a healthy representation of death in the images that we know stand behind a certain amount of skaldic poetry, namely the shield poems. Bragi's *Ragnarsdrápa*, in which the form apparently emerges full-blown, has the moment when Jǫrmunrekkr awakes to terror and widespread death when Hamðir and Sǫrli attack, and also the Hjaðningavíg, which certainly represented the fate of the warriors doomed to participate in the endless battle over Hildr.

This is hardly the place to discuss Germanic or Viking Age or even mediaeval notions of fate.[49] If, however, we view fate as including not just our deaths but the significant things that happen during our lives, then the fishing battle between Þórr and the Midgard serpent is part of the fate of both. This point will help to

[48] Preben Meulengracht Sørensen, "Thor's Fishing Expedition," in *Words and Objects: Towards a Dialogue between Archaeology and History of Religion*, ed. Gro Steinsland (Oslo: Norwegian University Press, 1986), 257-78.
[49] Compare the dueling "weird" books: Ladislaus Mittner, *Wurd: Das Sakrale in der altgermanischen Epik*, Bibliotheca Germanica 6 (Bern: Francke, 1955), and Gerd Wolfgang Weber, *Wyrd: Studien zum Schicksalsbegriff der altenglischen und altnordischen Literatur*, Frankfurter Beiträge zur Germanistik 8 (Bad Homburg v. d. H.: Gehlen, 1969). Dated but still of value are Walther Gehl, *Der germanische Schicksalsglaube* (Berlin: Junker & Dünnhaupt, 1939), and Åke V. Ström, "Scandinavian Belief in Fate: A Comparison between pre-Christian and post-Christian Times," in *Fatalistic Beliefs in Religion, Folklore, and Literature: Papers Read at the Symposium on Fatalistic Beliefs Held at Åbo on the 7th-9th of September 1964*, ed. Helmer Ringgren, Scripti Instituti Donneriani Aboensis 2 (Stockholm: Almqvist & Wiksell, 1967), 63-88.

underline the point I want to make about how the norns fix fate if we entertain the notion that *skera á skíði* means to carve images. The textual record for this myth suggests various outcomes, although all agree that the event was to occur. The visual record, including the Gosforth cross and the Altuna stone, suggests only one thing, namely that Þórr got the worm on his hook. These images present, or fix, an immutable fate for each of them. No other interpretation is possible. Perhaps it would be possible to unravel a kenning or two in such a way as to suggest that Þórr fished up not the serpent but, say, Hymir, or that he did not fish up the beast but met him on a battlefield, but if I were to assert either of these interpretations, the visual evidence would trump my reading of the textual evidence. This is important because we must assume that skaldic poetry changed less in oral transmission than did other forms. If we are dealing with a more malleable, self-correcting oral tradition, the fixed visual representation becomes even more important.

The progression in *Vǫluspá* 17-20 is clear: the gods can give whatever is needed for life – the mysterious *lá ok læti ok litir góðir*, but only the norns can give fates. There are thus two principles, one with a set of things that are in effect changeable. While I don't pretend to be certain about what exactly *lá ok læti ok litir góðir* refer to, they certainly look like aspects of the living body, and with our current state of knowledge I hardly think we can improve upon Dronke's translation "film of flesh, cry of voice, and comely hues."[50] These are indeed mutable. Our films of flesh wither as we age, our voices waiver and go up in pitch, and sudden changes in our comely hues indicate emotion.

I now will contend that these principles are bound up with different media: the mutable gifts of the gods with oral tradition and the fixed fates of the norns with something visual, either images as I have just argued or, less likely in my view, scorings on a piece of wood, as Holtsmark argued (or, least likely in my view, even the "lottery" that Dronke puts forth). The *frœði* of the gods is an

---

[50] Dronke, *Poetic Edda*, II: 11; cf. also 124.

unwritten control of the history and structure of the cosmos, couched especially in verse.[51] Óðinn, who is its master, brings it forth in *Vafþrúðnismál* and *Grímnismál*, in both cases in oral performances according to the frames of the poems. When the norns fix fate, I am arguing, they do it not with mutable words but with immutable visual representations.

In this instance it may be profitable to revisit the expression *kviðr norna*. In the legal language a *kviðr* is a panel or a panel verdict.[52] More generally, in effect a *kviðr*, whether used purely legally or not, is kind of oral statement that tries to be immune to change, since it is issued not by one person but by a group (panel). There is oral safety in numbers here: the words cannot be changed by one person alone, since the others in the group are available to correct misspeaking. This notion is captured in the noun *mis-kviðr*, for a mistake in legal pleading, that is, for changing something.

If the traditional dating of the genesis of *Vǫluspá* to just before A.D. 1000 is correct – and no compelling alternative exists, despite the multiple hypotheses[53] – then the issue of oral versus written retrieval would have been particularly acute. According to the tripartite scheme of Anders Andrén, the way the norns fix fate, by scoring onto wood, might look back to an "object-created" discursive context in which words are powerful and associated with material artifacts, but it would in fact fit perfectly into an integrated discourse in which words and objects presuppose each other.[54] Here, Andrén argued, inscriptions flourished. However, the

[51] John Lindow, "Íslendingabók and Myth," *Scandinavian Studies* 69 (1997): 454-64, at 455.
[52] Andrew Dennis, Peter Foote, and Richard Perkins, Laws of Early Iceland: *Grágás: The Codex Regius of Grágás with Material from Other Manuscripts*, vol. 1 (Winnipeg: University of Manitoba Press, 1980), 272.
[53] Most recently, see the essays in *The Icelandic Apocalypse: Approaches to Vǫluspá and Nordic Days of Judgment*, ed. Terry Gunnell and Annette Lassen, Acta Scandinavica 2 (Turnhout: Brepols, 2013).
[54] Anders Andrén, *Between Artifact and Text: Historical Archaeology in Global Perspective* (New York and London: Plenum, 1998), 150-53.

slow and laborious practice of rune carving, especially in stone, was no way to record a narrative, as in fact the dearth of narrative in the inscriptions shows clearly. But if a narrative can be captured in a few shorthand strokes, or in an image, then it can be fixed just as runes fixed short texts that mostly focus on the fact of a death and on family relationships to the deceased. Runes are not the right technology for such fixing, but an image might be. If our fate is just the day of our demise, a system of strokes indicating months and years will do.

In this context it is difficult not to think of the images on door panels that tell life stories, such as those rescued from the Hylestad stave church in Setesdal showing screens from the legend of Sigurðr. I am fully cognizant of the danger of arguing back from a medieval church to *Vǫluspá*, and I would not insist that this parallel be added to the dossier of *Vǫluspá* 20. I would note, however, that in both instances we are clearly dealing with a mixture of pre-Christian and Christian.

Holtsmark is able to show that the marks she proposes as parallel to the norns' incisions use the verb *skera* or cognates. As we have seen, *Laxdœla saga* used *merkja* and *skrifa* to indicate the "stories" carved at Hjarðarholt. While both verbs are helpful here, in that they suggest a semantic component, we may wonder whether the use of *skera* rather than some other verb is significant. I turn now to that verb and how it might be understood in *Vǫluspá* 20.

The Indo-European root **(s)ker* and all of the Germanic cognates of the verb *skera* mean "to cut."[55] In Old Norse-Icelandic, the implement used to *skera* is usually a knife or some other sharp tool, as is consistent with the secondary meaning "to slaughter," one of several.[56] In poetry there are such metaphorical senses as

---

[55] Pokorny, *Wörterbuch*, I:938-40; de Vries, *Wörterbuch*, 490.

[56] See, for example, the six tight columns in Johan Fritzner, *Ordbog over det gamle norske sprog*, new ed. (Oslo: Universitets forlag, 1973), II:310-13.

cutting through enemy forces in battle or through the waves with a
ship.[57] Within the corpus of Eddic poetry, however, the meaning is
more restricted: *skera* means to cut human bodies, to wound them.
It is regularly used to refer to the cutting out of Hǫgni's heart,
specifically in *Oddúnargrátr* 28, *Atlakviða* 22 (there Hjalli's heart
instead of Hǫgni's), 24 ("Hló þá Hǫgni, er til hjarta scáro" ["Hǫgni
laughed when they cut out his heart"]), *Atlamál* 59, and *Guðrúnarhvǫt*
17.

The latter passage itself is not wholly clear and is worth further
investigation.

> Enn sá sárastr,   er þeir Sigurð minn,
> sigri ræntan,   í sæing vágo;
> enn sá grimmastr,   er þeir Gunnari,
> fránir ormar,   til fiǫrs scriðo;
> en sá hvassastr,   er til hiarta fló[gu]
> konung óblauðan   qviqvan scáro.

And the most poignant, that my Sigurðr, stripped of
triumph, they slew in his bed – and the most terrible that
those glittering snakes slid towards Gunnarr to take his
life – and the most cutting that they flayed to the
heart the fearless king – slit his living body.[58]

One must infer that Hǫgni is the object of the last pair of long
lines, since the previous two sorrows are the loss of Sigurðr and
Gunnarr. Although Hǫgni is not technically a king, Kuhn
understood the term here to expand to include the blood relation of
one, and by skaldic usage of noun substitution a king can of course
be a man. More important is the textual problem posed by
manuscript *fló* at the end of the next to last long line. Neckel and
Kuhn relegate it to the apparatus, but Dronke emends it to the

---

[57] Finnur Jónsson, *Lexicon Poeticum*, 505-06.
[58] Text and translation from Ursula Dronke, *The Poetic Edda*, vol. 1, *Heroic Poems* (Oxford: Clarendon Press, 1969), 149-50.

plural *flógu*, from *flá* ("flay"). Her eloquent translation captures the violence of the scene. If this emendation is correct, and I believe it is, there is a direct collocation between *flá* and *skera* and therefore, as Dronke notes, a connexion with the slaughtering of animals, a base meaning of *skera* in prose.

The murder of Sigurðr finds expression through the use of *skera* in Guðrúnarkviða I, stanza 14, and the entire scene is far from pleasant.

Á leit Guðrún   eino sinni;
sá hon døglings scǫr   dreyra runna,
fránar siónir   fylkis liðnar,
hugborg iǫfurs   hiǫrvi scorna.[59]

Guðrún looked on one time; she saw the princes' hair run with blood, the king's bright eyes gone away, the breast of the chieftain cut with a sword.

What the norns do, literally, is *skera á*. As I noted above, *Atlamál* 79 offers a direct parallel, when Guðrún murders her sons: "scar hon á hals báða."[60] She cut both their throats, separating them not only from their childhood, as the poet has it, but from their lives.[61] If one's death is one's fate, Guðrún has cut their fates onto her sons, just as the norns cut the fates for Askr and Embla. The norns seemingly cut those fates on some piece of wood, but these other Eddic passages, and stanzas 17-20 in *Vǫluspá* taken as a whole, suggest a parallel and metaphorical reading for the *skíð* they cut. Dronke expressed the progression in these stanzas most eloquently.

---

59 *Edda*, ed. Neckel and Kuhn, 204.
60 *Edda*, ed. Neckel and Kuhn, 259.
61 "Brá þá barnæsco / brœðra in kappsvinna / scipit scapliga, / scar hon á háls báða" (*Edda*, ed. Neckel and Kuhn, 259) ("Then the bold woman separated the brothers from childhood, arranged it fittingly; she cut both their throats").

So the poet moves, conjoining, from *Askr* to *Askr*, from *brunnr* to *sær*, to the three lake-maidens, wise from the oracular element they inhabit, who come to cut upon the material of man himself – a piece of wood – *á skíði*, the lottery mark, the rune, that decides his fortune.[62]

Although I propose emending Dronke's lottery mark or rune, as well as Holtsmark's hypothetical scorings, to my hypothetical images, the result is the same. Fate is cut directly into the wood that in this mythology is the proto-material of humans. I have argued that the stories of the first people's fates were there to be read on the wall, unchangeable. If I am right, then the *Vǫluspá* poet expressed that fact directly. His use of the verb *skera* shows that receiving a fate is painful; what must be must be, in life and at life's end. As the *Hávmál* poet famously put it: "Deyr fé / deyja frændr / deyja sjálfr it sama" ("Cattle die, kinsmen die, just the same one dies oneself"). The norns cut the pain of life and death onto wood, the raw material of human beings. For warriors, fate might hold a painful tearing of the flesh by another man's axe or sword, but as *Egils saga* among others shows us, old age was no picnic either. This too the *Vǫluspá* poet captured in those three words, "skáru á skíði."

---

[62] Dronke, *Poetic Edda*, II:40. Dronke's understanding of the passage follows the idea of casting lots (Dronke, *Poetic Edda*, II:128-29), which in my view is unlikely. In line with that interpretation, she completes the thought with a lovely image. "The original condition of fatelessness of the two wooden pieces—*ørlǫglausa*—which seemed so pathetic at the opening of the sequence, finds ironic rectification at the close, with the institution of the fatal lottery, ørlǫg seggia, into which the marked man, the wood lot, is cast" (Dronke, *Poetic Edda*, II:40).

Swimming in the Flax Field, *verða at gjalti,* and Related Motifs

Marvin Taylor

In addition to signaling my affection and respect for Fred Amory, the present article makes good a promise I made in an earlier one[1] to examine the motif complex "Swimming in the Flax Field" in greater detail from the perspectives of folklore, literature, and historiography. As it happened, shortly after the appearance of that article I read one by William Sayers on the phrase *verða at gjalti* in descriptions of battle panic[2] that was to give me additional inspiration to write. Sayers is interested in the linguistic usage of the phrase and its scenic manifestation in Old Norse narrative, but he restricts his survey to text passages containing the expression in question, omitting descriptions of panic phrased in other words and leaving most textual genres outside the *Íslendinga sögur* unexamined. Instead, Sayers presses his evidence into serving the thesis that for speakers of Old Norse, the half-Irish phrase *verða at gjalti* functioned as a "derogatory ethnic descriptor" of the Celts, even though he himself calls this thesis "speculative" and admits that "in our extant textual evidence we find no explicit linking of the phrase *verða at*

---

[1] Marvin Taylor, "On Gizurr Þorvaldsson's Speaking Style," *Saga-Book* 24 (1994-1997): 311-28, at 314-15.

[2] William Sayers, "Deployment of an Irish loan: ON *verða at gjalti* 'to go mad with terror'," *Journal of English and Germanic Philology* 93 (1994): 157-82. In this phrase, the Irish word *geilt,* denoting a victim of battle-panic, was borrowed as *gjalt,* which may have been perceived as a byform of *goltr* ("boar").

gjalti with the Irish or Scots (except Nagli [of *Eyrbyggja saga*], who
may have been of mixed ancestry)."[3] I shall have occasion to point
to observations made by Sayers himself that lead to different
conclusions.

The text passages assembled in the present article are by no
means intended as a complete catalogue, but rather examples
chosen to represent the wide spectrum of variants, inversions, and
functional analogues of the "Swimming in the Flax Field" complex.
Secondary sources are drawn on to document the history of
relevant folkloristic scholarship, but otherwise cited sparingly.

I. DELUSIONS OF WATER

In a series of carefully crafted scenes, some with dialogue, the
eighth-century historian Paulus Diaconus narrates the fateful
conflict between the Herulians and Langobards at the beginning of
the sixth century. In the final scene of the sequence, with King
Rodulf dead and the battle as good as lost, panic breaks out in the
Herulian army:[4]

> Herolorum vero exercitus dum hac illacque diffugeret,
> tanta super eos caelitus ira respexit, ut viridantia
> camporum lina cernentes, natatiles esse acquas putarent;
> dumque quasi nataturi brachia extenderent, crudeliter
> hostium feriebantur a gladiis.

> While the Herulian army was fleeing this way and that,
> such was the divine wrath that fell on them, that when
> they saw blooming flax fields they took them for water to
> be swum over; and while they were spreading their arms

---

[3] Sayers, "Deployment," 157, 178.
[4] *Pauli Historia Langobardorum*, ed. Ludwig Bethmann and Georg Waitz
(Hannover: Hahn, 1878), §1.20, 67; my translation.

as if to swim, they were fiercely cut down by the enemies' swords.

The only other medieval attestation of the anecdote is found in Aimoinus of Fleury, who copied it from Paulus Diaconus for his history of the Franks,[5] but by the Early Modern Period, "Swimming in the Flax Field" had become a staple comic tale told of numerous ethnic groups, including the Swabians and the men of Mols in Jutland.[6] In international folklore studies, it bears the tale type number (AaTh/ATU) 1290 and the motif number (TMI) J1820.[7]

---

[5] *Historia Francorum libri quatuor,* in J.-P. Migne, ed., *Patrologia Latina,* vol. 139 (Paris: Garnier 1880), cols. 627-798, at §2.13, col. 675: *Tanta autem consternatio ac (ut verius dicam) mentium alienatio ejus invasit exercitum, ut virides segetes, lini campos, flumina crederent. Dumque brachia quasi nataturi extenderent, a supervenientibus sine difficultate cædebantur hostibus* ("For such was the panic or (to put it more truthfully) mental aberration that came over the army, that they believed green meadows, fields of flax, to be rivers. While they were spreading their arms as if to swim, they were cut down by the oncoming enemies without difficulty"; my translation).

[6] [Ludwig Aurbacher], *Die Geschichte von den Sieben Schwaben* (Stuttgart: Brodhag, 1832), 29-30; Arthur Christensen, ed., *Molboernes vise Gerninger* (Copenhagen: Schønberg, 1939), 120-21. The first scholar to link the medieval reports with the Early Modern numskull story seems to have been Wilhelm Wackernagel, "Die Spottnamen der Völker," *Zeitschrift für deutsches Alterthum* 6 (1848): 254-61, at 257-58.

[7] AaTh = Antti Aarne, *The Types of the Folktale. A Classification and Bibliography,* trans. and enlarged by Stith Thompson, 2nd revision (Helsinki: Suomalainen Tiedeakatemia, 1961); ATU = Hans-Jörg Uther, *The Types of International Folktales. A Classification and Bibliography Based on the System of Antti Aarne and Stith Thompson,* 3 vols. (Helsinki: Suomalainen Tiedeakatemia, 2004); TMI = Stith Thompson, *Motif-Index of Folk-Literature,* rev. and enlarged ed. (Bloomington: Indiana University Press, 1955-58). The most extensive original discussion and bibliography is that of Johannes Bolte and Georg Polívka, *Anmerkungen zu den Kinder- und Hausmärchen der Brüder Grimm,* rev. ed. by Ernst Schade, 5 vols. (Leipzig: Dieterich, 1913-31), s.v. no. 149: "Der Hahnenbalken," III:201-05, at III:203-06. Some additional material is provided by Christensen, *Molboernes*

Ia. Delusions of Water through Magic

In the "pure" form just described, "Swimming in the Flax Field" is not attested in Old Norse or Modern Icelandic.[8] A closely related motif complex, however, which also goes back to the eighth century,[9] has a much wider medieval distribution, including Old Norse: it is the illusion of water caused by magic, not stupidity. Students of the Grimms' fairy tales know the motif from tale number 149, "The Rooster's Beam" (AaTh/ATU 987), in which a wizard (as the second of two tricks) makes a flax field appear as a rushing stream, so that his victim makes ridiculous wading motions to pass through it,[10] and in their commentary, recognizing in this tale type an important family of variants on "Swimming in the Flax Field," Bolte and Polívka provide extensive documentation of delusory floods in medieval epic and modern folklore – mostly lacking the flax field connection, but characteristically involving the

---

vise Gerninger, 195-96, and Viera Gašparíková, "Schwimmen im Flachsfeld," in *Enzyklopädie des Märchens,* ed. Kurt Ranke and R. W. Brednich, 14 vols. (Berlin: de Gruyter, 1976-2013), vol. 12 (2005-2007), ed. R. W. Brednich, cols. 444-7. As sole substitute for waving fields of flax or grain, Gašparíková names the shadows of poplars in a Slovakian variant (*ibid.*), but there are also variants with fog, mist (see, for example, the listings in the TMI entry, which Gašparíková does not cite), or – at somewhat further remove – a moonlit pavement viewed from above (see the Arabic tale cited by Christensen, *Molboernes vise Gerninger,* 31: befuddled by opium, a man mistakes such a pavement for a pond, throws out his fishing line, and catches a dog).

[8] At least, it is not registered in Inger M. Boberg, *Motif-Index of Early Icelandic Literature* (Copenhagen: Munksgaard, 1966), or Einar Ól. Sveinsson, *Verzeichnis isländischer Märchenvarianten* (Helsinki: Suomalainen Tiedeakatemia, 1929).

[9] Bolte and Polívka, *Anmerkungen,* III:203.

[10] Jacob and Wilhelm Grimm, *Kinder- und Hausmärchen,* 3 vols. (Frankfurt: Insel, 1984), no. 149, "Der Hahnenbalken."

humiliation or panic of those duped.[11] Among the Icelandic tales told of Séra Eiríkur Magnússon of Vogsósar are at least two representatives of this group: in one, Séra Eiríkur creates an illusory brook with the same purpose and effect as in "The Rooster's Beam," in the other he makes a river swell as miserly travelers are crossing, so that they lose their barrel of liquor and Séra Eiríkur can salvage it, while a generous traveler has no difficulty crossing.[12]

The relevant headings in TMI are D2031.1 "Magician makes people lift garments to avoid wetting in imaginary river" and D2031.1.2 "People swim in imaginary river," and Boberg cites several Old Norse examples,[13] which we shall review before adding others. The first is a passage in *Magus saga jarls* in which Magus, under the name Skelja karl, prophesies and then proves that the swaggering courtier Ubbi jarl, far from being brave and loyal, would in fact be the first to desert the emperor in an emergency:[14]

Þa leit karl niðr fyrir sik. I þui varð gnyr ogurligr; ok þui nest brestr hallar veggrinn at bak[i] Vbba; uarð hann þá nockuð skiopuleygðr; þar streymir inn ogurligr forss með faðomligu boðafalli. Varð Ubbi fyrstr at bragði at hlaupa framm undan borðinu, oc þegar a sunnd, oc lagðiz ut or hollinni. Þar nest fyllir hollina, sva at þar er hverr maðr asunndi, iafn vel keisari ok sua Skelia karl. Þeir Sueinn ok

11 Bolte and Polívka, *Anmerkungen*, III:203-05; see also Arthur Dickson, *Valentine and Orson: A Study in Late Medieval Romance* (New York: Columbia University Press, 1929), 222, n. 18.
12 Konrad Maurer, ed., *Isländische Volkssagen der Gegenwart* (Leipzig: Hinrichs, 1860), 162-63. Strictly speaking, the second example does not seem to involve illusion but rather genuine control over the river, so it might more properly be registered under the motif D2151.2 "Magic control of rivers." Boberg's *Motif-Index* lists several texts under this heading, which will not be discussed further here.
13 Boberg, *Motif-Index*, s.vv. D2031.1 and D2031.1.2.
14 *Magus saga jarls* ch. 12, in Gustaf Cederschiöld, ed., *Fornsögur Suðrlanda: Isländska bearbetningar af främmande romaner från medeltiden* (Lund: Berling, 1877-83), 1-42, at 22-23; my translation.

Helgi lǫgðuz þegar abraut afętr Ubba. Þat undraðiz
keisari, er honum varð sundit sua erfitt, ok þat annat, at
hann fat eigi til dyranna. Engum veitti erfiðra enn Skelia
karli, þar er hann barðiz um; enn þo var hann leingstum
skamt i brǫtt fra keisara. Skelia karl mællti: "Hvart er, at
ek em sua oskygn, eða er hann Ubbi ibrǫttu?" Keisari
mællti: "Vist er hann ibrǫttu; enn alldri ętlaða ek, at hann
munndi sua illa fylgia mer." Skelia karl mællti: "Sua mun
fara, sem ek gat til." Keisari mællti: "Kostaþu ok giǫr at
þessu, ef þu mátt! þuiat ek se, at mer mun ei enndaz."
Karli quez ei meira fyrir at taka þetta ibrott enn veita. Þa
litaðiz keisari um; hann sa, at Skelia karl leit niðr fyrir sik;
þa varð gnyr mikill ok vndarligr hlutr; þa hliop aptr ilag
hallar veggrinn; ok þar nęst var þurr hǫllin.

Then Skelja karl bent his head down. At that moment
there was a terrible roar; and then the wall of the hall
breaks open behind Ubbi; his face took on a somewhat
shaken expression; then a terrible waterfall with frightfully
big waves rushes in. Ubbi was the first to react and run
away from the table, and he immediately entered the
water and swam out of the hall. Then the hall fills up, so
that everyone was swimming, even the emperor and
Skelja karl. Sveinn and Helgi swam away immediately, on
Ubbi's heels. The emperor was surprised that the
swimming was so difficult and that he could not find his
way to the door. No one had a worse time of it than
Skelja karl, in the place where he was struggling valiantly,
but nevertheless he was close by the emperor most of the
time. Skelja karl said: "Is it just my nearsightedness, or
can it be that Ubbi is gone?" The emperor said: "He
certainly is; though I never expected that he would serve
me so poorly." Skelja karl said: "It is as I predicted." The
emperor said: "Try to do something about this, if you
can! For I see that my own strength won't be enough."
Karl said it would be no more trouble to take this away
than it was to cause it. Then the emperor looked around;

he saw that Skelja karl was bending his head down; then there was a great roar and a strange thing: the wall of the hall closed again; and after that the hall was dry.

(We shall return to this example in a moment.) The second passage cited by Boberg is in *Sörla saga sterka;* here, too, the victims are deluded into helpless swimming motions in what they see as a rushing stream with steep banks, as a sorceress induces a *sjónhverfing* for purposes of defense:[15]

En er þeir Högni hugðu þangat at vitja ok þeir váru komnir at þeim skíðgarði, er var í kring skemmuna, laust á svá mikilli þoku, at engi sá annan, ok fundu þeir hvárki skíðgarðinn né skemmuna. Fetuðu þeir þá hvergi. En um síðir varð svá mikil móða fyrir hernum, at margir duttu þar ofan í á kaf ok svömluðu þar svá innan um þá nótt alla með stórum erfiðismunum. Varð þeim torsótt at klifrast neðan þá hamra, er tveim megin váru móðunnar. Gekk þetta allt til dags. En sem dagaði, sjá menn enga móðu, ok höfðu þeir verit at klórast neðan skíðgarðinn allt um kring, þar þeir hugðu hamra vera, duttu svá þar ofan fyrir ok gátu eigi at gert.

But when Högni and his men decided to go over there and had come to the palisade surrounding the ladies' house, so much fog arose that they couldn't see each other, and they found neither palisade nor house. They couldn't find their way anywhere. After a while such a great river appeared to the troops that many fell down into the water headfirst and paddled around in it with great effort all through the night. It was very difficult for them to climb up the cliffs that were on both sides of the river. This went on all night. But at daybreak the men see

---

[15] *Sörla saga sterka*, in Guðni Jónsson, ed., *Fornaldar sögur Norðurlanda*, 4 vols. (Akureyri: Íslendingasagnaútgáfan, 1954), III:367-410, at III:400; my translation.

no river, and they had been climbing up the palisade on
all sides, where they thought there were cliffs, and they
fell down and couldn't do anything about it.

In the third and final text cited by Boberg, *Egils saga einhenda ok
Ásmundar berserkjabana*, we again encounter a sorceress's *sjónhverfing*
involving steep cliffs leading down to water (the sea), as in *Sörla
saga*, but the scenic construction is different here, since the narrator
and protagonist (also a sorceress) welcomes the water:[16]

> "en því næst var brúðguminn út leiddr. Tók ek hann þá í
> fang mér, ok þóttumz ek hlaupa fram á sjóvarhamra, ok
> ætlaða ek at drekkja honum, svá engi skyldi mega njóta
> hans. En þá er ek þóttumz sleppa honum ofan fyrir
> hamrana, þá varð eigi betr en svá, at ek kastaði honum þá
> upp yfir fortjaldit, ok kom hann niðr í sæingina hjá
> brúðinni."

> "and after that the bridegroom was led out. I grabbed him
> with both arms, and I seemed to be running toward
> seacliffs, and I intended to drown him so that no one
> would have any pleasure from him. But when I thought I
> was dropping him down over the cliffs, it turned out that
> I was just throwing him up over the curtain, and he
> landed down in the bed next to the bride."

In the introduction to his edition of *Magus saga*, Cederschiöld
compares the passage from that saga cited above with two others,
neither of which is registered in Boberg's index entry.[17] The contest

---

[16] *Egils saga einhenda ok Ásmundar berserkjabana*, in Åke Lagerholm, ed., *Drei
Lygisǫgur. Egils saga einhenda ok Ásmundar berserkjabana, Ála flekks saga, Flóres
saga konungs ok sona hans* (Halle: Niemeyer, 1927), 1-83, at 58; my
translation.
[17] Cederschiöld, *Fornsögur*, lxxxiv (*Karlamagnús saga*), xcv (*Króka-Refs saga*).
Karlamagnús saga, which does not even appear in Boberg's bibliography,
may have been omitted from her study (or put off till later) as a translated

of supernatural feats in chapter 7 of *Karlamagnús saga* offers a very close parallel to the illusory flood in *Magus saga*:[18]

> Þá sagði Turpin erkibyskup sína íþrótt: Í morgin skal ek ganga til ár þeirrar er fellr hjá borginni, ok skal ek vísa henni ór stað sínum ok láta hana renna yfir allan Miklagarð ok fylla hvert hús; en keisari sjálfr skal vera svá hræddr, at hann skal flýja upp í enn hæsta turn, ok skal hann aldri ofan koma, nema því at eins at minn vili sé til.

> [. . .] Þá mælti Turpin við Karlamagnús konung: Bið bœn þína til guðs, at ek koma þessu á leið. Síðan gekk hann til ok signdi vatnit. En þar gerðust miklar jarteignir: sjá hin mikla á rann ór stað sínum yfir akrlönd ok eng ok fyldi öll hús. En borgarmenn tóku at at hyggja ok undrast. Hugon keisari varð svá hræddr, at hann flýði undan upp í enn hæsta turn at forða sér. Karlamagnús konungr var utan borgar á velli nokkurum undir tré einu, ok 12 jafningjar með honum ok þeirra lið, ok hlýddu til rœðu Hugons keisara, ok heyrðu, at hann óttaðist mjök vatn þat ok ætlaði sér bana ok sínu liði. Ok því næst mælti Hugon keisari við Karlamagnús konung, er hann sá hvar hann var undir trénu: Karlamagnús konungr, segir hann, hver er ætlan þín við mik, er þér alhugat at drekkja mér í vatni þessu? Ek vil gjarna gerast maðr þinn ok vera skattgildr undir þik, ok gefa þér alt fé mitt ok svá gripi, er þú kemr þessum vanda af oss. En Karlamagnús konungr mælti svá:

---

work – although *Magus saga* derives from the Charlemagne romance cycle, too, and neither *Magus saga* nor *Karlamagnús saga* is a word-for-word translation. In any case, it goes without saying that translations can be influential, and anyone interested in reception and intertextuality must take them into account.

[18] *Karlamagnús saga* §§7.9 and 7.16, in *Karlamagnús saga ok kappa hans. Fortællinger om Keiser Karl Magnus og hans jævninger i norsk bearbeidelse fra det trettende aarhundrede*, ed. C. R. Unger (Kristiania [Oslo]: Jensen, 1860), 475, 480-81; my translation.

Verðr er hverr miskunnar er hennar beiðist. Síðan bað
Karlamagnús konungr guð þeirrar bœnar, at vatn skyldi
aptr snúast í sinn farveg, ok þegar jafnskjótt sem hann
bað, þá veitti guð þat, at vatnit snerist aptr til staðar síns,
ok gerði þá guð mikla jarteign fyrir sakir Karlamagnús
konungs.

Then Archbishop Turpin named his feat: "Tomorrow I
shall go to the river that runs beside the city, and shall
turn it from its course and make it flow over all
Constantinople and fill every house, and the emperor
himself will be so frightened that he will flee to the top of
the highest tower, and he will never come down unless I
want him to."

[. . .] Then Turpin said to King Charlemagne: "Say your
prayers to God that I can manage it." Then he went and
made the sign of the Cross over the water. Then great
wonders took place: the great river flowed out of its
course, across fields and meadows, and filled every house.
The citizens began to be concerned and astonished.
Emperor Hugo was so frightened that he fled to the top
of the highest tower to save his life. King Charlemagne
was outside the city wall on open land under a tree, and
the twelve peers with him together with their men, and
they listened to the speech of Emperor Hugo and heard
that he was very frightened of that water and thought it
would be the death of him and his people. And then
Emperor Hugo spoke to King Charlemagne, when he
saw where he was under the tree: "King Charlemagne,"
he says, "what do you intend to do with me? Are you
determined to drown me in this water? I shall gladly
become your vassal and pay you tribute, and give you all
my money, and possessions, too, if you get us out of this
trouble." And King Charlemagne said: "Everyone
deserves mercy who asks for it." Then King Charlemagne
prayed to God with the request that the water return to

its course, and immediately, just as soon as he had said the prayer, God granted that the water turned back to its course; and God worked a great miracle for the sake of King Charlemagne.'

Here and in *Magus saga* the motif of the magic flood is used in the same drastically exaggerated fantasy version of the "king-Icelander theme": the foreign emperor and his haughty courtiers are put in a ridiculous position by the resourceful (and, in Charlemagne's case, pious) newcomers and even beg for mercy. Otherwise, the scenes differ only in the topography of the flood description, and perhaps in that the flood in *Magus saga* seems to be an illusion (the "flood in the hall" is repeatedly attested as a wizards' parlor trick in medieval European and Oriental romance), while the corresponding "miracle" in *Karlamagnús saga* seems physically real.

The second "magic flood" parallel mentioned by Cederschiöld[19] is considerably more distant: in *Króka-Refs saga,* Refr's fort is saved from attackers' fire by a kind of sprinkler system so technically advanced that the attackers suspect magic (*fjölkynngi*). There is no suggestion of swimming or helplessness on the part of the attackers, except that later a second technical marvel built into the fort kills some of them when it is deployed: part of the outer wall functions as an emergency escape drawbridge, allowing a ship on wheels to roll down into the sea.[20]

There is a further Old Norse text not listed by Boberg that describes, with more than a slight touch of slapstick, the protagonist's initial panic (subsequently overcome) in a magically swollen river: it is the story of Þórr's encounter with Geirrøðr's daughter Gjálp at the river Vimur, told by Snorri with the aid of

[19] Cederschiöld, *Fornsögur,* xcv.

[20] *Króka-Refs saga,* in *Kjalnesinga saga, Jökuls þáttr Búasonar, Víglundar saga, Króka-Refs saga, Þórðar saga hreðu, Finnboga saga, Gunnars saga Keldugnúpsfífls,* ed. Jóhannes Halldórsson, ÍF 14 (Reykjavík: Hið Íslenzka fornritafélag, 1959), 138-48.

Eilífr's *Þórsdrápa*.[21] However great the scholarly disagreement on the mythological ramifications of this story, no one disputes the indebtedness of Snorri's version, in this form, to medieval comic narrative; the relevant stanzas in the *drápa*, on the other hand, despite their obscurities, are clearly more serious in tone and emphasize the strenuousness of Þórr's battle with the elements.[22]

Before closing this section, it remains to cast a glance, by way of contrast, at Chaucer's "Miller's Tale," for the frame of this tale constitutes in essence an extravagantly staged "tub" variant of the water delusion motifs under study here. What is the final scene, after all, but the natural climax of an extended "Swimming in the Flax Field" story, with the dupe John waiting in his tub, hearing the frantic cries of "Water!" and trembling at the flood he imagines to be filling his house, then cutting the rope to lower the tub, only to crash ridiculously down to earth?[23]

II. DELUSIONS ON WATER

---

[21] *Skáldskaparmál* ch. 18 (= ch. 26 in the numbering of the Codex Regius), in Snorri Sturluson, *Edda,* ed. Finnur Jónsson, 2nd ed. (Copenhagen: Gad, 1926), 88-90, at 89.

[22] Lotte Motz reviews the issues from the point of view of folklore and mythology in "Þórr's River Crossing," *Saga-Book* 23 (1990-93): 469-87.

[23] I am not aware of any previous analysis of "The Miller's Tale" in terms of "Swimming in the Flax Field," though I do not pretend to command more than a fraction of the pertinent Chaucer scholarship. Folklorists analyze the tale into other constituent elements: the complete tale of the sham flood (usually without a tub) is AaTh/ATU 1361; "Vergil in the Basket" (without water) is TMI K1211, and so on. Along with the standard motif and type indexes, see Stith Thompson, "The Miller's Tale," in W. F. Bryan and G. Dempster, ed., *Sources and Analogues of Chaucer's Canterbury Tales* (Chicago: University of Chicago Press, 1941), 106-23; Larry D. Benson and Theodore M. Andersson, ed., *The Literary Context of Chaucer's Fabliaux: Texts and Translations* (Indianapolis: Bobbs-Merrill, 1971), 3-77; Elfriede Moser-Rath, *Lustige Gesellschaft. Schwank und Witz des 17. und 18. Jahrhunderts in kultur- und sozialgeschichtlichem Kontext* (Stuttgart: Metzler, 1984), 432.

Another narrative subtype concerns delusions in or on real water. Since Liebrecht,[24] folklorists have recognized that "Swimming in the Flax Field" also exists in an *inverted* form: numskulls mistake the calm surface of a body of water for dry land, the entrance to Heaven (the clear sky is reflected in the water), the entrance to a church (the twinkling reflections of stars are taken for candlelight), and so on, and they fall in.[25]

An Old Norse example of this inverted subtype may be the report given by Snorri of the behavior of Óláfr Tryggvason's crew in the sea-battle of Svǫlðr, if one accepts Ian McDougall's reading of it as a "battle-weary delirium":[26]

Var þá mikill vápnaburðr á Orminn, at varla mátti hlífum fyrir sik koma, er svá þykt flugu spjót ok ǫrvar, þvíat ǫllum megin lǫgðu herskip at Orminum. En menn Óláfs konungs váru þá svá óðir, at þeir hljópu upp á borðin til þess at ná með sverðhǫggum at drepa fólkit, en margir lǫgðu eigi svá undir Orminn, at þeir vildi í hǫggorrustu vera. En Óláfsmenn gengu flestir út af borðunum ok gáðu eigi annars, en þeir berðisk á sléttum velli, ok sukku niðr með vápnum sínum[.]

---

24 Felix Liebrecht, "Zu den Avadânas," in his *Zur Volkskunde. Alte und neue Aufsätze* (Heilbronn: Henninger, 1879), 109-21, at 114-16.

25 The inversion has a separate section, for example, in Bolte and Polívka, *Anmerkungen*, III.206, and Gašparíková, "Schwimmen," col. 445, but the folklore indexes make no provision for it as such.

26 *Óláfs saga Tryggvasonar*, in Snorri Sturluson, *Heimskringla: Nóregs konunga sǫgur*, ed. Finnur Jónsson (Copenhagen: Gad, 1911), 105-81, at 177; my translation. McDougall draws attention to this passage in his tongue-in-cheek catalogue of Viking-Age water disasters, "Slippery under Foot: A Case of Accidental Death in the *Anglo-Saxon Chronicle*," in *Fótarkefli rist Peter Foote 26.v.99*, ed. Alison Finlay et al., 2 vols. (London: n. pub., 1999), I:21-27, at 25, though he admits that it may just be an "elaboration of the accompanying verse from Hallfreðr Óttarsson's *erfidrápa* on Óláfr Tryggvason: *sukku niðr af Naðri . . .*"

The Ormr came under heavy attack, and there was hardly any protection to be had since the spears and arrows were flying so thickly; warships were approaching the Ormr from all sides. But King Óláfr's men were so enraged that they ran up onto the gunwales in order to be able to kill the people with swordstrokes, but many did not come alongside the Ormr for fear of a swordfight. But most of Óláfr's men went overboard and paid no attention to the fact that they were fighting anywhere other than on dry land, and they sank down with their weapons.

The flight of the Hebridean Nagli in *Eyrbyggja saga* is comparable at least from a topographical point of view, though the premises are different: Nagli flees a battlefield at great speed, and out of sheer panic seems to be heading "into the sea," but his confederates rescue him at the last minute, while the two slaves running with him do in fact throw themselves over a cliff like lemmings.[27]

Í þessu kómu þeir Þórarinn eptir, ok varð Nagli skjótastr; en er hann sá, at þeir ofruðu vápnunum, glúpnaði hann ok hljóp umfram ok í fjallit upp ok varð at gjalti.

[. . .] Þeir Þórarinn tóku hesta þeira Þorbjarnar ok ríða þeim heim, ok sá þeir þá, hvar Nagli hljóp it efra um hlíðina; [. . .] Þá tóku þeir Þórarinn at hleypa, því at þeir vildu hjálpa Nagla, at hann hlypi eigi á sjó eða fyrir bjǫrg; ok er þeir Nagli sjá, at mennirnir riðu œsiliga, hugðu þeir, at Þorbjǫrn myndi þar fara; tóku þeir nú rás af nýju allir inn til hǫfðans ok runnu þar til, er þeir koma þar, sem nú heitir Þrælaskriða; þar fengu þeir Þórarinn tekit Nagla, því

---

[27] *Eyrbyggja saga*, in *Eyrbyggja saga, Brands þáttr ǫrva, Eiríks saga rauða, Grœnlendinga saga, Grœnlendinga þáttr*, ed. Einar Ól. Sveinsson and Matthías Þórðarson, ÍF 4 (Reykjavík: Hið Íslenzka fornritafélag, 1935), 1-186, at 37-38, 45-46; trans. Judy Quinn, "The Saga of the People of Eyri," in *The Complete Sagas of Icelanders Including 49 Tales*, ed. Viðar Hreinsson, 5 vols. (Reykjavík: Leifur Eiríksson, 1997), V:131-218, at 146-47, 150.

at hann var náliga sprunginn af mœði, en þrælarnir hljópu
þar fyrir ofan ok fram af hǫfðanum ok týndusk, sem ván
var, því at hǫfðinn er svá hár, at allt hefir bana, þat er þar
ferr ofan.

[. . .] Þórarinn kvað:

12. Nágǫglum fekk Nagli
nest dáliga flestum,
kafsunnu réð kennir
kløkkr í fjall at støkkva;
[. . .]

13. Grátandi rann gætir
geira stígs frá vígi,
þar vasat grímu geymi
góð vón friðar hónum,
svát merskyndir myndi,
men-skiljandi, vilja,
hugði bjóðr á bleyði
bifstaups, á sjó hlaupa.

At that moment, Thorarin and his men came upon them,
with Nagli at the forefront. But when Nagli saw them
brandishing their weapons he lost his nerve and ran away
up onto the mountain, scared out of his wits.

[. . .] Thorarin and his men took Thorbjorn's horses and
rode them home. On the way, they saw Nagli running
along the hillside. [. . .] Thorarin and his men began to
gallop because they wanted to help Nagli and stop him
from jumping into the sea or over the cliffs. When Nagli
and the slaves saw that the men were riding furiously
towards them they assumed it must be Thorbjorn and his
men. They all raced off again towards the promontory
and ran until they came to the place now called
Thraelaskrida. Thorarin and his men finally caught up

with Nagli there because his lungs had almost exploded
from panting, but the slaves ran ahead and jumped off
the promontory and were killed, which was to be
expected because the cliff is so high that everything
perishes that goes over it.

[. . .] Thorarin replied:

12. Most of the corpse-geese
got a poor feed from Nagli;
faint-hearted, the knower
of the sea's sun fled into the hills;
[. . .]

13. Crying, the keeper of the swords' path
ran away from combat.
There seemed little hope of peace
to the guardian of the helmet,
so the mare-driver
preferred to dive into the sea;
cowardice was on the mind
of the cup-bearer, wreck of a man.

Since Sayers devotes considerable space to this episode in *Eyrbyggja
saga* in his article on battle panic,[28] we shall return to it in sections
IV-V below.

For now, however, let us examine military anecdotes in which
other, specific delusions are linked with panic in or on water.
Wackernagel mentioned one such military anecdote in connection
with "Swimming in the Flax Field" already in his article of 1848:[29] in
2 Kings 3:22-23, the Moabites mistake the red light of dawn on the
water for the blood of the armies allied against them, whom they
suppose to have quarrelled and decimated each other during the

---

[28] Sayers, "Deployment," 169-73.
[29] Wackernagel, "Spottnamen," 257-58.

night, and, perhaps not unlike the crew of Ormrinn langi in their battle fury, they make a fatal rush (on land, in this case) into the hands of their enemies. A more common motor for disorganized action is fear. Latin and Greek historians attributed to various barbarian populations a fear that the sky might fall,[30] and in a passage in Bede, the Britons' battle-cry of "Alleluia" causes precisely this delusion to arise in the opposing Saxon and Pictish forces, so that the latter throw off their weapons, flee in panic into a river, and many drown in the attempt to cross it.[31] Centuries later, an anecdote of a similar narrative type surfaces in Iceland as a cautionary tale told by Gizurr Þorvaldsson to his men before the battle of Ørlygsstaðir, according to Sturla Þórðarson's *Íslendinga saga.*[32]

> Gizurr talaði þá fyrir liðinu ok eggjaði menn til framgöngu. "Vil ek eigi," sagði hann, "at þér hafið mik á spjótsoddum fyrir yðr, sem Skagfirðingar höfðu Kolbein Tumason, frænda minn, þá er hann fell í Víðinesi, en runnu sjálfir þegar í fyrstu svá hræddir, at þeir vissu eigi, er þeir runnu yfir Jökulsá, ok þar er þeir þóttust skjöldu bera á baki sér, þar báru þeir söðla sína."

> Gizurr addressed his troops then and exhorted them to valor. "I do not want you to have me at your spearpoints," he said, "the way the Skagfirðingar had my kinsman Kolbeinn Tumason, when he fell at Víðines and they themselves ran, so scared at first that they didn't know it when they ran through the river Jökulsá, and

---

[30] Herwig Wolfram, *History of the Goths* (Berkeley: University of California Press, 1988), 113, 129.
[31] *Bede's Ecclesiastical History of the English People,* ed. Bertram Colgrave and R. A. B. Mynors (Oxford: Clarendon Press, 1969), §1.20, 62-65.
[32] *Íslendinga saga* ch. 137, in *Sturlunga saga,* ed. Jón Jóhannesson et al., 2 vols. (Reykjavík: Sturlunguútgáfan, 1946), I:229-534, at 429-30; my translation. In *Íslendinga saga*'s own account of the Battle of Víðines (I:129), no such panic is reported.

when they thought they were carrying their shields on
their backs, they were carrying their saddles."

Although the panicked confusion of shields and saddles is
unparalleled in those military anecdotes known to me, even this
motif displays a certain affinity to Bede's report, for example, which
also describes the abandonment of arms in a panicked flight
through a river. The narrative – and topographical – frame of the
two stories is virtually identical, except that Sturla Þórðarson (and
Gizurr himself, we may assume[33]) employs the more sophisticated
rhetorical tool of embedding the anecdote in a finely constructed
formal speech.

III. SWIMMERS MOCKED

To complete our investigation of the block of "Swimming in
the Flax Field" variants that include the motif of water, let us now
direct our attention to narrative constructs that focus on panicked
or otherwise ridiculous swimmers but lack the motif of delusion.
The theme of delusion is picked up again in §IV.

IIIa. Swimmers in Water

It is only natural that clumsy or panicked swimming also exists
as a simplex motif, so to speak, in narrative: it can be described for
its own sake, without attention to causes or results. In the words of
a commentator on the Breca episode in *Beowulf*:[34]

> The image of swimming seems to be ancient, ubiquitous,
> and inevitable. Cf. the shipwreck scenes in the *Odyssey* and
> the *Aeneid*. Lucretius' famous lines (De Rerum Natura
> II.1-2) on the pleasure of watching from the shore a

---

[33] Cf. Taylor, "On Gizurr," 324, n. 27.
[34] Edward B. Irving, Jr., *A Reading of Beowulf* (New Haven: Yale University
Press, 1968), 75, n. 23.

swimmer struggling in rough waters are often quoted by
the theorists of tragedy.

As it happens, we have a Carolingian text that carries the above-
cited tradition of Homer, Vergil, and Lucretius explicitly into the
Middle Ages. In his epic-length encomium on Louis the Pious, the
court poet Ermoldus Nigellus describes how the people of Orléans
made fun of travellers whose haste induced them to swim the Loire
in the year 814:[35]

Flumina non retinent trepidos, nec horrida silva,
Nec glacialis hiemps, nec pluviosa dies.

Qui rate non valuit, satagens hic forte natatu
Trans fluvium Ligeris certat abire prior.
O quantos populos celsa de rupe videres
Absque rate in fluvium se dare praecipites!
Aurelianenses illos risere natantes;
Turre vocant summa: "Litus amate, viri."

Neither rivers nor wild forests hold the hurrying people
    back,
nor icy winter, nor a rainy day.

Whoever was unable to get a boat, has his hands full with
    struggling
to be the first to get across the River Loire by strong
    swimming.
Oh, how many people one saw plunging headlong
from a steep cliff into the river without a boat!

---

[35] Ermoldus Nigellus, *In honorem Hludowici* §2, ll. 127-34, in *Poetae Latini aevi
Carolini*, ed. Ernestus Duemmler *et al.*, 4 vols. (Berlin: Weidmann, 1881-
1923), vol. 2 (1884), ed. Duemmler, 5-79, at 28; my translation. The
passage is cited as an example of epic comedy in Ernst Robert Curtius,
Europäische Literatur und lateinisches Mittelalter, 1st ed. (Bern: Francke, 1948),
Exkurs IV:5, 430.

The Orléanais made fun of those swimmers;
They call from the highest tower: "Love the shore, men!"

This is a *pasticcio*, including a fragment of the *Aeneid* in practically every line; the penultimate line of the passage, for example, echoes Vergil's *labentem [...] risere natantem* ("made fun of the foundering swimmer").[36]

In the literature of medieval Northern Europe this motif is more difficult to find than in the South.[37] The reason may simply be that swimming in the less temperate latitudes is (for a considerable part of the year) no laughing matter, even for good swimmers, and thus more generally avoided; and in the case of involuntary immersion the water temperature makes it unlikely that there will be any long story to tell. The *Beowulf* poet's treatment of the hero's swimming feat – first mocked by Unferþ, then presented in its proper light by Beowulf himself – is the artistically brilliant exception that proves the rule.[38]

In the Old Norse corpus, a clear – though brief – example of swimming mockery faintly reminiscent of Unferþ's exchange with Beowulf is found in the famous *mannjafnaðr* of the Magnús-synir Eysteinn and Sigurðr:[39]

---

[36] See Dümmler's notes, *ibid.*

[37] To be sure, the vernaculars all possess translations of Matthew 14:28-31, in which Peter "of little faith" tries to walk on water but sinks after a promising start. One of the Old Norse renderings is cited in David McDougall's article *"Pétr gekk þurrum fótum,"* in *Fótarkefli rist Peter Foote,* I:18-20, at 19.

[38] By contrast, Beowulf's second swimming adventure (the dive to the cave) is presented in full heroic seriousness, as is the wading and swimming in the corresponding episode in *Grettis saga* (chs. 64-66); there is not the slightest doubt about the hero's skill.

[39] *Magnússona saga*, in Snorri Sturluson, *Heimskringla*, ed. Finnur Jónsson, 532-54, at 543; my translation.

Þá mælti Sigurðr konungr: "mantu, hversu fór um sundit
með okr; ek mátta kefja þik, ef ek vilda." Eysteinn
konungr segir: "ekki svam ek skemra en þú, ok eigi var ek
verr kafsyndr; ek kunna ok á ísleggjum, svá at engan vissa
ek þann, er þat kepði við mik, en þú kunnir þat eigi heldr
en naut."

Then King Sigurðr said: "Do you remember how our
swimming went? I was able to dunk you if I wanted to."
King Eysteinn said: "I did not swim any shorter distance
than you, and I was no worse in swimming underwater; I
could also ice-skate so well that I didn't know of anyone
who could compete with me, but you couldn't do that any
more than an ox could."

The simile employed about Sigurðr's ice-skating (not swimming)
ability has few parallels in medieval texts, though many are attested
in the modern languages: *Zahlreich sind die Vergleiche, die einen
ungeschickten Schwimmer oder einen Nichtschwimmer verspotten* ("Numerous
are the similes that make fun of an awkward swimmer or a non-
swimmer"), declares one of the foremost authorities on German
idioms, and lists comparisons with leaden fish, leaden ducks,
grindstones, bricks, and millstones.[40]

Old English and Latin reports of troop drownings in the
Thames in 1013 and 1016 that appear to have been caused by
foolhardiness have been collected in an article by Ian McDougall.[41]
Because the reports are so short, it is difficult to say whether
mockery or irony were intended; "the spare account in [the *Anglo-
Saxon Chronicle*] is open to different interpretations."[42] The drowning

---

[40] Lutz Röhrich, *Lexikon der sprichwörtlichen Redensarten* (Freiburg: Herder,
1973), s.v. *schwimmen*, 931.

[41] I. McDougall, "Slippery," 21-24.

[42] *ibid.*, 22. As a humoristic experiment, McDougall tries to squeeze the
maximum amount of irony out of the texts, but his article also contains
serious source criticism, and experimental readings are labeled as such.

in 1016 is explicitly attributed to the English troops' "own
carelessness" (*heora agenre gymeleaste*) in rushing ahead, but, as
McDougall points out, the entry for 1013 is less clear: Danish
troops drowned on their way to attack London, *forðam hi nanre bryge
ne cepton* ("because they did not bother to look for [or: did not seize]
a bridge [or: ford]"). Instructive is in any case McDougall's
discussion of the interpretation of this chronicle entry in
subsequent reworkings in Latin, especially that of William of
Malmesbury, who introduces a slanderous twist at the Danes'
expense: he reorders the sequence of events so that the Danes first
attack London, are repelled, and flee *in panic* into the Thames, where
they drown.[43]

IIIb. Ridiculous Swimming Motions on Land

Some of the words and phrases that we have seen employed in
unflattering descriptions of swimmers in water are also used for
similar motions on land, or figuratively for certain types of
confusion, helplessness, or slow, irresolute activity. The Icelandic
verb *svamla*, used in the passage from *Sörla saga* cited above, is an
excellent example;[44] as are the English verbs *founder, flounder,* the
idioms *to be at sea, to be out of one's depth,* and so on. Equivalent to the
latter expressions is the German idiom *mit etwas schwimmen,* the
origin of which Röhrich explains as follows:[45]

Sie beruht auf der Beobachtung, daß jemand, der nicht
weiterweiß, dies durch schwimmartige Armbewegungen
offenbart. Er verhält sich unwillkürlich dabei so, als habe
er den festen Boden unter seinen Füßen verloren und
müsse seine Unsicherheit durch entsprechende
Schwimmbewegungen überbrücken.

---

[43] *ibid.,* with literature.
[44] Árni Böðvarsson, *Íslensk orðabók handa skólum og almenningi,* 2nd ed.
(Reykjavík: Menningarsjóður,1988), s.v.
[45] Röhrich, *Lexikon,* s.v. *schwimmen,* 931; see also the idioms *ins Schwimmen
geraten (kommen)* and *jemanden ins Schwimmen bringen, ibid.*

It [the expression] is based on the observation that someone who is at a loss about what to do reveals this fact through swimming-type motions of his arms. In this, he behaves involuntarily as if he had lost his footing and had to compensate for his uncertainty by means of swimming motions.

Psychological speculation of this sort is nothing new. Chapter 12 of Hugh of St. Victor's *De institutione novitiorum* is devoted to observations of and rules for what we today would call body language, including the following passage on annoying and ridiculous arm mannerisms:[46]

Alii navigant brachiis incedentes, et duplici quodam monstro, uno et eodem tempore pedibus deorsum in terra ambulant et lacertis sursum in aere volant. Quod est quaeso monstrum hoc, quod simul in se fingit et hominis incessum, et navis remigium, et avis volatum?

Others row with strokes of their arms; and like some twofold monster at one and the same time they walk on the ground below with their feet and fly in the air above with their arms. What is this monster, I ask you, that simultaneously displays in itself the gait of a man, the rowing of a boat, and the flight of a bird?

Chapter 53 of the Middle English *Cloud of Unknowing,* on "vnordeynde & vnsemely contenaunces," has a similar structure and purpose. Some of the images may have been borrowed from Hugh, but many are evidently original.[47] One of the closest parallels

---

[46] Hugo de Sancto Victore, *De institutione novitiorum,* in J.-P. Migne, ed., *Patrologia Latina,* vol. 176 (Paris: Garnier 1880), cols. 925-52, at §12, col. 942; my translation.

[47] Phyllis Hodgson, ed., *The Cloud of Unknowing and The Book of Privy Counselling* (London: Oxford University Press, 1944), lxxvii. My attention was first drawn to these sections of *De institutione novitiorum* and *The Cloud*

happens to be precisely the description of arm mannerisms, but even here, the English writer has employed an original image: "Som rowyn wiþ þeire armes in tyme of here spekyng, as hem nedid for to swymme ouer a grete water."[48]

With these similes we arrive back at the description of the panicked Herulians in Paulus Diaconus (*dumque quasi nataturi brachia extenderent*), having come full circle, as it were, in our examination of "Swimming in the Flax Field" from various angles in sections I-III. From both the anthropological and the narratological points of view it would be helpful also to investigate stock descriptions of aimless or helpless movement that use images other than swimming, beginning with the biblical "groping at noonday as the blind" (Deut. 28:29) and proceeding through images of wavering, falling, lurking, and so on; a few examples will be encountered in section V.[49]

IV. DELUSIONS (UNRELATED TO WATER)

Several of the Old Norse texts cited in the preceding sections describe *sjónhverfingar*, that is, optical illusions caused by magic. In 1943, Hilda R. Ellis began her study of the phrase *verða at gjalti* by stating that it "is interesting as an example of a borrowing from the Irish, but more interesting because of the problems bound up with

---

of Unknowing by R. W. Chambers, "The Continuity of English Prose from Alfred to More and his School," supplementary article in *Harpfield's Life and Death of Sir Thomas More*, ed. E. V. Hitchcock and R. W. Chambers (London: Oxford University Press, 1932), xlv-clxxiv, at cvi.

[48] *The Cloud of Unknowing*, §53, 98-99.

[49] An analytic survey of many types of pejorative description in *Egils saga Skalla-Grímssonar* and *Íslendinga saga* (and two non-Icelandic texts), including coordination problems (falling), confusion, physical symptoms of fear, irresoluteness (beating about the bush, cowering, wavering, etc.), hiding, and flight, appears in Marvin Hunter Taylor, Jr., "Verbal Aggression in Early Germanic Prose," (Diss. University of Minnesota, 1992), see especially 198, 200-01, 211-12.

its interpretation and their bearing on a subject which held great fascination for the Norse saga-tellers, that of abnormal states of mind."[50] This subject is indeed exceptionally well represented in Old Norse literature,[51] and Ellis devoted special attention to "certain lines of association" linking *verða at gjalti* with concepts of shape-changing and magic: *sjónhverfing, fylgjur, hamremi, berserksgangr,* and *herfjǫturr*.[52] In his 1994 article, Sayers names Ellis's article in a bibliographical footnote,[53] but is otherwise silent about it. His stated purpose is, in fact, diametrically opposed to hers: he is interested in the phrase *primarily* as a borrowing from the Irish, since this aspect is imperative for his hypothesis of latent xenophobic prejudice. There are only occasional signs that he might have recognized the value of Ellis's approach and of her conclusion that "abnormal states of mind" held a special fascination for the saga-writers: he observes that *verða at gjalti* is repeatedly linked with "sensory disequilibrium," "optical illusions," "logical and ocular illusion," "cognitive disorientation," and magic,[54] and admits that "the idea of unsettling optical illusions and their potential consequences for military action" may have had "native origins."[55] At one point he cites Snorri's list of synonyms for *óvitr,* but only in order to argue that the loan *verða at gjalti* never achieved full native status, since it is not in the list.[56]

---

[50] Hilda R. Ellis, "'Gjalti': A Study of Battle-Panic in Old Norse Literature," *Comparative Literature Studies / Cahiers de littérature comparée* [Cardiff] 11 (1943): 21-29.

[51] Cf. Anatoly Liberman, "Mistaken Identity and Optical Illusion in Old Icelandic Literature," in his *Word Heath / Wortheide / Orðheiði. Essays on Germanic Literature and Usage (1972-1992)* (Rome: Il Calamo, 1994), 165-75, at 173, on optical illusion: "Icelandic had a remarkable number of words for a concept that hardly existed in the other old Germanic languages."

[52] Ellis, "'Gjalti,'" 24-27.

[53] Sayers, "Deployment," 157, n. 1.

[54] *ibid.,* 169, 171, 173, 176.

[55] *ibid.,* 177.

[56] *ibid.,* 178, n. 44.

Sayers reserves his most extensive textual analysis for the *Máhlíðingamál* episode in *Eyrbyggja saga,* emphasizing (as he must, given his thesis) Nagli's Scottish ancestry and membership in a "marginalized social group," together with the themes of gender ambiguity, magic, and panicked flight,[57] but does not see that the magic and the hints of gender ambiguity in the story are just some of its many variations on the general theme of misapprehension, deception, and delusion. I shall name here a few important points overlooked by Sayers. This whole theme, including, but not limited to, the attractive Katla's later *sjónhverfingar,* is explicitly foreshadowed in Geirríðr's warning *eru ok opt flǫgð í fǫgru skinni* ("many a witch wears a fair face").[58] Appearances deceive, and it takes some time before Katla's malevolence becomes evident to the reader. Oddr Kǫtluson deliberately slanders both mother and son, Geirríðr and Þórarinn, and he succeeds each time – at first – in deceiving the community into believing his perfidious untruths; the story of the *klámorð* against Þórarinn – first accepted, apparently even by his mother, then disproved – runs parallel to this double *rógmæli* motif. Finally, Nagli's panicked flight has nothing to do with magic, though instances of magic are named in contiguous segments of the same story, but with a *series of misapprehensions.* First, Nagli seems to experience a sudden and illogical perception of danger on the battlefield ("Nagli had made no attempt to avoid the battle, and had been well to the fore in the attack on Thorbjörn" when the panic overcame him, observes Ellis[59]), second, he tells the slaves he meets that his comrades (including their master) have certainly been killed, although "he had no reason to believe this when he began his flight,"[60] third, he mistakes his victorious comrades, when they appear, for his enemies, and fourth, he seems to mistake the sea for dry land and seek death instead of life. Moreover, as Ellis points out, Þórarinn's slaves are equally guilty of an absurd misapprehension when they join Nagli in his flight, since, even if

---

[57] *ibid.,* 169-73.
[58] *Eyrbyggja saga,* ÍF 4: 28-9; trans. Quinn, V: 142.
[59] Ellis, "Gjalti," 21.
[60] *ibid.*

Þórarinn had been killed, as Nagli told them he had, his slaves "would have been in no danger from the victors. The story implies blind, utterly illogical panic, which proved contagious."[61]

I have dwelt on the *Máhlíðingamál* here at some length for methodological reasons, since the text irrefutably confirms Ellis's position; its theme is the misperception of reality.[62] Within the confines of the present article, it is out of the question to attempt a catalogue of types of delusions or other "abnormal states of mind," important as this task is,[63] but we shall examine one particular motif in some detail in what follows.

IVa. Delusions of Battle

Structurally comparable to many of the anecdotes we have examined so far, though lacking the motif of swimming, is Livy's report of the panic of the Bastarnae on the mountain Donuca. As

---

[61] *ibid.* One is reminded of one of the most frequently cited numskull stories in Old Norse, the report in *Gautreks saga* (chs. 1-2) of the hillbillies throwing themselves off their *ætternisstapi*. The description of this cliff is practically identical with that of Þrælaskriða: *Hann er svá hár ok þat flug fyrir ofan, at þat kvikendi hefir ekki líf, er þar gengr fyrir niðr* ("It is so high and [has] such a sheer drop that any living thing that goes over it loses its life") (*Gautreks saga,* in *Fornaldar sögur Norðurlanda,* ed. Guðni Jónsson, IV:1-50, at 5; my translation).

[62] A similar conclusion is reached by Liberman in a different context, "Mistaken Identity," 175: "The motif of mistaken identity and optical illusion allowed Icelandic storytellers and singers of tales to explore the disharmony between the perceiver's view of things and reality." In these terms, the *Máhlíðingamál* episode is a symphony of disharmony.

[63] Ellis's statement that this region of Old Norse literature remains to be fully explored ("'Gjalti'," 28) is echoed by Liberman fifty years later: "I was unable to discover general works on the aberration of vision in medieval literature" ("Mistaken Identity," 175, n. 1).

they are scaling the mountain in pursuit of the Thracians, a severe
thunder- and hailstorm breaks out, with disastrous consequences:[64]

> Neque enim imbre tantum effuso, dein creberrima
> grandine obruti sunt cum ingenti fragore caeli
> tonitribusque et fulguribus praestringentibus aciem
> oculorum, sed fulmina etiam sic undique micabant ut peti
> viderentur corpora, nec solum milites sed etiam principes
> icti caderent. Itaque cum praecipiti fuga per rupes
> praealtas improvidi sternerentur ruerentque, instabant
> quidem perculsis Thraces, sed ipsi deos auctores fugae
> esse caelumque in se ruere aiebant. Dissipati procella cum
> tamquam ex naufragio plerique semermes in castra, unde
> profecti erant, redissent, consultari quid agerent coeptum.

> For not merely were they assailed with a deluge of rain
> and then masses of hail, along with tremendous crashes in
> the sky and thunders and lightning-flashes blinding their
> eyes, but also the bolts flashed all about them so that their
> own bodies seemed to be the targets, and not only the
> common soldiers but even the chieftains fell stricken on
> the ground. So when in headlong flight in their blindness
> they were rushing about and falling over lofty cliffs, the
> Thracians too came upon them in their panic, but they
> themselves said that the gods were the causes of their
> flight and that the skies were falling upon them. Scattered
> by the tempest, as if after a shipwreck, when many of
> them, half-armed, had returned to the camp whence they
> had set out, they began to consider what they should do.

The sequence of events bears a striking resemblance to that in
Paulus Diaconus. Instead of the delusion of water in Paulus, we

---

[64] *Ab urbe condita* §40.58, in *Livy with an English Translation*, ed. Benjamin
Olive Foster, 14 vols. (Cambridge: Harvard University Press, 1919-51),
vol. 12 (1938), ed. and trans. Evan T. Sage and A. C. Schlesinger, 176;
translation *ibid.*, 177.

have here the delusion of a heavenly attack induced by weather phenomena;[65] instead of the panicked flight through imaginary water, we have the panicked flight "over cliffs"; in both historians' reports, the enemy (who has hitherto not been on the scene) is then able to exploit the panic and strike. There are rhetorical effects, but there is no comic exaggeration; the formal tone of tragic realism is the same one we encounter in Paulus, or in Gizurr Þorvaldsson's speech as quoted by Sturla Þórðarson.

In the fourteenth-century Florentine Franco Sacchetti's novella number 132, the delusion of an attack appears as a full-blown, explicitly comic anecdote, though presented as a true story of the town of Macerata in the war year 1377.[66] As in Livy, the cause is a storm, but the chain reaction leading to the panic is as long as in "The Miller's Tale": the runoff from a heavy downpour clogs a drain, so that rainwater floods several houses in the street, an unsuspecting housewife goes downstairs to get wine for supper and is trapped in thigh-deep water, she calls to her husband for help, he calls in turn to the neighbours, the cry that "there are people inside" is misunderstood to mean that the enemy has entered the town, and the alarm (*All'arme!*) spreads to the town clerk, the prior, the bell-ringer, and the militia. When a friar bearing a large shield falls and cannot get up, since his arm is stuck in the shield, he is taken for the first casualty of battle, and so on.

Agnete Loth has drawn attention to an Old Norse version of the "delusion of battle" motif, in this case a military anecdote in a form somewhere between the earnest tone of the classical historians and the novellistic exuberance of Chaucer or Sacchetti; she

---

[65] Cf. n. 30 above. Panic is predicted to result from supernatural weather phenomena (visible and audible signs in the heavens and the sea) in Luke 21:25.

[66] *Il Trecentonovelle* ch. 132, in Franco Sacchetti, *Opere,* ed. Aldo Borlenghi (Milano: Ruzzoli, 1957), 405-09, with Borlenghi's notes. This tale is given its own heading, J1837* "The false alarm," in D. Rotunda, *Motif-Index of the Italian Novella* (Bloomington: Indiana University Press, 1942).

identifies it, quite rightly, as a numskull story and cites modern parallels.[67] Since the anecdote is attested in *Hákonar saga Ívarssonar* (that is, the surviving Latin-Danish summary), *Morkinskinna,* and the *Heimskringla* version of *Haralds saga harðráða,* it can be no younger than the beginning of the thirteenth century.[68] Snorri's version follows:[69]

Lǫgmaðr Gauta hét Þorviðr; hann sat á hesti, ok var bundinn taumrinn við hæl einn, er stóð í mýrinni; hann talaði ok mælti: [. . .] Í því bili hljóp upp herr Norðmanna ok œpði heróp ok bǫrðu á skjǫldu sína; tók þá Gauta-herr at œpa; en hestr lǫgmannz hnykkir svá fast, er hann fældisk við herópit, at hællinn gekk upp ok hrøkði honum um hǫfuð, lǫgmanninum; hann mælti: "skjóttu allra Norðmanna armastr." Hleypði lǫgmaðrinn þá í brot.

The lawman of the Gauts was named Þorviðr; he was sitting on horseback, and the tether was made fast to a stake in the moor. He spoke and said: [. . .] At that moment the Norwegian army ran up and sounded their battle-cry and banged on their shields; then the Gautish army began to shout; but the lawman's horse shies so hard, when it is startled by the battle-cry, that the stake went up and hit the lawman in the head; he said: "Curses on the Norwegian that made that shot!" Then the lawman galloped away.

The comic irony is amplified by the fact that when he is hit, Þorviðr is giving a pre-battle speech (omitted in the quotation) admonishing his eager men not to charge too early or too far – an effective type of scenic irony in battle anecdotes. Here is a speech

---

[67] Agnete Loth, "Et 'Molbo'-motiv i Hákonar saga Ívarssonar," in *Opuscula* 1 (Copenhagen: Munksgaard, 1960), 361-62.

[68] *ibid.,* 362.

[69] *Haralds saga harðráða,* in Snorri Sturluson, *Heimskringla,* ed. Finnur Jónsson, 447-513, at 494; my translation.

scene from *Íslendinga saga* with a similar slapstick ending, though without the motif of delusion, as the lone shot really does come from the enemy:[70]

> Biskup biðr nú stöðvast bardagann, ok fóru menn þá um allan kirkjugarðinn ok sögðu, at Órækja vill eigi berjast láta. Kallar þá engi meir en Eiríkr birkibeinn ok hleypr fyrir framan kirkjugarðinn. Þá flýgr steinn ór kirkjugarðinum ok kemr við eyra honum, svá at þegar kastaði fótunum fram yfir höfuðit, ok var lokit hans kalli at sinni.

> The bishop now asks for the battle to be stopped, and then men went around the whole churchyard and said that Órækja did not want there to be any fighting. No one is calling more loudly than Eiríkr birkibeinn, and he runs in front of the churchyard. Then a rock flies out of the churchyard and hits him on the ear, so that he immediately threw his legs up over his head, and that was the end of his calling for the time being.

This same chapter in *Íslendinga saga* begins, in fact, with a genuine "delusion of battle" anecdote: when Órækja's men approach just before dawn, Gizurr's men respond with battle-cheers and shield-banging, but do not advance to meet them.[71]

> Órækju menn þeir, er síðar fóru, hyggja nú, at þeir Gizurr hlaupi út á þá, bregða vápnum ok berjast nú sjálfir. [. . .] En er þeir, er vitrari váru, sáu, hvat títt var, hlaupa þeir til ok fengu stöðvat þá.

> Those of Órækja's men who were in the rear now think that Gizurr's men are running out at them, they brandish

---

[70] *Íslendinga saga*, in *Sturlunga saga*, ed. Jón Jóhannesson *et al.*, I:464; my translation.
[71] *ibid.*, I:461-62; my translation.

their weapons and begin to fight one another. [. . .] But
when those who were wiser saw what was going on, they
run over and managed to get them to stop.

We have now seen delusions of battle caused by
misunderstanding audible signals (such as storms or shouting) or
tactile signals (such as a blow); but this delusion can also arise
through misunderstood *visual* signals. Another of Sacchetti's
wartime anecdotes (set in the Florentine-Pisan war of 1362-64) tells
of three Florentine numskulls who are convinced that they have
encountered the enemy troops, although everyone knows that these
are one hundred miles distant. One numskull has heard "a great
noise," for example, which – as he is forced to admit – must have
been wind or water instead of cavalry, while another claims to have
seen the enemy troops on the gravel flats of the Arno and fired a
shot into their midst, but the driving rain and "the damned fog"
prevented him from making out any details.[72]

The motif of visual delusion leading to fear of imminent attack
brings us back into the orbit of "Swimming in the Flax Field," since
one of its officially recognized subtypes is just such a motif: waving
fields of wheat are taken to be a marching army.[73] What the
folkloristic indexes fail to mention is that precisely this motif
appears in inverted form – soldiers are taken for trees – in one of
the most famous historical *ruses de guerre,* later immortalized in quite
a different form in Shakespeare: the marching trees of Birnam

---

[72] *Il Trecentonovelle* ch. 36, ed. Borlenghi, 146-48, again with Borlenghi's
notes. Rotunda's *Motif-Index* registers this anecdote under J1805* "Three
frightened Florentines think they see doings of the enemy one hundred
miles away."
[73] See Gašparíková, "Schwimmen," col. 446, on AaTh 1290* "Man thinks
undulating wheat fields are marching."

Wood. Here is the original military anecdote as related in the eighth-century *Liber historiae Francorum*.[74]

Brinnacum villa veniens, multa dona et munera Francis ditavit, eosque ad pugnandum contra inimicos eorum coortans. Cum dedicisset, quod nimis esset exercitus Austrasiorum, coniunctis simul, consilium dedit Francos, qui cum ea erant, dicens: 'De nocte consurgamus contra eos cum lucernis, portantes socii, qui nos precedunt, ramis silvarum in manibus, tintinnabolis super equos legatis, ut nos cognoscere ipsorum vigiles custodes hostium non queant. Inluciscente inicium diei, inruamus super eos, et forsitan eos divincimus.' Placuitque hoc consilium. [. . .] Cum autem custodes hostium Austrasiorum ramis silvarum quasi in montibus in agmine Francorum cernerent et tinnitum tintinnabulorum audirent custodes, dixit vir ad socium suum: 'Nonne crastina die in illo et illo loco campestria erant, quomodo silvas cernimus?' Et ille inridens, dixit: 'Certe inebriatus fuisti, modo deleras. Non audis tintinnabula equorum nostrorum iuxta ipsam silvam pascencium?'

Coming to Berny-Rivière, [Fredegund] enriched the Franks with many presents and money, exhorting them to fight against their enemies. When she had learned that the Austrasian army was too great, she assembled everyone together and gave advice to the Franks who were with her, saying: "We shall sally forth against them by night with lanterns, while comrades of ours precede us, carrying branches of trees in their hands and with bells on the horses, so that the enemy guards on watch will not be

---

[74] *Liber historiae Francorum* §36, in *Fredegarii et aliorvm chronica, Vitae sanctorvm*, ed. Bruno Krusch (Hannover: Hahn, 1888), 215-328, at 304-05; my translation, using the partial translation by Joaquín Martínez Pizarro, *A Rhetoric of the Scene. Dramatic Narrative in the Early Middle Ages* (Toronto: University of Toronto Press, 1989), 94.

able to recognize us. When the first light of day begins to shine, we shall charge upon them, and perhaps we shall defeat them." This advice was accepted. [. . .] The watchmen of the Austrasian army saw branches gathered as in a forest in the middle of the Frankish camp, and heard the jingle of the bells. One of them asked his companion: "Weren't there open fields yesterday in this place and in that one there? How come we now see woods?" The other one, laughing, replied, "You must have been drunk, and now you are raving! Can't you hear the bells of our horses that are grazing by the forest?"

When the first light of dawn comes, it is too late (the dialogue breaks off here, and impersonal narration is resumed). In this text, the dramatic irony of the trick is drawn out by means of the watchmen's dialogue,[75] and an additional layer of irony accrues through their argument: the one who, in fact, perceives things correctly is judged by the other to be delirious. The early twelfth-century Irish epic *Mesca Ulad* contains a teichoscopy with practically the same motif and the same scenic construction, although it is much more extensive.[76] The principal difference is that the warriors approaching before dawn are taken for trees not through their own design, but through the stupidity of the two druid watchmen on the castle wall. It is a numskull story, and just as in the *Liber historiae Francorum,* one of the numskulls, Crom Darail, is stupider than the other, Crom Deróil. I quote from Watson's translation:[77]

---

[75] Martínez Pizarro, *ibid.,* emphasizes the scenic aspect of the "ingenious" narrative technique employed here: an invented dialogue "between anonymous individuals" in a crowd serves "to illustrate a reaction or state of mind in which every person present is assumed to share."

[76] I became acquainted with this text through the discussion in Kathryn Sue Campbell, "The Lyric Moment in Pre-Romance Verse" (Diss. University of Illinois at Urbana-Champaign, 1973), 88.

[77] "Mesca Ulad," trans. J. C. Watson, *Scottish Gaelic Studies* 5 (1938): 1-34, at 12-16. In Watson's edition, *Mesca Ulad* (Dublin: Stationery Office, 1941), the druid episode occupies ll. 346-505.

To these then it befell to be at that time on the wall of Temair Luachra, watching and keeping guard, contemplating and gazing afar upon every side around them. Then said Crom Deróil: "Has to thee appeared the thing that has appeared to me?" "What thing?" said Crom Darail. "Methinks they are multitudes of red weapons and the marching here and there of companies that I see coming across the slopes of the Eastern Luachair from the east." "A draught of gore and blood I would not deem too much in the mouth that so asserts," said Crom Darail; "for that is no host or company, but the huge oaks past which we came yesterday." [The discussion extends to other features. Crom Deróil sees royal chariots, shields, spearpoints, and horse-teams, but Crom Derail explains them away as features of the landscape, too: forts, pillars, the antlers of deer in the forest, herds of cattle, and so on. Then the tree image is taken up anew:] "And do not thou at all contradict me," said Crom Deróil, "for with me does the truth lie. As they come past the tips of the oaks of the Eastern Luachair, what would make them stoop if they were not men?" [. . .]
"It is not right for thee to dispute with me on every count.
Thou sayest that unmoving bushes are bent men."
"If they are bushes that are silent there,
they would not arise, unless need were, to go away.
If they are a grove of alder wood, over the wood of a cairn,
they would not go a guileful way, if they were dead. [. . .]"
[As the sun rises, it becomes clear that Crom Deróil had been right, and the first band of warriors arrives and charges the castle.] The hues of countenances were changed and there was chattering of teeth in Temair Luachra within. The two druids fell in trances and in weaknesses and in swoons, one of them fell over the wall outward, Crom Darail to wit, and Crom Deróil over the

wall within. And despite that Crom Deróil arose and cast
an eye over the first band that came into the green.

From the point of view of the epic, this episode is merely a comic
prologue to the real teichoscopy, which now begins: the attackers
are described in serious heroic style and identified, one by one, as
the men of Ulster. But it is remarkable for its explicit comedy and
its large-scale dialogic and prosimetrical composition; the slapstick
ending belies the careful linguistic and scenic construction of the
whole.

V. PANIC AND DISORGANIZATION

For his argument on Nagli's panic in *Eyrbyggja saga,* Sayers cites
saga passages in which men of Celtic descent are identified as fast
runners and in which slaves are said to have run away from
danger.[78] Not only Nagli's ethnic heritage, but also his behavior is in
a certain sense un-Icelandic, writes Sayers: Nagli is "a
disappointment in terms of manliness" and has proved to be
"substandard" for the "Icelandic social construction."[79] This is all
true enough, and the evidence adduced by Sayers could be
multiplied manifold. But such xenophobic associations were hardly
as automatic as Sayers seems to envision them, not even in *Eyrbyggja
saga,* since, after all, Þórarinn goes out of his way to save Nagli, a
Hebridean of indeterminate social status, and praises Nagli's
Hebridean colleague Álfgeirr explicitly for his conduct in the battle.

And the existence of other ethnic slurs proves nothing about
how – if at all – the phrase *verða at gjalti* as such differed in usage
from other expressions denoting panic; there are many, and Sayers
gives no evidence of having examined them. That the writers of any
extant Old Norse documents regarded *gjalti* as a loanword or
"foreign descriptor," let alone as an ethnic slur, is pure conjecture
on Sayers's part. It is that which is to be proved, which is why his

---

[78] Sayers, "Deployment," 171, n. 32.
[79] *ibid.,* 171.

conclusion seems perilously close to circular reasoning: "The use of the foreign descriptor [verða at gjalti] clearly labels certain actions as non-Icelandic."[80]

Let us pursue some of Sayers's other observations further. In *Rémundar saga keisarasonar* (why only there?), he finds that the phrase in question is used for "hyperbolic effect";[81] I agree. And the *Íslendinga sögur* examples are, he finds, "so successfully executed [. . .] that one is tempted to conclude that their authors reserved the *geilt* motif for incidents to which they wished to give additional artistic profile."[82] Sayers gives an excellent example: the figure of Nagli provides a foil for the hero Þórarinn in that he "adds a bathetic coda to the encounter, while Þórarinn is unexpectedly successful."[83] This idea is developed a few pages later:[84]

> It seems allied to the techniques of irony and understatement, in that it has a lightly deflating effect on the heroic environment, a means of pulling bold acts back into an everyday frame of reference: the tramps who rush off in disarray, the big Scotsman who fails his first test in Iceland. Heroic deeds, instead of being played out in the modal vacuum of the epic, are lent human perspective when framed by unheroic deeds.

This is, in my opinion, a fruitful – and necessary – line of argument, one that is capable of doing justice to the narrative complexity of the texts and that, in the long run, is compatible with literary, folkloristic, historiographical, even psychological and sociological analysis.

---

[80] *ibid.*, 179.
[81] *ibid.*, 175.
[82] *ibid.*, 173.
[83] *ibid.*, 171.
[84] *ibid.*, 176.

Not the act of becoming *gjalti* as such (however the word was understood), but many kinds of panic and confusion are attributed to "marginalized social groups" in the history of European narrative and ethnography. Let us take a look at just a few examples. The topos of panicked fear of the sky falling has already been mentioned. Clearly related to it is the ethnographical topos of disorderly (or nonexistent) government or military discipline: Roman historians attributed it to barbarians, while medieval Western Europeans attributed it (for example) to the Slavs or the Celts.[85] Military historiography not only permits, it demands stock descriptions of flight, often combined with panic.[86] Gizurr Þorvaldsson's *svá hræddir, at þeir vissu eigi, er þeir runnu yfir Jökulsá* 'so scared that they didn't know it when they ran through the river Jökulsá' in his battle address in *Íslendinga saga* ch. 137 echoes Flosi's *svá hræddr, at eigi mun vita, hvert hlaupa skal* 'so frightened that he won't know which way to run' in his battle address in *Njáls saga* ch. 130, and innumerable other literary and colloquial instances, beginning with the Bible.[87]

---

[85] One example of many: the unflattering description of Scottish warfare in *Egils saga Skalla-Grímssonar* ch. 54 would have been grist for Sayers's xenophobia mill. See the section on "confused organization" in Taylor, "Verbal Aggression," 200-01. An extreme form of the disorganization topos involves suicide, as in an early fourteenth-century ethnography of the Baltic Prussians: *Quando ex inopinato rerum eventu aliquam immoderatam incurrerunt turbacionem, se ipsos occidere consueverunt* ("When through an unforeseen turn of events excessive confusion has befallen them, they have usually killed themselves"), (Peter von Dusburg, *Chronik des Preußenlandes* §III.5, ed. Max Toeppen [Darmstadt: Wissenschaftliche Buchgesellschaft, 1984], 104; my translation). The thematic affinity of the passages in *Eyrbyggja saga* and *Gautreks saga* cited above is obvious.

[86] Numerous examples in Taylor, "Verbal Aggression," 212.

[87] *Íslendinga saga* ch. 137 and translation as in n. 32. *Njáls saga* ch. 130 in *Brennu-Njáls saga*, ed. Einar Ól. Sveinsson, ÍF 12 (Reykjavík: Hið Íslenzka fornritafélag, 1954), 337; trans. Robert Cook, "Njal's Saga," in *The Complete Sagas of Icelanders*, III:1-220, at 159.

A similar phrase is employed in the report of the demise of the wizard Eyvindr kelda in *Óláfs saga Tryggvasonar,* here cited after Snorri:[88]

Þá sǫmu nótt kom þar við eyna Eyvindr kelda; hann hafði langskip alskipat; váru þat alt seiðmenn ok annat fiǫlkyngisfólk. Eyvindr gekk upp af skipi ok sveit hans ok mǫgnuðu fiǫlkyngi sína. Gerði Eyvindr þeim hulizhiálm ok þokumyrkr svá mikit, at konungr ok lið hans skyldi eigi mega sjá þá. En er þeir kómu mjǫk svá til bœjarins á Ǫgvaldznesi, þá gerðisk lióss dagr; varð þá mjǫk annan veg, en Eyvindr hafði ætlat; þá kom mjǫrkvi sá, er hann hafði gǫrt með fiǫlkyngi, yfir hann ok hans fǫruneyti, svá at þeir sá eigi heldr augum en hnakka, ok fóru alt í hring ok kring.

That same night Eyvindr kelda came to the island; he had a fully manned longship; they were all wizards and other practitioners of magic. Eyvindr and his crew went up from the ship and practiced their magic. Eyvindr made them a cloak of invisibility and a dark fog so thick that the king and his followers wouldn't be able to see them. But when they came close to the farm at Ǫgvaldznes, it became broad daylight; things turned out then quite differently for Eyvindr than he had supposed; for the darkness that he had created by magic now came over him and his followers, so that they couldn't see with their eyes any better than with the napes of their necks, and they wandered around in circles.

After this the wizards are easily caught and put to death. In his source-criticism of this passage, Dag Strömbäck says two important things about its motifs. First, in Oddr Snorrason's version, which

---

[88] *Óláfs saga Tryggvasonar* in Snorri Sturluson, *Heimskringla,* ed. Finnur Jónsson, 150; my translation.

was Snorri's source, Eyvindr and his men are said to have been
struck with blindness at the sight of the church in which Óláfr is
staying (after which they run around in circles, as in Snorri);
according to Strömbäck, Snorri may have preferred to substitute the
motif of the fog because it was more secular and tied into a folk
belief that a practitioner of black magic could be forced by a
superior magician to suffer what he had intended for others.[89]
Second, the literary models for both Snorri's and Oddr's versions
must be sought in the large group of medieval saints' legends in
which sacrilegious thieves are caught by a sudden thick fog (or
invisible agency) that renders them blind, so they wander helplessly
in circles, thus literally fulfilling the prophecy of Psalm 12:9.[90]
Clearly, under some circumstances, the list of the "marginalized"
must be amended to include wizards, druids, the sacrilegious, and
so on.

Similarly mixed paths of influence must also be responsible for
a passage in Snorri's *Skáldskaparmál* for which no model – or even a
convincing explanation – has been found.[91]

Óðinn fór heiman ok kom þar, er þrælar níu slógu hey;
hann spyrr, ef þeir vili, at hann brýni ljá þeira. Þeir játa
því. Þá tekr hann hein af belti sér ok brýndi ljána; en þeim
þótti bíta ljárnir miklu betr ok fǫluðu heinina; en hann
mat svá, at sá, er kaupa vildi, skyldi gefa við hóf, enn allir
kváðusk vilja ok báðu hann sér selja, en hann kastaði
heininni í lopt upp; en er allir vildu henda, þá skiptusk
þeir svá við, at hverr brá ljánum á háls ǫðrum.

---

[89] Dag Strömbäck, *Sejd: Textstudier i nordisk religionshistoria* (Stockholm:
Geber, 1935), 47. It is well known that Snorri preferred to secularize his
material. Aimoinus, similarly, translated the "divine wrath" of his source
Paulus into secular and scientific terms as an "aberration of the mind"
(see n. 5 above).

[90] *ibid.*, 48.

[91] *Skáldskaparmál* §1 (= §6 in the numbering of the Codex Regius), in
Snorri Sturluson, *Edda*, ed. Finnur Jónsson, 72; my translation.

Óðinn set out and came to where nine slaves were
making hay; he asks if they want him to sharpen their
scythes. They say yes. Then he takes a whetstone from his
belt and sharpened the scythes; and they thought that the
scythes cut much better and asked to buy the whetstone;
and he declared that whoever wanted to buy it should pay
a fair price, but all of them said they wanted to and asked
him to sell it to them, but he threw the whetstone up into
the air; and when all of them tried to catch it, the end of
their dealings was that each of them brought his scythe
down onto the neck of another.

Parallels to Óðinn's role and to the deadly confusion of the slaves
can be found in the folktale complex "The Dangerous Sickle"
(AaTh/ATU 1202-1203A, including TMI J2422): numskulls who
have previously harvested grain by an absurdly inefficient method
observe how a wayfaring stranger uses a sickle or scythe; when he
leaves this tool behind (or sells it), the suspicious numskulls throw a
stone at it, causing it to fly up and injure one or all of them
(sometimes they decapitate themselves or each other in trying to
remove the sickle from around their necks). Folklore scholarship is
unaware of any form of this tale older than the sixteenth century,
however, so Snorri's version stands alone chronologically;[92]
moreover, Snorri does not portray the slaves as ignorant of scythes.

Snorri's ending is much easier to understand in the context of
religious legends of the aforementioned type. Gregory of Tours, for
example, employs a very similar image repeatedly in describing the
divine punishment of sacrilegious thieves: either in confusion or in
sudden rage, they transfix each other (or themselves) with their

---

[92] Ulf Palmenfelt, "Sichel: Die gefährliche S.," in *Enzyklopädie des Märchens*,
vol. 12, cols. 635-38, at col. 636.

lances. The first and most complex of the group involves an attempted escape in a boat:[93]

> Ingressique fluvium, protinus vibrante carina, huc illuque feruntur. Cumque amisso solatio remorum, hastilia lancearum in fundum alvei defixa, remeare conarentur, navis sub pedibus eorum dehiscit, et uniuscuiusque ferrum, quod contra se tenebat, pectore defigitur, transverberatique cuncti a propriis iaculis interimuntur.

> Then they pushed off into the stream, but their keel began to sway to and fro, and they were carried round and round. They had lost their oars, which might have saved them. They tried to reach the bank by pushing the butts of their spears into the bed of the river, but the boat split apart beneath their feet. They were all pierced through by the points of their lances, which they were holding against their bodies; they were all transfixed and were killed by their own javelins.

The next speaks for itself: *Ille vero, qui beati Martini iumenta abduxerant, commota altercatione, se invicem lanceis transfixerunt* ("These men who had stolen Saint Martin's animals then quarrelled among themselves and started thrusting each other through with their spears").[94] In the third text of the group, the lance motif appears at the end of a catalogue of punishments:[95]

> Nam plerisque manus divinitus urebantur, emittentis fumum magnum, sicut ex incendio surgi solet. Nonnulli arrepti a daemone, per inergiam debachantes martyrem

---

[93] *Histories* §IV.48, in *Gregorii episcopi Tvronensis libri historiarvm X,* ed. Bruno Krusch and Wilhelm Levison, 2nd ed. (Hannover: Hahn, 1937-51), 185; *The History of the Franks,* trans. Lewis Thorpe (Harmondsworth: Penguin 1974), 245.

[94] *ibid.,* §VII.21 (ed. Krusch and Levison, 340; trans. Thorpe, 402).

[95] *ibid.,* §VII.35 (ed. Krusch and Levison, 356; trans. Thorpe, 418-19).

declamabant. Plurimi vero semoti a seditione propriis se
iaculis sauciabant.

Many of their hands caught fire supernaturally and gave
forth a great smoke, like the pall which rises from a
conflagration. Some were possessed by a devil and rushed
about screaming the martyr's name. Others fought with
each other and wounded themselves with their own
javelins.

The first of these three legends explicitly describes not only the
lance motif, but also the same confused and pointless motion that
we have seen in other texts: the boat drifts helplessly this way and
that (*huc illucque*). And even in the other two, movement is implied
in the words *commota* (not translated) and *debachantes* (which Thorpe,
in fact, renders with "rushed about").

Having examined the end of Snorri's anecdote, let us return to
its beginning. The act of throwing the whetstone into the air to bait
the greedy has two analogues in very well known Old Norse texts.
The first is the tale told by Saxo and by Snorri himself in
Skáldskaparmál of how Hrólfr Kraki "sowed gold" on the road in
order to distract the pursuing Swedes. The second – even closer to
Snorri's scythe anecdote, since it includes both a comparable
premise and a comparable ending – is Egill Skalla-Grímsson's plan
to "sow silver" at the þing and watch the ensuing commotion. In
words suggestive of a number of texts we have reviewed in this
section (note especially the verb *skipta*, which appears in the same
place in the scythe tale), Egill envisages the result as a potentially
deadly confusion of numskulls:[96]

"ætla ek at sá silfrinu, ok þykki mér undarligt, ef allir
skipta vel sín á milli; ætla ek, at þar myndi vera þá

---

[96] *Egils saga Skalla-Grímssonar*, ed. Sigurður Nordal, ÍF 2 (Reykjavík: Hið
Íslenzka fornritafélag, 1933), 297; my translation.

hrundningar ok pústrar, eða bærisk at um síðir, at allr
þingheimrinn berðisk."

"I intend to sow the silver, and I have my doubts whether
they will all share it fairly; I suspect that push will come to
shove and fists will fly, and it may turn out that the whole
assembly ends in a pitched battle."

Expanded in this saga to a veritable meta-novella, the numskull
story is embedded in a matrix of several narrative levels: Egill's
vision of the future (the novella *in nuce*), his description of the plan
to Þórdís, her sarcastic answer to Egill, her report of the plan to
Grímr, Grímr's conversation with Egill, and finally, overseeing the
whole business, the saga narrator. This is the exquisitely developed
art of Snorri and his school.

Masculinity and/or Peace?
On *Eyrbyggja saga*'s *Máhlíðingamál*

Ásdís Egilsdóttir

In his preface to his classic edition of *Eyrbyggja saga*, Einar Ólafur Sveinsson writes that the saga is *fyrst og fremst karlmannasaga*, first and foremost a saga about men.[1] Indeed, feuds and disputes between men form the major part of the saga.[2] One of the first significant episodes of the saga, known as *Máhlíðingamál*,[3] tells of the witch Katla in Holt and her son Oddr Kǫtluson, the *ójafnaðarmaðr* Þorbjǫrn digri and his son Gunnlaugr, the knowledgeable Geirríðr

---

[1] "Þó að sagan sé þannig fyrst og fremst 'karlmannasaga' (eins og norska skáldið Kinck kemst að orði)," *Eyrbyggja saga*, ed. Einar Ól. Sveinsson, Íslenzk fornrit 4 (Reykjavík: Hið íslenzka fornritafélag, 1935), xl.

[2] On the episodic structure of the saga, sociological and ideological analysis, see Elín Bára Magnúsdóttir, "Et samfunn preget av kaos. Presentasjonen av Snorri goði og sagaens samfunn i Eyrbyggja saga," *Nordica Bergensia* 14 (2000): 139-64; Elín Bára Magnúsdóttir, "An Ideological Struggle: An Interpretation of Eyrbyggja saga," *The Fantastic in Old Norse/Icelandic Literature. Preprint Papers of The 13th International Saga Conference Durham and York, 6th-12th August, 2006*, ed. John McKinnell et al., 2 vols. (Durham: The Centre for Medieval and Renaissance Studies, 2006), 208-216. See also Bernadine McCreesh, "Structural patterns in the Eyrbyggja saga and other sagas of the Conversion," *Mediaeval Scandinavia* 11 (1978/79): 271-80; R. McTurk, "Approaches to the Structure of Eyrbyggja saga," *Sagnaskemmtun: Studies in Honour of Hermann Pálsson* (Vienna: Hermann Böhlaus Nachf., 1986), 223-37; Paul Bibire, "Verses in the Íslendingasögur," *Alþjóðlegt fornsagnaþing, Reykjavík 2-8 ágúst 1973: Fyrirlestrar*, 2 vols. (Reykjavík: n.p., 1973), 1-28, at 9-13.

[3] *Eyrbyggja saga*, 33-54.

in Mávahlíð and her son, the poet Þórarinn svarti. Þórarinn is a central figure in the *Máhlíðingamál.* Katla and Geirríðr are presented as rivals. Katla is portrayed as sexual, evil and dangerous, whereas Geirríðr is depicted only as a wise woman. Young Gunnlaugr spent some time in Mávahlíð learning magic from Geirríðr, and consequently making Katla jealous. When Gunnlaugr is found unconscious and injured near his father's farm, Geirríðr is accused of injuring him by riding him as a *kveldriða* ("night-rider hag"). Oddr Kǫtluson spreads the rumour that Geirríðr was the cause of Gunnlaugr' s injury, which was actually caused by his mother's witchcraft. Arnkell goði, Geirríðr' s brother defended the charge on her behalf and swore an oath that she was not guilty of the accusations. Geirríðr and Katla, and indeed other women, play a significant role in the *karlmannasaga.* When introduced in the saga text, Þórarinn, the son of Geirríðr, is described thus:[4]

> [. . .] mikill maðr ok sterkr, ljótr ok hljóðlyndr, vel stilltr hversdagsliga; hann var kallaðr mannasættir. Hann var eigi fémikill ok hafði þó bú gagnsamt. Svá var hann maðr óhlutdeilinn, at óvinir hans mæltu, at hann hefði eigi síðr kvenna skap en karla.

> [. . .] a big, strong man, ugly and taciturn, but usually self-composed, and he had a reputation as a peace-maker. He was not a rich man, although he had a profitable farm. Thorarinn was so impartial that his enemies said his disposition was as much a woman's as a man's.

---

[4] *Eyrbyggja saga,* 27. "The Saga of the People of Eyri," trans. Judy Quinn, *The Complete Sagas of the Icelanders,* ed. Viðar Hreinsson, 5 vols. (Reykjavík: Leifur Eiríksson, 1997), 5:131-218, at 142. I shall refer to the *Eyrbyggja saga* (1935, hereafter ÍF 4) and "The Saga of the People of Eyri" (1997) in this article.

Þórarinn's personality makes him unmanly, at least in the eyes of his enemies.[5] Recently, medievalists have shown increased interest in men and masculinities. It can be argued that research has always focused on men, the subjects of traditional scholarly discourse were for the most part men, but then, the hegemonic males were seen as generic, human history.[6] Modern studies see gender as relational and put emphasis on culturally constructed masculinity, difference and diversity. Feminist studies have paved the way for modern studies of masculinities, where men have been studied and discussed as gendered. Feminist scholars have shown that gender roles put restrictions upon women, but scholars are now beginning to ask questions about how men reacted to the demands that were made on them. In his influential book *Making Sex: Body and Gender from the Greeks to Freud*, Thomas Laqueur discusses the idea of the 'one-sex model' in European history, which, according to Laqueur, prevailed in Western culture until the eighteenth century. The one-sex model implied that femininity was simply a lack of masculinity and that women should therefore be understood as a lesser man.[7] Preben Meulengracht Sørensen and Carol J. Clover have studied the interaction of power and gender in the Icelandic sagas.[8] Sørensen pointed out that masculinity and femininity should not only be seen as opposites but also in relation to each other. A man's honour and prestige depended not only on himself but also on the appreciation of the women in his family.

---

5 For a psychological analysis of Þórarinn's character, see Torfi Tulinius, "Is Snorri goði an Icelandic Hamlet? On Dead Fathers and Problematic Chieftainship in Eyrbyggja saga," *The Fantastic in Old Norse/Icelandic Literature*, 961-70.
6 Thelma Fenster, "Preface: Why Men?" *Medieval Masculinities: Regarding Men in the Middle Ages*, ed. Clare A. Lees, Medieval Cultures 7 (Minneapolis: University of Minnesota Press, 1994), ix-xiii.
7 Thomas Laqueur, *Making Sex: Body and Gender from the Greeks to Freud* (Cambridge MA: Harvard University Press, 1990).
8 Carol J. Clover, "Regardless of Sex: Men, Women, and Power in Early Northern Europe," *Speculum* 68.2 (1993): 363-87; Preben Meulengracht Sørensen, *Fortælling og ære* (Oslo: Oslo University Press 1995), 212-27.

The men played an active part in society, but the women watched over their honour and prestige, evaluated them and often encouraged fight and revenge with their *frýjur*. Although there was a clear distinction between manliness and unmanliness in Old Icelandic society, both categories, male and female, were movable. A woman could be encouraged to adopt the mental toughness normally associated with men, but a man would be degraded to the sphere of women if he showed any inclination towards femininity. But while Sørensen sees power as a metaphor for sex, Clover argues that sex can be a metaphor for power. The terms Clover suggests in her dynamic analysis to present the opposites instead of man versus woman are *hvatr* ("vigorous") versus *blauðr* ("soft, weak").[9] *Hvatr* and *blauðr* can also mean masculine and feminine.

Sixteen uniform verses, the so-called *Máhlíðingavísur*, are attributed to the quiet and peaceful Þórarinn svarti.[10] As Roberta Frank has pointed out, he "seems extraordinarily sensitive to what women were expecting of him."[11] The *Máhlíðingavísur* contain seven references to women, beginning by stating that the poet warded off reproaches from women and ending with a plea to a woman that he did not break any law when he killed his enemy. Several scholars have discussed the age of the verses in relation to the prose text of the saga. Based on their vocabulary, the verses were believed to old

---

[9] Clover, "*Regardless of Sex*," 377. See also Bjørn Bandlien, *Man or Monster: Negotations of Masculinity in Old Norse Society*, Acta humaniora 236 (Oslo: Unipub, 2005) and Henric Bagerius, *Mandom och mödom: Sexualitet, homosocialitet och aristokratisk identiet på senmedeltida Island* (Göteborg: Göteborgs Universitet, 2009).

[10] The verses are also fragmentarily preserved and referred to in the *Hauksbók* version of *Landnámabók*. *Íslendingabók: Landnámabók*, ed. Jakob Benediktsson, Íslenzk fornrit 1, 2 vols. (Reykjavík: Hið íslenzka fornritafélag, 1968), 115. Snorri Sturluson quotes the opening lines of the first verse in his *Háttatal* and ascribes them to Þórarinn.

[11] Roberta Frank, "Why Skalds Address Women," *Poetry in the Scandinavian Middle Ages: Atti del 12° Congresso internazionale di studi sull' alto Medioevo* (Spoleto: Centro Studi, 1990): 67-83, at 77.

enough to be authentic and the narrative surrounding them a good example of oral tradition. Using linguistic evidence, Russell Poole has argued that the verses cannot be any older than the 11th or 12th century. The verses possibly formed a part of a narrative about Snorri goði and were later interwoven into the *Eyrbyggja* text.[12] Vésteinn Ólason finds Poole's dating convincing, but he also argues that details of the narrative strengthen the belief that it is based on oral tradition.[13]

The verses are found in chapters 18-22, according to the Íslenzk fornrit edition.[14] The prose text tells of Þorbjǫrn digri, who was "mikill fyrir sér ok ósvífr við sér minni menn" ("an unbalanced man who bullied weaker men")[15] had many horses grazing up on mountain pastures and used to choose a few of them for slaughter each autumn. One cold autumn his horses could not be found. Oddr Kǫtluson asked Spá-Gils, who had a sixth sense for solving

---

[12] Russell Poole, "The Origins of the Máhlíðingavísur," *Scandinavian Studies* 57.3 (1985): 244-285.

[13] Vésteinn Ólason, "Authorship and tradition in Eyrbyggja saga," *Úr Dǫlum til Dala: Guðbrandr Vigfússon Centenary Essays*, ed. Rory McTurk & Andrew Wawn (Leeds: School of English, University of Leeds, 1989), 187-203, at 198-200.

[14] Forrest S. Scott has pointed out that scholarly editions of *Eyrbyggja saga* have relied mainly in a single paper manuscript, AM 448 4to (Aa), a copy made by Ásgeir Jónsson in Copenhagen in 1686-88. All surviving manuscripts of *Eyrbyggja saga* are fragmentary. Scholars who have studied the structure of *Eyrbyggja* have "measured the saga by means of the chapter numbers found in Einar Ól. Sveinsson's edition in Íslenzk fornrit." Although there is no great difference between the chapter divisions of Aa and the vellum manuscripts, they are not identical. *Eyrbyggja saga: The vellum tradition*, ed. Forrest S. Scott, Editiones Arnamagnæanæ Series A 18 (Copenhagen: C. A. Reitzel, 2003), xiii. Scott's edition of the *Máhlíðingavísur*, at 58-59.

[15] *Eyrbyggja saga*, ÍF 4: 29; "The Saga of the People of Eyri," 142.

thefts, for help. Spá-Gils said that the horses did not stray far from their usual pasture implying that the horses may have been stolen:[16]

. . . sagði Oddr ok, at hann hefði svá mælt, at þeir væri líkastir til hrossatǫku, er sjálfir váru févana ok hǫfðu þó aukit hjónum ór því, sem vanði var til; í þessum orðum þótti Þorbirni kveðit á Máhlíðinga.

Oddr added that Spá-Gils had said that those most likely to be horse thieves were those who were short of money themselves, but who had a larger household than usual to provide for. It seemed to Þorbjǫrn that this wording implied the people of Mávahlíð.

Þorbjǫrn accused Þórarinn of the theft and established a so-called *duradómr* ("door court")[17] where he brought the charge against him. At that moment his mother, Geirríðr, stepped out and said:[18]

"Ofsatt er þat, er mælt er, at meir hefir þú, Þórarinn, kvenna skap en karla, er þú skalt þola Þorbirni digra hverja skǫmm, ok eigi veit ek hví ek á[19] slíkan son."

That judgement is all too true, she said, that you, Þórarinn, have as much a woman's disposition as a man's, when you tolerate every disgrace from Þorbjörn the Stout. I do not understand why I have such a son.

Þórarinn and his men ran out intending to break the court and a fight followed. The women tried to separate the men and threw clothes upon their weapons. A woman's hand was found in a

---

[16] *Eyrbyggja saga*, ÍF 4: 34; "The Saga of the People of Eyri," 145.
[17] A *duradómr* is not mentioned in other sagas but is referred to the *Gulaþingslög*. The door court was held at the home of the defendant.
[18] *Eyrbyggja saga*, ÍF 4: 36; "The Saga of the People of Eyri," 145.
[19] *Skylda eiga, Melabók*, AM 445 4to, AM 309 4to. *Eyrbyggja saga* (2003), 56.

hayfield near the farm where the battle had taken place. Þórarinn found out that his own wife had been injured in that way; her hand had been cut off. When Þórarinn discovered this, he ran after Þorbjǫrn and his men. Þorbjǫrn remarked that Þórarinn had fought boldly but Oddr said that Þórarinn had accidentally cut off his wife's hand, and they all laughed and ridiculed him. Þórarinn then killed Þorbjǫrn. When Þórarinn returned home his mother was waiting in the doorway. The first verse is a reply to the mother when she asks how the fight had gone:[20]

Varðak mik þars myrðir
morðfárs vega þorði
hlaut ǫrn af ná neyta
nýjum, kvinna frýju.
barkak vægð að vígi
valnaðrs í styr þaðra.
Mælik hól fyr hœli[21]
hjaldrsgoðs af því sjaldan.

I warded off reproaches from women, where the warrior dared to fight; the eagle had the luck to avail himself of a new corpse: I did not flinch from the swordplay there in the battle; I seldom make boasts in the presence of a person who praises the god of battle.[22]

Þórarinn begins by telling that by taking part in the fight he had defended himself against women's reproaches.[23] He draws a traditional picture of the battle, the eagle was well fed, but ends by saying that he didn't boast about it before the people that wished

[20] *Eyrbyggja saga*, ÍF 4: 38.
[21] *Mælik ljóð fyrir fljóði*, AM 309 4to. *Eyrbyggja saga* (2003), 59.
[22] English prose translations of the *Máhlíðingavísur* are according to Poole, "The Origins of the Máhlíðingavísur," 244-85.
[23] When Þórarinn is mentioned in the following text, I refer to the voice of the poet in the saga, not the "historical" Þórarinn.

for war. In this context the image of the vulture becomes ironic.
Geirríðr then asks if Þorbjǫrn had been killed and Þórarinn replies
with another verse:[24]

Knátti hjǫrr und hetti[25]
hræflóð, bragar Móða,
rauk of[26] sóknar sœki,
slíðrbeittr staðar leita.
Blóð fell, en vas váði
vígtjalds náar skaldi
þá vas dœmisalr dóma
dreyrafullr, um eyru.

The skald's lethally sharp sword struck home beneath the
hood; blood spouted forth over the warrior: the blood
streamed down over his ears and then his mouth was full
of it, but his sword came close to the skald.

The verse seems to please Geirríðr who responds by saying:
"tekit hefir þá brýningin"[27] ("the whetting paid off, then"). The
verse describes the terror of the battle, flowing blood and a sharp
sword, and Þórarinn claims that his life was in danger.

The morning after the battle Þórarinn recites a verse, which is a
reply to the worrying words of Þórarinn's wife, Auðr, who fears
the aftermath of the fight. Þórarinn tells her that he is going to seek
help from Vermundur, his brother in law.[28]

Myndit vitr í vetri

---

[24] *Eyrbyggja saga*, ÍF 4: 39.
[25] *i hofi*, *Melabók*, *i hofði*, AM 309 4to. *Eyrbyggja saga* (2003), 58-59.
[26] Rann um, *Melabók*, AM 309 4to. *Eyrbyggja saga* (2003), 58-59.
[27] *Eyrbyggja saga*, ÍF 4: 39. *tekit hefir þá brýningunni*, *Melabók*, AM 309 4to,
AM 447 4to. *Eyrbyggja saga* (2003), 60-61.
[28] *Eyrbyggja saga*, ÍF 4: 40.

vekjandi mik sekja
þar ák lífhvǫtuð leyfðan
lǫgráns, um þær vánir,
ef niðbræði næðak
nás valfallins[29] ásar (alfalldins)
Hugins létum nið njóta
nágrundar, Vermundi.

The cunning man who instigates the robbery of my legal
rights would not outlaw me this winter – there I have
praised my protector, because of those expectations – if I
reached the warrior Vermundr; I caused the raven's kin to
benefit from the battlefield.

Þórarinn travels to Vermundr and the following eight verses are
supposedly recited at his farm. Vermundur asks Þórarinn for news
and he answers by reciting verses where he describes the attack on
him and the dangerous battle.

Blood and a hand are dramatically emphasized in the
concluding lines of the next verse, and the kenning used for sword,
"Hrundar handa hnigreyr" ("the valkyrie's hand-reed")[30] reminds
the audience of the severed female hand found in the field: "roðin
sák Hrundar handa / hnigreyr, lǫgum dreyra"[31] ("I saw swords red
with blood"). In the next verse the poet concludes by telling that he
had been unwilling to break the truce: "sleitka líknar leiki lostigr"
("I did not break the sport of comfort willingly").[32] Guðný,
Þórarinn's sister, asks him if he had cleared himself of the women's
taunts. Her question corresponds to Þórarinn's reply to his mother
in the first verse. He paints a disgusting and appalling pictures of
the fight in close-ups, making use of traditional poetic language:

---

[29] *alfalldins, Melabók. Eyrbyggja saga* (2003), 64.
[30] "The Saga of the People of Eyri," 148.
[31] *Eyrbyggja saga*, ÍF 4: 41.
[32] *Eyrbyggja saga*, ÍF 4: 42; "The Saga of the People of Eyri," 149.

"hrafninn naut líkanna" ("the raven enjoyed the dead bodies"), in a similarly effective way as the first verse. Another battle-verse follows, where danger is emphasized from the very beginning.[33]

Then Vermundur asks: "Hvárt vissu þeir hvárt þú vart karlmaðr eða kona?" ("Have they found out yet whether you are a man or a woman?")[34] His words express an approval, by now other men must have realized that Þórarinn behaved correctly as a man and accepted him, even those who had humiliated him with their laughter. He adds yet another verse to prove further that he had fought off any suggestion of cowardice.[35] The following verse is difficult to interpret but the latter half tells that cowardly men, who abused the law, had accused him of having hurt his own wife, but he also remarks "eggjumk hófs" ("my aim is moderation").[36]

In the next two verses (Íf 12 – 13) Þórarinn describes two other men who also took part in the battle, one brave, but another a coward. The latter is said to have run crying away from the battle. The poet uses non-military kennings to describe him: *merskyndir* ("mare-driver") and *bifstaups bjóðr* "cup bearer"). Although peaceful, he shows his contempt for a man who fled from the fight.[37]

Some time has passed when Þórarinn and Vermundur travel together to see Arnkell, Þórarinn's uncle. While travelling, Þórarinn recites a verse.[38] In the first half the poet addresses Vermundur and thinks back to the happy days they had together before the killing of Þorbjǫrn. An unidentified woman is addressed in the second

---

[33] Vésteinn Ólason points out that skaldic imagery describing battle is indeed horrific if understood literally, Vésteinn Ólason, "Authorship and tradition in Eyrbyggja saga," 201. However, the characterization of Þórarinn and his poetry is unique, as Vésteinn also demonstrates.

[34] *Eyrbyggja saga*, ÍF 4: 43; "The Saga of the People of Eyri," 149.

[35] *Eyrbyggja saga*, ÍF 4: 43-44; "The Saga of the People of Eyri," 149.

[36] *Eyrbyggja saga*, ÍF 4: 44; "The Saga of the People of Eyri," 150.

[37] *Eyrbyggja saga*, ÍF 4: 45-46; "The Saga of the People of Eyri," 150.

[38] *Eyrbyggja saga*, ÍF 4: 47; "The Saga of the People of Eyri," 151.

part. *Máhlíðingavísur* contain seven references to women. The poet begins by telling that he warded off reproaches from women and ending with his plea to a woman that he did not break any law in killing his opponent. All these references show the importance of fulfilling the expectations of women. As Roberta Frank has pointed out, the first half of the verse describes happy male bonding, in the latter half the poet turns to the judge of his action, a woman.[39] In the closing words of the verse he tells that he dislikes strife: "leið erum randa rauðra regn" ("The rain of the red shields is repugnant to me").

When the two travellers arrive at Arnkell's farm, Arnkell welcomes his guests and asks their news. Þórarinn replies with a verse which describes the atrocities of the battle, emphasizing fear in the first half: "Vas til hreggs at hyggja /hrafn-víns á bœ mínum" ("It brought fear, to think of storm of the raven's wine at my farm").[40]

The next verse is a response to Arnkell's remark: "Reizk hefir þú nú frændi, svá hógværr maðr sem þú ert" ("You really must have been angry, kinsman, since you are usually such a moderate man"). In this verse the poet claims that he avoids feuds. Men have accused him of easy living, but "opt kemr ævifúrs æðiregn ór dúri" ("a cloudburst often comes in still weather"). The concluding words of the verse tell that a woman will now hear of his message.[41]

In his article "On Being a Male in the Middle Ages," Vern Bullough writes:

> Though what constitutes manhood has varying definitions according to a society or culture or time period, the most simplistic way of defining masculinity is

---

[39] Frank, "Why Skalds Address Women," 77.
[40] *Eyrbyggja saga*, ÍF 4: 47; "The Saga of the People of Eyri," 151.
[41] *Eyrbyggja saga*, ÍF 4: 48; "The Saga of the People of Eyri," 151.

as a triad: impregnating women, protecting dependents, and serving as provider to one's family. Failing to do so challenges a man's masculinity and can even be seen as feminine weakness.[42]

In the beginning of the *Máhlíðingamál* narrative, Þórarinn is accused of neglecting his duties as a man. It is implied that he doesn't provide enough for his family and he is said to have accidentally chopped off his wife's hand, therefore also seriously neglecting his duty to protect her. He was supposed to take care of the lives of his family and upholding the family's honour. Their honour is in danger when he is accused of cowardice.

Þórarinn needs to establish his masculinity, before other men and before women. The women watch over and judge his behaviour. Interestingly, his wife, Auðr, is peaceful like himself, but his strong-minded mother takes on the role to egg him on. He states clearly that he dislikes the behaviour which is expected of him and battles are not shown in a glorious light in the *Máhlíðingavísur*. The poet seeks balance in trying to be a man of peace and reconciliation and taking care of his masculine honour. Paradoxically, he has to prove himself by means of violence. Masculinity is the central theme of the *Máhlíðingamál* narrative and the verses are interwoven accordingly.

---

[42] Vern Bullough, "On Being a Male in the Middle Ages," *Medieval Masculinities*, 31-45, at 34.

Interpreting the Sagas before the Sagas

Theodore M. Andersson

We might gladly sacrifice one or two middling sagas for the minutes of a conversation in which a group of twelfth- or thirteenth-century Icelanders exchange ideas about the nature of the sagas. Alas, no such set of minutes is extant, but I will propose that we do have some fragments that give us a tantalizing insight into what such a conversation might have sounded like. These fragments suggest, ever so obliquely, how the medieval Icelanders thought about the sagas and how they construed meaning at the dawn of the saga-writing era. The fragments I have in mind come from a chronicle of Norwegian kings known as *Morkinskinna*, composed around 1220, that is, at a date prior to the great emergence of saga composition in the thirteenth century. These fragments pertain to two mid-eleventh-century kings, Haraldr Sigurðarson harðráði of Norway and Sveinn Úlfsson (or Svend Estridsen) of Denmark, kings who were for a time persistently at war with one another.

We may begin with King Haraldr, or Harald Hardrule, as the English convention prescribes. King Harald seems to have been reputed among the Icelanders as the most resourceful and deeply perceptive of all the Norwegian kings. A passage in *Morkinskinna* is quite explicit:[1]

---

[1]*Morkinskinna*, ed. Ármann Jakobsson and Þórður Ingi Guðjónsson (Reykjavík: Hið íslenzka fornritafélag, 2011), Íslenzk fornrit (hereafter ÍF) 23: 204, and *Morkinskinna: The Earliest Chronicle of the Norwegian Kings (1030-*

Haraldr konungr var ríkr maðr ok stjórnsamr innanlands, spekingr at viti, ok þat (er) vitra manna mál at engi maðr hafi verit djúpvitrari á ǫllum Norðrlǫndum en Haraldr konungr ok manna ráðsnjallastr, svá at honum varð aldri ráðfátt.

King Harald was a powerful man and a firm ruler in Norway. He had a profound intelligence, and it is the opinion of well-informed men that no one in all the northern lands was more penetrating than King Harald. He was the most resourceful of men so that he was never without a remedy.

Many of his adventures, which are told at greater length in *Morkinskinna* than those of any other king of Norway, apart from Saint Olaf, serve to illustrate Harald's special intelligence. That is the nature of the first anecdote I submit.

At one point during the hostilities with Denmark Harald is trapped in a fjord by the Danish fleet and deprived of access to drinking water. He remedies the situation by landing on an island and devising a stratagem to find water. He locates a snake, dehydrates it by the fire, fastens a thread to its tail, and lets it lead him to a hidden spring that only the snake can find. The author comments: ". . . ok varð af þessi ráðspeki konungs vatnit fundit, ok því at minnum haft eptir at ráðit þótti vitrligt ok hugkvæmligt" (because of the king's intelligence the water was found and [the device] was preserved in memory because it seemed wise and ingenious).[2] Tradition seems therefore to have clung not only to deeds of valor but to intellectual feats as well. The intellectual category could also include particularly chiseled verbal exchanges.

1157), trans. T. M. Andersson and Kari Ellen Gade (Ithaca: Cornell University Press, 2000), 204 (hereafter abbreviated "trans.").
[2] ÍF 23: 240; trans., 226. Cf. a similar comment on the ingenuity of Sigurðr slembir, ÍF 24: 207; trans., 386.

This type of tradition is illustrated by a little epilogue to the Battle of Niz (1062), during which King Harald captures his enemy Jarl Finnr Árnason but offers to spare Finnr's life. The dialogue runs as follows:[3]

"Viltu hafa grið nú," segir konungr, "þótt þat sé ómakligt?" "Eigi af hundi þínum" svarar jarl. "Viltú þá," segir konungr, "at Magnús frændi þinn gefi þér grið?" Magnús, sonr konungs, stýrþi þá skipi ok var þó á ungum alldri. Þá svarar jarl: "Hvat muni hvelpr sá griðum ráða?" Þá þótti konungi gaman at erta jarl ok mælti: "Viltu taka grið af Þóru, frændkonu þinni." Þá spurði jarlinn: "Er hon hér?" "Hér er hon," svarar konungr. Þa mælti Fiðr jarl orðskrǫk þat er síðan er uppi haft ok frá segir hversu reiðr hann var, er hann fekk eigi stillt orðum sínum: "Eigi er nú undarligt at þú hafir vel bitizk, er merrin er með þér."

"Do you wish to be spared," asked the king, "even though you hardly deserve it?"

"Not by a dog like you," answered the jarl.

"Are you saying that you want your kinsman Magnús to spare you?" asked the king. The king's son Magnús was in command of a ship but was still very young.

Then the jarl asked: "What sort of reprieve can that whelp manage?"

The king found it amusing to tease the jarl and asked: "Will you accept a reprieve from your kinswoman Þóra?"

Then the jarl asked: "Is she here?"

---

[3] ÍF 23: 251; trans., 232.

"Here she is," said the king.

Then Finnr made a vicious comment that was later remembered because it indicates that he was so angry that he could not control his words: "No wonder you bit so well since you have the mare looking on."

The jarl's parting shot relates to the spectator sport of horse fighting in Iceland, a contest in which two stallions were pitted against each other. Icelandic research has established that stallions do indeed fight more fiercely if a mare is present.[4] For our purposes, however, the authorial comment is more important than the matter of equine behavior. What the author does in this passage is to advance a theory on why the incident was remembered, and presumably retold: because, he says, it suggests that Finnr Árnason was so angry that he could not control his words. The episode thus becomes a parable on self-discipline. The author suggests that the incident was remembered and repeated for the moral of the story: Jarl Finnr cannot contain himself, but King Harald remains calm. Modern readers may find that moralization of the anecdote somewhat implausible, but the author returns to it a second time, as we shall see.

Before finalizing the moral of the story, however, the author adds a second anecdote, this time about the defeated king Svend, who barely escapes from the Battle of the River Niz and takes refuge in disguise in a remote cottage in the Danish forest. The woman who resides there, unaware of the king's identity and conforming to the tradition of the sharp-tongued harridan, questions him about the outcome of the battle. When she learns the truth about the Danish disaster, she voices her opinion in no

---

[4] Bjarni Vilhjálmsson, "Postulínsgerð og hestavíg," *Gripla* 7 (1990): 20-21.

uncertain terms:[5] "Vesǫl erum vér konungs ok æ vei verði oss. Vér eigum konung hvártveggja haltan ok ragan" ("Woe to us—we are miserably provided for since our king is both halt and cowardly"). As a matter of historical interest, it should be pointed out that a modern medical examination of King Svend's bones revealed that he may well have been lame.[6] The author now goes on to comment on the woman's malicious sally in the following words:[7]

Þetta er gamans frásǫgn ok eigi sǫguligt eins kostar, nema fyr þá sǫk at hér er lýst grein speki ok óvizku. Ok í annan stað, er sagt var áðr frá orðaviðskiptum þeira Haralds konungs ok Finns jarls; þar líknaði sá er valdit átti, ok vegr var þat en eigi lítilræði. En jarlinn sýndi þat hversu óhræddr hann var. Hann mátti þá ekki gøra annat en mæla þat er í skapi bjó ok sýndi í því jafnlyndi, mælti ekki til Sveins konungs nema þat er vel var, er hann hafði honum áðr þjónat, en mælti hermiliga til Haralds konungs er hann hafði móti verit. En Haraldr konungr virði þat allt sem barnsorð, ok hafa svá allir síðan virt.

This tale is only for the fun of it and worth telling only because it distinguishes wisdom from witlessness. Moreover, when the exchange of words between King Harald and Finnr was told [referring back to the previous episode], the man who had the power showed mercy, and there was honor in that action and no lack of authority. But the jarl showed how fearless he was. He was unable

---

[5] ÍF 23: 252; trans., 232. On the motif in general see Joseph Harris, "The King in Disguise: An International Popular Tale in Two Icelandic Adaptations," *Arkiv för nordisk filologi* 94 (1979): 57-66.
[6] Finnur Jónsson, "Sannfræði íslenskra sagna," *Skírnir* 93 (1919): 183-92 (esp. 184-85).
[7] ÍF 23: 252-53; trans., 232. Cf. the author's similar comment on angry words spoken to King Eysteinn Magnússon (berfœtts) in ÍF 24: 113 (trans., 333).

to do otherwise than to speak what was on his mind, and in that he demonstrated consistency. He spoke only well of King Svend since he had been in his service, but he spoke angrily to King Harald, whom he had opposed. But King Harald treated what he had to say like so many childish words, and that has been the view of everyone ever since.

This passage exhibits an interpretive stance very rare in Old Norse-Icelandic literature, but it raises a number of confusing problems. The conclusion of the paragraph makes it clear that the interview between king and jarl was known from oral tradition since it is assumed that there was a continuity of opinion, that the jarl's words had always been considered childish. Such pointed exchanges were therefore the stuff of tradition. They must have been considered saga-worthy and deserving of retention, perhaps as demonstrations of mental or verbal agility. Furthermore, it appears that people not only remembered such incidents but also voiced opinions about how they should be understood. This author believes that Finnr's rejoinders had always been considered "so many childish words," and, by implication, that King Harald's tolerance was viewed as a model of moderation.

This opinion may, however, be the perfect illustration of why authors should not be believed on matters of interpretation. The construction our author puts on the episode seems in fact to be quite eccentric. In the total context of Old Icelandic letters it is evident that stinging repartee is not reported in the sagas because it established a contrast between wise and foolish behavior but because it was amusing and had entertainment value. In particular it was a way for the underdog to even the score when confronted with overpowering force. Episodes in *Bandamanna saga*, *Njáls saga*, and *Ọlkofra páttr* illustrate the point.[8] The response of reader or

---

[8] See ÍF 7, ed. Guðni Jónsson (Reykjavík: Hið íslenzka fornritafélag, 1936), 347-57; ÍF 11, ed. Jón Jóhannesson (Reykjavík: Hið íslenzka

listener would have been to laugh at the honed wit, in this case the insulting comparisons to animals and the escalation from dog to whelp to stallion to mare, with the lurking insinuation that King Harald is getting his sexual satisfaction with a mare.[9]

This interpretive indeterminacy is no less characteristic of the anecdote about King Svend's refuge in a lowly cottage. Here too we find a moralizing stance; we are told that the story serves to illustrate "wisdom and witlessness." But that summation is a little cryptic. It is clear that the woman's comment describing the king as "both halt and cowardly" exemplifies witlessness, but who exemplifies wisdom? *Morkinskinna* (ÍF 23:252; trans., 232) implies that the king ("the man who had previously said less") parries her thrust with the words: "I suspect, old woman, that the king is not cowardly, but neither is he very fortunate in battle." *Heimskringla* makes it quite explicit that the king speaks these words, but is it the king who demonstrates wisdom?[10] Are his words wise because they are moderate? The problem is that he is constrained to be moderate if he wishes to maintain his disguise and protect his identity. Clearly no moral credit accrues from a moderation that is imposed by the circumstances.

In a sequel to the story in *Heimskringla* the king turns out to be anything but moderate.[11] He summons the old couple who

---

fornritafélag, 1950), 91-93; ÍF 12, ed. Einar Ól. Sveinsson (Reykjavík: Hið íslenzka fornritafélag, 1954), 297-305.

[9] The persistent animal references are somewhat reminiscent of the jokes about the nickname of King Harald's father Sigurðr sýr (sow) in "Hreiðars þáttr" (ÍF 23: 163; trans. 178) and "Stúfs þáttr blinda" (ÍF 23: 291; trans., 256).

[10] *Heimskringla*, ed. Bjarni Aðalbjarnarson, ÍF 28 (Reykjavík: Hið íslenzka fornritafélag, 1951), 153. The author of *Fagrskinna* takes the account over from *Morkinskinna*, including the moralizing: *Ágrip af Nóregskonunga sǫgum; Fagrskinna—Nóregs konunga tal*, ed. Bjarni Einarsson, ÍF 29 (Reykjavík: Hið íslenzka fornritafélag, 1985), 270-71.

[11] *Heimskringla*, 155-56.

harbored him to his court, rewards the husband richly, but refuses his request to take his wife with him, offering instead to give him "a much better and wiser wife." The author of *Morkinskinna* does not recount this sequel and may not have been aware of it, although *Heimskringla* (p. 156) states that the story came north to Norway and became famous. We could, as an alternative, imagine that the author of *Morkinskinna* thinks that the husband, by dint of saying nothing, is the one who exemplifies moderation, but since the husband is not mentioned in the *Morkinskinna* version, we cannot be certain that the author even imagined him to be present.

This is not the only difficulty in the passage. The moralizing begins with the remark that the tale is only a "gamans frásǫgn" (a tale for the fun of it) and not at all worth telling except that it makes a moral point. Again, other listeners and readers may have disagreed with this narrow reading and might have emphasized the entertainment value of a story in which a king is demeaned to his face but, under the circumstances, is unable to respond. Such readers could have pointed out that the moralizing option is unclear and perhaps beside the point. What the passage therefore illustrates, once again, in not a clear-cut interpretation but possible avenues for discussion. The author of *Morkinskinna* could have explored these avenues with any number of readers, including the author of *Heimskringla*, who made extensive use of his book. Such discussions would no doubt have produced as much disagreement as agreement.[12]

---

[12] Indicative of the interpretive latitude is a reading of the encounter between King Harald and Finnr jarl offered by an anonymous reader of this paper: "It seems to me that the comedy resides largely in the fact that Finnr is furious at being offered mercy because he has made up his mind to have a heroic death by defying Harald, only to be deprived of it by Harald's determination to spare him whether he wants mercy or not. Harald then humiliates him further by offering him the mercy of a boy and then of a woman. The angrier Finnr becomes, the more ridiculous he seems."

Some years ago Carol Clover theorized about the audience of the sagas, more properly about two audiences, a general audience of listeners, and a highly skilled audience composed of other saga authors. She wrote as follows:

> To concede the literary artistry of the saga is to concede a self-conscious artist, one who presumably studied the work of others with an eye to imitation or improvement. Just as, according to *Egils saga*, Einarr skálaglamm and Egill Skallagrímsson met at the Althing and conversed at length and pleasurably on the subject of poetry, 'a topic they both found enjoyable,' so must saga authors have known one another and formed their own literary society. At some level, each individual saga is a response to the sagas preceding it and a standard for those to come.[13]

We may perhaps pursue Clover's observation one step further. If there was an audience interested in, and able to discuss, literary technique, so too there must have been an audience ready to discuss the significance of a story. That much emerges from the authorial asides in *Morkinskinna*, but we have also seen that not even the asides of one author in a single passage are necessarily reconcilable with one another. How much more divergent would have been the views of several authors in conversation with one another, not to mention the disparities among nonspecialist listeners.

Morkinskinna affords us a quite novel insight into the interpretive perspectives that were to be found in medieval Iceland. These perspectives attach to individual episodes and do not embrace whole sagas. We may bear in mind, however, that an important genre of early Icelandic prose fiction was also episodic. I refer to the so-called *þættir*, the little stories about adventurous Icelanders, often in their encounters with foreign kings. These

---

[13] Carol J. Clover, *The Medieval Saga* (Ithaca: Cornell University Press, 1982), 188-204, here 200-1.

stories seem to lend themselves particularly well to generalizing interpretation. If episodes in *Morkinskinna*, which may be regarded as the chief repository of Icelandic *þættir*, were subject to interpretation, we can hardly doubt that interpretation was readily practiced. In addition, it would perhaps be artificial to argue that episodes were interpreted but whole sagas were not. Nor is it likely that interpretation was restricted to an elite composed of saga authors. When the author of *Morkinskinna* states that such and such "has been the view of everyone ever since," he is in all likelihood not referring to a literary clique but is suggesting that common listeners and common readers had an opinion as well.

In the twentieth century we took to writing books about the Icelandic sagas, sometimes large, interpretive books. We may well have done so with some hesitation, because the sagas do not offer much interpretive guidance, and we may feel that our efforts bring extraneous categories to bear. We are perhaps haunted by the suspicion that our approaches have no foothold in medieval Icelandic thinking, that Icelanders in the thirteenth century would have found our surmises strange and irrelevant, for example, our peculiarly inconclusive readings of *Hrafnkels saga*. But perhaps the authorial reflections cited above from *Morkinskinna* will be sufficient to convince us that thirteenth-century Icelanders would have recognized the interpretive impulse. They too could ponder the moral of the story. They may in fact have found our speculations no stranger than those they had heard from their countrymen and contemporaries. They would have disagreed with us of course, but perhaps no more than they would have disagreed with their fellow readers in their own day.

A Voyage Round Egill Skalla-Grímsson

George Clark

I owe my title to John Mortimer, but dedicate this paper on Egill and his saga to the memory of Fred Amory, a wise and generous friend for more than half a century.

The "sagas of Icelanders" or "family sagas" create a theatre that allows no soliloquies and precludes a direct view into the inner lives of the actors. A usually impassive narrator, rather like a chorus, comments briefly on actors, actions, and public opinion or report. Those narrators remind us frequently that the actors in the drama are historical persons with whom the Icelandic audience has a real connexion and that the actions took place in historical time even though modern scholarship may object that invention has played an important role in the sagas' making. The narrators' interventions leave to the audience the major task of understanding the actors and actions as real persons in a still familar world. Egill Skalla-Grímsson ranks among the most intricate and fascinating characters represented in the sagas.[1] His adventures abroad occupy most of the saga and dominate critical assessments of his character, but we do not see Egill in full until his final return to Iceland. The part of the saga from that return to his last meeting with his only surviving son, Þorsteinn, completes the development or revelation of Egill as a "rounded" character. Only in the familial, social, economic, and political context of Iceland can we finally discern the historical-

---

[1] Throughout I have cited *Egils saga*, ed. Bjarni Einarsson (London: Viking Society, 2003) simply by chapter (ch. or chs.) but where the chapters are long and the reference to a brief passage, also by page. Since many libraries will have *Egils saga Skalla-Grímsonar*, ed. Sigurður Nordal, Íslenzk fornrit 2 (Reykjavík: Hið íslenzka fornrifélag, 1933), I have added his chapter numbers (Nordal, ch. or chs.) in parentheses where they differ from Bjarni Einarsson's. All translations are my own.

legendary figure the saga creates as a whole person. In Iceland, Egill proves intensely loyal to his family even when that loyalty runs counter to his immediate desire not to survive the death of his most-loved child or his earlier bias against his least-loved. And we recognize this Egill from a past in which his love of violence, revenge, plunder and the composition of poems celebrating his skills and success dominates the story.

Egill and his popular and handsome brother, Þórólfr, seem to desire the same woman, but Þórólfr, the older, has the advantage of success in the worlds of trade and piracy, while Egill has only his youthful promise. Þórólfr asks for Ásgerðr and, as an appropriate match, wins her. Some time after the wedding, Þórólfr and Egill set out on a Viking cruise culminating in a visit to the court of the English king, Athelstan, who just then badly needs good warriors.[2] Egill, though disappointed in love, attempts to assure Þórólfr's life and deeply mourns the battle-field death of his brother and rival. This implicit *psychomachia* between brotherly and romantic love, and indeed Egill's capacity for love and his loyalty to his family become central to the saga's representation of its complex hero.

Halvdan Koht acutely remarked that Egill's story "is the study of a character in action, constantly revealing new traits of a highly fascinating individuality and, with great art, uniting them in a portrait of strong psychological effect."[3] Jónas Kristjánsson sums up on Egill in greater detail:

> the call to adventure out in the world rings in Egill's ears and is slow to fade. Óðinn has bestowed on him the craft of poetry that brings him relief after the death of brother and sons. Under his cloak he dreams of the lovely lady who had been the wife of his dashing brother, and in the end he wins her. He appears a mixture of god-given

---

2 Ch. 50.
3 Halvdan Koht, *The Old Norse Saga* (New York: American-Scandinavian Foundation, 1931), 71.

inspiration, human sensitivity, and brutish coarseness and greed."[4]

Kristjánsson concludes that such a complex characterization implies that a literary genius like Snorri Sturluson must have created this version of Egill Skalla-Grímsson,[5] but the saga cloaks its authorship and requires us to understand Egill from its materials, narrative action, dialogue, the reactions of other characters to him, and his relationships with them.

Theodore Andersson maintained the sagas were "written against excess: excessive self-seeking (*Egils saga*). . ."[6] Andersson's main example of this "excess," Egill's uncle, Þórólfr Kveld-Ulfsson, has a major role in the saga's opening but seems more of a parallel to his other nephew, Þórólfr Skallagrímsson, than to Egill. The earlier Þórólfr dies in a conflict with Haraldr hárfagri ("fairhair"), in part because of Þórólfr's concern to remain own man even as he enjoys the position as one of the king's men, a subordinate.[7] But Þórólfr's brother, Grímr (later called Skalla-Grímr for his bald head), impolitely declines subordination to King Haraldr, and with his father and their allies avenges Þórólfr's death, and escapes to Iceland where he becomes one of the first settlers.[8] In the next generation, Egill's brother, Þórólfr (named for his uncle) gets on well with Eiríkr blóðöx ("bloodaxe") and later subordinates himself to the authority of the English king Athelstan. As a good follower, he accepts Athelstan's plan of battle which Egill predicts he will often regret. The first Þórólfr's independence becomes part of the pattern leading to his death, but the second Þórólfr's soldierly

---

[4] Jónas Kristjánson, *Eddas and Sagas: Iceland's Medieval Literature*, trans. Peter Foote (Reykjavík: Hið íslenska bókmenntafélag, 1988), 269-70.
[5] Jónas Kristjánson, 269.
[6] Theodore Andersson, "The Displacement of the Heroic Ideal in the Family Sagas," *Speculum* 45.4 (1970): 575-93, at 588.
[7] The crucial point comes in chapter 16: Þórólfr refuses to join the king's court under Haraldr's constant surveillance. Þórólfr has challenged his superior.
[8] Chs. 25, 27-28.

obedience proves fatal. Having seen his brother's recklessness in the first day of battle, Egill wants to alter the royal strategy so that he and Þórólfr will fight together—presumably giving Egill a chance to protect his brother or die with him.[9] After the battle of Vinheiðr or Brunanburh, Athelstan promises Egill rank and wealth to stay in England, but Egill gains Athelstan's permission to go to Norway because of his obligations to support Þórólfr's children, if any survive, and his right to claim his inheritance in the event Þórólfr died without heirs. As they part in friendship, the king insists ever more urgently that Egill quickly return to England, but Egill answers that his return is "very likely." When the king restates his wish, Egill asserts he must return, but a fragment of the oldest manuscript adds his condition that binding obligations might prevent him.[10] After winning his brother's widow, Egill returns to Iceland where his father, now growing old, is very glad to see him. For some years thereafter, Egill occupies himself entirely in the work of the farm at Borg apparently without a thought about the position and wealth he might have held in England.[11] When Gunnhild's spell draws Egill back to England, he seems to rationalize his restlessness and desire to travel to his wish to visit Athelstan and collect on those generous promises. His voyage ends in York where Arinbjörn and Egill's poem, *Höfuðlausn*, save his life despite Eiríkr's wrath and Gunnhildr's witchcraft.[12] Granted his life, Egill rides south with Arinbjörn; Athelstan again offers Egill a position and wealth, but after promising to return once his affairs are in order, Egill never comes back to England.[13]

True to the family tradition, mutual hostility marks most of Egill's long relationship with a king of Norway, in this case Haraldr's son, Eiríkr blóðöx ("bloodaxe"); like his father, Skalla-Grímr, Egill avenges his losses on his royal enemy and survives to continue a line of independent and prominent landholders in

---

[9] Chs. 53-54.
[10] Ch. 54 and 83, note b.
[11] Ch. 55, at 83-86.
[12] Chs. 61-63 (Nordal, chs. 59-61).
[13] Ch. 64 (Nordal, ch. 62).

Iceland.[14] Andersson notes that both Þórólfr, Egill's uncle, and Egill himself feud with a Norwegian king, but claims that the "eminently attractive" Þórólfr perishes while but the "eminently unattractive Egill . . . Þórolfr's antithesis . . . survives," but "gains nothing in stature; he remains a surly, aggressive, and acquisitive giant."[15] In this reading, Egill ultimately failed because of his self-centered and excessive desire for personal gain and dominance. Kennedy regards Egill not as a failure in life but as one who survived into irrelevance while remaining an object of nostalgic admiration. Kennedy suggests Egill regarded the office of a *goði* "as part of the developing legal and administrative structure of a society which was increasing ordered—and increasingly uncongenial to Egill whose splendid, incorrigible, and sometimes anarchic spirit dominates so much of the saga."[16] In a similar vein, Harris claims that " the saga clearly treats Egill as the last of an epoch. With his old age, the theme of opposition to the Norwegian throne is allowed to lapse, but in the purely Icelandic setting of the close of the saga it remains clear that the old man is the last of his kind."[17] The saga (and this paper) closes with a brief account of Egill's grandson, Skúli Þorsteinsson, whose career triumphantly reprises Egill's.[18]

Byock accurately notes that once Egill has returned to Iceland, the saga "turns from the wanderings of an epic poet and mercenary warrior" to the typical concerns of the family sagas including

---

[14] After Eiríkr has denied Egill justice in Ásgerðr's inheritance, Egill kills both Ketill höðr, probably Eiríkr's illegitimate son and Rögnvaldr, a legitimate son of Eiríkr and Gunnhildr, see chs. 58 and 59, at 94-7. See Nordal, ch. 56 and 57, at 161 and 170.

[15] Andersson, "Displacement," 578.

[16] John Kennedy, "The *goðar* in *Egils saga Skalla-Grímsson*," *Words and Wordsmiths: A Volume for H. L. Roger*, ed. Geraldine Barnes et al. (Sydney: University of Sydney, 1989), 70-76, at 76.

[17] Joseph Harris, "Saga as Historical Novel," *Structure and Meaning in Old Norse Literature*, ed. John Lindow, Lars Lönnroth, and Gerd Wolfgang Weber, Viking Collection 3 (Odense: Odense University, 1986), 187-219, at 213.

[18] Ch. 89, at 182 (Nordal, 87).

conflicts and their resolution, power politics, the arranging of marriages and alliances.[19] Neither a social misfit nor a kind of living antique or memento of days gone by, Egill acts effectively within the context of Icelandic society when the island was fully settled and the competition for productive land intense; his actions link his own moment in history to the narrator's present time.

In his role as an Icelandic landowner and head of a family, Egill acts decisively to assure the futures of his surviving children. He makes good marriages for his step-daughter and his daughters and resolves a dispute over land so as to give his son Þorsteinn a significant advantage over a dangerous local rival, a son of Egill's contemporary, Önundr sjóni ("seer," "clearsighted"). Egill's father, Skalla-Grímr, gave Önundr's father, Áni, a part of his original claim of land in Iceland, but in the third generation, Áni's descendent attempts to encroach on valuable pastureland belonging to Skalla-Grímr's family.

As Egill settles ever more definitively into Iceland and his role as an independent and influential landowner, we see the same man in another light and see more of him and in him. In Iceland Egill first appears as a wilful, unruly but gifted child, abroad he becomes a savage and reckless viking, a lover of plunder and tangible wealth (who extravagantly places two golden arm rings on his brother's body), and as a poet home again in Iceland Egill's greatest poem expresses his grief at his greatest loss and becomes his consolation for that loss. Profound grief arises from the loss of what was deeply loved; love makes us vulnerable to sorrow. In the course of the saga Egill mourns his brother's death, his apparently unrequited love, and finally the death of his most loved child and expresses those griefs in his poetry. We come to see Egill as intensely loyal to his friends, his family and a man capable of love, not just for the woman in his life, but also for his brother, his step daughter, the child his brother never saw, and his own children. He takes considerable effort to assure the success of his least loved child and

---

[19] Jesse L. Byock, *Feud in the Icelandic Saga* (Berkeley and Los Angeles: University of California, 1982), 196-97.

at the last a warm, even loving, relationship as father and son replaces their former coolness.

At home in an Iceland, the wild viking acts as a good, indeed exemplary, stepfather should. Grímr, a man destined to become *lögsögumaðr* or "law-speaker," asks to marry Þórdís Þórólfsdóttir. We are told that Egill loved Þórdís, his late brother's daughter—and the daughter of Ásgerðr, Egill's wife—no less than he loved his own children.[20] Near the end of his life, when Ásgerðr has died, Egill hands the farm at Borg over to Þorsteinn and retires to Mossfell where Þórdís—the person he loved most of those still living—and Grímr were settled.[21] In Þórdís, Egill could have have seen both the image of the brother he loved and the woman loved and with whom he shared a large part of his life. Egill accepts Grímr's request for Þórdís knowing Grímr to be rich, influential, and well able to support Þórdís properly and a good man who will not, therefore, abuse her. And with this, Egill, an avid lover of wealth, transfers to Þórdís her paternal inheritance. This property would, of course be Þórdís's own, not her husband's. She is a very fortunate young woman to be so well provided for by a stepfather. Though Grimstad calls him "a miser," Egill's desire to gain and keep, illustrated by his refusal to share Æthelstan's two chests of silver, proves less strong than his love for Þórdís.[22] Egill can be generous: he gives Arinbjörn two gold rings for sucessfully persuading Eiríkr to hear Egill's panegyric rather than immediately executing the poet. The panegyric persuaded Eiríkr to let Egill leave York alive. Egill also placed two gold rings on his brother's body after the battle of Vinheiðr or Brunanburh, no miserly act. In a later adventure, a rich and eccentric old man, Álfr, gives Egill a night's hospitality and abundant information. Egill repays his host with a fur jacket, that makes a full-length cloak for the smaller man.[23]

---

[20] Ch. 79, at 144 (Nordal, 77).

[21] Ch. 81, at 167 (Nordal, 79).

[22] Kaaren Grimstad, "The Giant as Heroic Model: the Case of Egill and Starkaðr," *Scandinavian Studies* 48.3 (1976): 284-98, at 294.

[23] Ch. 63 (Nordal, ch. 61) and ch. 76 (Nordal, ch. 75).

Egill maintained his estate, according to the narrator, magnificantly because he had both the necessary wealth, and a good disposition for living largely.[24] In this spirit of confident estate management, Egill bought a lot of building timber when a trading ship from Norway came in and ordered that it be brought to his estate. The small eight oared boat which was to transport the timber was swamped in in rough water with the loss of all hands including Egill's favourite son who had asked to go along. When he finds and buries his son's body, Egill's dress includes imported cotton, his splendid and well-armed appearance at the assembly (where his sole surviving son faces a dangerous lawsuit) also attests to his willingness to use his wealth.[25] After Þorgerðr has persuaded him to abandon his suicidal plan, Egill sees his daughter off with gifts as befits a generous host.[26]

Shortly after Þordís's marriage, Óláfr pái ("peacock," for his fine dress), asks for Þorgerðr in marriage and Egill agrees because he knows Óláfr well and realizes this was an excellent match. *Egils saga* reports that the new couple went home and then names their children and gives some details regarding their lives.[27] *Laxdæla saga* complicates this plain tale: Óláfr and his father ask for Þorgerðr at the assembly. Egill approves the match, but leaves the decision to Þorgerðr who objects strenuously saying that Óláfr is a maidservant's son. Egill argues that Óláfr's mother was the daughter of a king and thus very well born though enslaved by misfortune.[28] Þorgerðr seems noncommittal; Egill reports to Höskuldr and Óláfr how matters stand. Óláfr then proposes to talk with Þorgerðr personally and his father agrees. After a long day's private conversation between the two, Egill is sent for and Þorgerðr

[24] Ch. 80: "Bú hafði hann [Egill] rausnarsamligt, því að fé skorti eigi. Hann hafði ok gott skaplyndi til þess," 154 (Nordal, ch. 78, 257).
[25] Ch. 80, at 145 (Nordal, ch. 78) and ch. 83, at 172 (Nordal, ch 81, 283-84).
[26] Ch. 80, at 154 (Nordal, ch. 78, at 257).
[27] Ch. 80, at 144 (Nordal, ch. 78, at 242).
[28] *Laxdæla saga*, ed. Einar Ól. Sveinsson, Íslenzk fornrit 5 (Reykjavík: Hið íslenska fornritfélag, 1934), ch. 23, at 63-5.

leaves the decision to her father, who, as she knows, has already agreed to the match.[29] Or in short, she answers "yes," but indirectly and with appropriate decorum. Þorgerðr's modest conduct in *Laxdæla* echoes her mother's in *Egla*: Ásgerðr did not respond directly to Egill's proposal but left the matter up to her father (who owed Egill's family for their support) and Arinbjörn, Egill's best friend. Very possibly the author of *Laxdæla*, in which Þorgerðr has an important role, knew the story of *Egla* and modelled the daughter's conduct in this matter on her mother's. Egill gives his last unmarried daughter, Bera, to Özurr Eyvindarson, a man with good family connections since his brother was a *goði*.[30] Egill seems to have made a good match for his last single daughter, as a good father should.

That last marriage brings the story to Egill's favourite son, Böðvarr—even good parents have favourites. The brief narrative leading from the death of Egill's favourite child to the composition of the greatest of the poems attributed to him falls into three sections or even acts that create a sense of Egill's place within his family. Though surprising, the figure of Egill emerging from this dramatic scene resonates with earlier indications of his inner life and the response of others to him. Act one: learning that a boat with Böðvarr and six of his servants has been lost in Borgarfjord, Egill finds and buries his son's body, returns home, and enters his bedcloset. Act two: *in italics*, the events at Borg before Þorgerðr's arrival which flows into her appearance and entry into the house at Borg. Act three: Þorgerðr's risky plan which turns the action toward its denouement.[31]

Þann dag spurði Egill þessi tíðendi ok þegar reið hann at leita líkanna; hann fann rétt lík Böðvars. Tók hann þat upp ok setti í kné sér ok reið með út í Digranes til haugs

29 *Laxdæla saga* ch. 23, at 65.
30 *Kristni saga*, ed. Sigurgeir Steingrímsson et al., *Biskupa sögur*, Íslenzk fornrit 15-17, 3 vols. in 4 (Reykjavík: Hið íslenska fornritfélag, 2003), 1.2: 1-48, at 8, ch. 2 at 8.
31 Ch. 80, at 145-46 (Nordal, ch. 78, at 244-45).

Skalla-Gríms. Hann lét opna hauginn ok lagði Böðvar þar
niðr hjá Skalla-Grími; var síðan aptr lokinn haugrinn ok
var eigi fyrr lokit en um dagsetrs skeið. Eptir þat reið Egill
heim til Borgar, ok er hann kom heim þá gekk hann þegar
til lokrekkju þeirar er hann var vanr at sofa í. Hann lagðist
niðr ok skaut fyrir loku; engi þorði at krefja hann máls.

En svá er sagt þá er þeir settu Böðvar niðr at Egill var
búinn: hosan var strengð fast at beini, hann hafði
fustanskyrtil rauðan, þröngvan uphlutinn ok láz at síðu.
En þat er sögn manna at hann þrútnaði svá at kyrtillinn
rifnaði af honum of svá hosurnar.

En eptir um daginn lét Egill ekki upp lokrekkjuna; hann
hafði þá ok engan mát né drykk. Lá hann þar þann dag ok
nóttina eptir; engi maðr þorði at mæla við hann.

*En inn þriðja morgin þegar er lýsti þá lét Ásgerðr skjóta hesti
undir mann - reið sá sem ákafligast vestr í Hjarðarholt - ok lét
segja Þorgerði þessi tíðendi öll saman, ok var þat um nónskeið er
hann kom þar. Hann sagði ok þat með at Ásgerðr hafði sent henni
orð at koma sem fyrst suðr til Borgar.*

*Þorgerðr lét þegar söðla sér hest ok fylgðu henni tveir menn; riðu
þau um kveldit ok nóttina til þess er þau kómu til Borgar; gekk
Þorgerðr þegar í eldahús. Ásgerðr heilsaði henni ok spurði hvárt
þau hefði nóttverð etit. Þorgerðr segir hátt:*

"Engvan hefi ek náttverð haft, en engvan mun ek fyrir en
við Freyju. Kann ek mér eigi betri ráð en faðir minn; vil
ek ekki lifa eptir föður minn ok bróður."

Hon gekk at lokhvílunni ok kallaði: "Faðir, lok up
hurðunni; vil ek at vit færim eina leið bæði."

Egill spretti frá lokunni; gekk Þorgerðr up í hvilugolfit ok lét loku fyrir hurðina, hon lagðist niðr í aðra rekkju er þar var.

Þá mælti Egill: "Vel gerðir þú, dóttir, er þú vil fylgja feðr þínum; mikla ást hefir þú synt við mig. Hver ván er ek muna vilja lifa við harm þenna?"

Egill heard the news the same day and immediately set out to search for the bodies; he soon found Böðvarr's body. He picked it up and laid it across his knees and rode out to Digranes to Skalla-Grímr's grave mound. He had the mound opened and lay Böðvarr down next to Skalla-Grímr; then the grave mound was closed and it was nightfall by the time it was closed. After that Egill rode home to Borg, and when he got there, he immediately went to the bedcloset where he usually slept. He lay down and shot the bolt. No one dared to ask him to speak.

And it's said that when they put Böðvarr down, that Egill was dressed like this: his hose were tight, he was wearing red cotton tunic tight at the top and laced on the sides. And what people say is that that he swelled up so that his tunic ripped loose and his hose too.

The next day, Egill didn't open the bed-closet; he had taken no food or drink then. He lay there that day and the following night; no one dared to speak to him.

The third day, as soon as it was light, Ásgerðr quickly had a man horsed—he galloped west to Hjarðarholt as hard as he coul—and ordered him to tell Þorgerðr the whole story—and he got there about midday. And with all the news, he told Þorgerðr that Ásgerðr sent word that she was to come south to Borg at once.

Þorgerðr immediately had a horse saddled for herself and two men accompanied her; they rode that afternoon and into the night until

they reached Borg. Þorgerðr went immediately into the main room.
Ásgerðr welcomed her and asked if they had eaten supper. Þorgerðr
said loudly

"I have not eaten any supper and I won't eat any until I
do so with Freyja. I don't know a better course for myself
than my father's; I don't want to survive my father and
brother."

She went to the bedcloset and said "Father, unlock the
door, I intend that both of us should follow the same
path." Egill unlocked the door; Þorgerðr went in and
bolted the door behind her; she lay down in the other bed
there.

The Egill said "you do well, daughter, when you wish to
follow your father, you have shown great love for me.
How can I be expected to live with such a loss?"

The first act opens with direct narrative in chronological order,
this, then this, . . . and then that. Although Egill has just buried his
favorite son, the story gives no immediate indication of the depths
of emotion he feels, and feels in well-noted isolation. Egill had the
grave mound opened, but the servants who dug in to the mound
exist only in the pronoun *þeir* ("þá er þeir settu Böðvar niðr"
["when they laid Böðvarr down"]). After Egill places Böðvarr's
body in the mound, it is closed—*var síðan aptr lokat* ("afterwards it
was closed again,")—but the passive construction makes the
servants invisible and leaves Egill alone. Nothing seems done in
haste though we hear that on reaching home, "he went
immediately"—*gekk hann þegar*—to his *lokrekkja* or bed-closet
(lockable from within). Egill's self-imposed isolation admits only
the non-company of *engi* ("nobody,") "no one" dared try to
communicate with him. The words *loka* ("to close or lock"), *lok-*
("lockable-"), *loka* ("a bolt for locking a door"), and *lúka* ("to
lock"—with *upp* to unlock) become a leitmotif in this brief
narrative, beginning with the emphatic doubling of the closing of

Skalla-Grím's (now also Böðvarr's) grave-mound—"var síðan aptr lokinn haugrinn ok var eigi fyrr *lokit* en . . ." ("afterwards the grave mound was closed and it was [nightfall]. . . before it was closed . . ."). Thereupon "gekk hann [Egill] þegar til *lok*rekkju . . . ok skaut fyrir *lok*u": he went at once to his lockable bedcloset and shot the bolt. Egill's locked bedcloset and Böðvarr's closed grave mound begin to merge. When Þorgerðr arrives she addresses Egill: "*lúk* upp hurðunni" ("unlock the door"); then she enters the bedcloset and "lét *loku* fyrir hurðina" ("put the bar before the door"). Egill's father and son inhabit one closed space, he and his daughter another.[32]

On his arrival and self immolation in his bedcloset, the intensity of Egill's unvoiced but unmistakeable emotion shocks his household into a silence like his own. The middle of act one turns back in time to describe Egill's dress at the time of the burial; that description is introduced *svá er sagt* ("it is said") which does not create the sense of an individualised reporter. In apparent isolation, Egill places Böðvarr's body in the gravemound. Then the saga's neutral voice informs us that it's reported—*þat er sögn manna* ("what people say")—is that Egill's body swelled up so much that his tunic ripped apart and so did his hose.[33] That distant *sögn manna* leaves Egill alone in his grief; common report offers no human fellowship. The end of the first act dispassionately reports that Egill took no food or drink that or the next day and as a coda repeats the theme

---

[32] At the 2012 Saga Conference in Aarhus, Denmark, a young woman scholar suggested the parallelism between the grave-mound and bedcloset. I'm grateful for the suggestion. One might suppose that Þorgerðr was conceived in that same bedcloset.

[33] The prose narrative of *Völsunga saga* reports that Sigurðr's body swelled up so that his mail shirt split when Byrnhildr announced her intention to die and quotes a verse from the now lost part of the Poetic Edda making clear this swelling was caused by Sigurðr's grief, see *Fornaldarsögur norðurlanda*, ed. Guðni Jónsson and Bjarni Vilhjálmsson, 3 vols. (Reyjavík: Forni, 1943) 1: 64-65 (ch. 29). In *Beowulf* line 2401 the hero is *torne gebolgen* where *torn* seems to combine anger and grief and *gebolgen* may imply a psychological rather than physical reaction.

of impregnable silence. No one dared to speak to the unspeaking Egill who, as a three-year-old child described himself as *sögull*, "talkative, loquacious."[34]

However, *sögull* Egill has fallen strikingly silent on other occasions. He brooded wordlessly until Æthelstan compensated him generously for the death of his brother, Þórólfr. Not long thereafter, Arinbjörn had to persuade a strangely withdrawn, sombre, and silent Egill to speak up and admit the cause of his distant and uncommunicative behaviour, of which more later.

A sense of general urgency and anxiety pervades the second act (in italics here). All the actors share that urgency save, of course, Egill himself. As the eye of the storm, he remains fixed as everything else swirls around him. As soon as it lightens—in the white dawn—Ásgerðr at once has a man, that is a servant, horsed; we hear that he rode hard, if not wildly, all the way to Hjarðarholt where Þorgerðr and Óláfr pái are living. Ásgerðr's urgency might cynically be attributed to an awareness that a widow however rich may be vulnerable rather than love for her husband, but the servant rides hard all the way; servants may follow orders diligently while watched, but out of sight may slack off. Not in this case. His alacrity bespeaks the servant's loyalty and devotion (and by implication, the feeling of Egill's servants for him) just as Ásgerðr's urgency suggests her feelings about Egill. And indeed, the servant's loyalty predisposes the audience to see Ásgerðr's motivation as an expression of love and loyalty. Clearly Ásgerðr has made the right choice in sending for Þorgerðr whom the saga has described as *vitr ok heldr skapstór* "intelligent and possessed of a powerful personality" which power she does not assert for trifles.[35] When the servant reports the news to Þorgerðr, we discover that his commission included a request that she come to Borg right away. To review a few breakneck-paced sentences, we go from first light to the mounting of a messenger and his hard riding then back to his

---

[34] Ch. 31 where Egill's poem celebrates a gift of silent sea-shell given *söglum Agli*, "to talkative Egill."

[35] Ch. 80, at 144 (Nordal, ch 78).

commission and then forward to his arrival then back once more to his further commission and then to his statement of Ásgerðr's request that Þorgerðr come at once. The breathless narrative style, disrupted, jerky, back and forth, but energetic and compelling conveys the urgency and anxiety of the day's events. As if sharing the general anxiety, the usually impassive narrator seems affected by the sense of a desperate crisis and tumbles out the story like one overwhelmed by the matter that must be conveyed.

From the moment Þorgerðr enters the action until she speaks, the disconnected style gives way to a chronological this, then this, and finally that, but the events powerfully continue that sense of desperate urgency. On hearing the news and Ásgerðr's request, Þorgerðr immediately has a horse saddled and rides off accompanied by two servants. Unlike the messenger, they ride into failing light but continue until nightfall to Borg. Of course, in an Icelandic midsummer, the sun sets only briefly, but in the long twilight shadows cast by knolls and trees pose a hazard to riders. Since Þorgerðr dispatched the servant at first light, and Böðvarr's grave was not closed until near nightfall, the season is not midsummer. To reach Borg, or leave it, a rider must find the way through the marshes that give Skalla-Grimr's descendents the collective name *Mýramenn*. Egill arrived late at the party where he composed the first poems the saga attributes to him because Skalla-Grímr didn't want the unruly three year old at a drinking party. Egill then followed the rest but had some difficulty finding the way when his sight line to the other party was blocked by trees or knolls.[36] The messenger rode *ákafligast* ("very hard, furiously, recklessly") through all this to Hjarðarholt in half a day. Þorgerðr and her servants cover the distance in the second half of that day and finish riding through the marshes as night falls. Even in broad daylight, those who ride hard risk serious injury or death.[37] When she arrives at Borg,

---

[36] Ch. 31.

[37] A recent Canadian study indicates horseback riding causes more than three times as many injuries as motorcycle riding (.49 injuries per 1000 hours of riding versus .14 injuries per 1000 hours). "The Globe and Mail"

Þorgerðr goes at once—*þegar*—to the main room where Ásgerðr asks if she and her servants have eaten supper. Past that *þegar* nothing suggests an overpowering need for haste. Quite another mood dominates as the saga audience must realize that Þorgerðr risks her life on her ability to divert Egill from his suicidal course of inaction; she has promised they will both go the same way.

The first two acts of this passage have no direct discourse; the distant narrator reports the events and what was said. No one dares to speak to Egill; and the self-effacing narrator reports for the implied community—*svá er sagt, þat er sögn manna*—("it's said," "what people say is that . . ."). In this third act, direct speech dominates: Ásgerðr greets Þorgerðr, Þorgerðr replies. Then Þorgerðr addresses Egill directly, and Egill recognizes the depth of her love for him and justifies as best he can his desire for death. This act begins as Ásgerðr welcomes Þorgerðr and asks if she and her servants have eaten supper; Þorgerðr announces, loudly enough that Egill can hear, her intention not to eat until she can sup with the goddess Freyja, that is to starve herself into another world, and Egill hears that statement. Then she addresses him directly saying she wants them both to travel the same road. We must guess that she has another road in mind than the one Egill assumes. He praises Þorgerðr for her determination to follow her father and adds "mikla ást hefir þú synt við mig" ("you have shown great love for me") and she has. If her deception fails and Egill continues his fast, Þorgerðr can hardly withdraw from her commitment to die with him. As if aware that his sorrow for the loss of one much-loved child will lead to the death of another, Egill defends his decision against an unexpressed challenge: *hver ván er ek muna vilja lifa við harm þenna?* "how can I be expected to wish to live with this sorrow?" When he first entered that locked bedcloset, his decision seemed to need no defence and to preclude any request for explanation. Now Þorgerðr's announced determination to follow her father challenges his purpose, imposes a limit on his freedom of action. His rhetorical

(Monday, September 24), A3. In this study, about 7% of injuries sustained in horseback riding resulted in death.

question—"how can I be expected to live with this sorrow?" sounds defensive, even apologetic. The expectation (*ván*) Egill refers to implies a recognition of other peoples' hopes, expectations, and desires.

Þorgerðr's deception, if it is hers rather than Ásgerðr's, succeeds rather easily because Egill, we may suppose, realises that dying of grief for Böðvarr now means he will also lose Þorgerðr, as if he were to avenge the death on one child on another. Egill's position resembles Hreðel's in *Beowulf*—to avenge one son's death on another would simply double the loss to the family.[38] The ensuing poem, *Sonatorrek*, a lament for the loss of his sons, compares Egill's kingroup to a fence in which the sea has broken a gap. Böðvarr's death weakens the whole fence, the family.[39] And Þorgerðr, who is part of that fence, bears no responsibility for Böðvarr's death. After a period of silence in the bed-closet, Egill asks what Þorgerðr is chewing. She answers that she is chewing *söl* ("seaweed") in order to shorten her life, but *söl* in modern usage clearly means an edible seaweed.[40] When Egill asks if it is bad for people she asserts that it is *allillt*, "very bad." The sea weed makes them both thirsty and Þorgerðr calls for water. When Egill hears he has drunk milk, not water, he bites a mouthfull from the horn itself. Þorgerðr's claim that both of them have been tricked completes, we may suppose, a virtuous deception. Þorgerðr knew the seaweed was harmless though salty and the cup contained milk not water.

This brief episode in Egill's long history powerfully attests to the loyalty and devotion to him of his wife, daughter, and an

---

[38] *Klaeber's Beowulf*, ed. R. D. Fulk, Robert E. Bjork, and John D. Niles (Toronto: University of Toronto Press, 2008) ll. 2435-43; for an accurate translation, see *Beowulf*, ed. and trans. Michael J. Swanton (Manchester: Manchester University, 1978) and the notes on this passage in both.

[39] Ch. 80, verse 6 (Nordal, ch. 78 verse 6).

[40] Ch. 80, at 145-6; see Arni Böðvarsson, *Íslensk orðabók*, second edition (Reykjavík: Menningarsjóðs, 1985), and Richard Cleasby and Gudbrand Vigfusson, *An Icelandic English-English Dictionary* (Oxford: Oxford University, 1957), s.v. *söl*.

unspecified servant implying the loyalty of his servants generally. Egill's care in accepting marriage proposals for his daughters and step-daughter demonstrates his family loyalty to them. He concerns himself to see these young women have as secure a future as an uncertain world affords. Egill's last great action in the public sphere manifests his loyalty to his least-favored child, Þorsteinn. In a very serious case at law, Egill intervenes decisively on Þorsteinn's behalf. Bredsdorff refers to this episode claiming that "in a struggle between his sons and those of a friend, which was about to end in a settlement, [Egill] uses his power to have it his own way."[41] Bredsdorff believes this episode, like Egill's childhood killing of an older boy, illustrates Egill's desire for personal freedom even at the cost of the freedom of others.[42] In fact, the lawsuit pits Egill's only surviving son, Þorsteinn, against, Steinarr, one of Önundr's sons. Önundr, an older contemporary and friend of Egill's, was in youth a man of extraordinary strength whom common report called a berserker, a negative term the sagas rarely apply to Icelanders.[43] No settlement was in prospect in the case at Þorsteinn's choice. The event makes clear that Þorsteinn expected and depended on Egill's intervention in a dispute that could, and in the event did, expand Þorsteinn's power, prestige, and wealth at the expense of a rival.

Egill intervenes at the assembly to give Þorsteinn an initial victory which leads on to local dominance of Skalla-Grímr's descendants.[44] The story of Egill's support of Þorsteinn follows shortly after the latter's introduction into the saga which notes explicitly that Egill did not love Þorsteinn much and that Þorsteinn cared little for his father, but had a close relationship with his mother. A brief narrative illustrates both points and gives Egill some cause for annoyance with Þorsteinn: without asking leave, Ásgerðr gives Þorsteinn a long silk gown, a gift of Arinbjörn to

---

[41] Thomas Bredsdorff, *Chaos and Love: The Philosophy of the Icelandic Family Sagas*, trans. John Tucker (Copenhagen: Museum Tusculanum, University of Copenhagen 2001), 23.

[42] Bredsdorff, *Chaos and Love*, 23-24.

[43] Ch. 69 (Nordal, ch. 67).

[44] Ch. 84 (Nordal, ch 82).

Egill, to wear at the general assembly. The trailing gown is soiled
with mud at the assembly. Much later Egill discovers the damage;
Ásgerðr tells him the truth and Egill answers with a verse
complaining he lacks a proper heir since his son has betrayed him
living rather than waiting until he was dead.[45]

The conflict between Þorsteinn Egilsson and Steinarr
Önundarson pits members of the third generation of Icelanders
against each other in contrast to the friendships and cooperation in
the first generations. Þorsteinn's grandfather, Skalla-Grímr, gave
part of his original landclaim to Steinarr's grandfather; that gift
became the farm Ánabrekka.[46] When he takes over the farm,
Steinarr grazes his cattle on a particularly rich pasture belonging to
Þorsteinn and persists despite repeated warnings. Eventually
Þorsteinn kills two slaves whom Steinarr has instructed to keep his
cattle on Þorsteinn's pasture. Steinarr brings a suit against Þorsteinn
for the two killings, a charge that might lead to outlawry and
permanent exile or death for Þorsteinn.[47] At this point, Ásgerðr has
died and Egill has given Borg and apparently his *goðorð* and
authority to Þorsteinn and retires to Mosfell to live with his
stepdaughter Þordís (the living person he loves most) and her
husband, Grímr. John Kennedy accurately notes that we hear only
of Egill's *goðorð* as he gives it to Þorsteinn, nor was Skallagrímr
called a *goði*.[48] When messengers from Þorsteinn arrive at Mosfell,
Egill affects indifference, but privately inquires closely into the
matter and into the support Steinarr has gathered for the
prosecution. When the messengers return, their report pleases
Þorsteinn, but we have to guess that Egill has promised his support
in the coming lawsuit.[49] Naturally, Egill wants his arrival at the
assembly to take Önundr and Steinarr by surprise, hence his display
of indifference at the news of the lawsuit against Þorsteinn.

---

[45] Ch. 81 and verse 55 (Nordal, ch. 79).
[46] For the land grant, see ch. 28 and for Steinarr's accession, ch. 82
(Nordal, ch. 80).
[47] Ch. 83, at 171 (Nordal, ch. 81, at 282).
[48] Kennedy, "The goðar," 71.
[49] Ch. 83, at 171 (Nordal, ch. 81, at 282).

At the assembly, Þorsteinn arrives with a large force of supporters and acts with calm assurance. He prepares quarters for his followers and a still larger accommodation that remains unoccupied. Steinarr arrives with a large force and makes his case aggressively confident he has both the law and the balance of power on his side. Þorsteinn brings no counter-charge against Steinarr, offers no settlement, and tells those who urge him to make an offer of compensation for Steinarr's slaves that he proposes to accept the court's judgement, a risky decision. But if Þorsteinn compromises and pays compensation for the slaves, his claim to the fertile and highly valuable pasture will be weakened and his rival's claim strengthened. The struggle for productive land, whether forests, pastures, or arable land, runs through the sagas of the Icelanders.[50] At the crucial point, when both fully armed sides confront each other, a small army of eighty men fully equipped for battle and led by a large and impressively armed man rides to the assembly. They proceed to the accommodation Þorsteinn has prepared but left unoccupied. The man is, of course, Egill and his arrival does not surprise Þorsteinn who greets his father warmly. Egill has mustered up the most warlike young men in his district, all the sons of property-owners. At the assembly, Egill first enquires forcefully if Önundr sjóni is present. Önundr answers and expresses his pleasure that Egill has arrived. At this point, Önundr sjóni, whose nickname seems to mean Önundr the sharp-sighted, is nearly blind. If *sjóni* should mean intellectually "clear-sighted," that vision too has failed. Seemingly displeased that he and Önundr, men who grew up together, should let their sons engage in lawsuits and apprised that Önundr has attempted to persuade Steinarr to settle the suit rather than prosecute, Egill first persuades Önundr to take over the case from his son. Steinarr demurs at first but then reluctantly complies and releases his backers, whose support he had paid for, and agrees they have acquited their obligations to him.

With the balance of power significantly altered, Egill persuades Önundr to let him adjudicate the dispute. Again Steinarr demurs

---

[50] Byock, 143-160 and 223-31.

then accedes to his father's insistence that he has always decided matters for the two of them and will do so now. Steinarr adds prophetically or clear-sightedly "opt ætla ek at við iðrimsk þessa," ("I think both of us will often regret this"). Egill's persuasive powers carry the day with a show of indignation—why have we let things get to this?—a further suggestion Steinarr's supporters egged him for the sake of gain and a bit of entertainment or *Schadenfreude*—followed by a plea that the two fathers should settle the quarrel between their sons. When this multifaceted rhetoric wins Egill the power to arbitrate the matter fully, he rules that Steinarr deliberately violated Þorsteins landright and hence the slaves, Steinarr's agents, fell in a state of lawless activity rendering them outside the protection of the law even if they had been free men and not slaves. Further, Egill rules that Steinarr's suit wrongly attempted to deprive Þorsteinn of his rightful property. Egill then awards to Þorsteinn that the property at Ánabrekka which Skalla-Grímr gave Áni, Önundr's father, without financial compensation and further rules that Steinarr must vacate at the next moving-days and may not settle in the district south of Long River or failing that he could be killed by Þorsteinn or any of his supporters. Egill has asserted for Þorsteinn and future generations of *Mýramenn* the family's right to the fertile pasture, *stakksmýri,* and brought part of Skalla-Grímr's original land claim back into the family's control.[51] The father and son who formerly had little love for each other part at the end of this episode *með blíðskap* "with warm affection."[52]

The complete success of the lawsuit does not end the conflict, but Steinarr never again can rally the support of local leaders and after a serious battle between the rivals, Þorsteinn gives Steinarr the choice of quitting the district at once or falling before superior force.[53]

---

[51] The history of the conflict and lawsuit occupies chapters 82-84 (Nordal, chs. 80-82).
[52] Ch. 85 (Nordal, ch 83).
[53] Ch. 86, at 177 (Nordal, ch. 84).

Egill's support for Þorsteinn does not end at this assembly:
Þorgeirr blundr, a nephew of Egill's, supported Þorsteinn in the
case and asks for the farm at Ánabrekka when it becomes vacant.
Egill urges Þorsteinn to grant Þorgeirr the farm.[54] Þorgeirr proves a
very bad neighbour to Þorsteinn and later Egill and Þorsteinn meet
and discuss the matter and agree completely. Egill composes a
poem expressing his outrage at Þogeirr's betrayal of his kinsmen.
Whether the poem's effect drives Þorgeirr off as his earlier poem
seemed a cause of Eiríkr exile from Norway (along with Egill's
"scorn-pole" and curse) or inspires Þorsteinn to face Þorgeirr
down, the bad neighbour withdraws immediately.[55]

The dramatic episode following Böðvarr's death demonstrates
Þorgerðr's love for her father and suggests Ásgerðr's affection for
her husband. The saga has more than one example of the eternal
triangle, but the most important includes Þórolfr, Þorgerðr, and
Egill himself who deeply loves his brother, but also loves the girl
Þórolfr eventually marries and then leaves a widow. We can suspect
that Egill came to love Ásgerðr as they grew up at Borg and that the
attraction might have been mutual. Ásgerðr was born at Borg when
Þórólfr was old enough to have a full voice in family matters and to
undertake his first voyage abroad.[56] Þórólfr proposes to take
Ásgerðr back to her father when she has grown up, that is has
reached marriageable age, but Egill insists on going along. Þórólfr
demurs, but Egill demonstrates that if he doesn't go, he'll make sure
Þórólfr won' t go either. Þórólfr takes Egill on, though reluctantly,
because he intends to ask for Ásgerðr in marriage and may suspect
Egill wants Ásgerðr for himself since he knows the two youngsters
grew up together at Borg while he was adventuring abroad.[57]

---

[54] Ch. 85, at 175 (Nordal, ch. 83).
[55] For the poem see ch. 58, verse 28 (Nordal, ch. 56), for the curse and
scorn-pole, ch. 59, at 98 (Nordal, ch. 57 at 171) and for the poem
rebuking Þorgeirr, ch. 86 (Nordal, ch. 84).
[56] Ch. 34.
[57] Chs. 40-41, at 55-56.

In Norway, the relationship between the brothers seems strained even as Egill and Arinbjörn become friends, as it will turn out, for life.[58] Þórólfr seems rather old to be unmarried, but he may have had a compelling romantic attachment in Norway. He accompanied Eirikr the future king in an expedition to Bjarmaland where, the saga reports that Eirikr married Gunnhildr and further that, "kærleikar miklir váru með þeim Þórólfi ok Gunnhildi," ("there was great affection between Þórólfr and Gunnhildr").[59] Hermann Pálsson suggests this affection was *nánari og meiri en góðu hófi gegndi* "closer and greater than appropriate"—the critic here following the saga's lead in prefering suggestion to explicit declaration.[60] When Gunnhildr rebukes Eiríkr for his indulgence toward Egill and Þórólfr, he rejoins, "en hafði verit kærra við Þórólf af þinni hendi en nú er" ("there's been more affection for Þórólfr on your part than there is now").[61] Einarsson takes this remark to indicate that Eiríkr does not suspect any impropriety between Þórólfr and Gunnhildr, but Eiríkr may be incapable of challenging his powerful queen though he might aim an irony at her. Later, when Egill enquires as to who may be supporting Berg-Önundr in his seizure of an estate to which Ásgerðr has a claim, we hear that Egill "var sagt at Önundr var kominn í vináttu mikla við Eirik konung ok við Gunnhildi þó miklu kærra," that is, Egill was told that Önundr had become a good friend to King Eirikr and was nevertheless much dearer to Gunnhildr.[62]

Whatever his romantic past, Þórólfr takes the conventional approach in seeking Ásgerðr in marriage, mentioning the matter to his host, Þórir, a relative of Ásgerðr's. Þórir then brings the

---

[58] Ch. 41.

[59] Ch. 37.

[60] Hermann Pálsson, "Um kærleikan í Egils sögu," *Afmælisrit til Dr. Phil. Steingríms J. Þorsteinssonar,* ed. Aðalgeir Kristjánsson et al. (Reykjavík: Stofnun Árna Magnússonar, 1971), 59-62. at 61.

[61] Bjarni Einarsson, "Review of: Thomas Bredsdorff, *Kaos og Kærlighed,*" *Mediaeval Scandinavia* 5 (1972): 143-53, at 147, and for the comment on Gunnhild's fondness for Þórólfr see *Egils saga*, ch. 48.

[62] Ch. 57, at 96 (Nordal, ch. 56, at 152).

proposal up to Ásgerðr's father, Björn who accepts the proposal. The date is set, and Þórólfr's wedding party sets out, but Egill suddenly falls ill and cannot travel.[63] They leave without him of course—quite unlike the voyage to Norway—and Egill recovers rather quickly.[64] He asks to accompany Ölvir, Þórir's farm manager, who has now to collect Þórir's landrents. Ölvir accepts the offer gladly since Egill makes a valuable addition to the group which will be responsible for the safe conveyance of those rents. In the course of their journey, Egill acts violently and recklessly but not without provocation. An Icelandic audience familiar with Egill's story might reflect that the eternal triangle (if . . .) involving Egill, Þórólfr, and Ásgerðr pitted two brothers against each other and that Egill, even having lost Ásgerðr, loved and attempted to protect his successful brother. If Egill's desire conflicted with his brotherly love, Ásgerðr's feelings for the boy and man she had grown up with may have contended with her affection for her first husband, whose death caused her real pain.[65]

Death can resolve a romantic triangle; after Ásgerðr's marriage, Egill enters upon a dangerous course as if life or death no longer mattered. After a storm, Ölvir, Egill, and all, soaked and tired, find shelter with the king's servant, Bárðr who is "kær mjök Eiríki konungi ok Gunnhildi dróttningu," ("very dear to King Eiríkr and Queen Gunnhildr").[66] Barðr gives the storm-tossed sailors a good fire and supper, bread, butter, and skýr (yogurt), but regrets he has no beer to offer them. Just a little later, Eiríkr and Gunnhildr appear. On learning that Bárðr has taken Ölvir and company in, Eiríkr asks that they be bidden to join the festival. When they do so, the truth comes out that there's lots of beer. Bárðr now forces the company to drink hornfull after hornfull of the now-abundant beer. Some of Ölvir's men vomit in the hall, others make it to the door. Bárðr and Gunnhildr try to poison Egill who parries with a runic inscription (and a verse) that breaks the horn and spills the drink.

---

[63] Ch. 42.
[64] Ch. 43.
[65] Ch. 56.
[66] Ch. 43, the festival and Egill's escape, chs. 44-45.

Then he tries to lead Ölvir, already pale from an excess of alcohol, outside. Bárðr follows them and demands that Ölvir drink a farewell toast before leaving. Egill drinks it and in the dark hallway runs Bárðr through with his sword and departs leaving Ölvir and Bárðr respectively in pools of vomit and blood.[67] Egill escapes killing three more of Eiríkr's men and reaches Þórir's where the newly married Þórólfr has also returned. At bit later, Þórir approaches the king and gains permission to to lodge Þórólfr and Egill over the winter despite this *contretemps*. Eiríkr then allows Þórir to lodge the brothers another winter, but Gunnhildr protests that the sons of Skalla-Grímr present a clear danger to Eiríkr's family. Gunnhild claims Egill has spoiled his brother and now regards them as enemies. Both have offended her: Þórólfr has married and Egill has killed Bárðr, another favourite though perhaps less favoured than Þórólfr.[68]

A series of raiding adventures bring Þórólfr and Egill to England where they join Æthelstan's army, and fight in the battle of Vinheiðr or Brunanburh. In the first engagement, Þórólfr and Egill hold the line after the one of Athelstan's nobles takes flight for the second time in the same war. In the battle, Þórólfr fights with reckless courage slinging his shield over his back and laying about with both hands to great effect. In planning the order of battle for the following day, Athelstan intends to separate Egill and Þórólfr, but Egill objects and asks that they be together wherever the fighting is likely to be heaviest. Apparently Egill intends to make sure that Þórólfr survives the battle if either of them does, but Þórólfr insists on following the king's plan. Egill replies, "Þér munuð nú ráða, en þessa skiptis mun ek opt iðrisk" ("you will decide now but I will often regret this plan of battle").[69] Þórólfr's death might resolve the romantic triangle in Egill's favor, but as a loyal and loving brother, Egill tries to prevent Þórólfr's death or,

---

[67] The action occupies chs. 43-44 of the saga. For a radically different and generally inaccurate account of this episode, see Bredsdorff, *Chaos and Love*, 28-29.

[68] Ch. 48.

[69] Ch. 54, at 78.

failing that, to share his brother's fate. Egill's forbodings come true:
Þórólfr recklessly charges ahead of his company and falls. Egill
buries his brother with all his equipment and places two large gold
rings on Þórolf's arms, recites two poems of mourning, and enters
into a state of profound and melancholy silence. Æthelstan brings
Egill back to himself with rich compensation for his brother's
death, none of which Egill ever shares or spends.

Egill returns to Þórir and reports to Ásgerðr the news of
Þórólfr's death and offers to look after her, an oblique proposal.
This departure from convention suggests the depth of Egill's
feelings, but Ásgerðr takes the news of her husband's death with
sorrow and does not respond to Egill's hint. Later that fall, he
withdraws into silence, hides his face in his cloak, and seems deep
in sorrow. Arinbjörn draws him out knowing that Egill will have
acknowledged the cause of his grief in poems. He asks what Egill
has been composing and recognizes the first poem as a *mansöng*, a
love poem which seems to name the object of Egils love in rather
riddling diction.[70] Love poems and love melancholy have appeared
in the saga earlier: Ölvir hnúfa, a viking, falls in love with an earl's
daughter, Solveig, whom he saw at a fall sacrifice.[71] He asks for her,
but her father rejects the suit and Ölvir gives up his viking career
and composes many love-poems about her. This story might seem a
loose detail, but it anticipates viking Egill's *mansöng* and reminds the
saga's audience of the dangers love incurs. Egill confesses to his
love for Ásgerðr and asks if Arinbjörn will help arrange the
marriage. Arinbjörn likes the idea and promises his support. Egill
had, quite unlike his brother, proposed obliquely to Ásgerðr who
did not answer, but after a more conventional negotiation, she
leaves the decision to her father and to Arinbjörn, whom she knows
to be Egill's best friend and constant supporter. Björn receives the
proposal graciously, perhaps because he owes a debt of gratitude to

---

[70] Ch. 56.
[71] Ch. 2.

Skalla-Grímr's family with whom Ásgerðr grew up.[72] Improbable as it may seem, this may be a love-match; deferring a proposal to third parties certain to say "yes," seems a gracious way to answer "yes."

When Egill returns to his native Iceland and his farm for good, people were glad to see him home ("Egill fór heim til bús síns. Urðu menn honum fegnir") which we might not have expected given the turbulance of his early years there.[73] Despite his Viking ferocity, Egill won steadfast friends abroad and repaid their friendship well. The saga narrator reports that Egill lived at Borg to old age but engaged in no ligitation, fought no duels, and engaged in no killings once he had settled in Iceland. His wife and wisest daughter demonstrate their love for Egill whose loyalty and devotion to all members of his family merit theirs. His intervention on behalf of the son he initially loved little secured his descendents, the *Mýramenn*, prosperity and power in their district. In the last stanza of *Sonatorrek* he resolved to await whatever death was in store for him: the saga relentlessly makes real Egill's decline and the courage and self-mocking humour with which he faced it. But the story ends with a short account of Egill's grandson, Skúli Þorsteinsson. Skúli was in at the death of King Óláfr Tryggvason, fought in seven battles as a Viking, gained a reputation as warrior and hero, held the farm at Borg for a long time, and continued the line of Skalla-Grímr's family. That minature saga reflects Egill Skalla-Grímsson's career from his prime to his age; the story comes full circle and confirms Egill's heroic status in Icelandic memory.[74]

---

[72] For Ásgerðr's Icelandic birth and childhood in Skalla-Grímr's household, see ch. 35. She was not reunited with her father in Norway until she was of marriageable age (ch. 41).

[73] Ch. 82, at 154 (Nordal, ch. 78).

[74] Nordal includes the final sentences of the saga in a textual note (p. 300, n. 1) because the Möðruvallabók redaction reached the bottom of the sheet and left the saga wounded at the heel. Bjarni Einarsson prints the close in his main text citing manuscripts K and W for the "natural saga-ending" (182).

Grettir's First Escapades: How To Challenge Your Father And Get Away With It – A Case Study In Historical Dialogue Analysis[1]

Maria Bonner

When Fred Amory gave a lecture on speech acts and violence in the saga[2] at Bonn University back in 1989, I was intrigued by his attempt to apply modern linguistic methodology to literary texts, and even to mediaeval texts, asking questions that were different from topics in saga analysis at the time. His approach was of special interest to me as a linguist fascinated by Old Icelandic texts, but not necessarily with a strong interest in the literary analysis of these texts. With his pragmatic angle on the sagas Amory certainly succeeded in pointing out the importance of verbal interaction as "doing things with words" in a literary context, as well. Since that time interest in historical pragmatics[3] and historical anthropology[4] has increased considerably, yet in the field of Old Norse there is still

---

[1] I wish to thank Kaaren Grimstad for valuable comments on the draft of this paper and for her help with weeding out mistakes from my English.

[2] Later published as Frederic Amory, "Speech Acts and Violence in the Sagas," *Arkiv för nordisk filologi* 106 (1991): 57-84.

[3] The range of topics in the *Journal of Historical Pragmatics* or the bibliography compiled by Andreas Jucker provide ample proof for this development.   http://www.es.unizh.ch/ahjucker/HistPrag.htm   (last accessed August 28, 2013).

[4] See for example Peter Burke, *The Historical Anthropology in Early Modern Italy: Essays on Perception and Communication* (Cambridge: University Press, 1987).

very little work done that focuses on analysing character development or social order in the sagas by examining interaction between the characters as a means of gaining insight into the rationale of their behaviour from a perspective of their own time rather than an external view from the vantage point of our time.[5]

METHODOLOGICAL ISSUES: DIALOGUE ANALYSIS[6] AND MEDIEVAL FICTION

One might of course question whether we have licence to speak of interaction in saga texts at all. One might also object to using modern tools, designed to analyse naturally occurring authentic dialogues, for old texts without at the same time facing severe methodological drawbacks. In response I would like to argue that saga dialogues are authentic dialogues, as well, understood in such a way that they are dialogues that exist in a meaningful text for the Old Icelandic society and are not isolated sentences constructed or arranged for the sake of analysis. One has to bear in mind, of course, that they are not authentic in the modern sense of

---

[5] For examples of dialogue analysis in Old Norse texts see Marcel M.H. Bax and Tineke Padmos, "Two types of verbal duelling in Old Icelandic: The interactional structure of the *Senna* and the *Mannjafnaðr* in *Hárbarðsljóð*," *Scandinavian Studies* 55 (1983): 149-174; Maria Bonner and Kaaren Grimstad, "*Munu vit ekki at því sættask:* A closer look at dialogues in *Hrafnkels saga*," *Arkiv för nordisk filologi* 111 (1996): 5-26; and Kaaren Grimstad and Maria Bonner, "*Sá er svinnr er sik kann:* Persuasion and Image in *Hrafnkels saga*," *Arkiv för nordisk filologi* 118 (2003): 5-28.

[6] I use the term "dialogue analysis" here in a very broad sense as an umbrella term for a non purist methodological approach to analyse written dialogues, inspired by the whole spectrum from speech act analysis to conversational analysis and all "shades" in between. For a survey of a variety of approaches see for example Linda A. Wood and Rolf O. Kroger, *Doing discourse analysis. Methods for studying action in talk and text* (Thousand Oaks, CA: Sage, 2000), here appendix B; Gerd Fritz and Franz Hundsnurscher, ed., *Handbuch der Dialoganalyse* (Tübingen: Niemeyer, 1994); or Deborah Schiffrin et al., ed., *The Handbook of Discourse Analysis*, (Oxford: Blackwell, 2001).

authenticity of spontaneous speech,[7] uttered in real situations by real people. Yet they render a contemporary depiction of utterances in a concrete situation, albeit idealised and shaped by authors. Furthermore, as Bax[8] pointed out, dialogues in texts are our only access to verbal interaction in language communities that have ceased to produce speech events.

With this caveat in mind I claim that dialogue analysis is a powerful empirical tool for answering in detail the question of what is going on in the dialogues between the characters in the saga. A detailed analysis of the dialogues is a prerequisite for understanding when, how and maybe why the characters in the saga do things with words and when, how and why verbal (inter)action leads to nonverbal action. Whereas the question of the dialogues' development and dynamics is mainly a linguistic one, the literary and cultural explanation beyond the fabric of the dialogue calls for the literary scholar's expertise and thus is a wonderful field for interdisciplinary collaboration. Interpreting dialogues on the basis of their linguistic analysis can be expected to generate a range of new questions the more we become familiar with the world of Old Icelandic verbal behaviour. As a consequence results from dialogue analysis may very well contribute to a more multifaceted understanding of the cultural universe of the Old Icelandic society, its forms of communication, the function of verbal styles in different contexts, in short the ethnography of the dialogues as presented in Old Icelandic texts.

THE SCOPE OF THE ANALYSIS

---

[7] As a consequence we will hardly be able to examine some issues of central interest in dialogue analysis of authentic spoken discourse such as openings, turn-taking, repair etc.

[8] Marcel M. H. Bax, "Historische Pragmatik: Eine Herausforderung für die Zukunft," in *Diachrone Semantik und Pragmatik. Untersuchungen zur Erklärung und Beschreibung des Sprachwandels,* ed. Dietrich Busse, Germanistische Linguistik 113 (Tübingen: Niemeyer, 1991), 197-215, at 200.

With my contribution I want to provide an analysis of a set of saga dialogues and describe their fabric (the "what" and the "how") as input for literary scholars, leaving to them the literary interpretation (the "why") of these dialogues. I have chosen a series of dialogues from chapter 14 of *Grettir's saga*. This chapter contains three episodes considered by Russell Poole as "an incremental series of three examples that positively cry out for the attention of a structuralist"[9] and even more so, I would like to suggest, for the attention of a linguist with an interest in dialogues. After the introductory chapters which present the ancestors of Grettir's father Ásmundr, this chapter describes "a series of anecdotes about Grettir's childhood, when time and again he defies, violently, cruelly, and wittily the authority of his father, and is shielded by his mother."[10] In his reader-response oriented article Cook describes his own reactions to chapter 14 as follows: "By the end of chapter 14 [. . .] the reader is not certain whether he has met a tyrannous and unreasonable father, an incorrigible and sadistic ten-year-old, or a budding hero not content with menial tasks."[11]

The childhood episodes in chapter 14 are our first encounter with the hero of the saga, who exhibits a form of behaviour expected from adolescents in general, namely that he tries to challenge his father, tries to establish his independence, and tests his limits. In a sense these episodes display the pattern of Grettir's life in a nutshell, as well: again and again he tests his limits in a continuous battle against various opponents, both natural and supernatural. In all of these Grettir prevails until it comes to the

---

[9] Russell Poole, "Old Norse/Icelandic myth in relation to *Grettis saga*," in *Old Norse Myths, Literature and Society, Proceedings of the 11th International Saga Conference 2-7 July 2000, University of Sydney*, ed. Geraldine Barnes and Margret Clunies Ross (Sydney: Centre for Medieval Studies, University of Sydney, 2000), www.arts.usyd.edu.au/departs/medieval/saga/pdf/398-poole.pdf (last accessed August 28, 2013), 398-409, at 404-05.

[10] *Grettir's saga*, trans. Denton Fox and Hermann Pálsson (Toronto: University of Toronto Press, 1974), ix.

[11] Robert Cook, "The reader in *Grettis saga*," *Saga Book of the Viking Society* 21 (1982-85): 133-154, at 137.

final battle on Drangey where he is caught ill and weak and is subsequently killed. If one wants to adopt the idea that the "saga continually reveals the author's concern with the conflict between man's desire for individual freedom and the restrictive bonds imposed by society" as it has been summarised in the introduction to the English translation of the saga by Denton Fox & Hermann Pálsson,[12] then these first attempts of striving for independence from paternal authority can be assumed to set the tone for Grettir's interaction style, at least the verbal side of it.

My main interest is thus the reconstruction of the principles and the meaning of the verbal interaction between father and son in these dialogues and to account for my reading mainly relying on so-called grounding, i.e. how the characters are shown to have understood the previous turn.[13] The challenge in analysing their exchange lies in keeping an open mind for the linguistic details of the dialogues because otherwise we might easily be biased by preconceived ideas and interpretations of others.[14] Looking at the turns in the dialogues as much as possible through the eyes of the characters, paying attention to their reactions as guidance for the analysis will make us as modern readers less liable to rely on our own experience of social interaction in situations where we are less familiar with the world of the Old Icelandic saga. If we try to account for how the characters in the saga act, how they categorise themselves and others, we will get closer to an understanding of their mutual relationship since they show through their (re)actions

---

[12] *Grettir's saga*, viii.

[13] For the concept of grounding cf. Clark, Herbert H. and Susan E. Brennan, "Grounding in communication," in *Perspectives on socially shared cognition*, ed. Lauren B. Resnik, John M. Levine and Stephanie D. Teasley (Washington D.C.: American Psychological Organization, 1991), 127-149.

[14] This is a particular challenge for a language spoken several centuries ago and one should not be biased by Modern Icelandic understanding of certain passages; their pragmatic meaning might have changed considerably.

how they understand what their partners do with their words, what they think the other is trying to signal and to do.[15]

The analysis of each dialogue must therefore at first confine itself to the dialogue in its own right. This means that only the communication history of the characters will be taken into account as given knowledge at each turn in the dialogues. Later utterances that are not part of the characters' communication universe at each given point or our knowledge as readers of what will happen later in the saga will not be included as background for analysis unless this information constitutes general knowledge available to the saga characters as members of the Old Icelandic society and is not part of the plot later on in the saga. The following questions will be of central interest in the analysis: What are the characters doing in the dialogue? What are the goals of the interaction for each character and which verbal strategies (including the stanzas) do they use in order to achieve them?

On the basis of such a micro-level analysis of each saga dialogue, as Bax convincingly demonstrated, one can extrapolate descriptions of the structure of certain types of verbal interaction.[16] Therefore in retrospect I will compare the dialogues with respect to the potential pattern they share and discuss their structure. In this way I hope to contribute to a better understanding of the social interactions involving Grettir and thus provide crucial background information for further deliberations on him as the saga's main character.

---

[15] Dialogue analysis may thus reveal interesting aspects for an adequate translation, as well, as I briefly shall point out in some instances in the discussion of the dialogues.

[16] Bax, "Historische Pragmatik." See as well Grimstad and Bonner, "*Sá er svinnr er sik kann*" for a description of patterns in dialogues were one party asks for support.

ANALYSIS OF THE DIALOGUES[17]

In the process of the analysis I will discuss how the characters in the saga signal their understanding of the situation and their understanding of the utterances of the other characters involved. Thus it will be possible to access the shared knowledge or in other words the characters' common ground that is implied and make this explicit for potential literary analysis. The most difficult task in this process may be to understand the modality of the dialogues in the saga. As modern readers it is likely that we lack the competence to understand spontaneously the tone of the interaction as the contemporary audience might have (for example, to identify playfulness or irony). We therefore need to pay special attention to linguistic signals for emotional issues and stylistic subtleties. One of the goals of my analysis is thus to give evidence of how I weighed different factors against each other in order to arrive at a reasonable reading.

Dialogue I (Look after my geese)

At the beginning of chapter 14 we are told that Ásmundr has established his household at Bjarg. He has two sons, the older being Atli, who is described as a quiet and gentle man, liked by everybody. The second son, Grettir, is introduced as handsome yet taciturn and difficult. We may assume that his being taciturn is how the members of his family experience him, not just the narrator's assumption. His being difficult is a more general comment that might cover all kinds of behaviour on Grettir's part. Being a slow developer he is not well liked by his father, but loved dearly by his mother Ásdís, so the saga states. For this we have no direct evidence so far, and I will therefore not take this as a basis for my interpretation. At the age of ten he finally begins to develop

---

[17] The Icelandic text follows *Grettis saga Ásmundarsonar*, ed. Guðni Jónsson, Íslenzk fornrit 7 (Reykjavík: Hið íslenzka fornritafélag, 1936). The dialogues are divided into turns; indirect speech is underlined, narrative parts appear in parentheses.

strength. His physical development may be taken as a visible fact
and can be interpreted as an obvious reason why his father at this
point sees him as fit to be given a useful task and do some work
(*starfa nǫkkut*). The following dialogue develops.[18]

Á 1: <u>Ásmundr bað hann starfa nǫkkut.</u>
G 1a: Grettir <u>sagði sér þat eigi mundu vera vel hent</u>
G 1b: <u>ok spurði þó at,</u> hvat hann skyldi gera.
Á 2: (Ásmundr svarar:) Þú skalt gæta heimgása minna.
G 2: (Grettir svarar ok mælti:) Lítit verk og lǫðrmannligt.
Á 3a: (Ásmundr svarar:) Leys þú þetta vel af hendi,
Á 3b: ok mun þá batna með okkr.[19]

Asmund told him to get down to some work. Grettir said
he didn't think that was very good for him, but asked
what he was to do. Asmund replied: "You shall look after
my farm-yard geese." Grettir replied and said, "That is
mean and miserable work." Asmund replied, "You do
this job well, and then we shall get on better together."

The father asks his son to take care of some job to be done at
the farm (Á 1). We may assume that children at the age of ten or
even younger were considered to be able to share the duties in the
household and take over simple useful tasks.[20] Therefore Grettir's
claim that this does not suit him (G 1a) can only be seen as an
attempt to refuse involvement, mitigated, however, by his asking for
information about the kind of task his father has in mind (G 1b).

[18] Translation here and in the following dialogues taken from "The Saga
of Grettir," trans. Anthony Faulkes, *Three Icelandic Outlaw Sagas,* ed. and
introduced by Anthony Faulkes (London: Everyman, 2001), 71-272.
[19] *Grettis saga,* 37.
[20] Kirsten Hastrup, "Tracing tradition: An Anthropological Perspective on
Grettis saga Ásmundarsonar," in *Structure and Meaning in Old Norse Literature:
New Approaches to Textual Analysis and Literary Criticism,* ed. John Lindow et
al., Viking Collection 3 (Odense: Odense University Press, 1986), 281-313,
at 291, speaks of "an attempt to socialize Grettir to the work life of the
farm."

Asking for more information can be seen as postponing a final refusal or as consent to do as requested.

Ásmundr does not show any sign of having taken notice of Grettir's negative response but takes his answer as a whole for consent; otherwise he wouldn't explain what kind of job he has in mind (Á 2). Grettir's reply is an evaluation of the assignment in the first place; he downplays the work as an unworthy task, implying that he understands his father's negative evaluation of his talents, and also implying that he is not enthusiastic about being asked to do something beneath his capability and of no interest to him when he had already stated that he does not want to do any work in the first place. We may conclude that he either feels humiliated by the nature of the task, since a *lítit verk og lǫðrmannligt*, which means a job for an untalented or clumsy person,[21] does not agree with him or that he tries to protest against his father's giving him such an undemanding task and in this way tells him that it is no problem for him to perform the task as described. At the same time his turn might imply an indirect warning: It is your fault if you give me a job like this, and you have yourself to blame if I will not perform as well as you want me to.

Ásmundr's reaction does not unambiguously reveal how he understands his son's answer since he does not comment on its content. His lack of response to what Grettir has said can be understood as a display of paternal authority, telling his son that he as father calls the shots. We may conclude that Grettir's feelings about the job are of no matter to him. At the same time he makes a promise to his son, namely that a good performance in doing this job will improve their relationship (Á 3a, b), meaning that he will be

---

[21] The translation "mean and miserable" does not quite have the same flavour, since it omits the aspect of lack of ability that the Icelandic term implies. The translation by Denton Fox and Hermann Pálsson reads "shabby little job" which strikes me as still further away from the tone in Grettir's turn. They both conceal the possibility of a twofold message in Grettir's words.

more favourably disposed towards his son. Implicitly he thus expresses his disapproval of his son's performance so far and evaluates their relationship as not satisfactory. If we want to interpret what Grettir's being difficult might mean in the light of this exchange we may conclude that it consists in Grettir's not doing what his father wants him to do without resistance.

Dialogue II (Well then, let's try something different)

The second dialogue between father and son occurs after some time when the flock of geese is found partly dead and partly with broken wings. At this point as readers we have reason to believe that Grettir's comment about the nature of the job was indeed strategic and might have been meant as a warning to his father. We might therefore look out for cues in the dialogue that Ásmundr, too, begins to read his son's commentaries as part of a strategy.

Á 1: (Ásmundr líkaði stórilla) <u>ok spurði, hvárt Grettir hefði drepit fuglana.</u>
G 1a: <u>Hann glotti at</u> (ok svarar:)
G 1b: Þat gerik víst, es vetrar,
        vind ek hals á kjúklingum;
        enn þótt ellri finnisk,
        einn berk af sérhverri.
Á 2: Ok skaltu eigi lengr af þeim bera, (sagði Ásmundr.)
G 2: Vinr er sá annars, er ills varnar, (sagði Grettir.)
Á 3: Fásk mun þér verk annat, (sagði Ásmundr.)
G 3a: Fleira vet sá, er fleira reynir, (sagði Grettir,)
G 3b: eða hvat skal ek nú gera?
Á 4: (Ásmundr svarar:) Þú skalt strjúka bak mitt við eld, sem ek læt jafnan gera.
G 4a: Heitt mun þat um hǫnd, (sagði Grettir,)
G 4b: en þó er verkit lǫðrmannligt.[22]

---

[22] *Grettis saga*, 37-8.

Asmund was very displeased and asked if Grettir had
killed the birds. Grettir grinned, and replied:

Indeed I do when winter comes,
the goslings' necks I wring.

Even if some are older ones,
unaided I can win.

"Well you won't be winning with them any more," said
Asmund. "'That is a true friend who keeps you out of
harm's way'," said Grettir. "You must be found some
other work," said Asmund. "'The more you experience
the more you learn'," said Grettir, "and what am I to do
now?" "You shall massage my back by the fire, as I often
get someone to do." "That will be rather hot on the
hands," said Grettir, "but this is still miserable work."

Ásmundr's question (Á 1) can be understood as a question for
information or more likely as an accusation. He asks Grettir to
admit what he has done. Grettir's grin (G 1a) might be understood
as a cue; he is pleased with the situation.[23] His admission is rendered
as a stanza[24] (G 1b). He evaluates his doings as something that he
definitely (*víst*) did do. Not only did he manage to kill the goslings –
something a young boy or an untalented clumsy person might
achieve – he even managed all by himself (*einn*) to lame the fully-
grown birds, which might be a hint that he is aware of an unusual
strength. Telling in this way what he has achieved, depicting his

---

[23] If we are to judge from other instances in Old Icelandic literature,
grinning might have been understood as a contextualisation cue for
scornfulness, contempt, triumph or smugness to a contemporary
audience.

[24] For all stanzas in the saga we must assume that they actually were
understood by the characters they were spoken to. Whether they were
understood by the contemporary audience is not relevant for the analysis
of the dialogues. It will be relevant for a literary interpretation of the saga,
of course.

action in a stanza, a form normally reserved for heroic achievements, and showing no regret about a deed he must have known he was not supposed to do qualifies as bragging. Bragging about an action that upsets his father, bragging about jeopardising the chance to improve the relationship with his father is to be understood as a strong challenge to the paternal authority and at the same time a claim – whether meant sincerely or not we have no way of telling – that he is not willing to strive for his father's approval.

Ásmundr's statement that there will be no more chance to repeat the performance (Á 2) cuts the bragging short and might be interpreted as a strategy for getting control and asserting authority. Grettir's next turn consists of a proverb (G 2) with which he declares his father's behaviour to be the behaviour of a friend. This again can be seen as a challenge to the paternal authority. On the one hand – although this might be a modern idea about the paternal role – it seems inappropriate to reduce the father's contribution to keeping his son from harm;[25] on the other hand, Grettir is implying that because Ásmundr has failed to keep him from harm with the first task, he has failed as a father and therefore also bears responsibility for what has happened.

Again Ásmundr does not react to these words as challenges but persists in his plan from the first dialogue, namely to find a task for his son (Á 3). Grettir again hedges using a proverb (G 3a) that can be understood in two ways: it can refer to himself and be seen as consent to getting more experience or it can refer to his father and constitute a threat that he will get more experience of his son's ability to produce a bad outcome. On the basis of the experience so far I am more inclined to read it as a threat and a challenge, mitigated by Grettir's asking for more information about what his

---

[25] The translation by Fox and Hermann Pálsson reads here "evil" which in a way interprets Grettir's actions as ill intention and does not leave the possibility to see them as errors or consequences of juvenile bad judgment, an interpretation that seems more in tune with the proverbial lack of luck that follows Grettir throughout his life.

father has in mind as the next task (G 3b). This information is given in (Á 4). To a modern reader this looks like strange "work"; rather it gives the impression of a friendly gesture between family members. Without further knowledge of the practice of back-rubbing, we can only guess what this task means in terms of the relationship between father and son. I find it difficult again as a modern reader to understand all the implications of (G 4a). Grettir establishes here a contrast between this task and the previous one which he abandoned when it got cold (*es vetrar*), and, given the housing conditions of his time, warm hands might be desirable. From Grettir's evaluation of the task in (G 4b) we can be sure, however, that he sees the task as being in the same category as the first task, he constructs similarity by calling this task *lǫðrmannligt*,[26] as well. This evaluation again cues a challenge and a warning to his father. Since the saga ends this dialogue with Grettir's comment, we have no access to Ásmundr's understanding of Grettir's words.

Dialogue III (More commitment, please!)

Grettir has tried his hand at this new task for some time when the colder season approaches and Ásmundr found the warmth more and more alluring – as the saga puts it – *gerðisk Ásmundr heitfengr mjök*. One evening as they sit by the fire Ásmundr addresses Grettir as follows:

Á 1: Nú muntu verða af þér at draga slenit, mannskræfan, (segir hann.)

---

[26] There is though a difference between the two jobs. In the first case Grettir used the alliterating expression *lítit verk og lǫðrmannligt*; in this episode the task is not characterised as *lítit*. Three manuscripts (MS 556A, 4to, MS 152, fol., MS DG 10, fol.) have *vesalmannligt*, see *Grettis saga Ásmundarsonar*, ed. Richard C. Boer, Altnordische Sagabibliothek 8 (Halle: M. Niemeyer, 1900), 40, fn. 1. This word puts the second task in a somewhat different yet not more positive category. At the same time the alliteration *verk* and *vesalmannligt* can be read as proof for Grettir's rhetorical skills. It is interesting, too, that the three manuscripts that read *vesalmannligt* lack Grettir's commentary (G 1a) in dialogue I.

G 1: (Grettir segir:)Illt er at eggja óbilgjarnan.

Á 2: (Ásmundr mælti:) Aldri er dugr í þér

(Grettir sér nú, hvar stóðu ullkambar i setinu, tekr upp kambinn ok lætr ganga ofan eftir baki Ásmundar. Hann hljóp upp ok varð óðr við ok vildi ljósta Gretti með staf sínum, en hann skauzk undan; þá kom húsfreyja at ok spurði)

H 1: hvat þeir ættisk við

G 2: (Grettir kvað þá vísu þessa:)

    Mik vill menja støkkvir,
    mjǫk kennik þess, brenna,
    hodda grund, á hǫndum,
    hǫfugt ráð es þat bǫðum;
    lætk á hringa hreyti,
    hǫr-Gerðr, tekit verða
    gørr, sék gildra sára
    gǫgul, óskornum nǫglum.

H 2: (Illa þótti húsfreyju, er Grettir hafði þetta til bragðs tekit, ok kvað) hann ekki fyrirleitinn verða mundu.[27]

"You'd better buck yourself up a bit now, you useless creature." Grettir said, "'It's a bad thing to goad a stubborn person.'" Asmund said, "There's never any good in you." Then Grettir noticed that there were some wool-combs standing on the bench, picked up one of them and scraped it down Asmund's back. He jumped up and was furious at this and was going to hit Grettir with his walking-stick, but he dodged; then the mistress of the house came and asked what they were up to. Grettir uttered this verse:

The flinger of neck-rings [man] wants to burn my hands,
O ground of hoards [women], and I feel it greatly.
That is a bad thing for both of us.
Linen-Gerd [woman], I shall scratch

27 *Grettis saga*, 38-9.

the scatterer of rings [man] even harder
with uncut nails.
I can see blood from deep wounds.

The mistress of the house was annoyed that Grettir had
played this trick, and said he would never be careful of
what he did.

For the first time in the dialogues we see Ásmundr use strong
words, talking "irritably and insultingly"[28] when urging his son to
rub his back more vigorously (Á 1). The cues for his annoyance are
the adverb *nú* (now, finally), the modal *muntu* which carries the
meaning of obligation, the evaluation of his son's activity as lazy,
and finally the use of the invective *mannskræfa*, which carries the
meaning of miserable or worthless and/or coward with the definite
article adding contempt.[29] On the basis of the provocative tone we
may assume that he has not attributed an underlying warning to
Grettir's final turn in the previous interaction or that he does not
estimate that Grettir has a real chance for doing mischief in this
situation. Grettir in his turn answers his father's provocation with a
proverb that again contains a potential warning to his father (G 1).
He evaluates his father's words as bad and dangerous (*illt*) and
classifies them as provocation (*að eggja*). He refers to himself as the
addressee of the provocation as a fearless person who will not
tolerate an offence (*óbilgjarn*), thus contradicting his father's
depiction of him as a *mannskræfa* and constructing a different
identity for himself. This proverb thus carries a warning to his
father that he will have himself to blame for any unfortunate
consequences that his hot-headed son might inflict on him if
provoked in such a way. I do not share the opinion that warning his

---

[28] Cook, "The reader in *Grettis saga*," 137.
[29] See the comment in *Grettis saga Ásmundarsonar*, ed. Boer, 41: *der artikel in der anrede deutet geringschätzung an* ("the definite article in the address signals contempt"). The translation by Fox and Hermann Pálsson renders "coward," thus omitting the other nuances.

father is "far more impersonal and temperate"[30] than the father's
impatient urging; rather I think it constitutes a severe challenge to
the paternal authority in spite of the reference to the generally
accepted common sense expressed in the proverb.

Ásmundr obviously understands the challenge since he blames
Grettir for being completely useless (Á 2); never (*aldri*) is he able to
do something properly. Stating that a person never can perform
well is a general statement about a person's abilities and not a
comment limited to the actual occurrence of certain behaviour.
Such wide-ranging disapproval is a strong reproach based on the
evidence of the rather unpretentious task in this episode. Grettir's
reaction to the scolding is physical, not verbal. It almost appears to
be a stubborn and paradoxical attempt to prove that he can rub his
father's back more forcefully than with his hands and thus obey his
father, as if he were trying to declare: "Well, if that's what you want,
I'll give it to you." He grabs a wool-comb, scratches his father's
back with it and thus injures him.[31] Ásmundr, who in the previous
episode has shown rather moderate reactions to his son's verbal
challenges and has come across as calm and patient, now reacts
strongly to the physical challenge and pain and tries to beat Grettir.
He thus repays physical action with physical action, and at the same
time gives the impression that he has no verbal means to compete
with Grettir's rhetorical strategies.

At this point his mother (*húsfreyja* mistress of the house) enters
the scene and asks for an explanation of the uproar (H 1). It is
Grettir who once again demonstrates his verbal skills. Grettir's
answer is a stanza (G 2) addressed to his mother where he accuses
his father by claiming that he wanted him to burn his hands. In his
own defence he labels his father's desire for more heat as a bad

---

[30] Cook, "The reader in *Grettis saga*," 137.
[31] On an abstract level one might speculate about the symbolic value of
using a wool comb, a tool that belonged to the female domain. On a more
concrete level one might expect a lack of dexterity in performing
unfamiliar (female?) tasks like grooming.

intention (*hǫfugt ráð*)[32] that will hurt them both. With this reframing he constructs himself as a victim and justifies his own reaction as defence. At the same time this can be understood as a claim that it is his father's fault that they end up in this situation, which gives him every right to punish his father by injuring his back, as well. This again must be seen as a challenge since we may assume that the relationship between a father and a young son is an asymmetrical one where the son cannot claim the "right" to discipline his father.

With her comment that Grettir will never be a cautious man (H 2) the mother evaluates his trick as due to lack of foresight and blames her son for not having been careful. The saga states that the incident did not improve the relationship between father and son.

Dialogue IV (Maybe this finally will work…)

After a while the father tries once more to set his now somewhat older son to work.

Á 1: <u>Nǫkkuri stundu síðar talaði Ásmundr til, at Grettir skyldi geyma hrossa hans.</u>
G 1: <u>Grettir kvað sér þat betra þykkja en bakeldagǫrðin.</u>
Á 2a: Þá skaltu svá at fara, (sagði Ásmundr,) sem ek býð þér. Hryssu á ek bleikálótta, er ek kalla Kengálu; hún er svá vís at um veðráttu ok vatnagang, at þat mun aldri bresta, at þá mun hríð eptir koma, ef hon vill eigi á jǫrð ganga. Þá skaltu byrgja í húsi hrossin, en halda þeim norðr á hálsinn þegar er vetr leggr á;

---

[32] The translation leaves that out and loses a hint. The translation by Fox and Hermann Pálsson renders it as "stupid plan," *Grettis saga Ásmundarsonar*, ed. Boer suggests that *bǫðum* and *hǫndum* (on both hands) belongs together. On the basis of my analysis I prefer the interpretation in *Grettis saga*, ed. Guðni Jónsson, that *bǫðum* refers to both father and son which appears to be more in tune with the ambiguity that we encounter in Grettir's utterances.

Á 2b: þœtti mér þurfa, at þú leystir þetta verk betr af hendi en þau tvau, sem áðr hefi ek skipat þér.
G 2a: (Grettir svarar:) Þetta er kalt verk ok karlmannligt;
G 2b: en illt þykki mér at treysta merinni,
G 2c: því at þat veit ek engan fyrr gǫrt hafa.[33]

A little while later Asmund suggested that Grettir should look after his horses. Grettir said he would prefer that to the hot back-massage. "Then you must do this job as I tell you," said Asmund. "I have a chestnut mare with a stripe down its back that I call Kengala; she is so sensitive to the weather and the rain-fall that there will always be a storm without fail if she refuses to go out to pasture. If this happens you must shut the horses in the stable; but take them north up onto the ridge as soon as the winter frosts come. I should think it would be a good thing if you were to do this job better than the last two I gave you." Grettir replied, "This is a cold and manly work; but I think it's a bad thing to trust the mare, for I don't know that anyone else has ever done so."

Ásmundr assigns Grettir a third and more demanding task with a considerable amount of responsibility, namely to look after his horses (Á 1). Grettir evaluates this task by comparing it with rubbing his father's back which he characterises as setting the back on fire (bakeldagørðin) (G 1). The term can be understood as an ad-hoc-compound and thus an ironic comment and a challenging reminder to the earlier task. The whole utterance, on the other hand, signals Grettir's willingness to see this as more appropriate work for him, although tending the horses seems to be a task usually assigned to farm hands.

Ásmundr then gives detailed instructions on how to take care of the animals (Á 2a) which consist of practicalities. The last part of his turn (Á 2b), however, allows for several readings. Reminding

---

[33] *Grettis saga*, 39-40.

Grettir of his former failures can be understood as scolding, while expressing hope for a different outcome this time can be understood as a repetition of the promise in dialogue I (Á 3a) that he will reward his son by seeing him in a more favourable light if Grettir performs well. Grettir, who had been provoked by his father's scolding in dialogue III (A2), does not respond to that latter part of his father's turn. In his turn (G 2a) he does not evaluate the interpersonal message, but rather the factual nature of the task. By labelling it with an alliterating expression as cold and suited for a man (*kalt og karlmannligt*) he obviously evaluates it more positively than the former tasks, which we are to understand were not suitable tasks for a boy or young man of Grettir's status. He thus indirectly shares his father's assumption that a better outcome is likely. Yet he finds fault with his father's trust in a horse, which he criticises by stating that he does not like it (G 2b). He accounts for his opinion by categorising his father's confidence in the mare's foresight (G 2c)[34] as peculiar. The criticism constitutes a challenge to the paternal authority, on the one hand; on the other hand, it can be read as a warning based on the experience in the former dialogues where statements evaluating what Ásmundr had said in retrospect proved to imply a warning.

Dialogue V (Weather talk)

For a while things apparently go well until there is a cold spell and Grettir, clad badly and not used to the cold, is getting annoyed that he has to stay out in the most exposed areas where Kengala prefers to graze. One morning he slashes her back with a knife. As a result the horse seeks rescue in the shelter of the stable, and Grettir returns home where his father is inquisitive.

---

[34] Whether the contrast he constructs by specifically referring to *merr* and not to *hryssa* as Ásmundr does, or to *hross* as a generic term carries any particular meaning I see no way of accounting for from the dialogue. The implications will entirely depend on the underlying assumptions about the value of and associations connected with female horses in the rural society at the time and the connotations that go with *merr*.

Á 1: Ásmundr <u>spyrr, hvar hrossin væri.</u>
G 1: <u>Grettir kvezk geymt hafa í húsi eptir vanda.</u>
Á 2: <u>Ásmundr segir, at þá myndi skammt til hríðar, er</u>
<u>hrossin vildu eigi standa í þvílíku veðri.</u>
G 2: (Grettir segir:) Skýzk þeim mǫrgum vísdómrinn, er
betri ván er at.[35]

Asmund asked where the horses were. Grettir said he had
seen to them in the stable as usual. Asmund said it
wouldn't be long before there was a storm since the
horses wouldn't stay out in such weather. Grettir said:
"'Many who have been more reliable have been wrong.'"

When Ásmundr asks where the horses are (Á 1), Grettir claims
that he has followed the usual procedure (*eptir vanda*) (G 1). This
leads Ásmundr to assume that the weather will change (Á 2) since
he obviously understands the answer as providing the requested
information. With a proverb Grettir criticises his father's
assumption and thereby his ability to judge the situation properly.
As readers we already know that Grettir has played a trick. Since the
saga does not render any further exchange, we have no direct access
to Ásmundr's understanding of his son's turn. On the basis of the
other dialogues and because he fails to take immediate action it is
reasonable to assume that he does not understand the proverb as a
cue for a warning or an indirect claim that something already has
occurred.

Dialogue VI (You did it again)

When the weather does not change, Ásmundr goes out to the
stable on the third day in order to see for himself how the horses
are doing.

A1: Illa þykki mér hrossin við hafa orðit at jafngóðum
vetri; en þú munt sízt bregðask at bakinu, Bleikála.

---

[35] *Grettis saga*, 40-1.

G 1: Verðr þat er varir, (sagði Grettir,) ok svá hitt, er eigi
varir.
Á 2: (Ásmundr strauk bakit á hrossinu, ok fylgði þar
húðin; honum þótti undarligt, hví svá var orðit,) ok kvað
Gretti þessu valda mundu.
G 2: Grettir glotti at (ok svaraði engu.)[36]

"The horses seem to have been reacting very badly to
such a good winter, but your back will never let you
down, Kengala." "'Sometimes things turn out as you
expect,'" said Grettir, "'and sometimes as you don't
expect.'" Asmund stroked the mare's back, and the skin
came away in his hand; he thought it very strange that this
should happen and said it must be Grettir's doing. Grettir
grinned and said nothing.

Ásmundr clearly does not suspect any mischief since he only
expresses general concern over whether the horses are getting
enough to eat. He assumes that at least Kengala will be in better
shape than the other horses (Á 1). Grettir's commentary (G 1)
elicits no response from Ásmundr, and since he appears to have
failed to understand the ambiguity in the proverbs used previously
by Grettir we may assume that he also now regards it as elusive
rhetoric on Grettir's part.

Its meaning becomes clear when Ásmundr discovers the horse's
maimed back. At this point there's no question of who's to blame
and Ásmundr accuses Grettir (Á 2). Grettir's answer is nonverbal:
he grins silently (G 2). Without detailed knowledge to draw upon
for comparison it is difficult to identify the function of this grin.
When we compare it to Grettir's grinning in the first episode where
it was accompanied by bragging, the most likely interpretation is
that it signals the admittance of the deed and points to smugness.

---

[36] *Grettis saga*, 41.

Dialogue VII (Parents' talk)

When Ásmundr returns from the stable after the discovery of Grettir's bad trick, the saga reports that he is swearing heavily. He overhears his wife talking and the following dialogue develops:

H 1: Vel skyldi nú reynzk hafa hrossageymslan frænda míns.

Á 1: (Ásmundr kvað vísu:)
    Fyrst hefir flegna trausta
    fær prettat mik, Grettir,
    fljóð eru flest en prúðu
    fullmálug, Kengǫlu;
    víst mun venja flestar
    vitr drengr af sér lengi,
    hróðr nemi hrings en fríða
    Hlín, kvaðningar mínar.

H 2: (Húsfreyja svarar:) Eigi veit ek, hvárt mér þykkir meir frá móti, at þú skipar honum jafnan starfa, eða hitt, at hann leysir alla einn veg af hendi.

Á 2: Nú skal ok um enda gǫrt fyrir þat, (sagði Ásmundr,) en hafa skal hann viðrgǫrning verra.

G 1: Teli þá hvárigir á aðra, (sagði Grettir)[37]

"My son seems to have got on well with looking after the horses." Asmund uttered this verse:

Grettir has now flayed the trusty Kengala;
and has made a fool of me.
These fine women are always garrulous.
The clever child will soon make me tired
of giving him work to do.
May the fair ring-Hlin [woman, i.e.
Asmund's wife] hear my poem.

---

[37] *Grettis saga*, 41-2.

His wife replied: "I'm not sure which is worse, your always giving him work to do or his always doing it the same way." "Now we're going to settle accounts in this matter," said Asmund, "and he'll get the worst of it." "Then neither will have any reason to complain," said Grettir.

It appears strange that the mistress of the house should express the assumption that her son has performed well this time. From her husband's swearing Ásdís should be able to conclude that Grettir once again has failed to meet his father's expectations. Unless she has not at all heard her husband's swearing, in which case we can read her comment as a wish, her utterance could be interpreted as irony. The conditional (*skyldi*) together with the adverb (*nú*) point towards irony implying that the opposite of what she says is true. Yet as long as we lack pragmatic studies on the use of the conditional together with *nú* in saga dialogues accounting for the modality of Ásdís's utterance has to remain speculative. The same caution is advisable when interpreting her use of *frændi* (male relative) in reference to her son, which might express a certain distance.

The only support for a less ambiguous reading is to be obtained from Ásmundr's understanding of her turn: Ásmundr in his reply qualifies her words as an unwelcome commentary, categorising Ásdís as belonging to the multitude of women who talk too much, who are *fullmálug*. The reason for his criticism lies not necessarily in the proposition or the mode of her turn; he might just as well blame his wife for talking at all.

In the narrative part of the stanza Ásmundr informs her about Grettir's flaying the horse and admits that his son has outwitted him (*fær prettat mik*); by calling him *vitr drengr* he categorises Grettir as clever. This term, usually used in a positive sense, most likely expresses a certain amount of amazement over his son's skill to wiggle out of this task in such an unexpected way. He thus constructs an identity for himself as unwise that Grettir had already constructed for him in dialogue IV (G 2 b-c) and reiterated in dialogue V (G 2). Ásmundr's assumption that Grettir unquestionably will be able to evade any duties he might be assigning to him (*kvaðningar mínar*) provides reason to assume that he by now has recognised a pattern in Grettir's behaviour. In his stanza he also concedes that he has misjudged his paternal talent twice before. By explicitly addressing his wife with the demand that she pay attention to his words he adds weight to this admission, which at the same time serves as an announcement that he will spare Grettir his commands in the future.

Ásdís disregards Ásmundr's criticism of her as too talkative which only was mitigated through its reference to women in general. Instead she elaborates on Ásmundr's way of dealing with his son so far (H 2). By criticising her husband for always (*jafnan*) trying to prompt Grettir to work[38] she categorises Ásmundr's behaviour as wrong. At the same time she blames her son, as well, making explicit what she only alluded to in dialogue III (H 2). She thus constructs a similarity between the behaviour of father and son. Since the saga so far has only reported three episodes in which Ásmundr wanted to set Grettir to work, her choice of words either implies that Ásmundr has tried many times more or else contains an accusation of a more general nature. Her statement implies in addition that it is not at all unreasonable to expect a modicum of cooperativeness from a boy like Grettir. This in retrospect sheds light on Grettir's commentary in dialogue I (G1a). It allows us as readers to interpret that commentary as an inappropriate reply when summoned to work. As to Grettir, she classifies his pranks as the same way of doing or rather not doing the job, which is paraphrase for disobedience.

Ásmundr clearly interprets her utterance as criticism and backs away from what he just had expressed in the stanza where he

---

[38] This utterance obviously is the basis for Russell Poole's commentary "Ásmundr is not exactly pragmatic or tactful in the allocation of the tasks," Poole, "Old Norse/Icelandic myth in relation to *Grettis saga*," 404.

promised not to assign any more tasks to Grettir. With his reply he
declares that Grettir's behaviour will be terminated (Á 2). By
threatening with negative consequences (*viðrgørning verra*) for his son
he attempts to re-establish himself as paternal authority figure and
dismisses his wife's criticism of his paternal authority. Having just
admitted limited success in establishing boundaries for his son so
far his threat remains somewhat empty.

Grettir in his final turn indirectly admits that he has challenged
his father with his pranks since his statement (G 1) presupposes
that his father has reason to find fault with him. He reacts to his
father's statement that he from now on will exert his paternal
authority with other means as an announcement of an attempt to
get even. He thus assesses his interaction with his father so far to
have been a power struggle that will continue.

PATTERNS IN THE DIALOGUES/EPISODES

If we recapitulate what the characters are doing in the dialogues
we can on the part of Grettir observe a pattern of resistance and
challenge in form of ambiguous (proverbial) comments to what his
father asks him to do. In each episode Ásmundr summons his son
to work, whereupon Grettir evaluates this idea as bad or at least
unwelcome.[39] Ásmundr does not let his son's attempted challenge
get in the way of his plan to set him to work. After the practicalities
of the work have been explained by Ásmundr, Grettir categorises
the concrete task in each episode with reference to its being suited
for a weakling or a man. Ásmundr each time misreads or ignores
the challenge implied in his son's evaluation of his choice of task.
He insists on the task and urges Grettir to try to please him by

---

[39] The pattern of course depends on which manuscript we take as a basis
for our analysis. See fn. 24 for a crucial difference in the manuscripts of
Grettis saga. On the basis of this difference that might lead to a different
interpretation of the structure of the episodes I want to advocate very
strongly for editions that do not mix and match manuscripts according to
the taste of the editor but account for all readings and differences.

performing well. Yet each time Ásmundr has to declare failure indirectly by abandoning the original task and assigning a new one or by explicitly stating the obvious fact in the last episode. Grettir, however, does not give in; he has the last word and each time challenges his father by categorising his paternal abilities as insufficient.

As a boy in transition to young man Grettir has apparently the physical strength but not yet the psychological power of a *drengr*. In a way his behaviour speaks for the courage and strength expected of a *drengr* in that he both wants to challenge and to be challenged. Grettir reacts to the tasks his father assigns to him not as obligation but as challenges. The pattern thus might serve as supportive evidence for the idea that Grettir wants to be free of imposition, which Preben Meulengracht Sørensen has described as a necessary ingredient in the development from boy to a man: *Bondesønnen skal demonstrere, at han vil ikke lade sig træde for nær* ("the son of a farmer has to demonstrate that he will not allow anybody to invade his territory").[40] To judge from the episodes, however, things get out of hand, and Grettir obviously does not understand the necessity of defending his independence in harmony with the rules of society. The verbal exchanges turn into power struggles between father and son in which the son "wins" in the end and thus has managed to steer clear of his share of work at the farm. The father's endeavours to socialise his son to the life of a farmer have failed; the father thus comes across as the loser in this power struggle.

There is, however, one interesting difference in Grettir's conduct after the pranks, which sheds light on Cook's depiction of Grettir as potentially incorrigible. Grettir's behaviour after the pranks might be seen as the reflex of a learning process; in the first episode he has only a limited understanding for the implications of his deed, hence the bragging. In the second escapade Grettir defends himself by accusing his father of wanting to inflict physical

---

[40] See Preben Meulengracht Sørensen, *Fortælling og ære: Studier i islændingesagaerne* (Århus: Universitetsforlag, 1993), 220.

pain on him. In the third escapade Grettir's silence could imply that he fully understands what he has done both in terms of the material damage and the consequences for the relationship.[41]

Just as his admission of the deed moves from bragging to accusation and finally silence his closing challenge in each episode changes focus. In the first episode he frames his father as friend with a proverb that has a positive reading on the surface (*Vinr er sá annars, er ills varnar*); in the stanza in the second episode he accuses him of bad judgment referring to himself at the same time (*hǫfugt ráð es þat bǫðum*); and in the third episode, by implying that Ásmundr indeed will pay him back and get even (*Teli þá hvárigir á aðra*), he finally frames him as an opponent.

CONCLUSION

Although I do not want to engage in a literary discussion of the characters in the saga I nevertheless want to relate what we have learned about the principles and the meaning of the verbal interaction between father and son in chapter 14 of *Grettis saga* to Cook's comment mentioned above. Is it "a tyrannous and unreasonable father, an incorrigible and sadistic ten-year-old, or a budding hero not content with menial tasks" that we have met?

The notion of Grettir as incorrigible has already been discarded on the basis of the evidence from the analysis: The changes in the pattern of the dialogues speak for a character that slowly develops an understanding for his own role in the world. The portrayal of Grettir as sadistic cannot be supported by any utterances of the characters in the saga directly. It is a categorisation that depends on values outside the evidence of the saga. Judging from the amount of violence and cruelty depicted in the sagas, Grettir's behaviour – as

---

[41] Another detail that speaks for a depiction of a development in Grettir is the quality of the stanza. In the first episode the stanza is very straight-forward and easy to understand. In the second episode the stanza is syntactically rather intricate and contains four *kenningar*.

violent as it may seem to a modern reader – might have been considered rather 'normal' in his day and age.[42] Furthermore the pranks are not described as premeditated, which I take as evidence that cruelty is not the topic for these stories from Grettir's childhood. Rather one gets the impression that he mainly acts on impulse and that the situation each time gets out of hand. To judge by his mother's comment in dialogue III (H 2) he basically lacks what we might call prudence and considerateness.

When we turn to Cook's comment about Ásmundr, there isn't any clarifying evidence in the dialogues that allows us to call him tyrannous or unreasonable either; he might rather be characterised as prone to bad judgement and as a father who has forgotten his own childhood. The saga describes Ásmundr as difficult in his youth without giving any specific examples of his difficult behaviour. In spite of the trouble he caused when he was young when he like his own son did not want to work and had a bad relationship with his father, he developed into a first-rate farmer nevertheless. Based on Ásmundr's own career, his repeated attempts to set his son to work become a logical endeavour; he wants to train his son for his future occupation.

Also the question of whether Grettir shares this vision about a future as a farmer or whether we have met a hero in the making who needs bigger challenges than helping on the farm cannot be solved satisfactorily on the basis of the interaction in these dialogues alone. From Grettir's evaluation of the tasks it is obvious that he classifies all three of them as inappropriate; why he is not pleased with them he keeps to himself. The repeated use of ambiguous proverbs and the ability to create poetry on the spot are stylistic devices that serve to signal a heroic nature. Together with his challenging interaction style and his physical ability, these

---

[42] What constituted violence and cruelty to the contemporary saga audience is a difficult question. The prank with the geese might be a young boy's understanding of fun.

features signal to the audience that we have met a talented character with the potential to develop into a hero.[43]

With my analysis of the dialogues in chapter 14 of *Grettis saga* and my accounting for my readings I hope to have demonstrated how dialogue analysis results in a comprehensive micro-level and multi-faceted understanding of the characters' interaction. Such an in-depth understanding based primarily on internal evidence from the dialogues will most likely add a new dimension to saga research and may modify our perception of what the stories are about. We need to learn much more about how things are done with words in the sagas. This means that we, on the one hand, need to analyse many different dialogues in order to develop an understanding for the realm of interactions depicted in the sagas, and, on the other hand, need to analyse many dialogues of the same type in order to understand the individual patterns. The analysis of Grettir's verbal power struggle with his father has added to our understanding of the hero's interaction style. Further detailed analysis of all the dialogues in *Grettis saga* will without doubt reveal both more about how sagas were told in general and – most importantly – about this intriguing story of an outlaw with no luck.

---

[43] On the basis of this result Hastrup's psychological conclusion (Hastrup, "Tracing tradition," 291) does not convince me at all: "Largely because of the father, Grettir remains less than a man. What is more, he continues to behave in a stupid and asocial manner even as an adult."

Beowulf and *Njáls saga*:
A Trinitarian Approach

Rory McTurk

This paper is mainly about *Beowulf* and *Njáls saga*, as its title suggests, but I should like to begin with a discussion of the opening lines of *Cædmon's Hymn*, which I quote below from an edition based on one of the *Hymn*'s earliest known versions, the so-called Moore (or M) version, dating from the eighth century. I italicize the words which are relevant to my argument:[1]

Nu scylun hergan   hefaenricaes uard,
metudæs *maecti*,   end his *modgidanc*,
uerc uuldurfadur—   sue he uundra gihuaes,
eci dryctin,   or astelidæ!

I translate these lines as follows, again italicizing the relevant words:

Now we must praise heaven-kingdom's Guardian, the Creator's *powers* (*maecti*) and his *thought* (*modgidanc*), the *works* (*uerc*) of the Glory-father: how he, eternal Lord, established the beginning of every single wonder!

---

[1] Daniel Paul O'Donnell, *Cædmon's Hymn. A Multimedia Study, Archive and Edition*, Society for Early English and Norse Electronic Texts, Series A 7 (Cambridge: D. S. Brewer, 2005), 205. On the date of the manuscript containing this version, see O'Donnell, *Cædmon's Hymn*, 90, and n. 3, below.

I next quote these lines as paraphrased in Latin by Bede (†735) in Book IV, chapter 24, of his *Historia Ecclesiastica gentis Anglorum*, together with Colgrave's and Mynors's translation of Bede's text. Once again I italicize the relevant words:[2]

> Nunc laudare debemus auctorem regni caelestis, *potentiam* Creatoris et *consilium* illius, *facta* Patris gloriae: quomodo ille, cum sit aeternus Deus, omnium miraculorum auctor extitit [. . .].

> "Now we must praise the Maker of the heavenly kingdom, the *power* of the Creator and his *counsel*, the *deeds* of the Father of glory and how He, since he is the eternal God, was the Author of all marvels [. . .]."

Bede's Latin paraphrase is a contemporary translation of a version of the *Hymn* which may, for all we know, be closer to Cædmon's actual composition than its earliest surviving texts (of which the Moore text, quoted above, may even be the very earliest).[3] I have therefore felt entitled to be influenced by it in my own translation of the *Hymn*, at least to the extent of taking the form *uerc*, which could be either singular or plural in Old English, as plural: Bede's plural form *facta* leads me to translate it as "works" rather than "work." I have not gone so far as to translate the Old English plural form *maecti* ("powers") with a singular form, as Bede has done with his *potentiam* ("power"), but will pay respectful heed in what follows to Bede's interpretation of its meaning as singular rather than plural.[4]

---

[2] Bede, *Ecclesiastical History of the English People*, ed. Bertram Colgrave and R. A. B. Mynors (Oxford: Clarendon Press, 1992), 416-17.

[3] See O'Donnell, *Cædmon's Hymn*, 169-73.

[4] Compare the note to the form *maecti* in *Sweet's Anglo-Saxon Reader in Prose and Verse*, 15th ed., ed. Dorothy Whitelock (Oxford: Clarendon Press, 1967), 282, and see further A. Campbell, *Old English Grammar*, rev. ed. (Oxford: Clarendon Press, 1974), 242.

In 1959 Bernard F. Huppé suggested that the three words italicized in the *Hymn* as quoted above were open to a Trinitarian interpretation, from Bede's point of view, at least. According to Huppé, Bede would have been likely to see them as reflecting respectively, in the order in which they occur in the *Hymn*, the three Persons of the Holy Trinity: Father, Son, and Holy Spirit. Using the terms *Might* and *Work* for what have been translated above as "powers" and "works" respectively, Huppé writes: "the Might of God, the Creator, would represent the Father; the Thought of the Father, His plan and disposition of creation, the Son; the Work, the Holy Ghost."[5] It may be noted that, elsewhere in his discussion, Huppé translates *modgidanc*, not as "Thought," as in the passage just quoted, but as "Wisdom."[6] T. P. Dunning, C. M., in a review of Huppé, was prepared to agree that "Bede did indeed understand the opening lines" of the *Hymn* "as a Trinitarian invocation," but differed from Huppé in claiming that Bede, in his Latin paraphrase, took *metud* as referring to the Holy Spirit.[7] This would presumably mean that the *maecti*, or powers, of line 2 of the *Hymn* were seen by Bede as primarily an attribute of the Holy Spirit, rather than, as Huppé supposed, of the Father. Morton W. Bloomfield, in a note on the *Hymn* as discussed by Huppé, acknowledged that Bede's word for *maecti*, *potentia* ("power"), was "certainly traditionally connected with the Father." He also acknowledged that the concept of the Son might underlie the word *modgidanc*, but questioned Huppé's apparent equation of "wisdom" with "thought" as a translation of that word. He admitted that "wisdom" was "a possible translation and obviously suitable as an epithet for the Son," but maintained that the translation "thought" was preferable, as being more in line than "wisdom" with the findings of modern

---

[5] Bernard F. Huppé, *Doctrine and Poetry. Augustine's Influence on Old English Poetry* (Albany: State University of New York, 1959), 111.

[6] Huppé, *Doctrine and Poetry*, 109-11.

[7] T. P. Dunning, C. M., review of Huppé, *Doctrine and Poetry*, in *Review of English Studies* 12 (1961): 409-12, at 411.

lexicography and with Bede's use of the word *consilium*.[8] In maintaining that "wisdom" was a suitable epithet for the Son, Bloomfield may well have been thinking of I Corinthians 1:24, where Christ is indeed described as the wisdom of God (though also as the power of God: *Christum Dei virtutem et Dei sapientiam* "Christ, the power of God and the wisdom of God," as will be further noted below).[9] He went on to argue that Bede was here following the commentaries of St. Augustine (354-430) on the Book of Genesis in apprehending the creation of the world as an externalization of the Father's thought in the Son: as a virtual equivalent, in fact, of the Logos, or Word, even though Bede uses the word *consilium* rather than *verbum*. Bloomfield was thus prepared to accept a Trinitarian interpretation of the opening lines of the *Hymn* as far as the first two Persons were concerned, while differing from Huppé, not in linking the word *modgidanc* with the Son, but in the way he did so. He was decidedly critical, however, of Huppé's association of *uerc* ("work(s)") with the Holy Spirit, maintaining that Bede's past participle, *facta*, "hardly suggests the activating work of the Holy Ghost, but rather the completed work."[10]

It is interesting to note, not least in connection with this last point, that in 1974 D. R. Howlett found in the *Hymn* a Trinitarian pattern that differed considerably from the one identified by Huppé, and which depended on an understanding of the *Hymn* and of Bede's Latin that also differed markedly from what is reflected in the translations given above. Since *uerc* and *facta* are both neuter forms in their respective languages and could formally be either nominative or accusative, he took each of them as nominative and presented them as the subjects of *scylun* and *debemus* respectively,

---

[8] M. W. Bloomfield, "Patristics and Old English Literature: Notes on Some Poems," *Comparative Literature* 14 (1962): 36-43, at 41-42 and 41, n. 14.
[9] Latin and English quotations from the Bible in the present article are from the Vulgate and Douay-Rheims versions respectively.
[10] Bloomfield, "Patristics," 42-43 and 41, n. 14.

and gave a translation which he allowed to serve for both the Old English and the Latin text, as follows:[11]

> "Now ought we, the creatures of the Father of glory, to praise the Guardian of the Kingdom of Heaven, the Power of the Ruler, and His Counsel. Thus did He, the Eternal Lord, establish the beginning of every wonder [...]."

Here *uerc* and *facta* are no longer objects (along with *uard/auctorem*, *maecti/potentiam* and *modgidanc/consilium*) of the verbs *hergan* and *laudare* ("to praise") but have become the subjects of the auxiliary verbs *scylun* and *debemus* respectively and hence of the sentences in which they occur. This means that, for Howlett, they cannot be seen as reflecting any aspect of the Trinity, which, he nonetheless maintains, is the object of praise in these lines. He sees the Father, Son, and Holy Spirit as reflected, respectively, in the words *uard* ("guardian"), *maecti* ("power"), and *modgidanc* ("counsel"). I am not enough of an Old English specialist, or indeed of a Latinist, to say how far, if at all, Howlett's reading of these two texts stretches the rules of Old English and/or Latin syntax, but would note that in taking the words *uard* and *auctor* as each forming a three-part series with words meaning "power" and "counsel" Howlett is making both Caedmon and Bede guilty of the stylistic failing known as "mixed category," which offends against the principle that items in any kind of list should belong to the same category of ideas.[12] A word meaning "guardian" or "maker" could appropriately be applied to a *Person* of the Trinity, whereas words meaning "power" and "counsel" (as opposed to "power-wielder" or "counsellor") would surely be expected to refer to *attributes* of the

---

[11] David R. Howlett, "The theology of Cædmon's hymn," *Leeds Studies in English*, New Series 7 (1974): 1-12, at 7. See further D. R. Howlett, *British Books in Biblical Style* (Dublin: Four Courts Press, 1997), 262-74.
[12] Robert Graves and Alan Hodge, *The Reader over Your Shoulder: A Handbook for Writers of English Prose*, 2nd ed., abridged (London: Jonathan Cape, 1947), 114-15.

Trinity. I am not saying that this necessarily invalidates Howlett's argument, but that it is a consideration that he might profitably have taken into account. His view that the wording of the *Hymn* implies processsion of the Holy Spirit from the Father alone (rather than from the Father and the Son), and that this somehow justifies his associating *his modgidanc* ("His Counsel") with the Holy Spirit, also seems to me on the face of it questionable and in any case to require more argumentation than he gives it.[13]

What I do find interesting and attractive about Howlett's discussion is the fact that he sees Cædmon and Bede as associating power with the Son. In support of this Howlett quotes I Corinthians 1:24, where Christ is described as the power of God (*Dei virtutem*),[14] as shown above. Leaving aside for the moment the fact, already noted, that the passage in question immediately goes on to describe Christ as the wisdom of God – a fact which does not emerge from Howlett's quotation – we may point out that the vesting of power in the Son is consistent with two theological doctrines, both of which would have been known to Bede, at least. These are what Michel René Barnes has called the neo-Nicene and pro-Nicene doctrines of "one power." According to Barnes, "neo-Nicene theology identifies the Son as the single, proper 'Power' of God, while pro-Nicene theology understands the Father and the Son to share the 'Power' of God, and thus to share the same nature."[15] Of these two doctrines the former, the older one, is found in the *De virginibus ad Marcellinam* of St. Ambrose (†397), while the latter is found in the same author's *De fide ad Gratianum Augustum*, written some four years later; both works were known to Bede.[16] The section of the former work that most clearly illustrates

---

[13] See Howlett, "The theology," 8.
[14] Howlett, "The theology," 7.
[15] Michel R. Barnes, *The Power of God. Δύναμις in Gregory of Nyssa's Trinitarian Theology* (Washington, D. C.: Catholic University of America Press, 2001), 170.
[16] For the information that Bede was acquainted with Ambrose's *De virginibus*, and made use of it in his commentary on Genesis (and perhaps also in his *Historia Ecclesiastica*), I am indebted to the Fontes Anglo-

the neo-Nicene doctrine is *De virginibus*, Book III, chapter 1, parts 2-4, where Christ is described (in part 4) as *virtus Dei* ("the power of God"),[17] while the part of the latter work that is perhaps most germane to the pro-Nicene doctrine is *De fide*, Book I, chapter 1, parts 9 and 10, where Ambrose interprets Christ's words in John 10:30 (*ego et Pater unum sumus* "I and the Father are one") as meaning that there should be no separation of power and nature (*ne fiat discretio potestatis et naturæ*) between Father and Son, and presents Christ's injunction (in Matthew 28:19) to baptize the nations in the name of the Father, Son, and Holy Spirit as showing the Trinity to be of one power (*unius esse Trinitatem potestatis*).[18] Thus, whatever Cædmon's own theological position may have been, Bede would presumably have had no difficulty in associating the word *maect* ("power") in line 2 of the *Hymn* with the second Person of the Trinity, the Son; he might even have been likely to do so.

Enough has been said so far to show that there is considerable diversity of opinion among writers on the Trinity, ancient and modern, as to which of various possible attributes should be associated with which of its three Persons. This is hardly surprising. Believing Christians would no doubt point out that the properties of the Trinity cannot and should not be neatly pigeon-holed; and St. Augustine indeed makes the point, towards the end of his *De Trinitate* (Book XV, ch. 17, part 28), that if we think of the three

---

Saxonici Project, ed., *Fontes Anglo-Saxonici: World Wide Web Register*, http://fontes.english.ox.ac.uk/, accessed November 2007. As for Bede's knowledge of Ambrose's *De fide*, apparent not least in his commentary on St. Mark's gospel, this is clear from M. L. W. Laistner, "The library of the Venerable Bede," in *Bede. His Life, Times, and Writings. Essays in Commemoration of the Twelfth Centenary of his Death*, ed. A. Hamilton Thompson (Oxford: Clarendon Press, 1935), 237-66, at 240, 242, 247, 262, 263.

[17] *Sancti Ambrosii, Mediolanensis Episcopi, Opera Omnia* [. . .], ed. J.-P. Migne, *Patrologia Latina* 14-17, 2 vols., each in 2 parts (Paris: [Migne], 1879-87), vol. II, part 1 (1880), cols. 232-33.

[18] *Sancti Ambrosii* [. . .] *Opera*, ed. Migne, vol. II, part 1(1880), col. 553.

Persons of the Trinity as possessing (for example) the qualities of
memory, understanding, and love,[19] we should recognize "that all
together possess and each one possesses all three of these" (*ut omnia
tria et omnes et singuli habeant*).[20] It should be borne in mind here that
it is in the writings of the Church Fathers, rather than in the Bible,
that the doctrine of the Trinity becomes explicit: it is Tertullian
(?160-?220) who is believed to have invented the term "Trinity"
(*Trinitas*), as well as much other Christian terminology.[21] The
doctrine is nevertheless felt to have been implicit in the Bible, as
Alister E. McGrath has shown. McGrath cites a number of passages
from the New Testament – not least Matthew 28:19, quoted above
– to illustrate the Christian message that the Father is revealed in
Christ, the Son, through the Holy Spirit, finding that the earliest
Christian writers needed these three elements, Father, Son, and
Holy Spirit, to express the totality of God. He also finds that the
doctrine is adumbrated in the Old Testament, from which he
extrapolates three ideas, corresponding to what came to be regarded
as the three Persons of the Trinity. These are Wisdom, the Word,
and the Spirit. The first of these, Wisdom, is especially evident in

---

[19] I say "for example" because, earlier in the same work, Augustine offers
various other three-part series as aids to understanding, by analogy, the
threefold nature of the Trinity and the interaction of its three Persons. In
Book IX, ch. 5, he writes in this connection of mind, love, and
knowledge; in Book X, chs. 11-12, of memory, understanding, and will;
and in Book XI, chs. 3-5, of the memory, the inner vision, and the will. In
Book XIV, ch. 7, part 10, in the memory-understanding-will context, he
links the concept of will with that of love. For an edition and translation
of *De Trinitate*, see the next footnote.

[20] The translation is quoted from Saint Augustine, *On the Trinity*, trans.
Stephen McKenna, Fathers of the Church 45 (Washington, D. C.:
Catholic University of America Press, 1963), 493, and the original from
Sancti Aurelii Augustini, Hipponensis Episcopi, Opera Omnia [. . .], ed. J.-P.
Migne, *Patrologia Latina* 32-47; 11 vols. plus 1 supplementary vol., vols. III,
IV, V and X are in 2 parts each (Paris: [Migne], 1861-1902), vol. VIII
(1886), col. 1080.

[21]Alister E. McGrath, *Christian Theology. An Introduction*, 5th ed. (Oxford:
Blackwell, 2011), 238-44.

the Books of Proverbs, Job, and Ecclesiastes as a personification, most often in female form, of God's creative, shaping aspect. The second, the Word, is portrayed, particularly in the Psalms and in the Book of Isaiah, as the speech or discourse whereby human beings are made aware of the divine will and purpose. The third, the Spirit, which is referred to in the Books of Isaiah and Ezekiel in connection with the Messiah and the new order that will replace the old, is presented as the assurance of "God's presence and power within the creation."[22] The authors and audiences of *Cædmon's Hymn*, *Beowulf*, and *Njáls saga* are just as likely to have derived their knowledge of Christian doctrine from the Vulgate version of the Bible as from the writings of the Fathers, if not more so,[23] and it should not be thought that their conceptions of the Trinity were necessarily rigid or compartmentalized.

With the foregoing considerations in mind, I should like to suggest that the *modgidanc* ("thought"), *maecti* ("powers") and *uerc* ("works") attributed to God in *Cædmon's Hymn* represent the Father, Son, and Holy Spirit respectively. It is true that in this reading the *Hymn*, in placing the mention of *maecti* before that of *modgidanc* in line 2, is departing from the order in which the Persons of the Trinity are usually listed, but the *Hymn's* ordering here may, I believe, be explained on metrical grounds; it is difficult to see how the order of the two words could be reversed in the line without departure from the rules governing stress and alliteration in Old English poetry.[24] I am not persuaded that the concepts of

---

[22] McGrath, *Christian Doctrine*, 239. The Book of Ecclesiasticus in fact provides a rather better example than Ecclesiastes of the personification of Wisdom in female form.

[23] Cf. Svanhildur Óskarsdóttir, "Prose of Christian Instruction," in *A Companion to Old Norse-Icelandic Literature and Culture*, ed. Rory McTurk (Malden: Blackwell, 2005; rpt. 2011), 338-53, at 343-47.

[24] In seeking to substantiate this point I shall depart from the wording of the *Hymn* only to the extent of hypothetically reordering the wording of its second line. One such reordering might produce the line: **metudæs modgidanc,   end his maecti*, which would mean that the a-verse (*metudæs modgidanc*) exemplified Bliss's type 1D*4 (see Alan J. Bliss, *The Metre of*

"thought" and "wisdom" are quite so far removed from one
another as Bloomfield implies, and, while accepting his translation
of *modgidanc* as "thought," am encouraged by McGrath's apparent
association of Wisdom with the Person of the Father, and by
Bloomfield's reluctant admission that "wisdom" is "a possible
translation" of *modgidanc*, quoted above, to understand that word as
referring in *Cædmon's Hymn* to an attribute of the Father. The
association of *maect* ("power") with the Person of the Son is
justified, I believe, on the basis of Howlett's and Barnes's
observations, summarized above; and as for the word *uerc*
("works"), translated by Bede as *facta*, meaning "works performed
or completed," I am again not convinced by the rigid distinction
that Bloomfield evidently wishes to draw between "the completed
work" and the "activating power of the Holy Ghost" in this
context. The New Testament equivalent of "God's presence and
power within the creation" to which McGrath refers in the context
of the Old Testament's presentation of the Spirit, as shown above,
is surely the work or acts (*acta*, cf. Bede's *facta*) of the apostles, who
according to Acts 2 were enabled to speak various languages as a
result of the Holy Spirit descending upon them at Pentecost,[25] and

---

Beowulf [Oxford: Blackwell, 1958], 123), with resolution of the first two
syllables (though see Bliss, *The Metre*, 27-35), and that the b-verse (*end his
maecti*) would exemplify type a1b, a type which, however, would not be
expected to occur in a b-verse (see Bliss, *The Metre*, 123, 61). In my second
hypothetical reordering, **his modgidanc   end his maecti*, the a-verse (*his
modgidanc*) would be theoretically viable as a sub-type of type d4 (type d4a?
See Bliss, *The Metre*, 124), but the b-verse would be open to the same
objection as in my first hypothetical case. In my third and final
hypothetical reordering, **his modgidanc   end metudæs maecti*, the same would
hold true of the a-verse (*his modgidanc*) as in my second hypothetical case,
but the b-verse (*end metudæs maecti*) would be open to the objection that
double alliteration would not be expected to occur in a b-verse (see Alan
Bliss, *An Introduction to Old English Metre* [Oxford: Blackwell, 1962], 12).

25 Here and elsewhere in this paper I have been very much influenced by
Dorothy L. Sayers, *The Mind of the Maker* (7th ed., London: Methuen,
1944). I have avoided making specific reference to this book, however, as

so to begin the missionary work by which, according to Christian belief, the activating power of the Holy Spirit sustains the life of the Church. It will be seen that I am allowing here for a certain amount of breadth in interpreting the meanings of the three words in question, and I would stress that what I have suggested should not be taken to imply an assumption that Cædmon and/or his audience would necessarily have taken a rigid view of the distribution of divine attributes among the Persons of the Trinity, or would not have allowed for a measure of interchange or overlap among them.

As it happens, the noun *maect* ("power") is found (in its variant form *miht*) only twice in *Beowulf*, once (at line 940) with reference to the power of God, and once (at line 700) with reference to Beowulf's own power, strength, and physical courage.[26] R. E. Kaske readily associates other words in *Beowulf* meaning "power" or "strength" (notably *mægen* and *cræft*) with the concept of "courage,"

Sayers's terminology differs from mine in ways that might be confusing. She uses the terms *Idea*, *Energy*, and *Power* (see especially Sayers, *The Mind*, 26-35) for the concepts she sees as corresponding to the Father, Son, and Holy Spirit respectively, but also uses the term *Activity* (Sayers, *The Mind*, 30-31, 54, 97, 141, 162), apparently as an alternative to the second term, *Energy* (for what corresponds to the second Person). Her overall argument is that the creative process on the human level is Trinitarian in structure and reflects, albeit imperfectly, the creativity of the Trinity on the divine level. It is thus of great relevance, in ways that go far beyond the scope of this paper, to a study of the story of Cædmon, which she does not mention.

[26] The adjective *mihtig*, on the other hand, occurs six times in the poem, see *Klaeber's Beowulf and the Fight at Finnsburg*, 4th ed., ed. R. D. Fulk, Robert E. Bjork, and John D. Niles, Toronto Old English series 21 (Toronto: University of Toronto Press, 2008), 413. References in the present paper to the text of *Beowulf* are to this edition (which retains the traditional line numbering, while making use of findings which indicate that a case of dittography at ll. 2227-28 of *Beowulf* means that the poem is one line shorter than traditionally thought, lacking what was earlier regarded as l. 2229. See *Klaeber's Beowulf*, 4th ed. [2008], xxix, 76). Names of characters in *Beowulf* are given in slightly modernized spelling.

however, and if this association may be accepted (in much the same way as the concepts of "thought" and "wisdom" have been brought into relation with one another above), it is not difficult to correlate the first two members of the thought-power-works series found in *Cædmon's Hymn* with the ideals of *sapientia* ("wisdom") and *fortitudo* ("bravery"), which Kaske has seen as together constituting the controlling theme of *Beowulf*,[27] and which Michael Chesnutt sees as represented in *Njáls saga* by Njáll and Gunnarr respectively, and hence as helping to explain the two-part structure of this saga, with its first part celebrating the bravery of Gunnarr and its second the wisdom of Njáll.[28] The *sapientia et fortitudo* ideal evidently has a history going back as far as Homer, but the Latin terms used by Kaske and Chesnutt are taken from a passage in the first book of the *Etymologiæ* of Isidore of Seville (†636), where they refer to the qualities that are said to make heroes worthy of heaven.[29] It may be noted at this point that Frederich Klaeber, without using the Latin terms *sapientia* and *fortitudo*, sees the Germanic reflexes of the concepts they represent as corresponding, respectively, to the first and third parts of the three-part formula of thought, word, and deed.[30] It is surely tempting in the present context to correlate this latter series with the Persons of the Holy Trinity as discussed above, particularly if the Son is thought of as the Word of God, though it should be noted that Klaeber sees bravery as corresponding not to

---

[27] R. E. Kaske, "*Sapientia et fortitudo* as the controlling theme of *Beowulf*," *Studies in Philology* 55 (1958): 423-56, at 428. It may be noted that, in classical Latin, *fortitudo* has the meaning of "bodily strength" as well as of "courage"; see under *fortitudo* in Charlton T. Lewis and C. Short, *A Latin Dictionary* [...] (Oxford: Clarendon Press, 1879), 772.

[28] Michael Chesnutt, "Popular and Learned Elements in the Icelandic Saga-Tradition," in *Proceedings of the First International Saga Conference*, ed. Peter Foote et al. (London: Viking Society for Northern Research, 1973), 28-65, at 51-57.

[29] See Kaske, "*Sapientia et fortitudo*," 424.

[30] Frederich J. Klaeber, "Die christlichen Elemente im Beowulf," *Anglia* 35 (1911): 111-36, 249-70, 453-82; 36 (1912): 169-99. (Also published separately, *Die christlichen Elemente im Beowulf* [Halle: Niemeyer, 1912]). See Klaeber, "Die christlichen Elemente im Beowulf" (1911), 457.

the second member of the thought-word-deed series, as might have been expected if the Son were associated with power, as suggested above, but rather to the third, "deed," which it must be admitted lends itself to association with deeds of bravery no less readily than to an association with the Holy Spirit as reflected in the missionary acts, or deeds, of the apostles, such as the foregoing discussion might lead one to expect if the threefold correlation were made. Klaeber, who is here following Ernst Otto and Ernest J. Becker, does not however make this correlation, and neither does either of those two writers.[31] E. B. Cowell, indeed, to whom Becker refers in this context, shows that St. Augustine, far from correlating the thought-word-deed formula with the Trinity, criticized it in his account of the Manichean heresy, among whose adherents it was popular, as being confused and unphilosophical.[32] Cowell's many examples of the formula in question also show, incidentally, that the ordering of its three elements should in no way be regarded as fixed. Archbishop Hincmar of Rheims (806-882), on the other hand, a writer much closer in time and place than St. Augustine to the composition of *Beowulf*,[33] does seem to make the correlation in describing baptism in the following terms: *trina mersione* [...] *in nomine Patris, et Filii, et Spiritus sancti* ("by trine immersion in the

---

[31] Ernst Otto, *Typische Motive in dem weltlichen Epos der Angelsachsen* (Berlin: Mayer & Müller, 1902), 11-12, and Ernest Julius Becker, *A Contribution to the Comparative Study of the Medieval Visions of Heaven and Hell, with Special Reference to the Middle-English Versions* (Baltimore: John Murphy, 1899), 15.

[32] E. B. Cowell, "Thought, Word, and Deed," *The Journal of Philology* 3 (1871): 215-22, at 221-22. See further Charles D. Wright, *The Irish Tradition in Old English Literature* (Cambridge: Cambridge University Press, 1993), 79-84, with references.

[33] Here I simply note, with Andy Orchard, *A Critical Companion to Beowulf* (Cambridge, D.S. Brewer, 2003, 6), that "There is still no consensus on the date of the poem, with current estimates ranging from the seventh century to the eleventh (and indeed every century in between)." The earliest and latest conceivable dates of composition seem to be the late seventh and early eleventh century respectively. See *Klaeber's Beowulf*, 4th ed. (2008), clxii-clxxx, and further, Roberta Frank, "A scandal in Toronto: The Dating of 'Beowulf' a Quarter Century on," *Speculum* 82 (2007): 843-64.

name of the Father, and of the Son, and of the Holy Ghost"), and further stating: *omne peccatum, aut cogitatione, aut locutione, aut operatione efficitur; ideo triplici generi peccatorum trina videtur ablutio convenire (*"every sin is effected by thought, word, or deed. Wherefore the trine ablution seems to answer to the three classes of sins"). It may be noted that Hincmar does not specify which Person of the Trinity might be thought of as answering to which of these three types of sin; indeed he goes on to say that the purpose of threefold immersion in the name of each of the three Persons is to show "that the mystery of the Trinity may appear to be but one" (*ut Trinitas unum appareat sacramentum*), and he expresses this oneness with another three-part series: *unus est Deus, una fides, unum baptisma* ("One Lord, one faith, one baptism)."[34] Behind this seems to lie the view that the Persons of the Trinity should not be thought of as having rigidly demarcated domains. Hincmar of Rheims, it may here be added, had connections with Anglo-Saxon England and with viking Scandinavia: he solemnized the marriage of Æthelwulf, King of Wessex, the father of Alfred the Great, to his second wife Judith, the daughter of Charles the Bald, in 856, and, as the author of the Annals of St. Bertin for the years 861-82, chronicled viking activity in Francia during that period.[35]

While Klaeber, as already stated, does not correlate the thought-word-deed formula with the Trinity, it is interesting to note that his

---

[34] The Latin quotations from Hincmar are from his letter "Ad presbyteros Rhemensis parochiæ. De baptismo," as printed in *Hincmari Rhemensis Archiepiscopi Opera Omnia* [...], ed. J.-P. Migne, *Patrologia Latina* 125-26, 2 vols. (Paris: [Migne], 1879), vol. II, cols. 104-10, at col. 109. The English translation is quoted from the Rev. James Chrystal, *A History of the Modes of Christian Baptism: from Holy Scripture, the Councils Ecumenical and Provincial, the Fathers, the Schoolmen, and the Rubrics of the Whole Church East and West, in Illustration and Vindication of the Rubrics of the Church of England since the Reformation, and those of the American Church* (Philadelphia: Lindsay and Blakiston, 1861), 101-02.

[35] See Richard Abels, *Alfred the Great: War, Kingship and Culture in Anglo-Saxon England* (Harlow: Longman, 1998), 85, 107-08, 285-86, and *Hincmari* [...] *Opera*, ed. Migne, vol. I (1879), cols. 1203-1302.

examples of the formula include the description of the god Baldr in Snorri Sturluson's prose *Edda* as *vitrastr Ásanna ok fegrst talaðr ok liknsamastr* ("the wisest of the Æsir and most beautifully spoken and most merciful),"[36] and that Baldr has often been seen, whether rightly or wrongly, as a pagan counterpart of Christ.[37] His examples further include three from Bede's *Historia Ecclesiastica*, two of them found in contexts of virtuous behaviour, and one in a context of sin.[38] Klaeber also shows, with the help of further examples, that often only two of the formula's three elements are mentioned,[39] his implication being that mention of only two of them is enough to bring the three-part formula to mind. This is not so likely to be the case with the Trinity, at least as far as the first two Persons are concerned, since "father and son" is a pairing that would hardly give rise to thoughts of the Holy Spirit in any other than Christian theological contexts. The possibility that mention or implication of a father-son relationship in a medieval literary text might evoke thoughts in its audience of the first two Persons of the Trinity, other things being equal, is nevertheless one that deserves consideration in relation to *Beowulf* and *Njáls saga*, as I shall argue below. Enough has been said above, I trust, to suggest that the authors and audiences of these two works *may* have had a view of the Trinity comparable to what I have suggested in relation to

---

[36] See Klaeber, "Die christlichen elemente" (1911), 457. Snorri's *Edda* is quoted here from *Snorri Sturluson. Edda: Prologue and* Gylfaginning, ed. Anthony Faulkes (Oxford: Clarendon Press, 1982), 23, and the translation from Snorri Sturluson, *Edda*, trans. Anthony Faulkes (London: Dent, 1987), 23.

[37] See the items indexed under "Baldr" (sub-heading "Christ") in John Lindow, *Scandinavian Mythology: An Annotated Bibliography*, Garland Folklore Bibliographies 13 (New York: Garland, 1988), 508, and Heather O'Donoghue, *From Asgard to Valhalla: The Remarkable History of the Norse Myths* (London: I. B. Tauris, 2007), 94.

[38] See Klaeber, "Die christlichen elemente" (1911), 457, and *Bede's Ecclesiastical History*, ed. and trans. Colgrave and Mynors, 56-57, 494-95, 500-01.

[39] See Klaeber, "Die christlichen elemente" (1911), 457.

Cædmon's Hymn; this, at any rate, will be my assumption in what follows.

Before leaving *Cædmon's Hymn*, however, I would note that scholars have seen this work as reflecting the Holy Trinity not only in the words discussed above, but also in its overall structure, noting in particular its apparent preoccupation with the number three and its multiples: it has nine lines, shows a threefold chiastic patterning of words referring to the power and eternality of God, and to his act of creation, and consists (arguably) of three sentences, and (also arguably) of 81 syllables.[40] I shall not be looking here for a three-part structure in either *Beowulf* or *Njáls saga*, however; indeed I shall be arguing that these two works, insofar as they show a preoccupation with the Holy Trinity, give more emphasis to its first two Persons than to the third, and that this is reflected in the structure of each work. I agree with Chesnutt that the structure of *Njáls saga* is essentially bipartite, with its first part culminating (in the seventy-seventh of its 159 chapters) in the death of Gunnarr, who I would suggest reflects, albeit faintly and far from perfectly, the second Person of the Trinity, the Son, and with its second part culminating (in chs. 129-30) in the death of Njáll, whom I take to be similarly representative of the Father.[41] Precisely where the first part of the saga ends and the second begins is a matter of debate, but its essentially bipartite structure seems clear. To return for the moment to *Beowulf*, there is no doubt that in this poem there is a marked preoccupation with the number three, evident most especially in the prominence it gives to Beowulf's three great fights, each against a supernatural being: first Grendel and then Grendel's mother, both of whom he fights against and kills as a young man in Denmark, on

[40] See O'Donnell, *Cædmon's Hymn*, 179-86.
[41] References to *Njáls saga* are by chapter number to *Brennu-Njáls saga*, ed. Einar Ól. Sveinsson, Íslenzk fornrit 12 (Reykjavík: Hið íslenzka fornritafélag, 1954). It may be noted that the chapter numbers of *Njal's Saga*, trans. Magnus Magnusson and Hermann Pálsson, Penguin Classics: L103 (Harmondsworth: Penguin, 1960), and *Njal's Saga*, trans. Robert Cook, Penguin Classics (London: Penguin, 2001), coincide with those of the Icelandic edition.

behalf of the Danish king Hrothgar, and thirdly the dragon, against which he fights successfully, albeit receiving a fatal wound himself, as an old man, in his own counry, the land of the Geats, of which at that stage of the story he is king. It may be added that the second and third of these fights, those with Grendel's mother and the dragon, each have three clearly marked stages.[42] The three fights seem at first sight to invite a structural division of the poem into three, with the second part beginning at line 1251, shortly after which Grendel's mother is introduced, and the third beginning at line 2200, after which it is briefly explained, shortly before the dragon is introduced, that Beowulf has ruled the Geats for fifty years since becoming their king on the death of his cousin Heardred, the son of his uncle Hygelac. The trouble with this three-part division is that it imposes an unduly heavy burden on the second, central part of the poem. While the first and third parts thus envisaged are constructed neatly enough, with a prologue followed by the Grendel fight in the first and the dragon fight followed by an epilogue in the third, the second is relatively cumbersome: it begins with a recapitulation of the Grendel fight, and then covers the fight with Grendel's mother, Hrothgar's moralizing speech to Beowulf (known as "Hrothgar's sermon") and its postscript, Beowulf's return home to the land of the Geats, his reception by Hygelac, and his speech to Hygelac, which contains another recapitulation of the Grendel fight as well as one of the fight with Grendel's mother. In the face of this difficulty writers on *Beowulf* have tended to posit a division of the poem into two parts rather than three, with the second part beginning at line 2200. This division has however no manuscript authority, as far as I can see,[43] and imparts a certain imbalance to the poem in dividing it into two just over two-thirds of the way through a poem of 3,182 lines. It is

[42] See *Klaeber's Beowulf*, 4th ed. (2008), 207 (note to l. 1518) and 249 (note to ll. 2538-2711).

[43] See Julius Zupitza, *Beowulf: Reproduced in Facsimile from the Unique Manuscript British Museum MS. Cotton Vitellius A. xv*, 2nd ed., ed. Norman Davis, Early English Text Society, Original Series 245 (London: Oxford University Press, 1967), 101, and contrast the page referred to in the next note.

surely preferable to posit a two-part division with the second part of
the poem beginning at line 1888, with Beowulf's departure from
Denmark for his homeland. This division has manuscript authority
at least to the extent that it coincides with one of the divisions
between fitts, or numbered sections, that are marked in the
manuscript,[44] and credits the *Beowulf*-poet with more of a sense of
balance than is allowed by the traditional two-part division, since it
is relatively close, physically speaking, to the centre of the poem.
For the present argument it has the advantage of focusing attention
on a contrast in the poem between Beowulf abroad, among the
Danes, in the first part, and Beowulf at home, among his own
people, the Geats, in the second, a contrast just as important for
understanding the poem as the one between Beowulf's youth and
his old age, which is certainly present in the poem, and which the
traditional twofold division tends to accentuate.[45] The two-part
division here proposed draws attention in turn to yet another
contrast in the poem, the contrast between the roles of hero and
king, which is already apparent in the first part in the portrayals of
Beowulf and Hrothgar respectively. It is true that Beowulf's
accession to the Geatish throne is not reported until just after line
2200, as indicated above, but the lines leading up to this from 1888
onwards throw interesting light on the impression made by Beowulf
on his own people, the people over whom he is later to rule, raising
questions about his suitability for the role of king as opposed to
that of hero, in which latter role, he had, of course, functioned and
excelled among the Danes. We learn, for example (ll. 1993-97), that,
in spite of what Beowulf had implied to Hrothgar in the first part of

---

[44] See Zupitza, *Beowulf: Reproduced in Facsimile* (1967), 86.

[45] The latter contrast was strongly emphasized by J. R. R. Tolkien in his
famous lecture, *"Beowulf:* The Monsters and the Critics," *Proceedings of the
British Academy* 22 (1936): 245-95, at 271-72. In proposing a division of the
poem at l. 1887 – a division which Tolkien (*"Beowulf:* The Monsters," 273)
regarded as "secondary but important" – and in much else that I have
written here about *Beowulf*, I have been greatly influenced by discussions
with Alan Bliss, of whom I was fortunate enough to be a colleague at
University College Dublin from 1969 to 1978, and some of whose
seminars on *Beowulf* I was privileged to attend.

the poem, at ll. 415-18, Hygelac, at least, had not approved of Beowulf's expedition to Denmark, evidently considering it too rash an undertaking in the face of the threat posed by Grendel. We further learn (ll. 2183-89) that Beowulf had long been held in low esteem by his own people, including Hygelac; the impression given, indeed, is that in returning triumphant from Denmark he has at last proved himself.[46]

The hero-king contrast in *Beowulf* has been discussed by John Leyerle, with whose views I largely agree.[47] While agreeing also with Kaske to the extent that *sapientia* and *fortitudo* together constitute a major theme of *Beowulf*, I do not agree with him that Beowulf himself embodies these two qualities in virtually equal measure. I would see Beowulf as embodying *fortitudo* at the expense of *sapientia*, and would view Hrothgar, very much as Kaske does, as embodying *sapientia* at the expense of *fortitudo*.[48] Hrothgar, an aged king who is clearly held in the highest respect by his subjects (ll. 862-63), does not himself attack Grendel, presumably because it would be wrong for him to do so; as a king he must look after the interests of his people and not run the risk of leaving them leaderless as the result of a heroic death (which, to anticipate somewhat, is what Beowulf does at the end of the poem, as a result of the dragon fight; the two-part division of the poem, proposed above, also points up a contrast between Hrothgar and Beowulf in their roles as king). Leyerle, in contrast to Kaske, sees in the figure of Beowulf an example of bravery without *mensura*,[49] or a sense of proportion, which may surely be regarded as an aspect of *sapientia*, or wisdom. After Beowulf's victory over Grendel, Hrothgar expresses the wish to love Beowulf as a son, referring in this context to *nīwe sibbe*, the

---

[46] See Vilhelm Peter Grønbech, *The Culture of the Teutons*, trans. W. J. Alexander Worster, 3 vols. in 2 (London: Oxford University Press, 1931), I:118-19.

[47] John Leyerle, "Beowulf the Hero and the King," *Medium Ævum* 34 (1965): 89-102.

[48] Kaske, "*Sapientia et fortitudo*," 431-37.

[49] Leyerle, "Beowulf the Hero," 97.

"new kinship" between them (ll. 946-49), a relationship which
Hrothgar's wife Wealhtheow seems to confirm at ll. 1175-76, and to
which Beowulf himself refers at ll. 1474-79, just before embarking
on his fight with Grendel's mother. This is worth noting in the
context of what has been said above about possible echoes of the
Trinity in medieval literary references to father-son relationships.
After Beowulf's victory over Grendel's mother, Hrothgar addresses
Beowulf in the speech known as his sermon (ll. 1700-84). He begins
by referring to what he appears to see as Beowulf's combination of
sapientia and *fortitudo*, attributing to him *mægen mid mōdes snyttrum*
("strength with wisdom of the mind") (l. 1706), a phrase which
might almost be compared with the description in I Corinthians
1:24, referred to above, of Christ as the power and the wisdom of
God. He then goes on to contrast Beowulf with Heremod, an
earlier Danish king who was guilty of cruelty and avarice, urging
Beowulf to make the contrast his own, and then, after some general
reflections on the nature of pride, warns Beowulf against that vice
also. He further reminds Beowulf of the ultimate inevitability of
death, and concludes by reflecting on the misery he himself has
suffered as a result of Grendel's ravages. In the short postscript
which he adds after Beowulf's reply he once again seems to
attribute both *sapientia* and *fortitudo* to Beowulf, this time adding
eloquence as well. In a passage which Klaeber takes as his prime
example of the thought-word-deed formula, Hrothgar says: *Þū eart
mægenes strang ond on mōde frōd, / wīs wordcwida* ("you are strong in
might and mature in mind, wise in choice of words") (ll. 1844-45).[50]

Hrothgar's references to strength and wisdom might seem to
support Kaske's view that Beowulf combines *sapientia* and *fortitudo* in
more or less equal measure. It may however be noted, first of all,
that Hrothgar, a character in the poem, should not necesssarily be
thought of as expressing the views of the poet. Alternatively, even if
his words are taken as reflecting the poet's views, as they arguably
might be in recognition of the stylistic principle of what has been

---

[50] Klaeber, "Die christlichen elemente" (1911), 457.

called confirmation, whereby, in medieval literature, the vocabularies of narrator and character often coincide,[51] the references could be taken as hints at what is potentially rather than actually the case, and as parallel in this respect to the hints given later in the poem (as will be shown below) of Beowulf's comparability to Christ. Again, it should be remembered that the remarks in question are made at a relatively early stage of Beowulf's career, before his return to the land of the Geats and his accession to the throne. There are in fact indications in the second part of the poem that Beowulf has not fully assimilated the lessons of Hrothgar's sermon. Hrothgar had warned him against avarice and pride, and there is at least a case for saying that Beowulf by the end of the poem has succumbed to both these vices: to pride in scorning the help of followers in fighting the dragon (ll. 2345-47), and to avarice in what seems to be his inordinate preoccupation with the dragon's gold (ll. 2508-09, 2535-57, 2747-51, 2799-2800). While Beowulf may not have been cruel to his people in the same ways or degree that Heremod had been, there is perhaps an irony (on the part of the poet, at least) in the tribute paid to him in indirect speech by his followers at the very end of the poem (l. 3182), namely that he was *lēodum līðost ond lofgeornost* ("kindest to his people and most eager for praise"), since it was arguably his eagerness for praise as a hero rather than his concern for his people as their king that had led him to be less than kind to his people in attacking the dragon with only minimal help, and thus, in the event, leaving them without the protection of a leader.

As Leyerle shows, the heroic society portrayed in *Beowulf* calls for two different types of individual, the hero and the king. The hero is expected to be utterly fearless, and to enhance his reputation by undertaking avoidable adventures with a view to proving his fearlessness; the king is expected to be thoughtful, circumspect, and responsible, with a concern for the welfare of his people rather than for his own reputation. "[T]he fatal contradiction at the core of

---

[51] See Mark Lambert, *Malory: Style and Vision in* Le Morte Darthur, Yale Studies in English 186 (New Haven, Yale University Press, 1975), 8-16.

heroic society," which Leyerle sees as the major theme of *Beowulf*, means that an aspirant hero is most unlikely to grow up into the kind of man that this society requires to fulfil the role of king: "The greater the hero," he writes, "the more likely his tendency to imprudent action as king."[52] The hero's concern for his own reputation is indeed likely to lead to the irresponsibility that comes with pride, as suggested above in relation to Beowulf's disdain for help in fighting the dragon, and it is not difficult to see how the heroic code's emphasis on material possessions, the rewards that a hero might expect to receive from his leader, his *sincgifa* or "treasure-giver" (*Beowulf*, ll. 1342, 2311), for fearless action in his service, could be conducive to avarice. It is mainly against avarice and pride, as we have seen, that Hrothgar warns Beowulf in his sermon. This view of the poem's theme finds support in the numerous narrative digressions of the poem, most of which deal with topics not directly related to the three fights against monsters which form its main plot, and most of which point up, in one way or another, the tragic inadequacies of the heroic code. Several of them return to topics that have been treated in previous digressions, suggesting, perhaps, that the poet attached particular importance to those topics. It is noteworthy, for example, that two of them deal with Heremod, the first at ll. 901-15 and the second in the part of Hrothgar's sermon already referred to (ll. 1709-22). One of Heremod's faults, as already noted, was avarice. As many as three of them deal (at ll. 1202-14, 2354-66, 2913-21) with the death of Beowulf's uncle Hygelac on what seems to be have been a rashly undertaken raid on the territory of the Frisians, with whom Hygelac evidently opened hostilities *for wlenco* (l. 1206) ("on account of pride)." The longest of the digressions, the so-called Finn episode (ll. 1063-1160), the very length of which strongly suggests its thematic importance, illustrates the inevitably tragic consequences of the revenge ethic demanded by the heroic code with its account of the death of King Finn of the Frisians at the hands of enemies with whom he had tried to patch up earlier hostilities by negotiating

---

[52] Leyerle, "Beowulf the Hero," 89.

terms of peace: in other words, by behaving responsibly, as a king should.

If Beowulf has a tragic flaw, then, it is that he is not a sufficiently exceptional man to make a complete transition from the role of hero to that of king. The poem's overall portrait of Beowulf, however, is a sympathetic one. What is criticized in the poem is not so much Beowulf himself as the heroic code which he follows, as I hope I have given enough examples to show: his tragedy is not that he is an evil man, but that he is an ordinary man (as J. R. R. Tolkien wrote: "He is a man, and that for him and many is sufficient tragedy").[53] A consequence of this view, implicit in the poem rather than stated outright, is that the heroic code is inferior to the Christian code, which, arguably, is tailor-made for the ordinary man, to whom it holds out the promise of becoming both hero and king through being ultimately united with Christ, who, after his heroic triumph over death and hell, reigns as king in heaven.[54] What is particularly interesting in the present context is that the poem seems at times to hint at a comparison of Beowulf with Christ. We have already seen that such a comparison is hinted at in Hrothgar's sermon, where Hrothgar twice attributes strength and wisdom to Beowulf, thus recalling St. Paul's description of Christ as the power and the wisdom of God (I Corinthians 1:24). We may add here that Beowulf's injunction to his companions at ll. 2529-35 to wait and see the outcome of his single-handed engagement with the dragon has been compared to Christ's words to his disciples in Gethsemane: *sustinete hic et vigilate mecum* ("Stay you here, and watch with me") (Matthew 26:38; cf. Mark 14:34); that the disloyalty of ten out of his eleven followers in fleeing to save their skins after the first round of his fight with the dragon (ll. 2596-99) has been compared to Christ's desertion in Gethsemane by his disciples (Matthew 26:56; Mark 14:50); and that the loyalty of Wiglaf, the

---

[53] See Tolkien, "*Beowulf:* The Monsters," 260.

[54] This message is readily deducible from a careful reading of the Old English poem *The Dream of the Rood*. See Michael Swanton, ed., *Dream of the Rood* [3rd ed.] (Exeter: Exeter University Press, 1996).

eleventh man, to Beowulf (ll. 2599-2724) has been compared to the apostle Peter's resistance, shortly before his defection with the other disciples, to the High Priest's officers' arrest of Jesus (John 18:10; Matthew 26:51).[55]

What, then, are we to make of this poem in which the hero comes close to being condemned for his adherence to a code that is clearly at variance with Christian values, but in which he is also compared, at least by implication, with Christ? The echoes towards the end of the poem of the Gethsemane episode in the story of Christ are perhaps instructive here, since, as G. K. Chesterton noted, it is in Gethsemane, as well as at Golgotha, that the first two Persons of the Trinity come as near as they ever do to being in conflict.[56] In Gethsemane Christ says: *Pater* [...] *transeat a me calix iste* ("My Father, [...] let this chalice pass from me") (Matthew 26:39; cf. Mark 14:36); at Golgotha he says from the cross: *Deus meus Deus meus ut quid dereliquisti me* ("My God, My God, why hast thou forsaken me?") (Matthew 27: 46; Mark 15:34). One might also compare here Christ's words after his triumphal entry into Jerusalem and shortly before his arrest, as recorded in John 12: 27: *nunc anima mea turbata est et quid dicam Pater salvifica me ex hora hac* ("Now is my soul troubled. And what shall I say? Father, save me from this hour").

In *Beowulf* we have a thematic conflict between the roles of king and hero, represented respectively by Hrothgar, a greater king than Beowulf will ever be, and Beowulf, a greater hero than Hrothgar has ever been. The tension between the two roles is not resolved, however, because Hrothgar and Beowulf live in a pre-conversion world which has not received the gospel of Christ, who, as suggested above, provides a key to the reconciliation of these two roles. The *Beowulf*-poet is of course writing with an awareness of

---

[55] See *Klaeber's Beowulf*, 4th ed. (2008), 251 (note to l. 2596 ff.).

[56] Philip Yancey, intro., *Philip Yancey Recommends: Orthodoxy by G.K. Chesterton* (London: Hodder and Stoughton, 1999, first published as *Orthodoxy* [London: Bodley Head, 1908]), 204-06.

Christianity about pre-conversion people who are not aware of it, but is allowed by the stylistic principle of confirmation, described above, to combine the voices of narrator and character in such a way as to make his characters seem at times to express ideas of which they could not historically have been aware, as in the case, possibly, of Hrothgar's apparent attribution to Beowulf, in his sermon, of the power and wisdom of God as manifested in Christ. It will be remembered that Hrothgar, after Beowulf's slaying of Grendel, adopts Beowulf as his son. I would suggest that the poet sees these two figures, Hrothgar, with his *sapientia,* wisdom and thought, and Beowulf, with his *fortitudo,* courage and power, as embodying pre-Christian approaches to the properties associated by Christianity with the first two Persons of the Holy Trinity, the Father and the Son respectively. They symbolize those Persons only imperfectly, however, and there is a tension between the roles they represent in the poem, because they have not experienced the Third Person of the Trinity, the Holy Spirit, as manifested in the *acta* or *facta* of the apostles and their successors: the missionary work of conversion that would impart to them on the human level a unification of their roles that would in some measure reflect the harmony of the Trinity on the divine level. This view of the poem's theme accords well, I suggest, with the view of its structure offered above. It is essentially a two-part structure, which is in keeping with its primary concern with the first two Persons of the Trinity. Its preoccupation with the number three, also noted above, no doubt reflects the so-called Law of Three which in oral narrative often combines with the Law of Final Stress to make the events of a story rise to a climax in a tripartite sequence,[57] as Beowulf's three great fights do, but it may also be seen as serving to hint at the idea of the Trinity as thematically important in the poem.

In discussing the structure of *Beowulf* I have, I hope, given an idea of its plot that is sufficient for present purposes. I shall now attempt the well-nigh impossible task of briefly summarizing the

---

[57] See Axel Olrik, *Principles for Oral Narrative Research,* trans. Kirsten Wolf and Jody Jensen (Bloomington: Indiana University Press, 1992), 52-55.

highly complex plot of *Njáls saga*.[58] After recovering the dowry of his cousin Unnr Marðardóttir from her former husband Hrútr Herjólfsson, Gunnarr Hámundarson of Hlíðarendi becomes the third husband of Hallgerðr Hǫskuldsdóttir, Hrútr's niece (chs. 1-34). A quarrel between Hallgerðr and Bergþóra Skarpheðinsdóttir, the wife of Gunnarr's friend Njáll Þorgeirsson, results in the killing by Sigmundr Lambason of Þórðr Sigtryggsson, the former fosterer of Njáll's sons, and their killing of Sigmundr in revenge (chs. 35-45). Gunnarr's killing of Otkell Skarfsson in a feud initiated by Hallgerðr prompts Njáll's advice to Gunnarr never to kill twice in the same family, advice he is forced to disregard when, after a feud between himself and the brothers-in-law Starkaðr Barkarson and Egill Kolsson, in which the latter is killed, Gunnarr kills Otkell's son Þorgeirr when he and one of Starkaðr's sons, also named Þorgeirr, join forces against him. Banished from Iceland for three years, Gunnarr refuses to leave, and is slain by a group including Starkaðr, the latter's son Þorgeirr, and Unnr's son by her second marriage, Mǫrðr Valgarðsson, whose envy of Gunnarr has led him to plot against him from the time of Gunnarr's feud with Otkell onwards (chs. 46-81). Njáll's sons now kill Þráinn Sigfússon, who had been present at the slaying of their foster-father Þórðr, mentioned above, and who more recently had caused them trouble in Norway by involving them in the concealment of a wanted man. Njáll, anxious to keep the peace, adopts Þráinn's son Hǫskuldr as a foster-son (chs. 82-99). After the saga has paused to describe Iceland's (and Njáll's) conversion to Christianity (chs. 100-06), Njáll's sons, egged on by Mǫrðr's slanders, kill the innocent Hǫskuldr. This leads Flosi Þórðarson, the uncle of Hǫskuldr's wife, Hildigunnr Starkaðardóttir, to take revenge on Njáll's family by burning them to death with the help of a hundred followers (chs. 107-30). The one survivor of the burning, Njáll's son-in-law Kári Sǫlmundarson, starts legal proceedings against the burners, but when fighting breaks out at the *alþingi* as the result of a technical blunder in

---

[58] References to *Njáls saga* are as indicated in n. 41, above. Names of characters are given in their Old Icelandic nominative forms.

Mǫrðr's prosecution of the case against Flosi, Kári shoulders the responsibility of vengeance independently. He slays some of the burners and others fall in the defeat of the Norsemen by the Irish at Clontarf. Eventually, after Flosi and Kári have each made a pilgrimage to Rome, they are reconciled, with the marriage of Kári to Hildigunnr (chs. 131-59).

Whereas *Beowulf* portrays an exclusively pre-conversion society, *Njáls saga*, as will be clear from this summary, portrays a society which is converted to Christianity (nominally, at least) well over half-way through the action. There is manuscript evidence to suggest that the author of the saga attached particular importance to the chapters describing the conversion, and this has led Lars Lönnroth in particular to see the chapters in question as introducing the second of the saga's two main parts.[59] While this evidence should certainly not be ignored, considerations of balance as well as of theme, comparable to those adduced above in relation to *Beowulf*, suggest that the most natural dividing-line between the two parts of the saga comes at the end of ch. 81, where the story of Gunnarr is rounded off shortly after the account of his death in ch. 77.[60] If the first part of the saga is seen as the story of Gunnarr, and the second, beginning with ch. 82, as predominantly that of Njáll (who does, however, figure prominently in the first part also), this view accords well with the theme of *fortitudo* and *sapientia*, qualities which, as Chesnutt has argued, Gunnarr and Njáll respectively illustrate. Chesnutt indeed maintained that *Njáls saga* lays greater emphasis on *sapientia* than on *fortitudo*,[61] which is consistent with Njáll featuring in both of its two parts and Gunnarr only in one. In the portrayal of Njáll's friendship with Gunnarr there is nothing quite comparable to Hrothgar's adoption of Beowulf as a son; nor indeed is it certain

---

[59] See Lars Lönnroth, *Njáls saga: An Introduction* (Berkeley: University of California Press, 1976), 23-24, 28, with references.
[60] Compare the view of Cook as expressed in *Njal's Saga*, trans. Cook, xxxi-ii.
[61] Chesnutt, "Popular and Learned Elements," 53.

that Njáll is much older than Gunnarr.[62] His frequent advice to
Gunnarr, which is by no means always as cynical as my summary of
the saga may have suggested, may however be compared in general
terms with Hrothgar's sermon, to which it comes closest, perhaps,
in ch. 32, where Njáll warns Gunnarr, on the latter's triumphant
return from winning fame and fortune abroad, that he must expect
to encounter envy. Another of the many differences between
Beowulf and *Njáls saga* is that, whereas *Beowulf* does no more than
hint at the concept of the Holy Trinity, *Njáls saga* actually mentions
it: in the sixth of the conversion chapters (105) the chieftain
Þorgeirr Tjǫrvason of Ljósavatn, in a passage clearly influenced by
the Christian Laws section of the Old Icelandic law code *Grágás*,
proclaims at the *alþingi* that all Icelanders are to be Christians and
believe in one God: Father, Son, and Holy Spirit (*at menn skulu allir
vera kristnir* [...] *ok trua á einn guð, fǫður ok son ok anda helgan*).[63]

Until relatively recently, there was fairly general agreement
among writers on *Njáls saga* that the conversion of Iceland marks a
moral turning-point in the story, signalling a replacement of the
heroic ethic of the blood-feud by a Christian ethic of mercy and
forgiveness. One version of this view is that the structure of *Njáls
saga* is comparable to that of the Bible, with its first and second
parts (the second beginning with the conversion chapters)
corresponding to the Old and New Testaments, the death of
Hǫskuldr to that of Christ, the battle of Clontarf to Armageddon,
and the reconciliation of Flosi and Kári to the building of the New
Jerusalem.[64] Another is that Hǫskuldr's slaying, the burning, Njáll's
death, and Flosi's pilgrimage reflect a pattern of sin, punishment,
expiation, and atonement respectively.[65] In addition to the final

[62] Compare *Njal's Saga*, trans. Cook, xiv, xl.
[63] *Brennu-Njáls saga*, 272, and n. 3 on that page.
[64] Lönnroth, *Njáls saga: An Introduction*, 148-49.
[65] This view is not shared by Cook, but is well summarized by him in
Robert Cook, "The Effect of the Conversion in *Njáls saga*," *The Audience of
the Sagas: The Eighth International Saga Conference. Preprints*, ed. Lars
Lönnroth, 2 vols. (Gothenburg: Göteborgs universitet, 1991), I:94-102, at
97.

reconciliation, the noble gesture by the chieftain Hallr Þorsteinsson of Síða in rejecting compensation for the slaying of his son in the battle following the legal wrangle at the *alþingi* (ch. 145) has been pointed out as an example of the new Christian spirit.[66]

Recent writers have however demonstrated that *Njáls saga* is both simpler and more complex than this view suggests. Simpler, because it is easier to see the death of Hǫskuldr as part of a pattern of feuding and revenge than in terms of one of sin and expiation;[67] and to see the reconciliation of Flosi and Kári as due to a feeling by both that enough killing has been done to satisfy the demands of vengeance than as the result of any especially Christian impulse.[68] More complex, because, with the conversion chapters, the author seems to introduce into the saga an ironic tension between the requirements of Christianity on the one hand, and, on the other, the persistence of most Icelanders in the bad old ways. This only becomes gradually apparent. At first, indeed, it looks as though Christianity is on the side of blood-vengeance, as when, in ch. 106, just after the conversion has been described, Njáll's grandson Ámundi Hǫskuldsson the Blind, the son of Njáll's illegitimate son (confusingly named Hǫskuldr), receives the miraculous gift of sight for just long enough to kill the slayer of his father. As soon as he has done this, however, he becomes blind again for the rest of his life. What would have happened, one wonders, if he had resisted the temptation to kill?[69] The rejection by Hallr of Síða of compensation for his slain son, referred to above, is indeed a

---

[66] I. R. Maxwell, "Pattern in *Njáls saga*," *Saga-Book of the Viking Society* 15 (1957-61): 17-47, at 41-43; and Lönnroth, *Njáls saga. An Introduction*, 147-48.

[67] William Ian Miller, "Justifying Skarpheðinn: of Pretext and Politics in the Icelandic Bloodfeud," *Scandinavian Studies* 55 (1983): 316-44. Compare Cook, "The Effect of the Conversion," 98-99.

[68] Cook, "The Effect of the Conversion," 100.

[69] Andrew Hamer, "'It seemed to me that the sweetest light of my eyes had been extinguished'," *Introductory Essays on* Egils saga *and* Njáls saga, ed. John Hines and Desmond Slay (London: Viking Society, 1992), 93-101, at 99-101. Compare Cook "The Effect of the Conversion," 97-98.

handsome gesture, and wins such approval that he ends up receiving four times what is legally due to him – an ironic situation in itself; but its primary function in the narrative seems to be to throw into relief the contrasting attitude of Kári, who is set on vengeance for his own son, slain in the burning (ch. 147).[70] The prose text of the saga portrays the battle of Clontarf as a victory for the Christian Irish over the partly pagan forces of the Norsemen, whereas the poem known as *Darraðarljóð*, quoted just after the account of the battle (in ch. 157), presents it as a victory for the Norsemen.[71] This discrepancy effectively underlines the tension in the post-conversion part of the saga between Christian and pre-Christian values, raising for the reader the troubling question of whether Christianity really does finally triumph in *Njáls saga*'s world of ideas.

Most recently, Theodore M. Andersson has carried these arguments a stage further. Without especially emphasizing the Christian references in the saga, he argues that *Njáls saga*, standing as it does near the end of the period of classical saga writing, deliberately subverts the narrative positions of earlier sagas and offers instead a study in failure, not least the failure of the values of valour and wisdom, represented by Gunnarr and Njáll respectively.[72] These two characters, he maintains, "seem to be portrayed as paragons,"[73] but are nevertheless open to criticism on a number of counts. They are both introduced (in chs. 19-24) in the

---

[70] Cook, "The Effect of the Conversion," 99-100.

[71] This discrepancy might be seen as an example of what Mikhail Bakhtin has called heteroglossia, the dialogic interaction of conflicting interests and ideologies. See Mikhail M. Bakhtin, *The Dialogic Imagination: Four Essays*, ed. Michael Holquist; trans. Caryl Emerson and Michael Holquist, University of Texas Press Slavic Series 1 (Austin: University of Texas Press, 1992), especially 263, 428.

[72] Theodore M. Andersson, *The Growth of the Medieval Icelandic Sagas (1180-1280)* (Ithaca: Cornell University Press, 2006), 201, 203. Andersson clearly accepts the well-established view that *Njáls saga* was written around 1280; compare *Brennu-Njáls saga*, lxxxiv.

[73] Andersson, *The Growth*, 192.

context of what Andersson calls the "highly questionable legal trick"[74] whereby Gunnarr, on Njáll's advice, deceives Hrútr into reciting a legal summons, the recitation of which by Hrútr will enable Gunnarr to take him to court over the matter of Unnr's dowry, which Gunnarr is seeking to recover. When this stratagem fails, Gunnarr adopts the bullying tactic of challenging Hrútr to a duel which he, Gunnarr, is bound to win, thus forcing Hrútr to pay up. Also characteristic of Gunnarr is his tendency to make mistakes which turn out to have tragic consequences that in most cases might well have been foreseen. The most obvious example of this is his marriage to Hallgerðr, very much in the face of what seems an honest rundown of her character by her uncle, Hrútr, and Njáll's strong disapproval (chs. 33-34); another is his buying from Otkell, in place of the hay that Otkell churlishly refuses him, a slave, Melkólfr, whose presence in Gunnarr's household serves only to worsen his relations with Otkell when Hallgerðr persuades Melkólfr to steal food from Otkell's farm, thus initiating the feud which culminates in Gunnarr's killing of Otkell (chs. 47-54). Yet another is his accepting from the sons of Egill Kolsson their challenge to a horse-fight, the violent consequences of which lead to Gunnarr's killing of Otkell's son Þorgeirr, and so to his killing twice in the same family, in contravention of Njáll's express warning (chs. 58-72). Finally, there is his fatal mistake in deciding to stay in Iceland in defiance of the banishment from the country for three years that results from these killings (ch. 75).[75]

Before Andersson's view of Njáll is discussed, it may be noted that his strictures about Gunnarr, just listed, hardly detract from Gunnarr's strength and courage, the qualities that make him a hero. What Andersson mainly seems to be accusing him of is the kind of folly that is likely to arise from limited vision, interpretable in Gunnarr's case as a kind of innocence. Although Andersson does not use the Latin term *fortitudo*, he does not deny Gunnarr's status as a hero; indeed he notes that Gunnarr, in his journey abroad (in

---

[74] Andersson, *The Growth*, 190.
[75] Andersson, *The Growth*, 192-95.

chs. 28-32) after his success in recovering Unnr's dowry, "authenticates himself as a figure of truly mythic proportions" in warlike and athletic activity, and in his conduct at the courts of the Danish and Norwegian kings.[76] Andersson tends to de-emphasize, however, the *fortitudo* shown by Gunnarr after his return to Iceland, not least in his heroic last stand (ch. 77), and he gives insufficient credit to Gunnarr's magnanimity in, for example, his conscientious attempts to compensate Otkell for the losses resulting from the theft undertaken at Hallgerðr's instigation (ch. 49). Interestingly, Andersson does not accuse Gunnarr of pride, as Lönnroth, a proponent of the view that Christianity ultimately triumphs in *Njáls saga*, had done. Lönnroth had seen Gunnarr's "excessive pride"[77] as one of the reasons for his deciding at the last minute not to leave Iceland for his three-year period of banishment, a decision prompted, apparently, by his suddenly noticing the beauty of the hillside near his farm at Hlíðarendi, with its "pale fields and mown meadows" (*bleikir akrar ok slegin tún*, ch. 75). Andersson, who does not seem to have been influenced by either Peter Foote's[78] or David Ashurst's[79] criticism of this view of Lönnroth's, evidently accepts it no more than they do; he does not in any case see Beowulfian pride as prominent among Gunnarr's failings.

As for the character of Njáll, Andersson, while describing Njáll as "the quintessence of wisdom,"[80] emphasizes what he sees as the devious nature of his legal manoeuvering, not only in the case of Unnr's dowry, mentioned above, but also in his deliberately creating a situation of legal stalemate at the *alþingi* so that he can plausibly propose the establishment of a court of appeal, a Fifth Court (over and above the four courts already in operation), thus making it

[76] Andersson, *The Growth*, 190.

[77] Lönnroth, *Njáls saga: An Introduction*, 154.

[78] Peter Foote, "New Dimensions in 'Njáls saga'," *Scandinavica. An International Journal of Scandinavian Studies* 18 (1979): 49-58, at 56-57.

[79] David Ashurst, "*Bleikir akrar* – Snares of the Devil? The Significance of the Pale Cornfields in *Alexanders saga*," *Saga-Book of the Viking Society* 25 (1998-2001): 272-91.

[80] Andersson, *The Growth*, 201.

necessary for new chieftaincies to be established. His aim here is to secure for his foster-son Hǫskuldr the chieftaincy that will make him acceptable as a husband to Hildigunnr, who had made the chieftaincy a condition of her marrying him. Njáll is successful in this aim; the Fifth Court is indeed established (in the saga before, rather than, as happened historically, after the conversion),[81] and Hǫskuldr, having thereby become a chieftain, marries Hildigunnr (ch. 97). Andersson moreover does not entirely absolve Njáll of responsibility for the slaying of Hǫskuldr by his, Njáll's, sons (ch. 111). Without playing down the "consummate wickedness" of this act of theirs, he sees it as a not totally unforeseeable consequence of Njáll's fostering of Hǫskuldr, the son of his own sons' enemy, Þráinn Sigfússon, whom they had slain.[82] This departure from wisdom on Njáll's part, as Andersson sees it, is compounded, in his view, by Njáll's decision to retreat with his family into his house (against the advice of his son Skarpheðinn, ch. 128) when Flosi and his followers finally come to attack it.[83]

As with his remarks on Gunnarr, there is a certain selectiveness in Andersson's comments on Njáll. There is undoubtedly an element of cunning in Njáll's manipulation of the law, both in the case of Unnr's dowry and in that of the Fifth Court, but it should be remembered that Njáll's motivation is praiseworthy in both cases: in the former case he is seeking to help his friend Gunnarr in what he presumably sees as a worthy cause, and in the latter he is attempting to build on his charitable act of adopting Hǫskuldr as a foster-son, the purpose of which had clearly been to contain violence and preserve peaceful relations. His decision to retreat with his family into the house in the face of Flosi's attack is admittedly questionable, not least because it endangers others as well as himself; it is probably to be explained as due to combined

---

[81] See *Brennu-Njáls saga*, 246, n. 2; *Njal's Saga*, trans. Magnus Magnusson and Hermann Pálsson, 210 (note); and *Njal's Saga*, trans. Cook, 363 (under "Fifth Court").

[82] Andersson, *The Growth*, 198-99.

[83] Andersson, *The Growth*, 199, 201.

exhaustion and resignation, and as comparable in this respect, possibly, to Gunnarr's decision to stay in Iceland rather than obey the terms of his banishment. The fact that Andersson can describe Njáll as "the quintessence of wisdom" while at the same time making his criticisms, of which he has fewer in the case of Njáll than in that of Gunnarr, in any case hardly discourages the view that Njáll, whatever his failings, is an impressive representative of *sapientia* in the saga that bears his name.[84]

Andersson's discussion of *Njáls saga*, which is not confined to the characters of Gunnarr and Njáll, helps to show that the world portrayed in this saga is far from perfect, whether before or after the conversion of Iceland. Gunnarr of course dies unconverted, before the conversion takes place, and after his death is heard reciting verses in his burial-mound, proudly expressing the heroism he has shown in dying rather than yielding in battle (ch. 78). The conversion itself, as described in *Njáls saga* (chs. 100-05), hardly seems calculated to usher in an era of peace and love: the missionary Þangbrandr Vilbaldússon, sent to Iceland by King Óláfr Tryggvason of Norway to preach the new faith, and his companion Guðleifr Arason kill five people (not without provocation) while attempting to convert the Icelanders, and the eventual acceptance of the new religion at the *alþingi*, which makes provision for the continuation in secret of certain pagan practices, is presented as largely the result of a threat by King Óláfr to Icelanders in Norway and as a practical measure arising from the need for Iceland to have just one law (chs. 104-05). Njáll and his family are among those who accept Christianity (chs. 100, 102), and it is hardly surprising that Njáll, with his conciliatory, peace-loving instincts, finds the new religion congenial. More surprising is the case of his son

---

[84] In view of the fact, noted above, that Wisdom in the Old Testament is often personified as female, it is of some interest to note that in *Njáls saga* Njáll is presented as apparently unable to grow a beard (ch. 20), and as the target, consequently, of insulting remarks by Hallgerðr (in ch. 44) and Flosi (in ch. 123), the latter of whom says that few can tell by looking at him whether he is a man or a woman.

Skarpheðinn, who is very much a hero in the old mould, and on whose body are found, after the burning, indications that he, like his parents, had commended himself to God with the sign of the cross before dying (ch. 132; cf. ch. 129). Enough has been said above about Njáll's relationship with Gunnarr to suggest a comparison with a father-son relationship, even though such a comparison is not made explicit in the saga; and enough has been said about Njáll to show how, as a fount of wisdom, he might be seen as a human embodiment of certain of the characteristics attributed to the first Person of the Trinity, the Father. In looking for qualities in Gunnarr that might suggest the second Person of the Trinity, the Son (apart from such obvious "powers" as strength and physical courage), we may note his readiness to share hay and food with his neighbours in a time of famine (until his supplies run out, and he has to apply to Otkell, ch. 47); his professed aversion to killing at the end of ch. 54 (after circumstances beyond his control have led him to kill Otkell); and his reference in ch. 75, quoted above, to pale fields (*bleikir akrar*), which may reflect Christ's words to his disciples in John 4:35 about how the fields are already white for harvest, indicating that the time is at hand for the coming of the Kingdom of God[85] (if this is indeed a conscious reference to the gospel passage, it should naturally be viewed as a case of the narrator's voice merging anachronistically with Gunnarr's).[86] But neither Njáll nor Gunnarr is perfect, of course, and, strong and sustained though their friendship is, there is a conflict between the roles they represent in the saga, a conflict expressed by Vilhjálmur Árnason as follows: "The social need for peace and order calls for ways of acting which are in conflict with the heroic morality of honor, personal integrity, and vengeance."[87] This conflict, as will be evident, is comparable to that of the roles of king and hero in

---

[85] For commentary on the gospel passage, see John Marsh, *The Gospel of Saint John*, The Pelican New Testament Commentaries (Harmondsworth: Penguin, 1968), 221-27.

[86] Somewhat in the manner, that is, of the stylistic device of confirmation, briefly described above.

[87] Vilhjálmur Árnason, "Morality and social structure in the Icelandic sagas," *Journal of English and Germanic Philology* 90 (1991): 157-74.

Beowulf, discussed above. Taking Njáll and Gunnarr as representing *sapientia* and *fortitudo* respectively, Chesnutt writes: "the paths which they choose are estimable in themselves, but neither can lead to perfection."[88] If we take them also as imperfect human representatives of, respectively, the first and second Persons of the Holy Trinity, the Father and the Son, we might add that their paths can lead to perfection only if they are united with and by the third Person of the Trinity, the Holy Spirit, as manifested on the human level in the missionary work of conversion, the *acta* or *facta* of the apostles and their successors, of which Þangbrandr and Guðleifr, with their refusal to turn the other cheek, are woefully inadequate representatives, falling far short of the approximations of Njáll and Gunnarr to the other two Persons. Small wonder, then, that there is little moral improvement in the world of *Njáls saga* after Iceland's conversion.

In summary and conclusion: this paper took as its starting-point the idea that the Holy Trinity is an underlying theme of *Cædmon's Hymn*, in which words meaning "thought," "power," and "works" seem to refer to attributes of the Father, Son, and Holy Spirit respectively. The first two of these attributes, "thought" and "power," were correlated with the ideals of *sapientia* and *fortitudo*, represented in *Beowulf* and *Njáls saga* by Hrothgar and Njáll in the case of *sapientia* and by Beowulf and Gunnarr in the case of *fortitudo*. The third attribute, "works," was correlated with the missionary work of the Church, seen as inspired and sustained by the Holy Spirit. With the help of Hincmar of Rheims, the Trinity was further correlated with the thought, word, and deed series, the first and third members of which (though the ordering of the series was not taken as fixed) were in turn correlated with the ideals of *sapientia* and *fortitudo*. It was then argued that Hrothgar and Njáll on the one hand, and Beowulf and Gunnarr on the other, may be seen as Father and Son figures respectively, and that the unresolved tension between the roles they represent in each of the two works in which they appear is due to the fact that the Holy Spirit, as reflected in the

---

[88] Chesnutt, "Popular and Learned Elements," 54.

missionary work of conversion, has not entered the world of *Beowulf*, and has entered that of *Njáls saga* only partially.

Beyond *Grýla*

Þorleifur Hauksson

The searching characterization of Archbishop Adalbert by Adam, the poetic virtuosity of Saxo, or even the rhetorical speechifying of Dudo will stand comparison with the satirical oratory of Karl Jónsson and his patron, the principal authors of *Sverris Saga*, or the classic ironic reserve of Snorri and his assistants. For, despite divergences of taste, between these authors exist common literary forms and interests, a cross-cultural style which relates them together.[1]

In the preface to *Sverris saga*, the reader is told the name of the author: Abbot Karl Jónsson of Þingeyrar, who is said to have written the beginning of the saga while his patron, King Sverrir, "sat over him and settled what he should write."[2] Scholars have disagreed on how to interpret what the preface says about the origin and composition of the saga. Theodore M. Andersson sums this up in his survey of kings' saga studies:

The portion completed by Karl is known as "Grýla," but the exact parameters of "Grýla" have led to one of the most inconclusive debates in all of kings'saga studies. Scholars have often assigned only a brief section to Karl Jónsson, assuming that the

---

[1] Frederic Amory, "Saga Style in some Kings' Sagas, and Early Medieval Latin Narrative," *Acta Philologica Scandinavica* 32 (1978): 67-86, at 71.
[2] J. Sephton's translation. *Sverrissaga: The Saga of King Sverri of Norway* (London: D. Nutt, 1899), 1; *Sverris saga*, ed. Þorleifur Hauksson, ÍF 30 (Reykjavík: Hið íslenzka fornritafélag, 2007), 3.

remainder was written sometime after Sverrir's death in 1202. Exactly when this continuation was executed is another disputed question, with estimates ranging from 1204 to 1230.[3]

I have recently argued that this "beginning" of the saga, which according to the preface Karl Jónsson wrote in the presence and at the command of the king himself, and the "part of the book" called Grýla are in fact two different entities.[4] The preface to Sverris saga is written by a later scribe, and here the name *Grýla* refers to Sverrir's growing strength:

> Ok svá sem á líðr bókina vex hans styrkr, ok segir sá inn sami styrkr fyrir ina meiri hluti. Kǫlluðu þeir þann hlut bókar fyrir því Grýlu.

> And as the book advances, his strength grows, foreshadowing the greater events. They therefore called this part of the book *Gryla*.[5]

The word *styrkr* is the usual term for the cardinal virtue *fortitudo*, and the author of the expanded preface in Flateyjarbók follows this up by calling the second part *Perfectam fortitudinem*.[6] The ogress Grýla, who according to later folklore appeared at farms in the dusk around Christmas, seems to have been known in the Middle Ages, and already then the name is synonymous with something threatening. However, some scholars have found it difficult to relate this terrible ogress to the fortitude of an outstanding royal person and have searched for other explanations. Thus, in his

---

[3] Theodore M. Andersson, "Kings' Sagas (Konungasögur)," in *Old Norse-Icelandic Literature. A Critical Guide*, ed. Carol J. Clover & John Lindow (London: Cornell University Press 1985), 197-238, at 215.

[4] Þorleifur Hauksson, "Grýla Karls ábóta," *Gripla* XVII (2006): 153-166; Þorleifur Hauksson, "Formáli," *Sverris saga*, lv-lx; Þorleifur Hauksson, "Implicit ideology and the king's image in Sverris saga," *Scripta Islandica* 63 (2012): 127-35, at 128-129.

[5] *Sverris saga*, 3; Sephton, 1.

[6] *Sverris saga*, 286.

Altnordische Literaturgeschichte, Jan de Vries contemplates different
possibilities:

> Ist der wunderliche Name *Grýla* Ausdruck des Ekels vor
> der gewaltsamen Besitzergreifung des später als Tyrann
> verschrieenen Königs? Oder bezieht sich das Wort, das
> mit nhd *Greuel* verwandt ist, auf die Schreckenzeit vor
> 1184 als Sverrir im fortwährenden Kampf mit Erlingr und
> Magnús immer wieder Rückschläge erlitt? Wir können
> darüber nur Vermutungen aussprechen.[7]

> Is the strange name *Grýla* an expression of the revulsion
> caused by the violent seizure of power by the king, later
> proclaimed as a tyrant? Or does the word, which is related
> to New High German *Greuel*, refer to the period of terror
> before 1184, when Sverrir repeatedly suffered defeat in
> his incessant fights against Erlingr and Magnús? This is a
> matter about which we can only conjecture.

Even though one must agree with this last statement, some
conjectures are more far-fetched than others. There is no question
that the name *Grýla* alludes to Sverrir's battles during his first years.
At the time he is constantly fighting against an enemy always
superior by far in number, and all his victories can be ascribed to
the diverse ways he succeeds in surprising the enemy. One is
reminded of an episode in *Sturlunga saga* where Loftr Jónsson recites
a Grýla-verse before making his assault against the unsuspecting
"Breiðbælingar."[8]

In fact, there is hardly anything in *Sverris saga* which
substantiates either of de Vries' two hypotheses. The violence and
terror during Sverrir's ascent to power is greatly toned down by the

---

[7] Jan de Vries, *Altnordische Literaturgeschichte* II (Berlin: de Gruyter, 1967),
237.

[8] *Sturlunga saga efter membranen Króksfjarðarbók*, ed. Kristian Kålund, 2 vols.
(København: Gyldendal, 1906-11), I:344; Þorleifur Hauksson, "Grýla
Karls ábóta," 157.

author. It is much more natural to assume that we have here the same allusion as in the Loftr-episode, possibly a humorous one, to the threat of the ogress who lives in the wilderness, and has the habit of appearing unexpectedly in the dark. The name may bear witness to the admiration which this extraordinary Faroese priest and king enjoyed among the brethren at Þingeyrar, who were the first readers of the book which their Abbot brought with him upon his return from Norway in 1188. This book most likely contained the first 100 chapters of the saga, ending at a turning point in Sverrir's career when he had succeeded in defeating his powerful enemies – first Earl Erlingr and then his son King Magnús – and had become the undisputed king of the whole of Norway.[9]

King Sverrir died in 1202 and Karl Jónsson died in 1212 or 1213. Regarding the question of when the writing of the saga was continued, it is difficult to ignore Knut Helle's theory that the A-version of Bǫglunga saga was written after Sverris saga was completed, and that the latter accordingly must have been finished around 1210.[10] It is in fact possible that Karl Jónsson wrote not only the first 100 chapters of Sverris saga before his return to Iceland, but also the remainder of the saga at intervals during the remaining 25 years of his life. But there is disagreement about the extent of his authorship among scholars.

There have been widely divergent theories about the division between Grýla and the 'second part' of the saga. Grýla has been varyingly said to comprise the first 17, 31, 39, 43, 100, or 109 chapters of the saga, and many scholars have thought that the "second part" was written by a different author. A further complication is the assumption by a number of scholars that Sverrir's speeches are so vivid and correspond so well with his personality in the saga that they must have been dictated (after their

---

[9] Þorleifur Hauksson, "Grýla Karls ábóta," 160-164.
[10] Helle, Omkring Bǫglunga sǫgur (Bergen: J. Grieg, 1958), 98-101. The name Bǫglunga saga will be used here to refer to this saga, which describes the period between Sverrir's death and his grandson Hákon Hákonarson's ascent to power.

original performance) to Karl Jónsson and written down almost verbatim.[11] However, Karl Jónsson was a learned man and much in the saga bears witness to his rhetorical skill. He was acquainted with the king, and we can assume that he had no problems putting words into his mouth. Furthermore, the speeches form part of the texture of the saga. They play an important role in the course of the events in the saga, for example by prophecying the outcome of battles.[12]

In connection with the new edition of *Sverris saga*, the manuscripts containing the saga have been compared. It turns out that the saga exists in two distinct versions, not greatly different from each other, and that by analyzing them it is possible to reconstruct a somewhat earlier stage of the saga text. The new edition of the saga text attempts to present such a reconstructed version. This may be seen as an opportunity for scholars to look anew at the saga as a whole and to try to determine its structure as such, instead of looking at it as a compilation of two different parts with an uncertain line of demarcation.

Sverris saga is the oldest preserved secular kings' saga. There is evidence that it already enjoyed great respect in the Middle Ages as a historical document and an outstanding literary work. Research into the style and structure of the saga should be likely to yield valuable information concerning the evolution of secular saga-writing in Old Norse and Icelandic literature. The saga is clearly what has been called a contemporary saga (*samtímasaga*), based on eyewitness accounts shortly after the events. For example, the author did not feel the need to refer to any of the thirteen skalds known to have composed poems in praise of Sverrir. There are about 400 persons named in the saga, always without any formal introduction, as if it is taken for granted that they are known by the audience. The events are described in a coherent chronological order and the saga contains a detailed description of Sverrir's activities. Only in the middle section, chapters 101-128, covering

---

[11] Þorleifur Hauksson, "Grýla Karls ábóta," 160, note 4.
[12] James Knirk, *Oratory in the Kings' Sagas* (Oslo-Bergen-Tromsø: Universitetsforlaget, 1981), 107-109.

the years 1185-1195, is the sequence of events more sporadic, with just a couple of episodes mentioned for each year: in 1185 the rise of the Kuflungar, in 1186 the drunkenness of Sverrir's men in Bergen due to the import of German wine followed by Sverrir's brilliant temperance speech, etc. There is also a gap between the years 1190 and 1193 and another from spring 1195 to autumn 1196, and the dating of some episodes is vague, particularly in connection with the expedition of Sverrir's brother Eiríkr and Sverrir's excommunication. The remainder of the saga, from chapter 129 to the end, seems again to be precise and well documented; it is quite possible that this is because the Abbot sailed to Norway again around 1200 in order to complete his royal biography.

Compared with what has been called the classical saga-style, *Sverris saga* distinguishes itself by the use of some minor rhetorical embellishments: word-pairs, parallelisms and antitheses, similes and metaphors, and it turns out that these are more frequent in the narrative of the first chapters (i.e. speeches excluded) than later in the saga. As Carol J. Clover has pointed out, the first part is "almost wholly monothematic" compared with the saga in general.[13] The first chapters are told from Sverrir's point of view. Here we have descriptions of his youthful thoughts and dreams, as well as his worries and doubts concerning his mission during his first period in Norway. In this part there are also instances of the narrator's outspoken empathy with the protagonist, for example in the comments about God's intervention on Sverrir's behalf:

En svá mikla miskunn sýndi allsvaldandi Guð ok heilǫg María við Sverri konung at hann fekk af því fólki mikinn fagnað (21)

Ok þá er hann hafði fyrir skilt heitinu hafði Guð svá bráða ok háleita miskunn gǫrt við þá at þegar þóttisk engi vita hvaðan vindr var á (35)

---

[13] Carol J. Clover, *The Medieval Saga* (London: Cornell University Press, 1982), 165.

En svá lauk at Guð gaf konungi fagran sigr (39)

But Almighty God and Holy Maria gave such abundant
grace to King Sverri, that when the people heard his
words they furthered his progress (Sephton, 14)

but as soon as he had given utterance to the vow, God
granted them His gracious mercy so speedily that no one
at the moment could say from what quarter the wind then
blew (Sephton, 26-27)

and in the end God gave the King a glorious victory
(Sephton, 30)

The fact that God's name is used thus only in a limited part of
the saga has been seen by some scholars as one of the main criteria
for the demarcation of *Grýla*. These examples have even been
compared to Sverrir's "own words" in his speeches later on as
evidence that both sections reflect what Sverrir actually said.[14] Of
course, this part may well have been written according to the king's
own dictation. But it is also an essential part of the composition of
the saga. In these first chapters, Sverrir is beginning his struggle for
power. At the same time that his endurance is tested with great
difficulties and hardship, he is constantly under the obligation to
prove his vocation as a king and that he enjoys the grace of God.

The saga shows remarkable coherence, for example in the
depiction of Sverrir's character through his words and deeds, and
scholars have not been successful in their efforts to distinguish
between different portions of the saga on stylistic grounds. The
change from a monothematic to a richly stranded narrative
observed by Carol J. Clover is in fact due to a change in subject
matter and situation. Here we have a transition from Sverrir's lonely

---

[14] Halvdan Koht, "Norsk historieskriving under Kong Sverre, serskilt
Sverre-soga," *Edda* 2 (1914): 67-102, at 89-90; Ludvig Holm-Olsen, *Studier
i Sverres saga* (Oslo: Dybwad, 1953), 61-65.

ordeal as leader of a small group of outlaws to his becoming a strong commander, engaged in organized warfare. This leads to a narrative where we are "plunged alternately into Sverrir's camp and that of the enemy."[15] From chapter 28 onwards, we have a detailed narrative in chronological order containing descriptions of constant raids and battles, with shifts of focus from one camp to another, and the speeches of the leaders are interwoven with the episodes described. This pattern recalls the Latin historical monographs, as does the phrasing of the transitional formulas (which can also be found in the simultaneous narration of the later Icelandic family sagas).

In fact, there isn't any great difference in style between this part and the remainder of the saga. The rhetorical figures mentioned above are frequent in the speeches in other parts of the saga. And although after chapter 24, the author does not explicitly express sympathy with Sverrir, such sympathy is a part of the fabric of the text, and we will return to this later.

As already mentioned, the difficulties scholars have had in determining the boundaries between "Karl Jónsson's *Grýla*" and the "second part" of *Sverris saga* are mostly due to the saga's uniformity in vocabulary and style.[16] The oldest examples of a number of words registered in the card index of the *Ordbog over det norrøne prosasprog* in Copenhagen appear in *Sverris saga*. Among them are some words which occur more than once, both early and late in the saga, words like *bakslag, baksletta, koma dyn fyrir dyrr, mannfarmr*, and the hapax legomenon *vasikampr*. In addition, as Ludvig Holm-Olsen has pointed out, the author (and perhaps Sverrir himself?) seems to have been fond of special kinds of metaphors, namely those connecting warfare with hunting: *gildra til veiða, veiða í snǫru, veiðibráðr*, etc. The metaphor for battle as *fǫr, kaupferð, markaðr* occurs both in the narrative at the beginning, and in Sverrir's

15 Clover, *The Medieval Saga*, 165.
16 Ludvig Holm-Olsen, "Sverris saga," in *Kulturhistorisk leksikon for nordisk middelalder* XVII, cols. 553-554.

speeches later in the saga.[17] The differences between respective parts of the saga are inconsiderable and of such nature that they seem to be due to the author's varying access to sources.

Sverris saga has been labeled as propaganda writing, aimed at defending Sverrir and promoting the cause of his Birkibeinar.[18] Others have on the contrary emphasized the saga's objectivity and its "gentlemanly and fair" treatment of Sverrir's enemies.[19]

There is indeed a strong tendency to favour Sverrir in the saga. The bravery of his soldiers is often mentioned, but hardly ever that of the enemy. Sverrir's speeches are characterized by their sarcastic wit, but some of his adversaries are mocked in the narrative, such as the insurgent farmers on various occasions, and one of King Sverrir's mighty enemies, Bishop Nikolás Árnason.[20] Descriptions of his deeds, especially his assault on Bergen in chapter 150, are clearly meant to shed an unfavourable light on this man of God. In comparison, the representations of Earl Erlingr and Magnús Erlingsson are fairly objective on the surface, but that does not mean that they come across in a positive light, as I shall return to later.

The dreams which forebode Sverrir's birth and future vocation are a central theme in the first ten chapters of the saga. These early chapters are an undisputed part of *Grýla*, and so it has been a matter

---

[17] Ludvig Holm-Olsen, "Til diskusjonen om Sverres sagas tilblivelse," in *Opuscula Septentrionalia. Festskrift til Ole Widding* (Copenhagen: C. A. Reitzel 1977), 55-67, at 61-65; Þorleifur Hauksson, "Formáli," *Sverris saga*, lxi-lxiii.

[18] Egil Nygaard Brekke, *Sverre-sagaens opphav. Tiden og forfatteren* (Oslo: Aschehoug, 1958), 49-52.

[19] Lee M. Hollander, "Notes on the Sverris saga," *The Germanic Review* III.3 (1928): 262-76, at 262.

[20] *Sverris saga*, 202-203, 238-239; Sephton, 166, 196-197; Þorleifur Hauksson, "Isländskans *kveif*. Från 'biskopshuva' till 'kujon'," in *Från drasut till brakknut. Studier tillägnade Gerd Eklund* (Uppsala: Uppsala Universitet, 2007), 97-99.

of discussion whether Sverrir (and his mother Gunnhildr) really had these dreams or if they were his own fabrications.[21]

Gunnhildr dreams that she has "a wonderful and awful birth," namely a large white stone which "glowed fiercely, so that it emitted sparks in all directions like iron at a white heat in the fierce blast of a forge."[22] Ludvig Holm-Olsen seeks parallels in dreams preceding the birth of saints, in view of Sverrir's own education as a priest. Yet, as he acknowledges, these examples are far removed from the dream of Gunnhildr. Holm-Olsen only fleetingly mentions the dream of the mother of Alexander the Great, which must be considered the closest parallel in the context of the saga as Lars Lönnroth has pointed out.[23] Sverrir is not a saint, he is not even "well suited to be priest."[24] And the dreams which he has later on do not foretell the rise of a holy man, but rather a worldly ruler who enjoys the grace of God.

Sverrir's first dream occurs while he is still in the Faroe Islands. He dreams that he is staying in the court of Saint Ólafr in Norway, having "attained some position of honour, chosen to bishop most likely."[25] He is received with great joy and at one point, having washed in the same water as the King, he is summoned to arms against King Magnús Erlingsson and Earl Erlingr. Before this battle, King Ólafr hands him his sword and banner and protects him with his shield so that he is unharmed.

As Lars Lönnroth has shown, the scene where King Ólafr washes himself and then invites Sverrir to wash in the same water, "must be understood as a symbolic baptism, whereby Sverrir is inaugurated in the new sacred role as the saint's successor and as

---

[21] Ludvig Holm-Olsen, *Studier i Sverres saga*, 98-102.

[22] Sephton, 2; *Sverris saga*, 4-5.

[23] Holm-Olsen, *Studier i Sverres saga*, 100; Lars Lönnroth, "Sverrir's Dreams," *Scripta Islandica* 57 (2006): 97-110, at 99-100.

[24] Sephton, 3; *Sverris saga*, 6.

[25] Sephton, 4; *Sverris saga*, 8.

the true king of Norway."[26] When Sverrir has come to Norway and has agreed to become the leader of the Birkibeinar, he has a new dream where the Prophet Samuel appears before him in a church in Sarpsborg and anoints him and gives him God's blessing. Through this episode, which takes place close to the beginning of the saga, there are parallels between Sverrir and King David in the Bible. This happens again in his speech in chapter 99, after the battle at Fimreiti in 1184, where he sums up his fight against King Magnús. Here he quotes David's Psalm No 56: "Miserere mei, Deus, quoniam conculcavit me homo, tota die expugnans tribulavit me" ("Be merciful to me, O God, for man trod me under foot; all day he fought against me and tormented me").[27] And he continues: "At all times none have been so hated by God as the proud (*ofmetnaðarmenn*), and most sternly has He punished them." One of the examples which he quotes as parallels to his own predicament is when "King Saul raged against God" and "roamed over the land possessed by an unclean spirit."

The image of King David is thus strongly present in these first 100 chapters of the saga, in spite of the fact that his name is never mentioned. To quote Sverre Bagge:

> In contrast to St. Óláfr, David does not appear before Sverrir in his dreams. Instead, Sverrir is shown in a situation which makes every enlightened reader recognize his similarity to David. In addition to other direct references in the saga and other sources which allude to Sverrir's special relationship to David, Sverrir's whole career suggests such a parallel. Like David he was "a little and low man" from the periphery, like David he wandered around in the wilderness with a small number of men, and like David, who defeated the giant Goliath,

---

[26] Lönnroth, "Sverrir's Dreams," 103; Sverre Bagge, *From Gang Leader to the Lord's Anointed. Kingship in* Sverris saga *and* Hákonar saga Hákonarsonar (Odense: Odense University Press, 1996), 55.

[27] Sephton, 123-124; *Sverris saga,* 152.

he defeated enemies that were largely superior in numbers.[28]

The crucial question here, according to Bagge, is how much of the saga's narrative and ideology can be explained by this interpretation. His conclusion is that although the saga echoes Sverrir's political propaganda and the ideology later developed by Sverrir's dynasty, it "does not describe 'the ideal royal character' according to the tradition of European clerical historiography."[29] Instead, it presents a picture of a gang leader who leads his men to victory, not through God's grace and interference but through his own skill as a general.

This theory was challenged by Fredrik Charpentier Ljungqvist and Lars Lönnroth at the Thirteenth International Saga Conference.[30] Lönnroth analyzes Sverrir's dreams, both in the first 10 chapters and later in the saga (chapters 42 and 180), and his conclusion is that the purpose of the dreams "is obviously, and primarily, to establish Sverrir as a Christian *rex iustus* and as the only legitimate king of Norway."[31] Ljungqvist looks at *Sverris saga* in the light of medieval Christian learning. His conclusion is that even though Sverrir is not presented as the typical ideal of a *rex iustus*, this ideal is repeatedly referred to in the saga to justify him as the lawful king.[32]

In the dream in chapter 10, the Prophet Samuel concludes his message to Sverrir thus: "Be thou strong and valiant, for God will

---

[28] Bagge, *From Gang Leader to the Lord's Anointed*, 63-64.
[29] *Ibid.*, 65.
[30] Fredrik Charpentier Ljungqvist, "Kristen kungaideologi i Sverris saga," *Scripta Islandica* 57 (2006): 79-95; Lönnroth, "Sverrir's Dreams," 97-110.
[31] Lönnroth, "Sverrir's Dreams," 108.
[32] Ljungqvist, "Kristen kungaideologi i Sverris saga," 93; "Bannlyst kung av Guds nåde. Maktlegitimering och kungaideologi i Sverris saga," *Collegium medievale* 21 (2008): 3-66, at 30-36.

give thee help."[33] These words are recalled in Sverrir's speech in
chapter 94, after the battle at Fimreiti:

> Guð sjálfan skulum vér lofa fyrir sigr várn, er hann hefir
> nú miklu berara en fyrr veitt oss sinn styrk ok kraft í þessi
> orrostu.

> God Himself we must praise for our victory, for much
> more evidently in this battle than aforetime has He
> granted us strength and might.[34]

This strength (*styrkr, fortitudo*) is a gift from God and a proof of
His grace towards Sverrir. Throughout the saga, Sverrir is presented
as an embodiment of this regal virtue, through his undisputed
leadership among his men, his endurance in toil and hardship and
his calm authority in difficult situations.[35]

Sverrir is also endowed with *providentia*: foresight concerning the
outcome of battles and other events.[36] Moreover, his *prudentia* in the
ethical sense of the word – his ability to discern good from bad is
demonstrated in some of his speeches, such as the speech on the
mountain in chapter 20 and his temperance speech in chapter 104.[37]
Sverrir's *iustitia* is mainly demonstrated in his willingness to forgive
and grant truce to his enemies. Surely, we learn about his strong
retributions against the farmers, even to the point of burning down
their villages, but these actions are always justified by the farmers'
stubbornness and their unwillingness to make peace with him.

The predominant vice shown by Sverrir's enemies is *superbia*
(*dirfð, ofmetnaðr*). In chapter 15, the townsmen of Niðaróss showed
such audacity (*dirfð*) that they seized the banner of Saint Óláfr to

---

[33] Sephton, 12; *Sverris saga*, 17.

[34] *Sverris saga*, 145; Sephton, 118.

[35] William of Conches, *Das Moralium dogma philosophorum des Guillaume de
Conches*, ed. John Holmberg (Uppsala: Almqvist & Wiksell, 1929), 30-40.

[36] *Ibid.*, 9; *Sverris saga*, 44, 49, 66-67, 74, 84, 136.

[37] *Das Moralium dogma philosophorum*, 8.

bear it against King Sverrir. Here Sverrir is greatly outnumbered by the enemy, yet he defeats them and captures the banner, and "many came with meekness into the presence of Sverri who before, in excess of pride (*við miklum ofmetnaði*) had been loudest in their talk against him."[38] In Sverrir's funeral speech over Earl Erlingr in chapter 38, he concludes by advising the men to pray to God that the Earl's sins may be forgiven, especially the great sin of arrogance (*dirfð*). The Earl showed arrogance by giving the title of King to his own son, and by fighting against and destroying many lawful kings.[39] Erlingr's *superbia* is even known and admitted by his own men.[40]

Many scholars have observed how favourable the description of King Magnús is throughout the saga. He enjoys "the support of mighty men and of all the commons," is "beloved and popular,"[41] and "however disastrous it was to follow him, he never lacked men for his body-guard while he lived."[42] But does that also imply that he possessed the qualities that make a king in the eyes of the saga's medieval audience?[43]

Even though Magnús is a brave warrior, there is no comparison between him and Sverrir with regard to *fortitudo*. He is irresolute and not as wise as his opponent, and the times he decides against the advice of his chieftains it leads to disaster, as in the battles of Norðnes (ch. 53) and Fimreiti (ch. 89). Whereas Sverrir is nearly always willing to grant truce to his adversaries, Magnús, just like his father, is cruel and merciless towards the Birkibeinar. In his assault on Niðaróss in chapter 62, he does not even respect the sanctuary of the churches:

---

[38] Sephton, 18; *Sverris saga*, 25.
[39] Sephton, 51; *Sverris saga*, 63.
[40] Sephton, 52; *Sverris saga*, 64.
[41] Sephton, 3; *Sverris saga*, 6.
[42] Sephton, 122; *Sverris saga*, 151.
[43] Ármann Jakobsson, "Sinn eiginn smiður: Æventýrið um Sverri konung," *Skírnir* 179 (2005): 109-39, at 121-125.

Þá var þat gǫrt er aldri varð fyrr, at menn váru drepnir ok dregnir ór Kristskirkju.

Men were dragged out of Kristskirk and slain, a deed that had never been done hitherto.[44]

Before the battle of Norðnes, he exhorts his men in haughty words:

Vér hǫfum til móts við þá gǫfugmenni ok góða drengi, en þeir hafa ekki nema þjófa ok ránsmenn ok raufara þræla ættar ok stafkarla, sem Guð steypi þeim. En eigi er at réttu hefnt gǫfugra frænda várra þó at vér drepim þá alla, en brigzlalaust er oss at gera þat. Vil ek birta fyrir yðr minn vilja, at engi verði svá djarfr minna manna at einum gefi grið.

We bring to the fight men of high position and brave gentlemen; they have only thieves and highwaymen and robbers, the kin of thralls and beggars, whom may God confound. Our honourable kinsmen would not be any the more avenged should we slay every Birkibein, but we should free ourselves from reproach by doing it. Let none of my men presume to give quarter to one of them.[45]

Inevitably, the reader compares this speech with Sverrir's humble words at the same occasion, where he says that "our strength lies entirely in God and His Saints, and not in our numbers,"[46] and prays to God that He grant victory to those whom He knows to have the rightful cause.

King Magnús's speech bears witness to both *ira* and *superbia*, and the latter vice is the main theme of Sverrir's speeches after

---

[44] Sephton, 82; *Sverris saga*, 101.
[45] Sephton, 68; *Sverris saga*, 85.
[46] Sephton, 68; *Sverris saga*, 84.

Magnús's death. He prays God to forgive Magnús all his transgressions (*þat allt er hann varð offari í*), and subsequently, in one of his greatest speeches, he counts King Magnús among the proud, who have been most hated by God at all times and most severely punished.[47]

In the final descriptions of Sverrir and Magnús respectively, after their death, *temperantia* is contrasted with *luxuria*, on the one hand Sverrir who "never drank strong drink to the injury of his reason, and always ate but one meal a day," on the other Magnús, who "was fond of drinking-bouts and the society of women."[48] This *luxuria* is largely to blame for his humiliating defeat in Bergen in chapters 76-77, where his men are "roused up drowsy and drunk."

Sverre Bagge's last contribution to the dispute about Sverrir's image in the saga is an article in *Scripta Islandica* from 2007.[49] There he argues that when Lars Lönnroth and Fredrik Charpentier Ljungqvist interpret the ideology of the saga as being predominantly religious, they merely rephrase the author's explicit comments. The implicit ideology, he says, is quite different. According to Bagge's interpretation of the saga, the secular element in the image of Sverrir is predominant. The religious ideology, he claims, appears primarily in what he vaguely designates as the first part of the saga, which was written in the presence of Sverrir himself, and in the great speeches after the death of Earl Erlingr and King Magnús. Bagge compares the so-called *Speech against the Bishops*, which was written under Sverrir's auspices as a defence against the clergy, and the saga. The first is a rhetorical polemic, the second Sverrir's biography where various facts are played down, such as his being excommunicated until the day of his death.

---

[47] Sephton, 124; *Sverris saga*, 152.
[48] Sephton, 232, 123; *Sverris saga*, 280, 151.
[49] Sverre Bagge, "'Gang leader' eller 'The Lord's anointed' i *Sverris saga*? Svar till Fredrik Ljungqvist og Lars Lönnroth," *Scripta Islandica* 58 (2007): 101-119.

As has been demonstrated above, the religious ideology is also implicit in the image of King Sverrir in the saga itself. Furthermore, the import of the *Speech against the Bishops*, which Bagge considers to be characterized by a consistent *rex iustus*-ideology, is in fact not so dissimilar to the underlying ideology of *Sverris saga*, even though the presentation is totally different.

One should bear in mind that the privileges which the Norwegian church managed to secure itself in connection with the crowning of the young Magnús Erlingsson 1164 were, at least nominally, more liberal than those that any other church in Europe enjoyed.[50] There is hardly any doubt that the main reason for the serious conflict between Sverrir and the church was his unwillingness to accept them. As late as 1246, when Sverrir's grandchild, Hákon Hákonarson, was being crowned by one of the Pope's cardinals, there is evidence of an unsuccessful attempt by the Archbishop to reclaim those privileges.[51]

The *Speech against the Bishops* is a fierce and clever polemic, defending the idea of the king as the head, or rather the heart of the church. In the beginning, the church of Christ is pictured in the image of the human body, where the "eyes should be our Bishops, who should point us to the right way and the safe road, free from all erring paths." But now, the situation is such that each member of the body forsakes the office and service which it should perform: "The eyes look sideways and see dimly. The same scales have fallen upon the eyes of our bishops that fell on the eyes of the Apostles the night when God was taken."[52] A parallel can be seen in *Sverris saga*. Archbishop Eiríkr became blind, and his blindness is seen in the saga, in one of Sverrir's speeches, as a direct effect of the ban which Eiríkr has pronounced on him:

---

[50] Erik Gunnes, *Erkebiskop Øystein: Statsmann og kirkebygger* (Oslo: Aschehoug, 1996), 232.

[51] *Hákonar saga Hákonarsonar* in *Flateyjarbók*, ed. Guðbrandur Vigfússon and C. R. Unger, 3 vols. (Christiania: T. Malling, 1868), III:3-233, at 167-168.

[52] Sephton, Appendix II, 241, 242; *Sverris saga*, Viðauki, 287, 288.

"ok þat sama bann ok blótan," segir hann, "er hann
nefnir mik til, þat hefir nú drifit í augu hans, ok er hann
nú fyrir því blindr [...] En þó at hann hefði þar bæði augu
heil, er nú er hann báðum blindr, ok þar með sjálfu
hugskotinu at sjá it rétta, þá mun ek ekki brjóta lǫg ins
helga Óláfs konungs fyrir hans sakir, þó at hann bannisk
jafnan um eða blótisk."

"The ban and curse," he said, "which he has uttered
against me have fallen upon his own eyes and he is now
blind through them. [...] But if his both eyes were whole,
as surely as he is now blind of both, and blind also in the
judgment to recognise what is right, yet would I not for
his sake violate the law of King Olaf the Saint, though he
should ban and curse for ever."[53]

The main emphasis in the Speech is that the Pope's
condemnation will not touch the king or any innocent man in the
land,

því at Guð er jafnan réttdœmr, ok fara því Guðs dómar
jafnan eftir réttendum en eigi eftir ranglæti lyginna manna
ok svikfullra

For God is ever a righteous judge, and His judgments are
according to right, and not according to the iniquity of
lying and deceitful men.[54]

This reference to God's justice is repeated in the last sentence
of the Speech.

In the last scene in *Sverris saga*, God's justice is demonstrated.
On his deathbed, the king asks his men to leave his face uncovered
after his death, so that everybody may see if there is any mark on

---

[53] *Sverris saga*, 187; Sephton, 153.
[54] Sephton, Appendix II, 243-244; ÍF 30, Viðauki, 290.

his body of "the ban wherewith my foes have cursed and excommunicated me." Shortly afterwards, he dies:

> Nú var ok svá gǫrt sem konungr hafði beðit, at berat var andlit hans, ok sá allir þeir er hjá váru ok báru síðan allir eitt vitni um at engi þóttisk sét hafa fegra líkama dauðs manns en hans.

> His face was left uncovered, as he had commanded. All who were present observed, and all afterwards bore one and the same testimony, that they had never seen a fairer corpse than his.[55]

In the article by Fred Amory, quoted in the beginning, he examines aspects of the "cross-cultural style," by which he means the interplay between "the Old Norse language as it was spoken by the Norwegians and Icelanders of the Middle Ages and the literary adaptation of the same by Norwegian and Icelandic monks and clerks to the language and style of the Latin models of hagiography and historical biography upon which the kings' sagas were composed."[56] The style of *Sverris saga* is vernacular, with only minor rhetorical influence, but the ideology is continental and Christian. *Sverris saga* is a biography of a Norwegian king who had to fight his way to the throne. At the same time he is depicted not as a traditional heathen warrior but as the incarnation of royal and Christian virtues.

---

[55] *Sverris saga*, 280; Sephton, 231-32.
[56] Frederic Amory, "Saga Style in some Kings' Sagas," 68.

Gudbrand Vigfusson, Hugo Gering, and German Scholarship: Or, A Friendship Destroyed

Hans Fix

In his letter of 14 June 1884 Hugo Gering informed Theodor Möbius about a recent very kind letter he had received from Guðbrandr Vigfússon. "Sehr überrascht wurde ich in diesen tagen durch einen langen, sehr liebenswürdigen brief <u>Guðbr. Vigfússons</u> – eine verspätete danksagung für Æv[entyri]. II.," slyly adding, "Ich fürchte, es wird der lezte brief gewesen sein – die fussnote in der recension der cons. studier[1] wird er mir schwerlich vergeben." And he was obviously right, because there are no further letters kept in the authors' collections both at Kiel and Oxford.

The aim of this paper is to introduce the dramatis personae, to report upon the circumstances of their acquaintance, and finally to present the twelve letters by Vigfússon and Gering exchanged between 1877 and 1884 that reflect the development of their

---

[1] Julius Hoffory, *Oldnordiske consonantstudier* (Diss. University of Copenhagen, 1883); also *Arkiv för nordisk filologi* 2 (1885): 1-96. In his review of this Copenhagen dissertation (even Habilitationsschrift Berlin), Gering relentlessly calls the poems as printed in *Corpvs poeticvm boreale. The poetry of the old northern tongue from the earliest times to the thirteenth century*, ed., classified and transl. with introduction, excursus, and notes by Gudbrand Vigfusson, M. A. and F. York Powell, M. A. Vol. I: Eddic poetry. Vol. II: Court poetry (Oxford: Clarendon Press, 1883) "ihrer unzuverlässigkeit wegen für philologische untersuchungen überhaupt unbrauchbar" (*Zeitschrift für deutsche Philologie* 16 [1884]: 377-381, fn. 2).

relationship from enthusiastic beginnings to a sudden halt. Differing attitudes towards philological aims and principles alienated our correspondents in the course of time, and after the publication of the ominous *Corpvs poeticvm boreale* in 1883 the clash could no longer be avoided.

1. The distinguished author of the Oxford *Icelandic-English Dictionary* (1869-1874), Guðbrandr Vigfússon, and Hugo Gering, who was to become one of the eminent Edda scholars of his time, met in Copenhagen in the summer of 1877. His senior by twenty years, Guðbrandr took a deep interest in Gering's philological work and advised him on Old Norse texts to be edited. He obviously enjoyed the company of both the young German and of Gustaf Cederschiöld, an equally young Swede who became Gering's friend for lifetime. Their meeting was instigated by Theodor Möbius, professor of Scandinavian at Kiel university, who had become Gering's mentor on Nordic matters. Möbius was an old friend and correspondent of both Guðbrandr Vigfússon and Konrad Maurer, professor of law in Munich university, and is gratefully mentioned in Gering's edition of *Finnboga saga*, where the Copenhagen sojourn is recalled.[2]

Zunächst und vor allem bin ich herrn professor dr. Theodor Möbius in Kiel zu innigstem danke verpflichtet, auf dessen anregung hin das werk unternommen ward, der ihm fortdauernd die gröste teilnahme zugewendet, die revision des druckes übernommen und anfragen aller art stets auf das bereitwilligste beantwortet hat. Namentlich zeugt das glossar von seiner gütigen mithilfe. In zweiter linie gebührt der zoll des dankes zwei nordischen freunden: dr. Guðbrandr Vigfússon in Oxford und dr. Gustaf Cederschiöld in Lund, die ein glücklicher zufall zu gleicher zeit wie mich an Seelands gastliche küste geführt

---

[2] *Finnboga saga hins ramma*, ed. Hugo Gering (Halle a. S.: Buchhandlung des Waisenhauses, 1879), XL.

hatte. Dem mündlichen und schriftlichen verkehre mit beiden verdanke ich manche unschätzbare belehrung.

2.1. Guðbrandr Vigfússon[3] (1827-1889) was born in Breiðafjörður and brought up by his kinswoman, Kristin Vigfússdóttir. He graduated from Lærði skólinn in Reykjavík in 1849 and came to Copenhagen University to read Classics, History, and Germanic as a bursar in the famous Regense College. After his student course, he worked in the Arna-Magnaean Library and was appointed stipendiarius by the Arna-Magnaean trustees in 1856, although he never took a final university degree. During his time in Denmark he revisited Iceland twice where, on the occasion of his visit in 1858, he met Konrad Maurer again, whom he had taught Icelandic during the previous winter in Copenhagen. He had made a tour to Norway in 1854 and undertook several journeys to Germany, paying visits to Jacob Grimm in Berlin, to Möbius in Leipzig, and to Maurer in Munich in 1859.[4] Möbius and Maurer were revisited in 1861, in 1874 he travelled to Maurer again, and in 1877 – accompanied by Gustaf Cederschiöld – to Möbius meanwhile in Kiel.

---

[3] Various biographies, obituaries, and biographical sketches were printed, e. g.: "Gudbrandur Vigfusson," *Illustreret Tidende* 20, 17. Februar 1889, 237f.; F. York Powell, "In memoriam. Gudbrand Vigfusson," *The Academy* 877, Feb. 23, 1889, 131f.; repr. in: Oliver Elton (ed.), *Frederick York Powell. A Life and a Selection From His Letters and Occasional Writings* vol. 2: Occasional Writings (Oxford: Clarendon Press, 1906), 344-350; Jón Þorkelsson, "Guðbrandur Vigfússon," *Arkiv för nordisk filologi* 6 (1890): 156-163 and *Andvari* 19 (1894): 1-43; Páll Eggert Ólason, *Íslenzkar æviskrár frá landnámstímum til ársloka 1940*, vol. 2 (Reykjavík: Hið íslenzka bókmenntafélag, 1949), 114; B. S. Benedikz, "Guðbrandur Vigfússon: a biographical sketch," *Ur Dölum til Dala. Guðbrandur Vigfússon Centenary Essays*, ed. Rory McTurk and Andrew Wawn. Leeds Texts and Monographs New Series 11 (Leeds: University of Leeds, 1989), 11-33.

[4] Cf. "Ferðasaga úr Nóregi," *Ny félagsrit* 15 (1855): 1-83 [*Ein Islending i Noreg. Ei reiseskildring frå 1854*. Trans. Ingeborg Donali, afterword Hallfreður Örn Eiriksson (Vallset: Oplandske Bokforlag, 1990)] and "Ferðasaga úr Þýzkalandi," *Ny félagsrit* 20 (1860): 23-143.

In late summer of 1864 Guðbrandr Vigfússon was asked to finish Cleasby's dictionary and see it through the press;[5] after some months in London, he settled down in Oxford, which remained his home for the rest of his life; Gustaf Cederschiöld paid him a visit there in July 1878. Guðbrandr Vigfússon was given an honorary master's degree in 1871 and made Reader in Scandinavian at Oxford University in 1884; he was among the host of Jubilee Doctors of Uppsala in 1877. While some of his early editions were in cooperation with Unger, Maurer, and Möbius, most of his editorial work in England was carried out in cooperation with Frederick York Powell.

2.2. Hugo Gering[6] (1847-1925), had studied Classics, Germanic, and history at the universities of Leipzig, Bonn, and Halle from 1867-1873; a promising young scholar, he had done research on Gothic and Old High German[7] when he decided to expand his work in Germanic and also try his hand on Old Norse. Whether this was of purely academic interest or had to do with Gering's family history – his grandfather having remigrated from Sweden to Pomerania – or even with his own career planning, cannot be determined. Gering's career led him from professor extraordinary

---

[5] Cf. Elizabeth Knowles, "Notes on a First Edition of 'Cleasby-Vigfússon,'" *Saga-Book of the Viking Society* 20 (1978-81): 165-178.
[6] Cf. Hans Fix, "Gering, Hugo Carl Theodor Ludwig," *Internationales Germanistenlexikon* 1800-1950, ed. Christoph König, 3 vols. (Berlin-New York: de Gruyter, 2003), 553-555; Barend Sijmons, "Hugo Gering. Ein Nachruf," *Arkiv för nordisk filologi* 41 (1925): 339-345; Finnur Jónsson, "Hugo Gering 1847-1925," *Maal og minne* (1926): 65-70; K[auffmann], F[riedrich], "Hugo Gering," *Zeitschrift für deutsche Philologie* 50 (1926): 339-361 [with a list of his publications]. Cf. also Hans Fix, "Eine Freundschaft in Briefen. Hugo Gering und Barend Sijmons 1880-1925," *Amsterdamer Beiträge zur älteren Germanistik* 67 (2011): 343-382.
[7] *Über den syntactischen Gebrauch der Participia im Gotischen* (Diss. University of Halle; Halle a. S.: Buchdruckerei des Waisenhauses, 1873); *Die Causalsätze und ihre Partikeln bei den althochdeutschen Übersetzern des achten und neunten Jahrhunderts* (Habilitationsschrift Halle; Halle a. S.: Buchdruckerei des Waisenhauses, 1876).

of German in Halle in 1883 to succeed Möbius as ordinarius of Scandinavian in Kiel in 1889 where he spent the rest of his life. Although his task in Kiel was Scandinavian, Gering continued teaching various Germanic languages and literatures as the university's lecture catalogues amply demonstrate.

He edited and translated the *Edda*, collected its vocabulary both in a glossary and a "complete" dictionary, and commented on practically every line of the Eddic poems; he translated Beowulf, and put out many papers on Old Norse metres in particular. He was the leading editor of the text series Altnordische Saga-Bibliothek,[8] and, after his teacher's death, took over editing Zacher's *Zeitschrift für deutsche Philologie* for the next thirty years. Thus he kept an eye on Germanic philology as a whole, even if he primarily managed the journal's Nordic section and left the German section to his actual co-editor. While his strong editorial interference to "correct" the Eddic poems made a lot of his work obsolete, his editions of *Finnboga saga* and *Eyrbyggja saga* can still be worthwhile using, and his *Íslendzk æventýri* were never superseded.[9]

2.3. Theodor Möbius[10] (1821-1890), a son of the renowned mathematician and astronomer August Ferdinand Möbius, had studied Classics and Germanic in Leipzig and Berlin. He became a librarian in Leipzig University library in 1845, a professor extraordinary in 1859; called to Kiel University after the Second

---

[8] Initially edited by Gustaf Cederschiöld, Hugo Gering, and Eugen Mogk, cf. Hans Fix, "Die Anfänge der *Altnordischen Saga-Bibliothek*," *Verschränkung der Kulturen. Der Sprach- und Literaturaustausch zwischen Skandinavien und den deutschsprachigen Ländern.* Zum 65. Geburtstag von Hans-Peter Naumann, ed. Oskar Bandle et al. Beiträge zur Nordischen Philologie 37 (Tübingen-Basel: Francke, 2004), 305-330.
[9] *Eyrbyggja saga*, ed. Hugo Gering. Altnordische Saga-Bibliothek 6 (Halle a. S.: Niemeyer, 1897); *Islendzk æventyri. Isländische Legenden, Novellen und Märchen*, ed. Hugo Gering. 2 vols. (Halle a. S.: Buchhandlung des Waisenhauses, 1882-83).
[10] Cf. Konrad Maurer, "Theodor Möbius," *Arkiv för nordisk filologi* 7 (1891): 191-195.

Schleswig War, he was appointed professor of Scandinavian and *lector* of Danish in 1865. He retired in 1888 and returned to his beloved Leipzig where he died.

Concentrating on Germanic philology, Möbius did research on Old Norse in particular, on textual criticism, poetic metres, bibliography, and lexicography. His *Altnordisches Glossar* of 1866 with translations into German and Latin was obviously still considered handy and useful when reprinted by Wissenschaftliche Buchgesellschaft in 1963. Most of his editions, however, sank into oblivion. As a *lector* of Danish Möbius felt required to write his *Dänische Formenlehre*.[11] The only truly scientific primer of Danish in German was suffering, however, from the single fault, as Gering put it, that its rules were abstracted solely from books and neither controlled nor rectified by observing actual usage. Möbius never gained much proficiency in Danish pronunciation and reported facetiously himself, "welche heiterkeit sein Leipziger dänisch anfangs bei den nordschleswigschen studenten erregte."[12] Of great importance for philological research in Scandinavian even today is Möbius's most detailed *Catalogus* and its supplement.[13]

3. Advised by his Halle teacher Julius Zacher, Gering contacted Möbius at Kiel University, then the only chair of Scandinavian in Germany, asking for advice on some interesting research areas or some texts that needed editing. When Gering visited Möbius in Kiel

---

[11] Theodor Möbius, *Altnordisches Glossar. Wörterbuch zu einer Auswahl alt-isländischer und alt-norwegischer Prosatexte* (Leipzig: Teubner, 1866. Repr. Darmstadt: Wiss. Buchgesellschaft, 1963); Th. Möbius, *Dänische Formenlehre.* (Kiel: Schwers'sche Buchhandlung, 1871).

[12] Konrad Maurer & Hugo Gering, "August Theodor Möbius. Nekrolog," *Zeitschrift für deutsche Philologie* 23 (1891): 457-470 [with a list of his publications]; 463.

[13] *Catalogus librorum islandicorum et norvegicorum ætatis mediæ editorum versorum illustratorum Skáldatal sive poetarum recensus eddæ upsaliensis*, ed. Theodor Möbius (Leipzig: Engelmann, 1856); *Verzeichniss der auf dem Gebiete der altnordischen (altisländischen und altnorwegischen) Sprache und Literatur von 1855 bis 1879 erschienen Schriften*, ed. Th. Möbius (Leipzig: Engelmann, 1880).

in the beginning of May 1877 on his journey to Copenhagen, several letters had been exchanged and a pragmatic decision taken against editing a text connected to the German heroic plots;[14] these were either already being edited by other scholars[15] or deemed unsuitable for a newcomer not well versed in manuscript reading, as e.g. *Þiðreks saga*. After learning about Gering's preparation to work with Old Norse manuscripts Möbius suggested an accurate "literal" edition of *Finnboga saga*, a text not easy to come by although edited twice before, by Werlauff in 1812 and by Sveinn Skulason in 1860.[16] A "simple" saga without stanzas in the excellent 14th century manuscript *Möðruvallabók* would also save Gering from Kölbing's fate.[17] Gering is advised to buy Wimmer's *Formlære* and, under all circumstances, to take along Cleasby-Vigfússon's dictionary.[18] As a

---

[14] Cf. Hans Fix, "*Hochgeehrter herr professor! — Mein lieber Herr Doctor.* Ratschläge an einen jungen Philologen," *Studia Nordica Greifswaldensia*, ed. Jens E. Olesen. Publikationen des Lehrstuhls für Nordische Geschichte 5 (Greifswald: Ernst-Moritz-Arndt Universität, 2004), 195-223.

[15] *Die prosaische Edda im Auszuge nebst Volsunga saga und Nornagests-tháttr*. Mit ausführlichem Glossar, ed. Ernst Wilken. Th. 1. Text. Bibliothek der ältesten deutschen Litteratur-Denkmäler XI,1 (Paderborn: Schöningh, 1877).

[16] *Vatnsdæla saga ok saga af Finnboga hinum rama. Vatnsdølernes Historie og Finnboge hiin Stærkes Levnet*, ed. E. C. Werlauff (Copenhagen: Schubart, 1812); *Saga Finnboga hins ramma*, ed. Sveinn Skúlason. Íslendinga sögur 2 (Akureyri: H. Helgason, 1860).

[17] Eugen Kölbing's edition *Riddara sögur. Parcevals saga, Valvers þáttr, Ivents saga, Mirmanns saga*. Zum ersten Mal herausgeg. und mit einer literarhistorischen Einleitung versehen (Straßburg & London: Trübner, 1872) had been reviewed rather critically by Cederschiöld in *Germania* 20 (1875): 306-317, prompting Kölbing to apologize in *Germania* 21 (1876) 354-355, fn.

[18] Ludv. F. A. Wimmer, *Oldnordisk Formlære til Skolebrug*. 2. omarbejd. og forkort. Udg. (Copenhagen: Steen, 1876); *An Icelandic-English Dictionary*. Based on the MS. collections of the late Richard Cleasby, enlarged and completed by Gudbrand Vigfusson (Oxford: Clarendon Press, 1874). The preceding dictionaries by Erik Jonsson, *Oldnordisk Ordbog* ved det Kongelige nordiske Oldskrift-Selskab (Copenhagen: Qvist, 1863) and by

model for the *Finnboga saga* edition envisaged, Möbius not only
recommends Cederschiöld's *Jómsvíkinga saga*[19] that he had reviewed
but also furnishes Gering with a letter of introduction and expresses
his pleasure on 13 May 1877 when he learns about Gering's visit to
Lund:

> Auch das hat mich sehr in Ihrem Interesse erfreut, was
> Sie mir über Dr. Cederschiöld schreiben. Es wird ja nicht
> das erste u. letztemal gewesen sein, daß Sie bei ihm in
> Lund waren. (Suchen Sie ja ‹m›einen lieben Dr. Söderwall
> auf u. Prof. Wisén). [...] Das Beste, was ich Ihnen rathen
> kann, ist, daß Sie den überaus günstigen Umstand von
> Guðbr. Vigfússons Anwesenheit in Kph. möglichst
> ausbeuten und sich von diesem einen Vorschlag machen
> lassen. Werden Sie ihn nicht einmal in Skovshoved
> aufsuchen wollen? (Sagen Sie ihm, daß ich an ihn unter
> der Addr. von Jón ‹Si›gurdsson geschrieben, aber noch
> immer eine Antwort von ihm erwartete!!)

Of course, Gering followed the recommendation and advice to
meet the people Möbius named in his letters; greetings to both
Vigfússon and Cederschiöld are never forgotten, and Möbius is
rewarded with a short visit these two gentlemen paid him in Kiel in
mid-July 1877.

4. Let us turn to the manuscript work Gering began in
Copenhagen. Möbius had suggested *Finnboga saga*, which Gering
was to transcribe painstakingly and most thoroughly. And if this
would not fill out his time-schedule to the brim, Möbius suggested
transcriptions of *Bærings saga* or *Flóvents saga* from MS. AM 580 A B

Johan Fritzner, *Ordbog over det gamle norske Sprog* (Kristiania: Feilberg &
Landmark, 1867) are not mentioned.
[19] "Jómsvíkinga saga efter skinnboken 7 4to å Kungl. Biblioteket i
Stockholm," ed. Gustaf Cederschiöld, *Lunds Universitet Årsskrift* 11 (för år
1874, II. Afdelningen för philosophi, språkvetenskap och historia 3);
reviewed by Möbius in *Germania* 21 (1876): 103-109.

4°, and of *Ölkofra þáttr* because the existing editions[20] needed to be redone following *Möðruvallabók* more closely.

Gering's taking interest in Jón Halldórsson's ævintýri did not please Möbius very much. In his opinion, these stories were too late to consume the time and energy of a young philologist who ought to devote himself to the oldest transmission. Nevertheless he offered Gering the use of his own considerable preparatory work on the manuscripts AM 624 4° and 657 B 4° which he had postponed in 1869.

> Die Sammlung der kleinen Histörchen von und nach Jón Halldórsson [...] findet sich am besten in AM 624 4º – aus der spätern Hälfte des XV. Jhd. Sollten Sie wirklich dazu kommen, so schreiben Sie mir, da ich Ihnen in diesem Falle meinen ganzen Apparat von Abschriften ps. zur Verfügung stellen könnte; ich gedachte sie auch einmal herauszugeben. Nur fragt es sich, ob die Beschäftigung mit so späten Hdss. gegenwärtig in Ihrem Interesse liege.

He also incites him during the rest of his stay in Copenhagen, "das übersandte Material wo es Ihnen nöthig erscheint, mit den betreff. Hdss. zu vergleichen, naiv die einen u. andern Fragen, die Ihnen dabei erstehen, mit GV zu besprechen."

5. What our friends had talked about and discussed in Copenhagen, the mutual interest they took in one another's work, is recalled in the few letters exchanged between them in the course of time. These letters are kept among the letters to Guðbrandr Vigfússon in the Bodleian Library at Oxford and among Hugo Gering's literary

---

[20] *Nockrer Marg-Frooder Sögu-Þætter Islendínga*, ed. Björn Marcússon (Hólar: Halldór Eríksson, 1756), 34-37; *Krókarefssaga, Gunnars saga Keldugnúpsfífls og Ölkofra þáttr*, ed. Páll Sveinsson (Copenhagen: Louis Klein, 1866), 65-75.

remains in Kiel University Library.[21] For their publication they were
intertwined chronologically to maintain the impression of a
discourse; they are rendered in diplomatic print with abbreviations
expanded in [ ], and letters lost by hole-punching for a file-binder
added in ‹ ›, but without any sort of correction. Gering's notes on
Vigfússon's letters are in italics.

1
erh[alten]. 17/7 [recte 17/6] 77.   Skovshoved Skole
                                        Saturday June 16. 1877

Dear Dr. Gering.

Prof. Bugge is now arrived. He called here on Thursday
evening, and we had a pleasant walk & talk together. He
stays at <u>Bellevue Hotel</u> Kjöbenhavn. and leaves on
Tuesday or Wednesday.

In case you would call on him, my present note may serve
as an introduction. I am sorry to say that I am unable to
come to town to day or to morrow. On Monday I hope
to be there, and to see you.

Yours faithfully
G. Vigfusson
Hälsa Cederschiöld!

2
pr[aesentatum]. 7/11 772   St. John's Villas
antw[ort]. 14/1 78   St. John's Road

---

[21] I am grateful to both libraries for microfilms of these letters. While
GV's letters are numbered consecutively 1-10 (nos. 5, 8, and 10 being
Gering's neat yet not fully correct transcriptions of the negligent
handwriting of 4, 7, and 9) in the collection of fascicle 19, Gering's letters
to GV are entered in volume MS. German. d. 2, ranging from fol. 7r to
15r.

Oxford Nov. 1877

Kjære Dr. Gering,

Jeg skriver Dem blot faa Linjer denne gang for at erindre Dem om, at naarsomheldst De vil sende mig til gennemsyn Listen fra N° 1812, saa skal jeg være til Deres Tjeneste. Jeg seer af det sidste Hefte af Zacher's Zeitsch[rift]. at De har der leveret en Højtysk Liste.[22] maatte den Islandske komme snart efter. Jeg længes meget efter at see den trykt. Det var jo dog saa snildt af Dem at lægge den for. Jeg er nu beskeftiget med min Reader, navnlig med en kort Literairhistorie som Indledning.[23] Jeg arbeider sammen med en lærd dygtig ven Mr. York Powell.[24] Jeg dikterer til ham, som han noterer, og siden udarbeider, for at det Engelske kan blive bedre. Mange nye Ting kommer der for. Deriblandt kommer vi til at omtale Ölkofri og Finnbogi. Begge er, troer jeg, Fabrikerede Sagaer, fra det 13de Aarh. sidste Halvdeel. Ölkofra er gjort efter Bandamanna S[aga]., blot den ene kan jo være historisk, da jo the plot er det samme i begge. Den er dog interessant. 1. for de oplysninger den giver om Althing, Livet, Ölbryggeren, der har jo været mange successive Ölkofraer der, ogsaa (2) om Lagrettens Beliggenhed, som bedst sees af vor saga. 3. Hentydninger til tabte Sagaer & navnlig om Skapte, og Starre. Til Finnboge har der troer jeg ingen anden Tradition ligget til Grund, og intet meer end hvad vi veed af Vatsdæla. Sagaen citeres i Islendinga drápa. Begge Sagaer höre til vore ældste apocryphe. Ölkofra dog troer jeg den ældste.

---

22 "Mitteldeutsche Glossen," *Zeitschrift für deutsche Philologie* 8 (1877): 330-337; supplemented *ibid.* 9 (1878): 394.

23 Were the *Prolegomena* originally meant to accompany the *Modern Icelandic Reader*?

24 Frederick York Powell (1850-1904), lecturer of law, delegate to the Clarendon Press, became professor of Modern History in 1894.

– Dog nok om dette. Jeg havde hundrede Ting at fortælle
Dem fra min reise i Sverge, "Kroningen" o.s.v.[25] alt
herligt og uforglemmeligt. Jeg var siden kort Tid i
Christiania. Glem ikke "now & then" at tænke paa mig.
Jeg gjemmer paa Deres og Cederschjold's Korter i
Træklemmen som De kastede den ind af mit Vindue. Jeg
haaber at Deres Sommerrejse har baaret gode frugter for
mange aar. Deres Bekendtskab er mig en overmaade
venlig erindring. –

Dette i Hast. Deres altid
hengivne
Gudbrand Vigfusson
Mange Tak for Brev og Tilsendelsen af Specimenet af
Olkofra og Finnboga.

3

Halle ᵃ/S. 14 jan. 1878

Hochverehrter herr!

Was werden Sie nur von mir denken, dass ich Ihren
freundlichen, so überaus liebenswürdigen brief vom
november v[origen]. j[ahres]. immer noch nicht
beantwortet habe? Hoffentlich verzeihen Sie mir, wenn
Sie den grund meines schweigens erfahren. Ich wartete
mit der antwort, weil ich Ihnen gern eine sorgfältige
abschrift oder einen correcturabzug der glossen
mitgeschickt hätte, leider ist mir das aber noch nicht
möglich, und ich muss nun schreiben, damit Sie nicht
etwa denken, dass ich Sie und die schönen tage von
Seeland ganz vergessen habe. Ich warte von tage zu tage,

---

[25] An honorary doctorate of philosophy was bestowed on GV on 6
September during the celebration of the 400th anniversary of Uppsala
university, cf. *Upsala-Universitets fyrahundraårs jubelfest* (Stockholm: Norstedt,
1879), 110.

von woche zu woche, auf eine nochmalige collation der glossen, die ich herrn Gudmund Thorlaksson[26] übertragen, aber immer noch nicht erhalten habe, ebenso wie ich bis heute noch immer vergeblich auf seine abschrift der Finnboga s[aga]. aus AM. 510 4 lauern muss. Wir hatten uns damals in Kopenhagen nur mit einer seite in cod. reg. 1812 beschäftigt, erst hier in Deutschland erfuhr ich, dass noch auf einer zweiten Seite der handschrift ebenfalls lat.-isländ. glossen stehen. Es schien mir zweckmässig, wenn alles zusammen veröffentlicht würde, und so hat durch Cederschiölds vermittlung ein junger Schwede, Valdemar Steffensen, den zweiten teil der glossen für mich abgeschrieben. Meine abschrift, bei der Sie mich damals so freundlich unterstützten, sowie die von Steffensen, habe ich also noch einmal nach Kopenhagen geschickt. Hoffentlich bekomme ich das alles nun bald zurück, ich werde es dann so schnell als möglich zum drucke vorbereiten und nicht verfehlen, von Ihrem freundlichen anerbieten gebrauch zu machen, indem ich Ihnen einen correcturabzug sende.

Mit der ausgabe der Finnb. s. hoffe ich, wenn ich die abschrift aus Kopenhagen bald bekomme, bis ostern fertig zu werden, sodass der druck noch im laufe des sommers vor sich gehen kan. Es versteht sich von selbst, dass ich, wenn es soweit ist, Ihnen sofort ein exemplar zuschicke. In der einleitung werde ich ausführlich über die orthographie von AM 132 sprechen, wozu ich mir bereits recht dickleibige excerpte gemacht habe. Gegenwärtig arbeite ich an dem beizufügenden glossar, wobei mir Ihr dictionary die trefflichsten dienste leistet (NB Ihre vermutung s. 703[a] s. v. viðbeina ist richtig: die hs. hat deutlich viðbei̱na̱ð.)

---

[26] Guðmundr Þorláksson (1852-1910), stipendiarius of the Arnamagnæan commission in Copenhagen 1874-1896.

Was Sie mir über Ihre reise in Schweden und Norwegen,
sowie über Ihre arbeiten berichten, hat mich
ausserordentlich interessiert; hinsichtlich der letzteren
macht mich Möbius auf einen artikel in der Academy
aufmerksam, den ich leider noch nicht habe zu gesicht
bekommen können.[27]

Von Cederschiöld habe ich öfter briefe erhalten; in dem
letzten schreibt er mir, dass das erste heft seiner
"fornsögur Suðrlanda" demnächst erscheinen wird.[28]

Der schönen stunden, die ich in Ihrer und Cederschiölds
gesellschaft verleben durfte, gedenke ich stets in
dankbarer erinnerung. Das glück, auf meiner reise Ihre
bekantschaft gemacht zu haben, weiss ich nicht hoch
genug zu schätzen. Hoffentlich sehen wir uns bald einmal
wider "ved Skodsborgs voldsomme höi"

Mit herzlichen grüssen
Ihr
ergebenster
Hugo Gering.

4
pr. 26/5 78   Oxford 2 St. John's Villas
Antw[ort]. 30/5 78   St John's Road

---

[27] In his letter of 30 December 1877 Möbius advises Gering: "Wenn Sie
die 'Academy' (= engl. Centralbl.) in Halle halten, empfehle ich Ihnen
einen kleinen Artikel in nr. 291 (1. Dec. 1877), der über die Arbeiten
Vigfússons berichtet, von Mr. Skeat (?) in Oxf." In this contribution, A.
H. Sayce also mentions that GV "was one of the illustrious scholars who
received the degree of Doctor at Upsala in the summer" (514).
[28] "Fornsögur suðrlanda. Isländska bearbetningar af främmande romaner
från medeltiden. Efter gamla handskrifter," ed. Gustaf Cederschiöld,
Lunds Universitets Årsskrift 13 (för läsåret 1876-1877, II. Afdelningen för
philosophi, språkvetenskap och historia 3).

Kjære Dr. Gering,

Först om en undskyldning for at jeg ikke har skreven
Dem för nu, og takket Dem Deres venlige brev. Jeg har i
mit stille sind allerede tusinde gange lykønsket Dem til
Deres Verlobung.[29] Lad nu ikke græsset gro paa Deres vej
til heiraten; for som skalden siger None trotts hard with a
maid (a braut) between the betrothal & the wedding day.
Therefore make haste.

Deres Glossar[30] er jo ganske fortræffeligt; curious, at jeg
var ved at skrive Dem om þvetti, tænkende at det skulde
være þvætti, og nu staar det der. Ordet lǫn staar i
Lexikonet, det er et household word i Island, I have made
many a "hay-lǫn" myself. So altsaa nóra det staar i
Lexikonet. Gudmund Thorlaksson synes at have gort sine
sager godt. Jeg husker nu godt den ene side, da jeg i
sommers glemte at fortælle dem om

    Hvorledes gaar det med Finnbogi den Stærke, &
Ölkofri (Ale-hvad)? Jeg har i Pressen Prolegomena til en
Islandsk Literaturhistorie som min ven Powell og jeg
sætter sammen. Maa jeg ikke der omtale Finnb[ogi]. og
Ölkofri, samt Eventyrene, som being edited by Dr. Hugo
Gering of Halle? Lad os ikke vente for længe. Sturlunga
med disse Prolegomena vil komme ud inden få uger
herfra. En Reader er også i Pressen, og vil saa håber jeg
göre hurtige fremskridt.[31]

---

[29] That must have happened in April, as Cederschiöld's congratulations
are in his letter to Gering of 1 May 1878.
[30] "Isländische glossen," *Zeitschrift für deutsche Philologie* 9 (1878): 385-394.
[31] *Sturlunga Saga including the Islendinga Saga of lawman Sturla Thordsson and
other works.* Ed. with prolegomena, appendices, tables, indices and maps by
Gudbrand Vigfússon, 2 vols. (Oxford: Clarendon Press, 1878); dedicated:
"To the university of Upsala." Gering's forthcoming editions are

Med ærbodige hilsner til dem og Deres Allerhjertens kære
–

Deres altid hengivne
Gudbrand Vigfusson

5

Halle ᵃ/S. 30. mai 1878

Lieber herr doctor![32]

Recht vielen Dank für Ihren freundlichen brief und die
darin ausgesprochenen glückwünsche! Auf dem wege zur
hochzeit gedenke ich allerdings nicht gras wachsen zu
lassen, da ich meine liebste bereits im october heimführen
wil.

Dass Sie mit meinen glossen zufrieden sind, hat mich sehr
gefreut; das beste dabei habe freilich nicht ich getan,
sondern Sie und ihr landsmann Þorláksson. Ich wil nur
wünschen, dass Ihnen auch die Finnboga s[aga]. genügen
wird; dieselbe ist im druck (verlag des hiesigen
waisenhauses). ein bogen ist bereits fertig, damit der text
so correct wir möglich werde, lasse ich eine correctur
durch G[uðmundur]. Þorláksson in Kopenhagen lesen.
Auch prof. Möbius in Kiel hat die ausserordentliche
liebenswürdigkeit gehabt, die übernahme der revision mir
anzubieten. ølkofri und die märchen werden freilich noch
etwas warten müssen, der Finnbogi wird mich noch den
ganzen sommer über in anspruch nehmen: die einleitung

---

mentioned on pp. liv, lxiv, cxxxvi of the Prolegomena, his "Isländische
glossen" on p. cxli: *An Icelandic Prose Reader* with Notes, Grammar, and
Glossary by Dr. Gudbrand Vigfusson and F. York Powell, M. A. (Oxford:
Clarendon Press, 1879).
[32] After the bestowing of the honorary doctorate Gering changes to the
proper address.

habe ich noch nicht fertig, ich muss noch manches dazu lesen, jetzt bin ich bei der Ljósvetninga saga.

Auf Ihre isländ[ische]. literaturgeschichte bin ich sehr gespant, sie wird uns gewiss recht viel neue aufschlüsse bringen und bekantes von neuen gesichtspunkten aus beleuchten. Haben Sie in den reader die stellen aus Finnbogi und ølkofri aufgenommen?

Von Cederschiöld hatte ich kürzlich auch einen brief, es geht ihm gut. Wann die fortsetzung seiner fornsǫgur erscheint, schreibt er nicht. Er wird jetzt wol schon mit den vorbereitungen zu seiner reise beschäftigt sein; wolte er nicht auch nach England?[33]

Der sommer des vorigen jahres ist mir eine unerschöpfliche quelle freundlicher erinnerungen. Ich gebe die hoffnung nicht auf, dass wir und Cederschiöld uns noch einmal auf dem schönen Seeland zusammenfinden. Sie kommen doch gewiss bald einmal wider nach Kopenhagen? Mit der bitte, mich, wenn Sie zeit haben, einmal wider durch einen brief zu erfreuen und in der hoffnung dereinstigen fröhlichen widersehns

verbleibe ich herzlichst grüssend
Ihr
ergebenster Gering.

6

---

[33] Cederschiöld's journey to libraries and individuals began in June and led him to Halle to see Gering, to Weimar to meet Reinhold Köhler, to Munich to attend lectures of Konrad Maurer and Wilhelm Heinrich Riehl, he continued to Paris, to London and Oxford, where he met GV, in July; on his way back he visited Möbius in Kiel, spent some time in Copenhagen, and finally returned home at the end of August 1878.

pr[aesentatum]. 11/4 79   2 St. John's Villas
Antw[ort]. 24/5   St John's Rd.
                                                  Oxford Apr. 8, 1879.

My dear Dr. Gjering,

The Sturlunga with the Prolegomena is finished, and now
the last sheet of the Icelandic Reader was stru[ck] of on
the 1ˢᵗ hujus (viij + 560 pages).

Having unburdened my mind from these things I
remember with dismay how great my arrears are in
rendering thanks to absent friends. I have then to thank
you for your very excellent print of the Glosses, which I
was very glad to see done. Next the Finnbogi. The print is
neat and sober, and the spelling of AM 132 shows well
off. I think it is the first literal print from that important
vellum. I should have wished to see the <u>word division</u>
observed.[34]

As to the other questions arising I have only to remark
that I can not make out the number 216 leaves.[35] I once
calculated that when complete it would have scored 200
or 199. (Eight leaves of Njal beg[inning]; then the end of
Fostbr[æðra].; beside 2 leaves in Egil and 1½ in Njala
medio). – This is of small importance. – My thought also
has been that once of a time Egils S. was the leading Saga,
then Njála beginning a fresh sheet reverse. On the last

---

[34] GV seems to talk about the use of hyphens in compounds as he
arbitrarily applied them in his *Sturlunga saga* edition. The comment cannot
refer to the 85 word divisions at the end of lines in Gering's edition that
all but one comply to morphology; cf. e. g. <Þor- geirr> 10.16 or <agét-
ar> 71.18 (vs. AM 132 fol. 110va33f. <agé tar>), but <sæm- darfaur>
60.24 (vs. AM 132 fol. 108vb25f. <sæmdar faur>).
[35] Gering claims that AM 132 fol. originally consisted of "at least" 26
quires of 8 leaves = 208 leaves cf. *Finnboga saga*, I.

blank page of Egils s. is written the first half of
Arinbjarnar drápa; but how the end of that poem? that I
think ran on to the 1ˢᵗ blank page on the 1ˢᵗ Njála sheet.
This sheet has been [lost] time out of mind. The real loss
is, if my theory be right, the loss of Arinb[jarnar]. drápa. –
lost for ever!

Now, there is no use crying for spilt milk. I have not
heard from Möbius for an age, and do not know what he
is about; and what he has been about of late, I confess, is
not much to my mind.[36]

Are you married? or when is the happy auspicious event
to take place? Cederschiöld I fear is not, I wish he were,
and gave him a lesson to that effect last I saw him. But
lange Forlovelser seem to be the order of the day among
the students in Sweden. I like them not, they are unfair to
the better half of mankind.

---

[36] GV was quite irritated about a misleading reference of Möbius in his
Analecta norræna, 2nd ed. (Leipzig: Hinrichs'sche Buchhandlung, 1877),
VIII, to Konráð Gíslason to have attributed the First Grammatical
Treatise to Þóroddr Gamlason; in his "Berichtigung" in *Germania* 22
(1877), 508 Möbius corrected this attribution and asks for GV's pardon in
his letter of 24 January 1878 (MS Germ. d. 2 fol. 462):

Möchte es mir gelungen sein, Dich durch beifolgende
"Berichtigung" in Bartschs Germania XXII zu überzeugen, wie
fern es mir gelegen Dich verletzen zu wollen und wie sehr es
mir daran liegt, unsre alte Freundschaft – ungetrübt durch
diesen Zwischenfall – lebendig fort zu erhalten.

Wie kommst Du nur auf den Gedanken, daß ich für Prof.
Gíslason und Jón Þorkelsson so besondre Sympathie hege, die
mir doch beide – namentlich in wissenschaftlicher Beziehung –
nicht im Entferntesten das sein können, was Du für mich von
jeher geweßen bist und noch bist!

I have seen a draught of Jomsvíkinga drápa it is very well done.[37] Things from Germany have not all been so good. They write too long, and seem to take no account of distinguishing between irrelevant and relevant things. I am sad at reading Maurer's wearisome criticisms, leaden monotony, reasoning & juristerei and no soul or sympathy, and then our good Möbius his old song "erstens ... zweitens" and humble homages in season and out of season to Wimmer Gíslason and all that. I am tired of it.

Now, you may think I am setting out for a tilt "Kritische Untersuchungen" lest it be in "drei Bände" I break off at once, with every good wish to you & your bride (wife?).

Believe me to be very sincerly yours
G. Vigfusson
PS. Kölbing's Tristram is fair; he is much more gifted man than Brenner or Wilken. The Kristni S[aga]. I could not read.[38] 'Tis fatal!
G.V.

---

[37] *Jómsvíkinga Saga (efter Cod. AM. 510, 4:to) samt Jómsvíkinga Drápa*, ed. Carl af Petersens (Lund: Gleerup, 1879).

[38] *Tristrams saga ok Ísondar*. Mit einer literarhistorischen Einleitung, deutscher Übersetzung und Anmerkungen zum ersten Mal herausgegeben von Eugen Kölbing. Die nordische und die englische Version der Tristan-Sage. 1. Theil (Heilbronn: Henninger, 1878. Repr. Hildesheim-New York: Olms, 1978) [Dedication: Guðbrandr Vigfússon in Erinnerung an Kopenhagen und Oxford dankbar zugeeignet vom Herausgeber]; Oskar Brenner, *Über die Kristni-saga. Kritische Beiträge zur altnordischen Literaturgeschichte* (München: Kaiser, 1878). Oskar Brenner (1854-1920) had his doctorate from Munich University in 1877, Habilitation in Munich 1878, professor in Würzburg 1892-1919; cf. *Internationales Germanistenlexikon*, 269ff.; Ernst Wilken (1846-1927) had his doctorate from Greifswald University in 1867, Habilitation in Göttingen 1870, never gained a professorship because his scholarly work lacked recognition; he taught at Secondary Schools, cf. *Internationales Germanistenlexikon*, 2034f.

7

Halle ª/S. 24. mai 1879

Geehrtester herr doctor!

Recht freundlichen dank für Ihre Zeilen vom 8. v[origen].
m[onats]., aus denen ich mit vergnügen sehe, dass meine
arbeiten im grossen und ganzen Ihren beifall gefunden
haben.

Ihre Sturlunga Saga befindet sich schon seit längerer zeit
in meinen händen. Die "prolegomena" habe ich mit dem
lebhaftesten interesse gelesen und mich an der klaren und
geistreichen darstellung von herzen erfreut. Vielleicht
würden Sie sich den dank der gelehrten welt in noch
grösserem masse erwerben, wenn Sie sich entschliessen
könnten, das bild der altnordischen literaturgeschichte
noch einmal selbständig und in breiterer ausführung, mit
angabe des gesamten wissenschaftlichen materials zu
entrollen. Es gibt ja kein buch darüber, das den
ansprüchen der gegenwart genügte; geradezu ein skandal
ist es, dass eine so elende fabrikarbeit wie das werk von
Winkel Horn dem deutschen publicum angeboten werden
darf. Dass männer wie Zarncke, Möbius u. Maurer den
verfasser zur abfassung desselben aufgefordert haben, ist
natürlich eine dreiste lüge der verlagsbuchhandlung.[39]

---

[39] *Geschichte der Literatur des skandinavischen Nordens von den ältesten Zeiten bis
auf die Gegenwart* dargestellt von Frederik Winkel Horn (Leipzig: Schlicke,
1880); cf. VIII: "Das Buch ist den Herren Professoren Maurer, Möbius
und Zarncke gewidmet, als schuldigen Tribut für ihren mir bei meinem
Unternehmen geleisteten wohlwollenden Beistand. Ohne den

Da Sie so freundlich waren, sich nach meinen personalien zu erkundigen, so erlaube ich mir, Ihnen mitzuteilen, dass ich bereits seit dem october im glücklichen besitze meines lieben weibes bin. Cederschiöld wird wol noch nicht verheiratet sein, er hätte es mir sonst wol mitgeteilt. Ich fürchte, dass es die pecuniären verhältnisse sind, welche diese verzögerung veranlassen. Es ist das unglück der kleinen nationen, dass sie nicht im stande sind, für die hüter ihrer geistigen schätze in ausreichender weise zu sorgen.

Was Ihre auslassungen über Möbius und Maurer betrifft, so kann ich mich nicht entschliessen, darin etwas anderes zu erblicken, als die eingebung einer augenblicklichen und vorübergehenden verstimmung. Denn ich will nicht glauben, dass Sie Deutschland und der deutschen wissenschaft so entfremdet sind, wie Sie sich den anschein geben. Es ist ja wahr, dass blendende und formvollendete darstellung bei den deutschen gelehrten selten anzutreffen ist; eins aber muss das ausland, wenn es gerecht sein will, bei ihnen anerkennen: sorgfältige u. gewissenhafte forschung und sichere methode.

Die pflege der gemeinsamen wissenschaft, der altgermanischen philologie, ist eins der wenigen bänder, durch welche unsere nationen, die sonst leider feindlich genug sich gegenüberstehen, noch einigermassen fühlung unter einander erhalten. Lassen Sie uns dieses band nicht zerreissen!

In unveränderter freundschaft
verbleibe ich Ihr
ergebener

---

ermunternden Zuspruch jener Männer würde mir sicherlich der Muth dazu gefehlt haben." Frederik Winkel Horn (1845-1898), was a Danish archaeologist, historian and translator.

Gering

8 (postcard stamped: Oxford Ja 2 80; Halle 4 1 80)

Oxford Jan 1. 80

Kjære Doctor,

Mange tak for Deres vakre Ölkofri;[40] alt er rigtigt, blot
"word division" savner jeg; en hyphen eller lignende. Jeg
vilde önske Glum og Kormak paa samme maade udgivet
fra AM 132; den membran er orthographisk meget vigtig,
og deres Finnbogi og Olk[ofri]. er det eneste trykt. –
Deres venlige omtale i Anglia er jeg taknemmelig for.[41]
Men når Grendels moder er identificeret saa maa
Brydningen i hallen "follow suit," Parallelerne ere nok
ellers, the tearing of the "feld" and the tearing off of
Grendel's arm. Alene Glam er "good" i Sagaen, i Beowulf
derimod poor; mens Grendel's moder er et af de faa
Glanspunkter i det langspundne kjedsommelige Digt.
Havde andet for? – Kulturen skrider frem, Grendel og
Glam paa Union Postale Universelle Kort. –

Med mange lykönskninger til det Nye Aar Deres G.
Vigfusson

---

[40] Hugo Gering, "Þorhalls þattr Olkofra," *Beiträge zur deutschen Philologie.
Julius Zacher dargebracht als Festgabe zum 28. Oktober 1879*, ed. Ernst
Bernhardt et al. (Halle a. S.: Buchhandlung des Waisenhauses, 1880), 1-24;
even separately: *Olkofra þattr*, ed. Hugo Gering (Halle a. S.: Buchhandlung
des Waisenhauses, 1880).
[41] "Der Beowulf und die isländische Grettissaga," *Anglia* 3 (1880): 74-87.

9

Halle ª/S. 22 Decbr. 1881
22 Bernburger str.

Geehrtester herr doctor!

Meine ausgabe der isländischen legenden, märchen und
novellen, auf welche Sie mich vor 4 jahren zuerst
aufmerksam machten, ist unter der presse, und ich
erlaube mir Ihnen beifolgend einen correcturabzug des 4.
bogens zu übersenden, aus welchem Sie sich über die
einrichtung des buches ein urteil werden bilden können.
Es würde mir recht erwünscht sein, wenn Sie mich Ihre
meinung darüber hören liessen. Gleichzeitig habe ich aber
noch eine specielle bitte. Am anfange der 16. erzählung
werden zwei Isländer, Bergr Gunnsteinsson und Jón hestr
als verfasser einer biographie des bischofs Thomas Becket
erwähnt, über die ich nirgends, auch nicht in den beiden
ausgaben der Thomassaga, irgend welche auskunft finde.
Sie geben freilich in den prol[egomena]. zur Sturl[unga].
s[aga]. cxxxv an, dass Jón Holt, prediger zu Hitárdalr, eine
lebensgeschichte des heiligen verfasst habe, sagen aber
leider nicht, woher Sie diese notiz haben. Sie würden
mich sehr verbinden, wenn Sie mir nähere mitteilungen
hierüber machen könten. Ist Ihr Jón Holt vielleicht
identisch mit meinem Jón hestr?!

Ich war im frühling dieses jahres wider 6 wochen in
Kopenhagen, um das material für meine erzählungen zu
vervolständigen. Die zahl der stücke, die ich gebe, ist
dadurch auf 101 gestiegen. Erschöpfend freilich kann
meine ausgabe nicht werden, es wird immer noch eine
reiche nachlese übrig bleiben. Mehrere Stockholmer
handschriften konte ich in Kopenhagen benutzen, einer

derselben entnahm ich eine fast volständige isländische übersetzung der disciplina clericalis.[42]

Mit den herzlichsten wünschen für das neue jahr und in der hoffnung auf baldige antwort verbleibe ich

Ihr
ergebenster
Hugo Gering

10 (postcard stamped: Oxford 12 Ja 82; Halle Ankunft 14 1 82)

Oxford Jan. 12. 82

Dear Dr. Gering.

Am glad to learn of the Mediæval Legends; appropriate that they should appear in Germany the Promised Holy Land of Märchen: In these if not in every thing else Germany beats all nations. – What about the <u>hollt</u>, twenty years ago I read it out of AM 586; you read <u>hestr</u>, are you sure? I remember the letters were quite faded. remember not whether Jon Sig[urðsson]. also had it in hand and read it as I. I was the first to observe it. Is no great matter one way or another. A Jon hestr quite unknown entity, not to be identified under the sun. There were some

---

[42] *Disciplina clericalis* is the name of a well known collection of 34 "exempla" from the beginning of the 12th century by Petrus Alfonsi, a Jewish Spanish physician who converted to Christianity. The original Latin text (cf. *Die Disciplina Clericalis des Petrus Alfonsi (das älteste Novellenbuch des Mittelalters) nach allen bekannten Handschriften*, ed. Alfons Hilka & Werner Söderhjelm, Kleine Ausgabe, Sammlung mittellateinischer Texte 1 (Heidelberg: Winter, 1911) was translated into various vernaculars amongst which is the Old Norse version in MS. Holm. papp. 66 fol. This translation is in fact far from complete, containing parts of the prologue and of exempla 1-23 only.

misprints in your sheet, it is maybe a Correctur. I should gladly have perused sheets for you. Write on, never mind critics. – With kindest regards to you & family, yours faithfully & in haste

G. Vigfusson.

11
pr[aesentatum]. 11/6. 84.   Oxford. June 9. 1884.
resp[ondi]. 16/6.   (The Hill Dumfries)

My dear Professor Gering,

It is an eternity and a day since I have written to you to thank you for your kindness in sending me your new book, and at the same time to congratulate you on its completion.[43] You have indeed very nobly accomplished the task that I (if I remember right) was the first to put into your head at Copenhagen now seven years ago. Mr Powell has also been very pleased, and has, as I believe, written a little notice into the Academy[44] (for I never write myself), it has now long been at the Editors'; one has a great trouble to get notices in; we have to cut them brief, lest they be ever sated with Islandica; there has been of late false prophets abroad; the famine and other shameful jobbings, and now the innocent suffer. – In the long interval since I saw you much has changed; friends dead and gone, the bad ones alife, Mr. Sigurdsson gone, the only Icelander I cared for. As for yourselves there are

---

[43] *Islendzk Æventyri. Isländische Legenden, Novellen und Märchen,* Ed. Hugo Gering. I. Band: Text. II. Band: Anmerkungen und Glossar. Mit Beiträgen von Reinhold Köhler (Halle a. S.: Buchhandlung des Waisenhauses, 1882-1883).
[44] *The Academy* 576, 19 May 1884, 347 carries a one column notice on the contents of *Corpus Poeticum Boreale.*

only matters for congratulations, you are, since I saw you, married, probably have seen "pa-pa-papas kommen," professor, etcetera, have finished your work, I hope without hurt to your eyesight, for the Icel[andic]. vellums are dreadful you may go in Argus eyed, and may thank your fate if you do not go out dimsighted or blind. I being a farmer's son, nature's child on first hand, have escaped almost scotfree, though not quite without hurt.

In your book I met with a strange, old acquaintance. When child, about a six years old, in a little island, not bigger than your garden-plot, with my great-aunt, I remember bits of a story she told me, the first story I mind having heard, of an angel guiding a young man, they met with various adventures, whereof I clearly remember that of seeing a man hanging over a precipice (dauða-takit) holding a tuft of grass (gras-tó) upon which the guide, instead of pulling the man up, pulled up the tuft, on which the other's life hung; this struck me with horror, and so I can see it as it were; the other incidents I remember not, only there were several, nothing about lifting the silver, nor would I have understood that, being too young to know what it is to steal, nor do I remember the cow, which I wonder at; for we had in our islet one white cow and only one – I was with my old aunt like a young Parcival with his mother – with a little black dot on one side, just as a finger's print. Curious to know where my aunt got her story from: the rea[son] why she told it me you can understand, how the ways of God are inscrutable; the young man's horror at what the gentle guide did, and the explanations afterwards. Curious that in your msc. there is just at this point a blank, though the following shows that the precipice was one of the incidents; there is a similar one in Fostbr[æðra]. S[aga]. Flateybook text, only no angel there. I never heard or saw this story since, my aunt (who is now, as you may imagine, long since beyond the reach of any human inquiry) being my sole authority. – Your book is a very charming one, and in every way does you a great credit. The contributions of Dr. Köhler are quite delightful; what a wonderful fountain of all kind of good knowledge that man must be! Is he not Eckermann's successor?[45] I fare, I saw him in Oct. 1861, when I was in Weimar, walked with Mœbius (14th oct.) from Leipzig to Weimar; should like to be there again. Be so kind to give my best love to him. – I add as in a P.S. that I am now starting for Copenhagen, to prepare a fresh volume for the Clarendon Press (Mr. Powell & myself) this time the great Landnama, Kristni S[aga]., and Libellus, all in one volume, with Excursus Notes Indices, etcetera, like the Corpus.[46] I start from Edinb[ur]g[h] on Thursday, and this day a week I shall be deep at work copying, it is not the first time in my life, I am rather fond of it and hope I have not lost the skill;

I have not for an age heard from our friend Cederschiöld, he is a most genuine man, whom I much do like, now he is a married man, overseer at a Ladies' Institute in big commercial Gothenburg; do not know whether I shall see him this time; hardly I fear will, unless he do come down to Copenhagen.

This is a long winded idle letter, and I have to apologize twofold, for <u>not</u> writing so long time, and now for writing so ill; Be pleased to give my best love to your wife and the bairns, how so ever many they be; and be at all times

---

[45] Reinhold Köhler (1830-1892), a renowned and remarkably well read literary historian was a librarian in the Großherzogliche Bibliothek at Weimar; thus he was not Johann Peter Eckermann's successor.

[46] *Origines islandicae.* A collection of the more important sagas and other native writings relating to the settlement and early history of Iceland, ed. and trans. by Gudbrand Vigfusson and F[rederick] York Powell, 2 vols. (Oxford: Clarendon Press, 1905; repr. Millwood, NY: Kraus, 1976).

assured of my goodwill and respectful remembrance of
our short acquaintance at Copenhagen, now so many
years ago. There was lately a most gentle worthy young
German called hr Dr. Kluge of Jena, I am glad that there
be some young men of that sort, for I have lost my faith
and sympathy in your Mœbiuses & Maurers. If thing go
that gate, the studies of Northern things will become a
scare. One must never be dull, it is a mistake that a dull
scholar makes a deep scholar, though many seem now to
think so.

With every hearty wishes I remain, my Dear Mr. Gering,
ever sincerly yours
G. Vigfusson
P.S. Letters will now reach me only at Copenhagen.

12

Halle, 15. juni 1884

Sehr geehrter herr doctor!

Empfangen Sie meinen besten dank für Ihren
freundlichen und ausführlichen brief vom 9. d[es].
m[ona]ts. Die glückwünsche, welche Sie mir darbringen,
sind den tatsächlichen verhältnissen leider nicht ganz
entsprechend, da die professur, die ich seit einem jahre
bekleide, vorläufig noch eine unbesoldete ist, und ich von
den 4 jungen, die mir beschert waren, vor kurzem einen,
und zwar den liebenswürdigsten und begabtesten von
allen, habe begraben müssen. Indessen – d[er]gl[eichen].
erfahrungen bleiben kaum einem sterblichen erspart, und
ich will mit meinem schicksal, das mir auch manche
freude gewährt hat, nicht hadern.

Sehr interessant war mir Ihre mitteilung von der in
mündl[icher]. tradition fortlebenden parallele zu nr. C der

æv[entýri]., obwol ich daran zweifle, dass die erzählung
ihrer tante wirklich auf die legende des 14.
j[ahr]h[undert]s zurückzuführen ist. Der stoff ist ja
ausserordentlich verbreitet gewesen, und da Sie an das
vorkommen der <u>kuh</u> sich nicht mehr erinnern (diese tritt
ja nur in den <u>ältesten</u> belegbaren zeugnissen auf), so
dürfte die verwantschaft zwischen den beiden
erzählungen nur eine entferntere sein, zumal da auch das
herabstürzen eines menschen in einen abgrund
verschieden erzählt zu sein scheint.

Was Sie über Möbius und Maurer sagen, hat mich, offen
und ehrlich gestanden, verlezt. Dem lezteren müssen
doch sogar seine gegner nachrühmen, dass er 'der erste
kenner des nordischen rechtes ist und belesen in der
altnordischen u[nd]. dahin einschlagenden literatur und
mit ihrem inhalte vertraut, wie vielleicht im norden selbst
kein andrer'. Und was wir in Deutschland an einem
gelehrten am höchsten schätzen, treue und
gewissenhaftigkeit bis ins kleinste und scheinbar
unbedeutendste, sowie unbestechliche wahrheitsliebe –
<u>diese</u> eigenschaften wird <u>beiden</u> wol niemand absprechen
wollen; es sind dieselben vorzüge, die mir auch unseren
freund Cederschiöld so lieb und wert machen. Hierauf
beruht ja auch das ansehen, das die deutsche wissenschaft
noch heute im auslande geniesst. Warum hat die Early
English Text Society mit der herausgabe des Beówulf
einen Deutschen[47] betraut? Offenbar doch deshalb, weil
die englischen gelehrten – ein paar rühmliche ausnahmen
abgerechnet – es noch nicht gelernt haben, mit der
peinlichkeit und accuratesse zu arbeiten, welche man bei

---

[47] Julius Zupitza, *Beowulf*. Autotypes of the unique Cotton MS. Vitellius A
xv in the British Museum, with a Transliteration and Notes. Early English
Text Society, original series 77 (London: Trübner, 1882; 2nd ed. [with a
new reproduction of the manuscript], Early English Text Society, original
series 245, Oxford: University Press, 1959, repr. 1967).

uns – und im skandinavischen norden – heutzutage
fordert. Hiernach werden Sie es auch verstehen, dass ich
Ihre früheren arbeiten, die Eyrbyggja s[aga]., Fornsögur,
Biskupasögur, Flateyjarbók[48] etc. höher schätze als Ihre
lezten publicationen (Sturl[unga]. u[nd]. Corpus),[49] obwol
ich auch in diesen die glänzende combinationsgabe und
den reichtum an neuen und fruchtbaren gedanken
bewundere.

Ich hoffe, dass Sie mir meine offenheit nicht übel
auslegen, und wünsche Ihrem neuen unternehmen besten
fortgang und erfolg. Besonders bin ich auf Ihre ausgabe
der Landnáma gespant – an das buch knüpft sich ja noch
manche ungelöste frage.[50]

Cederschöld hat die absicht, während seiner ferien (mitte
juni – ende august), die er in Schonen bei seinen
schwiegereltern verlebt, auf einige tage nach Kopenhagen
zu gehen; Sie werden ihn also jedesfals begrüssen können.

---

[48] *Eyrbyggja Saga*, ed. Guðbrandr Vigfusson (Leipzig: F.C.W. Vogel, 1864);
Fornsögur: Vatnsdælasaga, Hallfreðarsaga, Flóamannasaga, ed. Guðbrandr
Vigfússon & Theodor Möbius (Leipzig: Hinrichs'sche Buchhandlung,
1860) [dedicated: Ihrem lieben Freunde Konrad Maurer ord. öffentl.
Professor des Deutschen Rechts an der Münchener Hochschule in
herzlicher Zuneigung und Hochachtung gewidmet von G. V und Th. M.];
Biskupa sögur, gefnar út af hinu íslenzka bókmentafèlagi. 2 vols.
(Copenhagen: Möller, 1858-1878); *Flateyjarbok*. En Samling af norske
Konge-Sagaer med inskudte mindre Fortællinger om Begivenheder i og
udenfor Norge samt Annaler. Udg. efter offentl. foranstaltning. 3 vols.
Det norske historiske Kildeskriftfonds skrifter, 4,1-3 (Christiania: Malling,
1860-68).
[49] Cf. fns. 1 and 31. – Cf. also Eugen Mogk's negative assessment in his
postcard to Finnur Jónsson on 16 April 1898, "Wie ich von Gering höre,
bereitet d. Samfund eine neue Ausgabe der Sturlunga vor. Das wird die
höchste Zeit, da die Vigfússonsche zu wissenschaftlichen Arbeiten
vollständig unbrauchbar ist."
[50] Cf. fn. 46.

An die übrigen bekanten in Kopenhagen (Wimmer, Þorláksson usw.) bitte ich empfehlungen auszurichten.

Mit besten grüssen
Ihr
ergebenster
Hugo Gering

6. There is no answer to this rather blunt letter of Gering, as he
surmised. Gradually the steady flow of information from Oxford to
Germany ceased, as letters to Möbius and Maurer became scarcer
and scarcer, too. Their replies to Vigfússon end in spring 1886.
There is only one additional letter by Maurer, dated 26 January
1889, an answer to York Powell, who had informed Maurer on 18
January that Guðbrandr Vigfússon had fallen seriously ill.

Let us sum up: After having given Vigfússon a piece of his
mind Gering continues his friendly discourse by mentioning future
plans and ongoings and even asks Vigfússon to pass on his
greetings to his Copenhagen acquaintances. His disappointment,
however, is immense: his friend's *Corpus poeticum boreale* does not live
up to the standards of scholarly publications towards the end of the
19th century and must therefore needs be rejected. In philological
matters Vigfússon became more and more idiosyncratic; he neither
cares about others' opinions, challenging Gering to do the same,
nor does he care about the correct references scholars want in order
to enable them to draw their own picture or to substantiate an
argumentation put forth.

It is not surprising that all reviews are basically negative,
claiming that the book is sagacious and ingenious, while the texts
contained are unreliable constructions. It was Konrad Maurer, who
in his obituary categorized these rejections based on Vigfússon's

lack of training in methodology as "feinere" or "derbere"[51] depending on the reviewers' dispositions.

Thus, Gustaf Cederschiöld is less negative in his letter to Gering of 17 February 1884, and, knowing the book's author, he can magnanimously overlook its shortcomings and be pleased by its merits.

Du frågade mig en gång om Vigfussons Corpus poeticum. Nu har jag sedan ett par veckor haft boken i min ego och studerat den med mycket intresse. På det hela tycker jag om den. Det är lätt att upptäcka en massa fel, godtyckligheter och vårdslösheter, och jag förutser, att samlingen kommer att mycket hårdt bemötas af kritiken (kanske har redan någon tysk tidskrift "nedgjort" den?). Men för mig verkar läsningen välgörande. Jag är van vid Vˢ suveräna förakt för detaljer och starka subjektivism, därför stöter jag mig ej på hans minnesfel och nycker, det uppfriskar mig att finna dessa gamla välbekanta "Stumper och Stykker" framstälda ur nya, ofta genialiska synpunkter. Ett och annat är säkerligen af bestående värde. Naturligtvis är det ledsamt, att icke V. själf eller någon annan kunnat underkasta arbetet den stränga sofring, som man nu fordrar af ett vetenskapligt verk; men den, som känner V., vet, att han icke kan arbeta på annat sätt, än han nu gjort. Jag tror altså, att man bör glädjas öfver den värdefulla gåfvan, som innehåller så många praktiska vinkar till en populär och njutbar framställning, och hvars fel lätt nog kunna varsnas af den,

---

[51] "Guðbrandur Vigfússon," *Zeitschrift für deutsche Philologie* 22 (1890): 219 alluding to reviews by Benedikt Gröndal *Tímarit hins íslenzka bókmentafélags* 5 (1884): 116-143; [Richard] Heinzel *Anzeiger für deutsches Alterthum* 11 (1885) 38-69; Julius Hoffory *Göttingische gelehrte Anzeigen* 1888, repr. *Eddastudien* von Julius Hoffory (Berlin: Reimer, 1889) 87-142; Barend Symons [= Sijmons] *Zeitschrift für deutsche Philologie* 18 (1886) 95-128. Cf. also Ursula Dronke, "The scope of the *Corpvs Poeticvm Boreale*," *Úr Dölum til Dala*, 93-111.

som vill bygga vidare. Hade jag mera tid och ro, så skulle jag anse det som en pligt att skrifva en utförlig recension af "Corpus," väsentligen i syfte att framdraga dess förtjänster. Men det skulle taga mycken tid och arbete, mycket mera, än jag får egna däråt.

What may not be known is that a *Corpus poeticum boreale*[52] had originally been planned as a joint publication by Möbius and Vigfússon about which Eugen Mogk reported to Gering on 2 June 1890 after having gone through Möbius's papers:

> Ferner sende ich Ihnen ein blatt, das ich ebenfalls in Möbius papieren fand. Es ist der entwurf eines Corpus poeticum boreale, den er 1863 mit Vigfússon festgestellt hat. Über dies werk hat er sicher auch mit Ihnen gesprochen. Das blatt zeigt so recht, wie ungleich exacter das Cpb. geworden wäre, hätte Vigfússon die arbeit mit Möbius unternommen. Meines wissens sollte damals das werk hier bei Weigel erscheinen. Das beigefügte manuscript zeigt, <u>was</u> wir in diesem werke zu erwarten hatten.

In his answer to Mogk of 10 June 1890 Gering is once again quite frank: "Das Cpb wäre allerdings ein anderes buch geworden, wenn sich Vigfússon nicht in seiner törichten verblendung von der deutschen wissenschaft abgewant hätte."

---

[52] "besser wäre: norrœnum," remarked Möbius in his letter to Gering of 30 July 1883.

Teaching Old Norse in the English-Speaking World

Anatoly Liberman

Despite the existence of some competitors, E. V. Gordon's *An Introduction to Old Norse* remains the most widely used book for teaching this language in the English-speaking world.[1] Although enrollments in courses dealing with Old Norse are small, the tradition of offering it has never been interrupted. Instructors teaching this course usually know the language very well, but a few sentences in the anthology can puzzle even them. The above remark, rather than being a sign of arrogance, is the result of bitter experience. With regard to Old Icelandic, most of us are self-taught; also, literary scholars may not have been trained in the niceties of grammar and are not always familiar with morphological and syntactic traps. Our colleagues in Reykjavík have developed excellent methods of teaching Modern Icelandic as a second language. By contrast, no one seems to have given much thought to the principles of teaching the old period.

I have written a detailed commentary on all the texts in Gordon's book, except those that deal with runic inscriptions. Several decades of teaching Old Icelandic have made me aware of students' initial enthusiasm (ranging all the way from "I have a Norwegian grandmother" to "I would love to read the sagas in the original") and their surprise at the discovery that even the simplest

---

[1] E. V. Gordon, *An Introduction to Old Norse,* 2nd ed., rev. A. R. Taylor (Oxford: Clarendon Press, 1957).

texts require an effort far beyond their expectations. English majors and all those who come to our courses with a smattering of Spanish and French (at best) get lost in endless paradigms. But Icelandic is difficult even to those who know some German and Latin. Fluency in Norwegian, Swedish, and Danish is of some use only in recognizing the vocabulary. Declensions and conjugations, with their multiple exceptions, have to be learned from scratch. It requires a heroic effort to keep students' enthusiasm alive.

Teaching Old Icelandic is a broad concept. One can study all or only the most important sound changes perfunctorily or in depth, learn the forms, and master the art of translating Old Icelandic prose and poetry (including the skalds). This is clearly not a minimalist program. Since Old Icelandic, unlike Old English, for example, is not a dead language, the rudiments of Modern Icelandic pronunciation are a useful addition to a course in "the language of the sagas." A dedicated following can finish Gordon's book (runes and all) in about three years. But in reality students seldom devote more than two semesters to Icelandic, and instructors have to cut their losses. I do not consider learning paradigms by heart a worthwhile task. To pass a test, students will agree to cram the series *sjá / þessi, þessa, þessum, þessa; kǫllumk, kallisk, kallisk, kallimk, kallizk, kallisk,* and so forth. No doubt, they will forget them on the next day. Even their lives are too short for such wasteful activities. But if they acquire sufficient expertise for understanding a tale in Old Icelandic and, while reading, consult the grammar, they will memorize the most frequent forms of even demonstrative pronouns and reflexive verbs. My requirement is that they identify all the forms occurring in the text, and here I am relentlessly consistent.

Gordon translated the first text (I A "Loki and Svaðilfari," 5-6) into English, but, in my opinion, it is better not to assign it too early. All the Icelandic passages in his book exist in readily available translations, and anyone can check them out and copy the passages, but those who enroll in our classes come with the intention to learn, not to cheat. "Loki and Svaðilfari" is not the easiest text in the book. I begin with XVI C and D (151: "The Founder of Scarborough" and "The Sword Skǫfnung") and spend two weeks or more discussing 15 (in fact, 14) lines. The next excerpt is V B ("Leif Eiríksson Sights America," 43), which occupies us for another two weeks or so. We talk about every form, and students get used to the glossary and begin to understand why Icelandic words change the way they do. Deciphering gradually turns into reading. V C ("Leif's voyage," 44-47) follows, after which the heroic age is left behind. Now any order is fine, for instance, Snorri (A, B, C) and "The Death of Gunnar" (87-92), with assignments growing to three pages a week. This brings us to the end of the first semester.

The second semester opens with *Hrafnkels saga*, and we read as many remaining texts as we have time for. If it is deemed desirable to introduce even those who will stop after the Fall semester to some poetry, then either I E ("The Doom of the Gods," 17-20) or XIII ("Þrymskviða") is appropriate. The same option exists for the Spring semester. At Minnesota, every two or three years, we try to offer a whole semester of poetry for which one semester of prose is a prerequisite. Twice in my experience students have asked me to substitute Old Norwegian (XVII "The Battle of Stamford Bridge," 157-161) and East Norse for the last passages in Old Icelandic, and I gladly acquiesced, but we spent minimal time on Haraldr's *vísa*. (Needless to say, while reading "Egil at York," we skip the *drápa*.)

After years of experimenting, I came to the conclusion that midterms and finals should be take-home open-book tests. Participants in the class get the assignment to comment on some grammatical phenomenon occurring in all the passages covered during the semester or to edit (with a complete essay on phonetics and grammar) a new excerpt. I am not trying to say that my method of teaching Old Norse is better than anyone else's, but I can state that it is efficient. Reading Icelandic becomes a source of pleasure. Attrition in my courses is small. Enough students return for the second semester to materialize, and in the past, when we had quarters, not a single time was the third quarter canceled.

Gordon's *Introduction*... is a splendid book. The mistakes Stefán Einarsson found in the first edition did not detract from its value,[2] though it is surprising that not all of them were corrected in the second edition by A. R. Taylor. The selection of texts and the notes are exemplary. However, *An Introduction to Old Norse* is not a graded textbook, and the compact outline of the structure of Old Icelandic makes no pretense of taking the learner from one step to another. Nor did Gordon find it necessary to highlight the most formidable difficulties of Icelandic morphology and syntax.

At the top of the morphological list is the neuter plural. Especially treacherous forms are the likes of *svik* and *jól* that exist only as plurals, but even such transparent phrases as *sterk vitni* need some attention because in (Old) Icelandic, as elsewhere in Indo-European, the endings of the neuter plural and of the feminine singular coincide. No less difficult are the forms of the *u*-stem (*vǫllr, vallar, velli, vǫll*, etc.) and of the second class of strong verbs (*bjóða, býðir*, etc.), along with contracted forms (*sjá – sá, liggja – lá*) and the verbs that lost *v* (< **w*) before back vowels (*vaða – œði, yrkja – orti*). Some such forms turn up in the glossary, others do not. A few more features of declension and conjugation also cause trouble, though not in translation. Among them are nouns whose -*r* belongs to the root. In such cases Gordon writes *hjaldr (rs)*, *hlátr (rs)*, *fingr (rar)*, and *fagr (ran)*. (Note the misleading notation *glǫggr (van)*, as though the accusative were **glǫggrvan* rather than *glǫggvan*.) Forms of weak verbs are usually easy to identify, but the roots ending in a dental often cause misunderstanding, for *elti, lesti, skipti*, and so forth do not look like preterits to beginners, as opposed to *seldi, vakði*, and especially *kallaði*.

---

[2] Stefán Einarsson, "Review of: E. V. Gordon, *A New Introduction to Old Norse*." *The Journal of English and Germanic Philology* 27.3 (1928): 412-24. (A shorter review of this book by him appeared in *Modern Language Notes* 43 [1928]: 542-45.)

However, the greatest difficulties are related to syntax. Three of them deserve special mention. English has a few verb adverb collocations of the *come to = come to one's senses* type: (*come by* can be amplified if needed: *come by our house*). In Old Icelandic, a suppressed, or an implied, object is the norm. The sentence ...*at hon skal kjósa sér mann af Ásum ok kjósa at fótum ok sjá ekki fleira af* (p. 7/ll. 89-90) is perfectly idiomatic: *af* at its end presupposes the unexpressed object *honum* after it. The meaning is clear, and the book provides no explanation; in English an object cannot be left out ("of him"). The next sentence is more difficult: *Bǫðvarr leiðir síðan hest sinn á stall hjá konungs hestum hinum beztu ok spyrr engan at* (27/2-3). *At* confuses beginners, and Gordon must have realized it, for in the glossary he translated the entire phrase: *spyrr engan at* "asks no one about it, asks leave of none." The impression is that we have something special here, though *spyrr engan at* is a counterpart of *sjá ekki fleira af*: there we have *sjá ekki fleira af* (*honum*), and here, *spyrr engan at* (*því*).

It is a moot question whether *sjá at* and *spyrja at* have the status of full-fledged verb adverb collocations or whether *á* and *at* are prepositions with an object implied. The second solution is probably closer to the truth, though intermediate cases exist. Knowing the history of such English compounds as *therein, hereafter*, and so forth, one may argue that in ...*at ekki nýtir þú hér af* (14/307), *af* goes together with *hér*, rather than being a preposition with *því* or *þessu* implied. *Koma á* and *koma í* look like cohesive units of the *come in* type. This quibbling should be left for seminars in theoretical grammar. Beginners should know that every time *at, af, til*, and the rest occur in the vicinity of a verb, an implied object has to be suspected. If its presence is denied, the function of the adverb should be explained. For example, in ...*at hann skyldi gøra til brauð þeira* (21/6-7), *til* does not govern *brauð* (otherwise, *brauð* would have been in the genitive) and there is no need to look for an object after it; consequently, we have the collocation *gøra til*, in which *til* performs its common function (emphasizes the completion of an action, as *up* and *down* do in English *eat up* and *slow down* – a typical *Aktionsart*).

Students who do not know that such nearly desemanticized objects as *it*, *this*, or *this matter* should be supplied in half of the sentences they see in Icelandic will always need help while translating *spyrr engan at* and other similar constructions. Gordon missed this peculiarity of Old Icelandic syntax and handled each case individually: he left *sjá ekki fleira af* without a comment, glossed the whole of *spyrr engan at*, and, having encountered *Nú hyggr konungr at fyrir sér...* (24/88), included *hyggja at* (*e-u*) in the glossary. It is unclear how *hyggja at* (*e-u*) should be interpreted, but I doubt that (*e-u*) indicates a possible omission of an object after *at*. *Hyggr at* has the same structure as *spyrr at*.

A tiny section (172) on impersonal sentences does not give the faintest idea of their importance and variety in Old Icelandic. They are ubiquitous, as though the syntax of Old Norse came into being at the time when people looked on themselves as the gods' playthings. The glossary specifies the impersonal use of *bera*, *taka*, *standa*, and the rest, but students concentrate their efforts on translation and care little whether the construction is personal or impersonal. *...svá at alt kom í heilann* (88/20) will yield nearly the same meaning regardless of how it is understood, and most beginners will take *alt* for the subject (approximately "all of it got into the brain," even though *øxi* is feminine!) instead of "it [the impersonal, 'dummy' it, as in *it snows*] went all the way into the brain."

A third outstanding feature of Old Icelandic syntax is what I call afterthought. Although the sentence *...þá settisk Þórr til náttverðar ok þeir lagsmenn* (8/114-15) will not baffle anyone, its word order is far from trivial. A sentence in an Icelandic narrative regularly falls into such segments: as much as possible is said about one "actor," and that information is followed by an afterthought. In translation, we automatically reshuffle the pieces. "...then Thor and his companions sat down to supper"; it is enough to say "...then Thor sat down to supper, and his companions" (instead of the bulky and unnecessary "and so did his companions") to realize how specific the Icelandic arrangement of the information is. The sentence poses no difficulties because it is so short, but not infrequently a whole line, if not more, separates the "theme" from *ok*. The next example is not so dramatic, but the bridge to be crossed is longer: *En bóndin gørði sem ván var ok ǫll hjónin* (9/131-32). So far "afterthought" has attracted relatively little attention, but see an article on this subject in my book of collected essays.[3] Consider the following sentence from that article (350): *Er þat ráð hans, at hann dregr saman lið ok Bǫðvarr, sonr hans, ok ríða þeir inn til Dala...* ("He is of the opinion that he should gather his forces—and Bothvar, his son—and that they should ride to Dalir..." = "He is of the opinion that he, together with his son, should gather his forces..."). *Hann* must have carried sentence stress: *at 'hann ...ok Bǫðvarr.*

I will skip many other recurring difficulties, such as transitive verbs governing the genitive and the dative; here sec. 156-158 give insufficient help to English-speakers without previous exposure to German or Latin. The few things mentioned below have been noticed more or less by chance. *Grafar* (pl.; sec. 83) is fine, but *grafir* (as in Modern Icelandic) is no less common; sec. 101: the neuter dative of *annar* is *ǫðru*, not *ǫðrum*; *yðar* (sec. 108) should be replaced by *yð(v)ar*; in sec. 111 *þessar* and *þessi* are listed, but *þessarar* and *þessarri* occur several times in the book; *nǫkkut* and *enskis* (sec. 115 and 116) have the variants *nǫkkurt* and *einskis*, both occurring in the texts; *bíða* may govern the accusative (then it means 'experience'); at *drjúgt*, the letter *j* is missing in *drjúgt manna*; under *mjǫðr*, *Óðins* is printed with a lowercase letter; in the glossary of names, at *Mjǫllnir* read 81 for 181; at *síð*, *um síðir* ("at last") should be added (24/85); *minnkast* (72/445) seems to have too many *n*'s; for *munum vér* (93/163) read *munu vér*; (100/6) read *hlýtir* for *hlytir*; *skepja* ("appoint") has been omitted; *vandr* ("difficult") has a short vowel, not *á*; *varðveita* also occurs with the sense "have in charge, administer" in the book; in sec. 89, 4th column (dative), read *vetri* for *vetr*; *viðskipti* is n. pl.; at *vætta*, the English gloss *expect* appears

[3] Liberman, Anatoly Liberman. *Word Heath. Wortheide. Orðheiði.* (Roma: Il Calamo, 1994), 336-55.

without final *-t*; read *bíða* for *biða* at *ró* (377); *vǫrð* occurs in
XVI/113, not XVI/112 (154; *ok eigut þær varðir vera* "and those
wives have no husbands"; *vera* confuses most, and all kinds of
nonsense are usually suggested about *varðir*, the plural of *vǫrð*), the
second occurrence of *menn* (108/33) appears in the form *men*; read
konungi for *konung* in 25/134. Gordon's long entries on heavy duty
verbs have an inconvenient arrangement. All, rather than some,
nouns should have been marked for declension, and all proper and
place names should have been "translated."

Among other things, the companion contains numerous
etymological hints that will help students to remember the words
with obvious cognates in English and occasionally in German.
Something is said about almost every line. The commentary is
unabashedly repetitive. For instance, the difference between *eptir þat*
and *eptir því* is explained again and again, whereas cross-references
are rare. Since I could not predict in what order other instructors
would read the texts, I thought it advisable to say the same things
more than once. Especially detailed notes have been written for the
passages with which I begin teaching Old Icelandic; this strategy is
self-explanatory. Some notes have a finger sign before them. Those
are either such as may not occur to some instructors or as I
consider controversial. The index gives a clear picture of the
subjects covered in the notes, and substitutes for the missing cross-
references. The companion is nearly eighty pages long. Below, I will
reproduce a few notes that may be of general interest.

6/57.   The ancient meaning of the root of Old Icelandic *lúka* and its
         cognates in other Germanic languages was "lend, twist"; hence
         the ambiguity of its meaning. In principle, *lúka* (like Engl. *lock*)
         means "close", but *lúka upp/fyrir sér* means "open" (the same
         holds for Dan. *lukke op* and Norw. *lukke op*; cf. Germ. *schließen*
         ("close") versus *erschließen* ("open") and see the note on 13/281).
         On the other hand, Old Norse had lost its prefixes long before
         the appearance of the earliest texts in it, and this circumstance
         created a good deal of confusion: cf. the seemingly incompatible
         meanings of *fá*, l. 74, below.

7/92.   The explanation given in the book is undoubtedly wrong. Choosing a spouse by his or her feet (the Cinderella motif) has nothing to do with hygiene. Njǫrðr was a fertility god (like the other Vanir) and his feet/legs must have held great attraction.

9/130. samt: an adverbialized neuter of *samr*; its most general meaning is "together"; here this meaning does not fit; in Cleasby-Vigfusson, this place is glossed as "yet, all the same";[4] the idea seems to be that the sight alone (*fyrir sjóninni einni*) was enough to frighten the farmer to death, but the word still looks like a filler.

9/138. lét eptir: it may be a collocation with a technical meaning ("give a pull": cf. p. 122/137); however, the direct meaning of *láta eptir* is "leave behind"; there is no reason why this sentence cannot be translated "he left the goats behind" (it does not seem that the company rode on and took the goats overseas).

9/150. leituðusk fyrir: the gloss in the book ("make a search before one") is unclear; *leitask fyrir* or *um* is *leitask* ("search") followed by *fyrir* or *um* with an implied (suppressed) object: "they searched" (for "things").

10/187. at miðri nótt: "in the 'middle' night" (= "in the middle of the night," not "at midnight"); the same usage in l. 189, and cf. ll. 194, 219, 242, and 266; the glossary translates *mið nótt* (194) as "midnight," but this is not necessary.

11/192. títt: it is hard to imagine that *títt* in l. 189 and here is not a deliberate pun; several interesting cognates cluster around OI *tíð*: the impersonal *tíða* ("desire"), *tíðr* ("usual" [? < "happening at any time"]), *títt* ("happening" [in *hvat er títt?*]), and *títt* ("quickly"); clearly, the abstract meaning "time" is late; cf. *stund* ("length of time, while" [partly as in German *Stunde* < *"the time spent learning a lesson"]), *stundum* ("sometimes"), and *stundar* ("very").

---

[4] *An Icelandic-English Dictionary*, initiated by Richard Cleasby, rev. Gudbrand Vigfusson, 2nd ed. by William A. Craigie (Oxford: Clarendon Press, 1957). (referred to henceforth as Cleasby-Vigfusson)

12/249-51. The sentence is translated in the note, but it is important to
understand why it means what it does; (l. 249) *þess* depends on
ván, which usually takes the genitive ("he says [*kallar*] [there to be]
greater hope of that [þess] that..."); hann: Þjálfi; of (l. 250) ("with
regard to"); hann (l. 251): Þjálfi; þessa: genitive n.; in l. 250, *þessa*
is f. sg. acc. (end of sec. 111).

13/272. vítishorn: the gloss "sconce-horn" (copied from Cleasby-
Vigfusson) must be incomprehensible to those who have not
been associated with Oxford and possibly Cambridge. The verb
sconce meant, in Oxford slang, "to fine." Hence *sconce* (noun) "a
fine of a tankard of ale or the like, imposed by undergraduates on
one of their numbers for some breach of customary rule when
dining in hall" (*OED*). Such punishments (for breaking the rules
or etiquette, usually at court) were common in Europe; a sconce
glass (bumper, tankard) would either have the form that
prevented it from being put on the table, so that it had to be
emptied all at once, or some abominable (or strong) homebrew
would be put into it, which incapacitated the victim. Old
Icelandic *víti* means "fine, penalty, damage" (Old Engl. *wīte*, Old
High Germ. *wīzzi*), and making one drink as punishment has
been attested in Old Icelandic texts. The entire scene is a comedy
of errors, but it is particularly amazing that the word *vítishorn* was
used in Thor's hearing. Note that the clause that follows does not
explain in what circumstances the retainers "were accustomed" to
drain this horn.

13/280-281. *lúta* means "bend, stoop," but *laut ór horninu* must mean
"raised his head from the horn." Mod. Norw./Dan./Swed.
lute/lude/luta and Old Engl. *lūtan* also mean "bend, stoop" (the
same holds for Mod. Icel. *lúta*). Fritzner quotes this passage and
translates it correctly (as a matter of course) but has no
comment.[5] In Cleasby-Vigfusson, only the first (easy) part of the
passage is glossed. It has to be admitted that OI *lúta*, like Germ.
steigen, referred to the movement both up and down, sometimes
depending on the adverbs following it. Later, all the languages

[5] Johan Fritzner, *Ordbog over Det gamle norske Sprog*, Rev. ed. Oslo-Bergen
(Tromsø: Universitetsforlaget, 1972-73).

having this verb retained a single specialized meaning. This place may be the only one in Old Icelandic that preserved the ancient ambiguity.

14/295. *á* seems to imply a suppressed object ("on, from it," not *á þér*); *hagr* is a noun; Útgarða-Loki is not asking whether Þórr is going to drink more than is good for him but rather whether Þórr won't (shouldn't) leave enough room in his stomach for one more drink, because the second was too big to make him comfortable (otherwise, how will he take a third drink, the biggest of them all?); in a cumulation of three attempts, the third is always the most important.

14/312-13. er...þykkja: the construction is ambiguous because the function of *at* is not immediately clear; it is tempting to connect *er...at* ("to whom," then "to whom it will seem to be a thing of no consequence"), but *lítit mark at* is a set phrase; under no circumstances can *at* go with *lítit mark*, for *at* rarely governs the accusative and, when it does, it means "after"; most likely, *at* in *lítit mark at* always presupposes the existence of a suppressed object: "little significance with regard to (the business at hand)"; cf. l. 328: þann mann...er eigi mun lítilræði í þykkja; thus, "young fellows to whom (*er*) little trouble (*lítit mark*) [it] will seem (*mun þykkja*) about (at: "the idea")."

22/15. hann: the boy is meant: "it seemed that he [the boy]" (that is, "segir Sigmundr at [honum] hann þótti..."); *at* goes with *manni*; the sentence is impersonal; þótt: it must mean something like "though yes, indeed, the boy..."

24/88-89. at: add an object; fyrir sér: cf. l. 44; þann er kendi lengst: impersonal (*kendi* can perhaps be understood as the form of the singular: "...death...that would be felt...").

24/93-94. eigi...komask: impersonal; the stone (slab) was put vertically in the middle of the mound, rather than laid flat, and since it touched both walls, the space was divided in two halves, with no communication between them.

24/95. The explanation in the book goes back to Axel Kock; yet it is
hard to understand how *þann vegin(n)* "was assimilated" to *þann
megin(n)*, even if **þann wegin(n)* is the etymon (Noreen, sec. 288,
calls the change "eigentümlich";[6] as to the pronoun *mér* < *vér*
("we"), the same change *mir* = *wir* is well-known from German
dialects and Yiddish; was the cause the same?).

29/66. Bǫðvarr's reply probably means "What went around came
around" (= he sent a bone and got it back = no one owes anyone
anything). Otherwise, the king would not have tolerated such a
saucy answer, but he seems to have appreciated the brilliant, pithy
response. (Literally: "he contributed to that which he received.")

30/83. at: see *at*, conjunction, in the glossary (the end of the entry). I
think the gloss is wrong: *at* is not redundant in any of those three
cases (just add a suppressed object *því* after *at* and see the note on
27/34).

34/4.   of ("over") with a suppressed object ("over the same 'journey'",
that is, covering the same ground); Konunga-ævi: *ævi* (or *æfi*)
means "lifetime," as opposed to *líf* (n., "life,") and for this reason
is not expected to occur in the plural; nor has its plural been
attested in Old Icelandic. *Ævi* belongs to the *ín*- declension (like
elli ["old age"] and other abstract nouns, *Kristni* among them; see
sec. 94); the few nouns of this type which did have the plural
formed it with the ending *-ar* (for instance, *gǫrsimar*). *Ævi* acquired
the meaning "biography"; yet the modern plural ("biographies")
is *ævir*. Konunga-*ævi* seems to occur only in this text. Since Konunga-
is the genitive plural ("of the kings"), -*ævi* must also be in the
plural ("biographies of the kings"). But then **ævar* could have
been expected. The word has no ending, however. This must
have been the reason -*ævi* in this compound has been labeled as a
neuter noun. Fritzner says *n.*, without adding *pl.*, and Gordon
followed Fritzner. However, Guðbrandur Vigfússon probably
could not imagine a neuter -*ævi* and marked Konunga-*ævi* as
feminine. The dictionaries, regardless of their treatment of this

---

[6] Adolf Noreen, *Altnordische Grammatik,* 2 vols. 5th ed. (Tübingen: Max
Niemeyer, 1970).

word, do not supply even the shortest comment. Noreen does not mention the possibility of *æfi* ~ *ævi* ever occurring in the neuter. Ari needed the plural of *ævi* but stopped short of coining **ævar* and left the word without an ending. The result was *ævi* (sg.) and *ævi* (pl.), but this did not change the noun's gender.

34/6. á þessi en á þeirri: both *þessi* and *þeirri* are feminine dative singulars and refer to the *Íslendingabók* (f.) in its first (*þessi*) redaction and the final version (*þeirri*) "I added what later became better known to me [*auka* takes the dative: *því*], and now it is said more fully (*gǫrr*) in this [revised redaction] than in that [first redaction, before Þorlákr and Ketill had seen it]"; see *þessi* and *þeirri* in sec. 111 (in Old Icelandic, *þeiri*, with one *r*, was more common; the modern form is *þeirri*); note that when Þór- is the first element of a name, the vowel is usually short if a consonant follows *r* (hence Þorlákr; cf. Þóríðr, l. 12); hvatki: the enclitics -*gi* and -*ki* have both a negative ("not") and a positive meaning; *hvatki* ("each separate thing,") but *hvatki er* always means "what(so)ever."

34/8. í þann tíð: *tíð* is f., so that *þann* is puzzling; the explanation in Cleasby-Vigfússon is fanciful ("the curious phrase *í þann tíð* is probably not to be explained as an old masc., but rather by *þan* = *þá* 'þan' being an obsolete pronoun form with a final *n*, cp. *þansi* on the Runic stone"). Noreen (sec. 390) says: "*tíð* scheint in den ausdrücken *í þann* oder *þenna tíð* 'zu jener zeit' mask. zu sein"; the expected form (*á þessi tíð*) is also common; Fritzner and etymological dictionaries are silent on this subject. Is it not possible that the common phrase *í þann tíma* influenced *á þessi tíð* and produced the ugly hybrid *í þann tíð*? In Middle High German, *zît* was f. or n.; the compound *sommerzît* was m.; also in Middle Dutch *tid* was m., but in Icelandic, *tíð* is m. only in this phrase.

34/13. óljúgfróðr "knowledgeable in things not based on lies" = "not given to telling fiction" (cf. *lygisaga*).

36/65. landa: landi; landa…þá; note the amusing gloss in the book for *fyrir* ("in retaliation") and cf. 130/49, with *fyrir* glossed as "in return"; this is the price dictionary makers pay for ignoring suppressed objects.

37/91-92. hafði svá nær: impersonal ("it came so near/close that they would fight"); at...miðli: impersonal; *of* presupposes a suppressed object ("that [one] did not see 'concerning [that matter]' between [fighting and an agreement]")

37/112. Nothing justifies the use of the weak form of the adjective *víss* here. The phrase *vís ván* is common. This is not a unique example containing *vísa* or of *vísa ván*. Hence the conclusion that Old Icelandic had an indeclinable adjective *vísa* (as said in Fritzner). All the other explanations (weak adjective, the genitive plural of *vísi* ["wise man"], *vísa ok ván* ["expectation"] with *ok* left out – this idiom did not occur in Old Icelandic – and anacoluthon) are much worse.

41/5.   á unga aldri: since there is no justification for the use of a weak form (*unga*) and since the indeclinable adjective *unga* does not exist, *unga* can be understood only as the genitive plural of the substantivized form *ungi* (at the age "of the young"), which is awkward; the dictionaries that follow Fritzner and list *ungaaldr* as a compound offer the best solution possible (the antonym is structured differently: *á gamals aldri*).

41/26.   bera af skipi: an extreme but not a rare case of a suppressed object; usually the suppressed object is vague ("it"), but here "cargo" is meant ("take [the cargo] from the ship"); the gloss *bera* (*af skipi*), "unload the cargo" is right, but it disguises the nature of the problem.

42/33.   landit var vatnat: *vatna* ("cover with water") occurs in a few nautical phrases (here: "until land merged with water" and, consequently, could not be seen), but it is not immediately obvious that *landit* stands in the accusative ("until [it] 'watered' the land"); the clause is impersonal; tók af byrina: impersonal (here the accusative cannot be missed: "[it] 'took off' the favorable breeze").

42/34.   Impersonal (and here unmistakable, because *lagði* is singular, whereas the nouns that follow are in the plural): "[it] laid..."; *at*: the glossary (the second *at*) says "redundant." Here perhaps *hvert at* ("where to") should be posited (cf. l. 39: *sigla at þessu landi*, and l. 65: *at landi halda*). See also the note on 126/57.

45/142. *kostr* is a cognate of Engl. *choose*, not of *cost*; its main meaning is "choice"; however, many other senses have accrued; *af kostum* "in accordance with the conditions"; cf. *landkostr* (l. 164); the sentence might be impersonal; impersonal *gefa* means "be obtainable, available, *etc.*": "to this land will the name 'be attainable' according to its conditions", but *kalla* cannot be impersonal, so that probably *ek* ("I") should be added: "I'll give...and call [it]..." [*mark* "mark, sign, feature"].

47/198. *sinn* (a possessive pronoun: sec. 110) is often used with *hvárt...eða,* "either...or" (it does not affect the meaning of the conjunction: *hvárt* is historically the neuter of *hvárr* ["which of two"], so that *sinn* means approximately "its": "[its] which or"); *mǫrk*, as in *Danmǫrk*, means "border"; in Norway, this word developed the meaning "forest," because forests traditionally "marked" the border between neighboring countries. Cf. Markland: 45/143.

47/200. ok þetta var ráðs tekit: an elliptical phrase for: þetta var *til* ráðs tekit (hence the genitive).

48/238. ørœfi: possibly a variant of *ørhæfi* (*or* is akin to *ór* ["out"], *hæfi* is related to *hǫfn* ["haven"]), unless *ørhæfi* is a folk etymological alteration of the obscure *ørœfi*. Although the form with *h* occurs only here, it may be the oldest one, and, if so, can there be any connection with West Germanic *ōbera-*, the etymon of Old Engl. *ōfer,* "edge, shore" (cf. Germ. *Ufer*)? "Shorelessness" fits well Cleasby-Vigfusson's gloss "immensity" for *oróf* ~ *orhóf* (*hóf* is "measure, proportion"; several near homonyms may have been confused.)

49/261. þeir þau: *þeir* is clear, but is *þau* the "hook-crook" couple or the ears of grain along with *vínberja*? Note the genitive *leiðar* (the genitive of place: cf. 137/7 and 9).

49/275-76. The sentence is translated in the note, but, as always in such cases, it is important to understand how the sense was obtained. *Láta* ("let") has numerous specific meanings, for example, "let something happen, grant"; *var...látit* is impersonal; *við* presupposes a suppressed object ("it", "prayer," understood from the previous sentence); thus "not so quickly was it answered" (only in the English gloss *it* is the subject, which makes the construction personal); *sem þeim var annt til* is also impersonal (*til* needs the same object as *við*, above); annt (past participle, neuter): unna (sec. 145).

51/337. þar sem holta kendi: impersonal (*holta*: gen. pl.); *kenna*, followed by an object in the genitive, means "feel; taste" (when *kenna* means "know," it takes the accusative), so that *holta kendi* means approximately "(where) [it] felt (like) wood" = "wher(ever) wood could be seen," that is, "grapes grew everywhere"; lœkr: one of several words in Indo-European having similar structure and designating a body of water (cf. *lake* and *lagoon*).

52/374. stœði: standa; in the Old Germanic languages rivers often "lie" and "stand," rather than "flow"; var...ǫllum: impersonal; rangsœlis: cf. sólarsinnis (l. 345); note the curious "iconicity" of these adverbs: when the meaning is "in the direction of the sun," the word for "sun" is the first; when the meaning is in the opposite ("wrong") direction, the corresponding word is at the end (both *-sœlis* and *-sinnis* are, from a historical point of view, genitives; in *sœlis*, the root vowel is umlauted before *-i*).

54/453. suðrœnn: *-œnn* is a suffix of direction (also in *norðrœnn, austrœnn, vestrœnn*) and otherwise a productive suffix in Old Icelandic (cf. Engl. *south-ern* and *extr-aneous*, the latter from Latin, where the suffix is *-aneus*); the neuter of *suðrœnn* is *suðrœnt*; *suðrœn veðr* is therefore in the plural (*veðr* is neuter: "southernly winds").

55/475. þá...koma: impersonal ("it seemed to become him"); létta mundi: impersonal (when impersonal, the word for the thing that must stop is in the dative; hence *óárani þessu*); óáran = ó-ár-an (*-an* is a suffix), and the idea is the same in *hall-œri* (*-aran* does not exist without the negative prefix).

60/34. An innocuous-looking but tricky sentence; *lengt* is not a form of *lengr* (it would have made no sense here) but of *lengja*, and the whole is impersonal, with *nafn* being in the accusative ("because of that, [it] was lengthened his name"); the rest is personal: "he was called…"

64/177. See the note in the book. It is also possible that *verða* alone may mean "happen as good fortune does"; or perhaps we are dealing with a remnant of an older verb that once had a prefix (verbs have no prefixes in Old Icelandic). See the article "The Gentle Fate of the Teutons…" in Liberman 1994, as in note 3, above, 117-28.

66/255. brýnt: related to *brúnn* ("shining"), perhaps a homonym of *brúnn* ("brown"), though opinions on this score differ; in any case, *brýnn* is "clear, plain, obvious" ("urgent" fits the context, but Þórbjǫrn seems to be saying that people like Sámr prefer *smásakar*, that is, cases requiring a subtle knowledge of minutiae, rather than obvious and therefore uninteresting cases; usually *smásakar* is glossed as "petty suits").

67/266. The punctuation here depends on the meaning of *víg*. If it means "killing," then "lýsir víginu; fær sér menn á hendr Hrafnkeli" also makes sense ("gathers people against Hrafnkell"); if, however, *víg* means "battle," then he "proclaims 'battle' (legal dealings)…against Hrafnkell," with *fær sér menn* in parentheses, as is done in modern editions of skaldic poetry; *lýsa* ("proclaim") takes the dative.

68/318. ná-ungi; sjá eptir: the gloss "look after" is misleading, but the overall meaning is clear: "he who had to 'see what remained after' his close relative"; *eiga* with an infinitive: "have to (do something)"; note the syntax of ll. 318-19 (which, in a way, is influenced by the pressure of "afterthought": first a whole block related to *margr*, then the subordinate clause).

71/413. þá ("then"); fá: 3rd p. pl. present (add the subject: *margir*); *fá* with a past participle means "get something done"; *gætt*: past participle of *gæta* ("watch, take care of" [it takes the genitive; hence *alls*]); *honum* is sg., like *mǫrgum*; *takask* ("fall out, result"); the change from the sg. (*mǫrgum*) to the pl. (*fá*) and back to the sg. (*honum*) may be a case of studied ("rhetorical") anacoluthon of excitement.

77/604. deyja frá: *frá* presupposes a suppressed object ("them"), that is, "if I die from them (my sons)" = "if I die and leave them behind."

81/730. hefir...til; *reka* takes the genitive (here: *þess réttar*); it is the same *reka* ("drive") as elsewhere, but here followed by *rettr* ("right thing, legal claim"): "and lacks trust [in oneself] to 'drive, pursue' one's right" (contextual glosses like "take one's vengeance," as in the book, *reka*, disguise the difficulty); *sinn* (n.) very often occurs in the dative (*sinni*), but its doublet *sinni* ("time, occasion" [n.]) also exists and occurs here in the acc. sg., as is obvious from *nǫkkurt*; ok eru... "by contrast"; nǫkkurt = nǫkkut (not mentioned in the book, 297).

81/738. lætr ganga af: lets go off; *kappi* is a form in the dative meaning approximately "with regard to the *kapp*" ("she lets herself go battle-like" = "full force, with a vengeance"); see the note (but it does not explain anything).

83/799. The gloss in the book is unclear. The sentence obviously means "a change has occurred (*á orðit*) among them," an understatement for "the battle was over" or reference to the fact that Sámr came too late to witness the fight.

88/30. hvers víss yrði: *yrði* is the past subjunctive of *verða* ("happen"); *hvers víss* is the genitive; without *hvers* the phrase would mean "(learn) what kind of a certain thing would happen to be"; *hvers* only reinforces *víss*.

93/164-65.   at ganga: *at* is adverbial (not the infinitival particle); afroð gjalda ("suffer loss"): the word *afroð* must have become obscure long before the Saga Age, for the forms *afrað*, *afráð*, and *afhroð* competed with it; they were connected with *ráða* ("advise") or perhaps with *rýðja* ("make a clearing," as in Germ. *roden* and Engl. *rid*), known from the law phrase *hrýðja dóm* ~ *hrýðja kvið* ("to challenge"), related to the noun *roð* ("clearing,") or even with *reiða* ("pay"); the phrase *afroð gjalda* occurred in legal texts, but here it is used metaphorically (approximately "the devil to pay"); segja frá "relate, report"; hvárir sigrask "who (which side) has won."

94/172. Impersonal. Some later reprints of Gordon's book have *Gunnari*. This emendation is wrong, for no one attacked *þeim Gunnari* (Gunnar defended himself alone). *Gunnar* is the subject, *sóttisk* ("advanced against"), *illa* ("with terrible results") (for the attackers: *þeim*).

98/307. fela ("hide," fourth class, strong, originally a third class verb; cf. Gothic *filhan* and the Old Icelandic past participle *folginn* "hidden," with the variation *h* ~ *g* being due to Verner's Law). The development seems to have been "place for safe keeping; bury," from there, possibly, "entrust," and, judging by German *befehlen*, "command," with the entire development being: "entrust" > "recommend" > "command, order."

101/32. þykki mér: *þykki* looks like the subjunctive of *þykkja*, but the status of the form is unclear. In the oldest period, the third person indicative of all verbs ended in some vowel followed by *þ*. The third person singular indicative of Gothic *þugkjan* (pronounced *þunkjan*) had the form *þugkeiþ* (*ei* = ī); in Old English, *þynceð* corresponded to it, and Modern German still has *dünkt*. In Old Norse, *-r* of the 2nd person was generalized, so that *þykkir* served for both persons; only in a few instances was the old ending supposedly preserved. Allegedly, it happened in *þykki-þ-þér*, simplified to *þykki þér*. From this form *þykki* is said to have spread to *þykki mér* and other contexts. Such is Noreen's explanation (sec. 530, note 2). Except for *þykki*, the few other examples Noreen cites are sporadic and not quite persuasive. It is more reasonable to suggest that *þykki* is indeed a subjunctive ("it would seem") used instead of the indicative (cf. Engl. *I would like* and so forth). This use of *þykki* must have been facilitated by *þótti* ~ *þætti*.

103/70. fœrði: perhaps there is no need to give such a concrete gloss as the book does; *fœra* is the causative of *fara* (the same relation as between German *fahren* and *führen*), that is, "make go; lead; put in a certain position"; see l. 76.

104/78. alt eitt atriðit (that is, *at-rið-it*): the idiom is overspecified in Cleasby-Vigfusson (Gordon took his gloss from them); it means only "the whole one pull"; that Grettir did two things at once

Teaching Old Norse

becomes clear from what follows; *sem* is regularly used with the superlative degree of adjectives.

104/90. þá...at...mœði: impersonal (*mœði*: acc.); af ǫllu saman: allt saman ("completely," here "from all these things"); the comma in the text is misleading (either delete it or add another comma after *honum*, or put it after *mœði*). The punctuation reflects the gloss in the book (see the note), which does not seem to be accurate.

104/91. Here, too, the comma after *því* is redundant: *því er* go together ("and for the reason [*því*] that [*er*]"); gaut: *gjóta* takes the dative.

105/121-22. ǫllum ... verk: impersonal; *verðr* takes the genitive (cf. p. 16/379: *minna* is the genitive), and the phrases *lítils verðr* and *mikils verðr* are common ("worth of little/much"); here *mikit* agrees with *verk* (n.); *um* often occurs in this phrase and implies an object; it is the repetition of *um* that makes the sentence confusing, but such repetition (which is probably not restricted to Icelandic, for in American English one often hears something like "This is the guy about whom I told you about") is not rare; literally "it seemed to all [to be] of great worth with regard [*um*] to that deed."

105/122. þeim er heyrðu: if the punctuation of modern editions is preserved, *þeim* occupies the place of the subject of the subordinate clause, but the subject should, naturally, be *þeir*; the comma can be put after *þeim* (then *ǫllum þeim*); if so, the defective subject of the next clause will be *er* − not a good candidate either (however, sometimes there is no other alternative; cf. l. 140: er mjǫk sýnisk annan veg en er: this is a common construction).

105/131. svá...sem: this collocation has several meanings "as...as," "so (such) as," and, when *svá* and *sem* stand together, "as if," but the syntax of the sentences with *svá...sem* varies; see the note on 13/268: "such great stories as" is added to the preceding part paratactically, whereas here *viðreign* echoes *aflraun* from l. 130 ("did not say [*kvazk* 'about himself'] what a trial of strength he had undergone, such big dealings that they had had"); the parataxis is evident, but it is not so striking.

108/21. af: the habit of using prepositions with suppressed objects was so strong that a preposition often occured where it could have been dispensed with; *sagði...um ferð* would have been sufficient without *af*; cf. 105/121-22.

110/108-09.   hefi aldregi beðit ró fyrir: *fyrir* needs an object ("on account of this"); *beðit*: the past participle of *bíða* (sec. 127); *bíða* takes the genitive when it means "wait" and the accusative when it means "suffer; experience."

119/48-49.   Put a comma after *þá* (instead of after *fyndi*). *Landsmenn* is in the accusative; segja til ("say," *til* is aspectual); hafask at (with a possible suppressed object) "do, deal". Thus: "Even though when (þótt) the vikings (nominative) might find (fyndi 'would find' = 'when the vikings managed to find') them (þá = landsmenn 'inhabitants'), they never told (sǫgðu til) the truth [about] what the earls (= Hákon and Eiríkr) were doing (hǫfðusk at)."

121/105.   *hugró* naturally means "peace of mind" (there also were a ship and an island bearing this name), but the gloss is "clinch on a sword's hilt" (German *Schwertknauf*); *ró* means "the rivet, or clinch of a nail," and *hug-* in this compound was associated by Old Icelandic writers with *hǫgg-*; yet the *hugró* does not strike! Other etymologies have also been proposed (unconvincingly); it is tempting to suggest that the *hugró* is what it seems to be (that is, "peace of mind"), a kenning; thus, *blóðrefill* (24/107) would be a sword with a sharp point, and *hugró*, the hilt that is the continuation of the hand, would indeed take care of the fighter's peace of mind.

130/46. ármaðr: from árr ("messenger"). Note the use of *þess* after the comma. As usual, two possibilities are open for resolving this syntactic difficulty. One is to transpose the comma (...á fund ármanns...þess, er...). But even if this was the original segmentation of such sentences, it was changed, so that a pause occurred before, rather than after, *þess*. This makes us formulate the following strange rule: "In subordinate clauses beginning with a demonstrative pronoun, the place of the subject was 'usurped' by this pronoun *repeating the case of the antecedent*" (antecedent "the word referred to earlier"). Thus, *ármanns* is in the genitive and *þess*, instead of being in the nominative is also in the genitive. This unexpected usage has been well attested in Old Icelandic and Gothic; see also the note on 105/122, above.

133/125. ek má eigi þat vita: perhaps a deliberate use of an anacoluthon (confused syntax, to express excitement, a rhetorical figure common in Latin and from there in Old Germanic literature): Auðunn begins "I am not sure, really cannot say ..." and finishes with the unexpected phrase "that I have been treated well ..."; the tortured gloss (at *vita*) ("I cannot bear to think that ...") must have been suggested in despair; apparently, another negation should be added to the subordinate clause or *eigi* expunged. I has been suggested to me that the unemended text means "I am unable to know that..." = "I cannot tolerate the knowledge that..."

150/4. Old Icelandic *sumar*, unlike Germ. *Sommer*, is neuter; when *geta* means "to be able to," it is followed by a past participle, so that *gæti at kaupa* cannot mean "was possible to obtain"; *geta* followed by an infinitive means "to happen to do something" (so here: "if grain 'happened to buy') = "if there was grain to buy"; the book uses *corn* in its British sense "grain").

151/34. *Rinna* is a strong verb; *renna* ("make run") is from a historical point of view weak (a so-called causative verb, as Engl. *lay*, *set*, and *drench* are to *lie*, *sit*, and *drink*). But early on the two forms merged, *rinna* became obsolete, and *renna* acquired both meanings: "run, *etc.*" and "make run." *Rinna* often occurs in Old Icelandic poetry. In our line, it is more "grammatical" to parse *runnu* as the past plural of *rinna*, but there is no harm in connecting it with *renna*, which will then split into *renna* (strong) and *renna* (weak). A similar merger happened to *brinna* and *brenna* ("burn").

170/30-31. Proverbial: "as dogs enjoy (njóta) grass", that is, "very little, not at all."

170/33-34. The last sentence has nothing to do with the previous text! (Ē "always").